HORIZONS IN THEORY AND AMERICAN CULTURE
Bainard Cowan and Joseph G. Kronick, Editors

Published with the assistance of the
V. RAY CARDOZIER FUND

Edgar Allan Poe, Wallace Stevens, and the Poetics of American Privacy

LOUIS A. RENZA

Louisiana State University Press
Baton Rouge

Designer: Barbara Neely Bourgoyne
Typeface: Galliard
Typesetter: Coghill Composition Co., Inc.
Printer and binder: Thomson-Shore, Inc.

ISBN 0-8071-2755-8

The paper in this book meets the guidelines for permanence and durability of the Committee on Production Guidelines for Book Longevity of the Council on Library Resources. ∞

IN PUBLIC:
to James M. Cox

IN PRIVATE:
to Alexandra Crista Rahmann

IN MEMORIAM:
Murray Krieger

Life itself is a bubble and a skepticism, and a sleep within a sleep. Grant it, and as much more as they will,—but God's darling! Heed thy private dream: thou will not be missed in the scorning and skepticism: there are enough of them: stay in thy closet, and toil, until the rest are agreed what to do about it.

—Ralph Waldo Emerson, "Experience" (1844)

I'm Nobody! Who are you?
Are you — Nobody — Too?
Then there's a pair of us?
Don't tell! they'd advertise — you know!

How dreary — to be — Somebody!
How public — like a Frog —
To tell one's name — the livelong June —
To an admiring Bog!

—Emily Dickinson, #288

Contents

Preface

One does not write for any reader except one.
—Wallace Stevens, "Adagia"

As a social topic, privacy has special import, especially regarding its eclipse today in the United States public sphere. I address certain aspects of that eclipse in my Introduction. The present book, however, does not propose to defend privacy or secure its value within the social economy. The kind of privacy I have in mind requires no such defense or protection, since of itself it eludes the very social configurations that effectively disclose or produce it.

It goes without saying that this thesis incurs a host of theoretical obstacles, some of which I also try to address in the Introduction. In *The Human Condition,* Hannah Arendt lucidly sums up the modern public's social-philosophical case against conceptions of a privacy unbound:

> Compared with the reality which comes from being seen and heard, even the greatest forces of intimate life—the passions of the heart, the thoughts of the mind, the delights of the senses—lead an uncertain, shadowy kind of existence unless and until they are transformed, deprivatized and deindividualized, as it were, into a shape to fit them for public appearance. The most current of such transformations occurs in storytelling and generally in artistic transposition of individual experiences. (50)

Prevailing critical theories today would likely waive Arendt's "unless and until," and also substitute "constructed" for "transformed." From their viewpoint, privacy remains a constitutively public matter, locked in place by specific historical-cultural contexts. In United States culture, for example, privacy most often appears synonymous with self-autonomy, or with the ability to control access to information about and surveillance concerning one's personal affairs. Conversely, privacy can also provide an alibi for anti-democratic behavior: for one's egregiously assuming, say, social privilege, for abusing others, or more generally, for fostering the unexamined life.

In short, most critical considerations of privacy situate it within variously defined public constellations. The following work disputes only their totalizing effect. I argue that those frameworks elide privacy's recurring otherness, which is not quite true with Arendt's depiction. She allows that private experience can exist in pre-public if "uncertain" form. Pressing her option, I instead regard such experience as a post-public phenomenon, holding that if public "reality" makes the private appear "shadowy," the private simultaneously shadows that reality. The "private" of private experience is what remains beyond its public codifications. It consists of an idiosyncratic or utterly singular surplus, always becoming *there* in the wake of inescapable efforts to express it.

From the last viewpoint, the public-private crossroads particularly pertains to acts of literary representation, which at once reflect and embody it. As Arendt points out, "storytelling" focuses on so-called private matters, constantly transposing them into publicly recognizable forms of subjective experience. But a private remainder, so to speak, continually appears alongside the "public appearance" or representation of experiences otherwise assignable to some determinate, private realm. Literary transpositions can educe just that: due to a slippage during writing, what one usually means by private experience ("the intimate life") can become *superfluously* private, precisely there and then *not* expressed, and contextually irrelevant to what is. It follows, I think, that if it can instantiate the "private," writing can paradoxically exploit its own public or communicational function to elicit nothing less.

I want to term this mode of privacy radical, inaugurated by but irreducible to cultural scripts. I find it most notably pursued in certain works by Edgar Allan Poe and Wallace Stevens, which to begin with self-evidently baffle public inquisitions. Riddled with referential loopholes, Poe's fiction has invited countless, hermeneutic "transformations" of the kind that Arendt speaks. Plying elusive tropes, Stevens' poetry has compelled similar exegetical exercises. Still, these interpretive conundrums by themselves fail to spell the kind of privacy I mean to discuss, and not least because, in principle or practice, one or another interpretive code always exists by which one can think to re-solve them. For example, one might surmise that, much as do other American literary works, the "private" effects a Poe tale or Stevens poem produces in-cipiently thematize a defense of privacy, given the perplexed, public-private dichotomy endemic to both writers' American, cultural environments.

I argue for something different: that Poe's and Stevens' works, at least those addressed in the present book, internally stage wholly to resist codify-ing appropriations. Both writers do so not to defend some inviolable, *a priori* privacy—abstention from public intercourse proffers no option for them—but as the sole means by which to access the anomalously private ambience of their compositional acts. Chapter 1 focuses on certain Poe tales, many rhe-torical practices of which I regard as private in exactly the last sense. I contend that these tales often script their own misreading, but as a redundant *mise en scène* that amounts to a crypto-rhetorical act. Of course, one might object that such practices in fact slyly manifest Poe's ambition for literary-public rec-ognition. Does he here play a game of literary concealment programmed for detection, or does he *mean* to go private, thus seeking to mute his ever-recur-ring ambition? Poe's tales, I propose, consistently permit readings that sup-port the second alternative.

In Chapter 2, I air his attraction to private maneuvers as they bear on the public-private concerns of his particular social-cultural milieu. If one can read those stratagems to support his tenuous, culturally representative status, other features of his tales transgress critical views that he either exploits *or* defends social notions of privacy. Poe, I maintain, opts for a more radical vi-sion of the private sphere, the theoretical ground of which he formulates in *Eureka,* which in Chapter 3 I read as a meta-literary text. *Eureka* allegorically figures an impersonal public sphere—not merely "all the world" but the uni-verse is a stage—wherein privacy at once means nothing and everything to everyone. *Eureka*'s thesis particularly redounds to Poe's imaginary nullifica-tion of his own literary ambition, which his fictional inscriptions of the private could never quite realize. In that sense, I see *Eureka* as privately inscribing Poe's poetics of privacy.

Among other American writers who at all engage the issue, Wallace Ste-vens, it seems to me, takes privacy to the same literary extreme in his 1923 *Harmonium* poems. Poe insists on the private by his rhetorical tactics and theory. In the last two sections of Chapter 3, I argue that Stevens non-aggres-sively theorizes a similar poetics, for instance in "The Comedian as the Letter C." Not only does he echo certain Eurekan principles in other *Harmonium* poems, in a Poesque manner he also frames his collection with poems that invoke and stage his literary public's misreading of it. Yet Poe's theory culminates his encrypted, rhetorical designs, whereas Stevens poeticizes his "private" theory to begin with. For Poe, the problem is how to go private in the face of his impulse to go public; for Stevens, how to include a public he instinctively wishes to occlude. Stevens recognizes that without any public, his "private" writing would entail not rigorous vision but mere aesthetic self-indulgence.

In Stevens' early-twentieth-century milieu, social and poetic figures of the "private" appear unstable in relation to continually shifting nodes of what comprises his American public realm. Chapter 4 holds that Stevens like Poe isolates certain of his period's public-private formations, each of which his *Harmonium* poems strive to elude. Different from Poe, however, Stevens must determine his private scenes of writing in relation to a protean public complex. In keeping with Modernist artistic practices, e.g., "thirteen ways of looking at" things, his lyrics thus adopt a variety of perspectives on the multiple cultural pressures that identify his sense of "the public" at any given moment. Since these pressures necessarily include artistic ones, I consider how Stevens' attraction to Modernist practices itself invokes another kind of public. This one appears indissociable from his immediate compositional acts, prompting his efforts to retrieve them from the context of literary-public performance.

Chapter 5 focuses on his use of poetic tropes evoking conventionally understood topics of private, personal experience. Stevens evokes them to conjure pleasurable because private scenes of writing his poems *while* writing them. In the poems I discuss here, his tropes specifically hint at submerged scenes of death and intimacy, erotic and autoerotic. Stevens deploys them not to conceal (let alone confess) intimate secrets, for example by constructing poems akin to resolvable cryptograms. He does so to delay the transformation of their compositional process into ersatz public artifacts, by which means he would keep his writing private. Yet within his acts of writing, none of those tropes helps realize his goal for long. Consequently, by expressive means not meant for public eyes, so to speak, Stevens also ends up violating his "intimate" designations of the private, personal sphere.

In sum, even as it acknowledges its "public" pull, the *Harmonium* poem traces Stevens' wish to hold readers at bay (Chapter 3). His poems go so far as to entertain the thought of not meaning *for* others at all (Chapter 4). Stevens sometimes writes to deny his sense of public reception altogether, whether "public" refers to an anonymous "they" or intimate "you" (Chapter 5). Carried to that extreme, his private impulses also induce intimations of poetic death, or of his own loss of poetic desire. Occluding others from his scenes of writing threatens to yield nothing more than an ephemeral, poetic experience, of no value, public *or* private, to others *or* to Stevens himself. Chapter 6 tracks how his *Harmonium* poems play out that particular worry. Some of them internalize Poe's Eurekan vision as a limit, to go beyond which would disable literature's beautification of the real or, the same thing for Stevens, upset the poetic frisson of disappearing from others.

In the end, Poe's precedent enables Stevens to envision a less vexed poetics of privacy. For him, writing positions a reading "other" as also possibly private rather than as exclusively representative of one or another public complex. Stevens can therefore assent to rather than feel threatened by readings contingent to his acts of writing. To be sure, he fashions his vision of the private in non-hierarchical terms. It exists, as I have suggested, on a revolving spectrum of the other private, poetic exercises that his *Harmonium* medium permits him to play. But with the last one, to change my metaphor, Stevens can imagine a way to make his poetic cake for public consumption, for anyone to enjoy, and simultaneously eat his piece of just, poetic desserts in private.

Acknowledgments

I could not have written the present book without the long-term good will and intellectual models of Murray Krieger and James M. Cox, to whom I owe the greatest debt for my academic career. I will miss Murray Krieger, the private man first of all, but then, as well, his faith in literature's illuminations and his exemplary work in critical theory to nourish those. The knowledge of James M. Cox regarding American literature and culture, and his force and style in expressing that knowledge, make him the one acquaintance who matches my understanding of Emerson's American Scholar. What I have learned from him knows no bounds, all of it trebled by my having taught with him at Dartmouth College for twenty years, and by my continuing friendship with him since that time.

Other academic colleagues and friends composed the good public sphere essential, in different and often private ways, for my having written this book. Its thesis originated, serendipitously, in a conversation with Bernard Bergen, whose later responses to my work inspired bold revisions. He and another close friend, John William Price, possess the kind of critical mind that I respect the most. In a manner often unbeknownst to them, both contributed to my particular discussions of ideas and texts. Blanche Gelfant and Donald E. Pease, English Department colleagues at Dartmouth College, did much the same, the former with her gracious encouragement and acute discussions of literature, the latter with his critically brilliant devil's advocacy. Both led me continually to rethink the privacy issue in line with their remarkably extensive knowledge of American literary and critical matters.

A number of people sustained the actual execution of my project during its various stages. More than once, Dartmouth College reference librarians, particularly Lois Krieger and John Cocklin, indefatigably tracked down sources for me, however obscure those were. Two teaching assistants allowed me to keep my writing and teaching in balanced nuance: Michelle Angers, with her native energy and intellectual wit, and Suzanne Semmes, with her sensitive attention to students and thought. I also wish to acknowledge those colleagues and friends who in various ways reinforced my resolve throughout the project. Sharon Cameron supported an early grant proposal. William Spengemann helped me sharpen the presentation of my general argument. William C. Cook, Patricia McKee, and John Jacobus voluntarily offered me information pertinent to my inquiries. Jack Morgan, Paul Sherwin, Horace Porter, Frank Gado, Donald Sheehan, and (too long ago) Ralph and Robert Colucci lent conviction to my critical instinct—to work out a line of thought, whatever its public cachet.

I especially want to thank Shawn J. Rosenheim, Cassandra Cleghorn, and John Limon, who generously afforded me the opportunity to discuss an initial version of Chapter 5 at Williams College. I also remain indebted to Burton R. Pollin and J. Gerald Kennedy for their generous advice on Poe matters, as well as to Hermann Josef Schnackertz and the conferees at the International Edgar Allan Poe Symposium, Eichstätt, Germany, September 1999, for their various critical responses to "The Pit and the Pendulum" section of Chapter 2. Several in camera readers of the book's earliest versions provided me with important recommendations for revisions. No less helpfully, Dartmouth College granted my proposal for the 1999 Summer Institute on "The Question of Privacy," the members of which—most notably its Senior Advisor, Jeff Weintraub—served to refine my awareness of different disciplinary perspectives on the privacy issue. I want to express my special appreciation to one member of this group, Milette Shamir, whose meaningful responses to my work come second only to the importance I place on her own study of literary privacy in antebellum American literature.

Edgar Allan Poe, Wallace Stevens, and the Poetics of American Privacy could never have come to public pass without the professional attention and incomparable, critical advice of Mark Bauerlein; without Kenneth Dauber's incisive understanding of my argument; and without the editorial interest and intellectual commitment shown by Joseph Kronick and John Easterly. Not least (and not at all in the mode of secret writing), I wish to thank Eivind Allan Boe for his patient, painstaking, eminently suggestive, and always cooperative copy-editing of my manuscript. Each of these persons made critical and stylistic recommendations for certain parts of the work, enacting the utmost of voluntary, academic generosity. If I have not always heeded their advice elsewhere in the book, the fault lies with myself alone.

And literally nothing of the book's private value for me would matter without the love of my wife, Crista, my mother, Anne, my son, Shayne, my nephew, Henry, and especially my niece, Alex.

The first section and a small portion of the second of my Introduction appeared in my essay "Edgar Allan Poe, Henry James, and Jack London: A Private Correspondence," published in *boundary 2* 27 (summer 2000). Chapter 1 is a considerably revised version of my former essay "Poe's Secret Autobiography," published by the Johns Hopkins University Press in *The American Renaissance Reconsidered* (1985). I used portions of Chapter 2's first section in my essay "Poe and the Issue of American Privacy," in the Oxford University Press *Historical Guide to Edgar Allan Poe* (2000). I thank these presses for permission to reprint the aforementioned materials. Lastly, I wish to convey my appreciation to Alfred A. Knopf, Inc., Random House Publishers, for permission to reproduce quoted materials from Wallace Stevens' works.

Abbreviations

EDGAR ALLAN POE

E&R   *Poe: Essays and Reviews,* ed. G. R. Thompson (New York: Library of America, 1984).

P&T   *Poe: Poetry and Tales,* ed. G. R. Thompson (New York: Library of America, 1984).

Mabbott   *Collected Works of Edgar Allan Poe,* 3 vols., ed. Thomas O. Mabbott (Cambridge: Harvard University Press, 1978).

WALLACE STEVENS

CP   *The Collected Poems of Wallace Stevens* (New York: Alfred A. Knopf, 1961).

CP&P   *Wallace Stevens: Collected Poetry and Prose,* ed. Frank Kermode and Joan Richardson (New York: Library of America, 1997).

L   *Letters of Wallace Stevens,* ed. Holly Stevens (New York: Alfred A. Knopf, 1966).

NA   *The Necessary Angel* (New York: Vintage Books, 1951).

OP   *Opus Posthumous,* ed. Milton J. Bates (New York: Alfred A. Knopf, 1989).

SP   *Souvenirs and Prophecies,* ed. Holly Stevens (New York: Alfred A. Knopf, 1977).

Edgar Allan Poe,
Wallace Stevens,
and the
Poetics of American Privacy

Introduction: Going Private

In this our talking America, we are ruined by our good nature and listening on all sides.
　　—Ralph Waldo Emerson, "Experience" (1844)

The vital distinction between what is private and what is public is obliterated, and everything is reduced to a kind of private-public gossip which corresponds more or less to the public of which it forms part. The public is public opinion which interests itself in the most private concerns.
　　—Søren Kierkegaard, *The Present Age* (1846)

1

Everywhere one turns today in academic journals, it is politics as usual: all texts are subject to political short-arm inspections. Not, as Jerry Seinfeld might have said, that there's anything wrong with that. Who wants to return to the closet claustrophobias enforced by prejudices of race, gender, class, ethnicity, and/or sexual orientation(s)? Or to discourage those still gripped by oppressive, dominant discourses and their endorsements of ignoble forms of behavior from breaking silence; from joining enclaves to air old and present social grievances; in short, from going public, and thereby introducing discursive cacophony, for strategic or cathartic purposes, into what passes for the prevailing public sphere of today's "humanities" profession? If no consensus exists about its particulars, this politicization—for instance of literary studies—surely stands for one in general. To be sure, I may choose not to regard imaginative, literary works for their political emissions or the "cultural work" they purportedly do. Yet in the present academic environment, that choice, too, will perforce appear political. The fact that this observation has become a virtual cliché simply proves the point.

So it is no surprise that a familiar type of critical practice opts for more exposés, more "outings," when it comes to, among other things, the culturally influential issue of canon-formation. For example, cultural imperatives dictate exposing Edgar Allan Poe for his alleged racist sentiments (although based on scattered evidence), not to mention his oft-proclaimed aesthetic ideology; Nathaniel Hawthorne for his misogyny or literary politicking regarding *The Scarlet Letter;* or Mark Twain for his use of the word "nigger" in *Huckleberry Finn.*[1] Conversely, other critics focus on recovering works and writers excluded for political reasons from the recommended, American literary canon, if only to show the political reasons why we should now include them. These reasons, too, are subject to further ideological revisions. With respect, say, to *Uncle Tom's Cabin*'s positive social effect at the time, how ought one assess Harriet Beecher Stowe's coterminous notion of Liberian colonization for freed slaves? But few expect such facts or canonical designs to go uncontested. Indeed, these contestations help fuel more political conversation,[2] often leaving uncontested only the issue of canonical thinking itself.

Strangely enough, however, from one perspective this critical zeitgeist or foregrounding of criticism as a performative activity exists in the historical mainstream of American social practices, the effect of which has been to dilute "private" considerations of most matters, including of literary texts. At first glance, those practices appear to value the privatization of everything from business enterprises to personal life. Yet the public-private binary in United States culture has usually meant the obeisance of the private to the public life. That was so for American-Puritan colonialists whose households "put no premium on privacy," or whose town governments "sought to control the people's private lives, forbidding profane language, lavish dress, excessive drinking."[3] In a different sense, early Republican leaders felt that public duty superseded inclinations toward the private life, which in any case soon became ripe material for scoring scandalous points against one's political opponents.[4]

More generally, for European-American settlers, geographical and social circumstances lent privacy the negative connotation it had assumed in Western antiquity, specifically the sense of "isolation, deprivation, and separation."[5] According to Hannah Arendt, in ancient Greek culture private life defined the site of social labor and natural process, the necessities of quotidian existence associable with the domain of women and slaves. In contrast, the public realm referred to the distinctive and privileged site of civic life, social decision-making, in which (some) males participated for honor and reputation, or for the special status of free citizenship.[6] To a certain extent earlier but especially with the incursion of nineteenth-century Western-industrial capitalism, privacy, etymologically linked to "privation," appeared gradually to shed its privative, social connotations. If still negatively framed, privacy, as Jeff Weintraub argues, nonetheless began to identify a zone of newly valued, intimate experiences as "defined in direct opposition to the ethos of the (equally new) 'public' realm of impersonal relations and institutions."[7]

As I maintain in Chapter 2, nineteenth-century American notions of domestic life affirmed one such zone of privacy. Yet domesticity's well-documented association with female activities simultaneously framed the private, middle-class household as at best a reactionary or imaginary refuge from the civic and commercial pressures—the patriarchal ethos—that dominated the American public sphere.[8] Moreover, domestic households arguably promulgated certain institutionalized practices of their own, in effect subsidizing the impersonal public sphere with which they were ostensibly at odds.[9] Contesting domesticity's pejorative reductions, recent feminist considerations of it argue that no "separate spheres" ideology existed at all. For one thing, many women actively engaged in public affairs. For another, by itself domestic ideology entailed a latent protest against an alienated public realm, or else proffered an alternate model for a more egalitarian one.[10] Revisionist or otherwise, however, these viewpoints of nineteenth-century domestic life self-evidently reconfigure it in terms of its public orientations.

From the late nineteenth century through the present, American liberal-individualist defenses of privacy also end up underwriting the very public sphere that makes privacy valuable for them in the first place. Most contemporary legal defenses and definitions of privacy take their cue from, even when they attempt to revise, Samuel Warren and Louis Brandeis' article "The Right to Privacy," published in the *Harvard Law Review* of 1890. Warren and Brandeis sought to limit the threats to a person's "right to be let alone" posed by technological innovations like photography, new commercial and bureaucratic practices, and especially a rapaciously intrusive late-nineteenth-century press. For Warren and Brandeis, the advances of modern civilization required an officially enforceable defense of privacy. Not simply one's physical

property but also one's personal "[t]houghts, emotions, and sensations de-
manded legal recognition," although "without the interposition of the legis-
lature." Along with common-law recognition of "a man's house as his
castle," their article defends personal privacy essentially on the liberal-individualist principle of one's "inviolate personality."[11]

For political skeptics of liberalism, this defense, of course, lacks persuasive
force. From a leftist viewpoint, defending personal privacy suspiciously serves
to defuse egregious economic versions of private self-interest. Distinguishing
between physical and personal forms of private property engages the same
ideological myth—a quintessentially public matter. Even on its own terms,
the Warren-Brandeis defense of privacy hinges on American-institutional
mechanisms, in particular a juridical if not legislative "recognition" to secure
it. Making one's right to an "intangible" personal privacy synonymous with
"the right to enjoy life" and "the right to liberty," Warren and Brandeis tie
privacy-rights to "the exercise of extensive civil privileges" sanctioned by the
American public realm. Moreover, linking privacy's status to either a "bad"
or "good" public clearly mitigates privacy's putatively "inviolate" ground.[12]

In any case, the Warren-Brandeis article's paradigmatic legal defense of
privacy argues only for a qualified and politically unthreatening kind of privacy. Even from a civic-republican viewpoint, the public assumes final authority in determining at what point privacy might afford a refuge for anti-social
behavior or anti-egalitarian self-interest. Summarizing the views of certain
critics on the issue, Patricia Boling notes that while a juridically defined privacy "protects us from scrutiny and interference," it "sometimes . . . shuts
off parts of our lives from public debate and prevents us from taking political
action to improve those parts of our lives." To the same end but with obverse
emphasis, many liberal arguments maintain that recovering or nurturing private experience is essential for establishing a meaningfully *civil* public
sphere.[13]

But as with the Warren and Brandeis article, both rationales inevitably suc-
cumb to more defensive views of privacy. Legal and politically oriented arguments for it inevitably respond to the power promoted by runaway
commercial and technological expansion. Rochelle Gurstein exemplifies the
dilemma in her nostalgic evocation of turn-of-the-century American proponents of social "reticence." For her, they possessed a "far richer appreciation
of the public realm" than the ultimately victorious, progressivist reformers
who touted media "exposure" of all types of private matters.[14]

In our time, of course, the manifest threats to privacy cited by liberals have become conspicuously exacerbated, thanks to the surge of a pervasive, late-capitalist commodity culture and revolutionary technological advances most evident in the area of communications. Whatever the public sphere once meant, it now also means "publicity," and in a more pervasive sense than encountered by Warren and Brandeis. Publicity consists of an amplified social space in which hyper-attention becomes trained on persons or events, with its most visible but certainly not sole aspect lying in the commercial exploitation of celebrities' private lives by the mass media—for example, the trials and travails of a president's penis.[15] If formerly the public took precedence over or egregiously threatened the private realm, it nevertheless assumed the appearance of an external, impersonal agency in relation to a separate or "other" sphere of existence. Now, however, one is additionally encouraged to regard the private as always already public.

For what can privacy mean in an era of publicly accessible, user-friendly, and electronically facilitated reproductions of what people once considered to be self-evidently private events: for instance, the camcordings of weddings, funerals, sex, deaths, and births? In effect, we ourselves internalize and regard our experiences in terms of an electronic public sphere and its instantaneous amplification of all such events. The ubiquitous cell-phone makes moot the sense of inaccessible places and time. Television and other video-technological options turn the illusion-demarcated movie people formerly watched into the "reality show" in which they always potentially exist: "Once we sat in movie theaters dreaming of stardom. Now we live in a movie dreaming of celebrity."[16] These internalized, technological tools of perception forecast "the end of privacy." They realize with a vengeance Foucault's famous interpretation of Jeremy Bentham's Panopticon, for they arguably comprise not an overt matter of social control, but a reflexive impulse beyond commercial considerations to witness and objectify—to represent—private affairs as newsworthy "secrets."[17]

This panoptic invasion manifestly concerns conventional notions of privacy, from physical solitude, domestic life, intimate relations, and conversations, to control over access to our bodies, work, and data-recordable profiles. These devolve on discernible activities or relations with others, but what about more subjective affairs like thinking or feeling? Here, too, twentieth-century thought, hardly in any mood to inhibit investigations into mental phenomena and the rapid distribution of its findings, propagates a "tell-all" ethos, which in effect duplicates the multiple, technological constructions of the public realm. One can readily cite a host of modern and postmodern theories that themselves contribute to the wholesale evacuation of privacy. Ludwig Wittgenstein eviscerated the possibility of private languages. Recent philosophers of mind like Thomas Nagel, not to mention "cybernetic" or positivist antagonists like Daniel Dennett, question the possibility of private experience. Psychoanalysts, too, "assume that it is possible to access and examine [persons'] motivations," thus placing "an agent's [subjective] intimacy claims" within "the reach of others." Not least, the academic-cultural criticism practiced today construes privacy as no more than a social-political construction. Even deploying postmodern, guerrilla-like strategies against panoptic procedures or hegemonic concepts like oedipal paradigms inversely legitimates the political cachet that such critiques simultaneously court.[18]

In short, phenomenological convictions about privacy can't pass critical muster. On one hand, privacy can denote whatever (including privacy itself) I feel, perceive, think, imagine, or do, beyond, but not necessarily excluding, the actual presence of others. On the other, a host of mediations—linguistic, cultural, political, gendered, familial, geographical, even architectural—continually qualifies this notion of privacy. Upon reflection, that is, whatever I feel, perceive, think, imagine, or do is never, strictly speaking, private at all. In that sense, "privacy" does not exist; instead, it remains deducibly pre-occupied by one or another public that happens to dominate my living and thinking environment at any given moment. The personal is indeed political, and not just as a political credo. So today's critical practitioners of "going public," whatever their different social agendas—egalitarian, anti-hegemonic, or even reactionary—seem right on, for both epistemological reasons and the social good they want to do. Who would want it otherwise?

2

Still, and beyond the fact that many of these same critics remain closet liberals regarding *certain* private matters, the public, at least from a literary-critical perspective, depends on the private as much as vice versa, if only not to implode into a realm of utter, aesthetic disinterest. Henry Sussman, for example, reflects a critical truism when he remarks how, "from a perspective of wish-fulfillment, [the blurring or] confusion between the public and the private accounts in part for the attraction that literature" in general "holds for its readers."[19]

So understood, literature can help defray the word *privacy*'s anti-social connotations, already implicit in many of its conventional definitions:

1.a. The state or condition of being withdrawn from the society of others, or from public interest; seclusion. . . .

b. The state or condition of being alone, undisturbed, or free from public attention, as a matter of choice or right; freedom from interference or intrusion.[20]

In Hannah Arendt's formulation, cited in my Preface, imaginative literature draws public attention to more specific synonyms of *privacy:* secrets and interpersonal intimacies. Literature lends them a public form, and in that way justifies as well as makes them interesting to others. Yet given our privy relation to fictional characters, literature can also sustain our illusion of private experience. Literary representations of identifiably private topics thus often finesse the otherwise either/or distinction between public and private spheres. Aesthetic interest lies primarily in the human slippage that the public-private topic inherently entails, such as how various registers of social meaning and value can fail to represent personal interests, wishes, and so on.

To a limited extent, I adopt that reasonable critical perspective in the following book. I argue that certain prose works by Edgar Allan Poe and Wallace Stevens' 1923 *Harmonium* poems not only thematize, but also rhetorically enact the public-private dichotomy in the above fashion. One can further claim, of course, that the issue of privacy possesses a social charge for both writers, although my thesis ultimately points in a different direction. Poe and Stevens surely pursue modes of literary privacy partly in critical response to certain oppressive, impersonal aspects of their respective social complexes. As already suggested, in Poe's mid-nineteenth-century world, the "public," the highlighted site of accepted or contested values, was coming into existence as a special, alienated category of social experience, particularly in the guise of the American capitalist marketplace and mass culture. Stevens' early-twentieth-century American world both took for granted a now heavily bureaucratized business economy and transformed the public sphere into a virtually hyper-self-conscious issue. Besides commercial enterprises, technological advances enabled and abetted a burgeoning array of disciplinary practices, most notably in relation to governmental, scientific, and mass-media affairs. More to the point, their conflation proffered new modes of cultural surveillance and helped instigate a "publicity" ethos on balance supported by because supporting American middle-class values.[21]

The historically different cultural formations of an American public sphere necessarily modify Poe's and Stevens' sense of the *literary*-public constituencies that their writing at once addresses and arguably resists. Poe writes for a mixed or an inchoately variable literary public: commercial-minded editors and publishers, a growing middle-class and mass-cultural readership (the "rabble"), along with an older, more honorific Romantic literary world. As a Modernist poet, Stevens writes in terms of a more delimited literary public. At the same time, his writing invokes an American literary past—an internalized, canonical public, as it were—from which Poe was comparatively free. In Poe's case, American-Republican literature existed in embryo, or as an issue more or less coming to the fore. His peer public largely consisted of geographically distant British writers, and in an era of delayed, scattered, and tenuously verifiable information.

Given these differences, one might infer that Poe exercised a less vexed, American right to literary privacy than Stevens could. Yet forced by economic circumstances to write magazine journalism, Poe, whose ambition for honorific, literary recognition lay primarily in writing poetry, emplots and mocks his mass readers in his tales. Poe's fiction, that is, includes the fiction of both his public's reading of it and his simultaneously witnessing, as if from some private or undetected position, the effect his emplotted readings will have on others. In that respect, he resembles Dupin, his fictional "private eye" in "The Purloined Letter." Like Dupin, Poe can unabashedly think to invade the privacy of readers encountering *his* tale or "letter," the better to annex that private position for himself: " 'I confess . . . that I should like very well to know the precise character of [Minister D——'s] thoughts when . . . he is reduced to opening the letter which I left for him in the cardrack' " (*P&T* 697).

Poe here inscribes an aggressive protest against a public complex, and no less so for its being a displaced or fictively framed, i.e., a privatized, wish not directly assignable to himself. Subject to the qualifications I raise in Chapter 4, Stevens' "Modernist" poems in *Harmonium* generally express something similar. His poems not only abjure thematic commonplaces of Romantic and Victorian credos, they also purvey an esoteric style that frames them as "private" in apparent reaction and resistance to utilitarian-, moral-, and/or consumerist-oriented reading conventions.

If they forfeit a mass-public audience in the process, Stevens' Modernist gambits nevertheless presuppose and appeal to a more specialized literary public, a surmise that his post-*Harmonium* poems tend to support. Among other things, they often theorize how the very medium of art includes its essentially public status. A poem, he states in his 1942 "Notes toward a Supreme Fiction,"

> refreshes life so that we share,
> For a moment, the first idea. . . .

Or the poet

> tries by a peculiar speech to speak
>
> The peculiar potency of the general

in relation to "the gibberish of the vulgate that he seeks" (*CP* 382, 397). If nothing else, such postulations suggest that Stevens deploys a less aggressive or more permeable sense of the public-private dichotomy than does Poe. Even in his pre-*Harmonium* years, Stevens occasionally worries about his personal proclivity for not sharing his thoughts with others, instead wishing for more "agreeable" public contexts where he could share at least some of them: "I must think well of people. After all, they are only people.—The conventions are the arts of living. People know. I am not the only wise man.—Or if I cannot think well, let me hide my thoughts.—It is of no consequence to explain or to assert one's self. . . . Life is not important.—At least, let's have it agreeable" (*SP* 176–77; 1907).

Stevens' early and later sentiments, in fact, might just as easily support an anti-private thesis about his *Harmonium* poems. It requires little interpretive effort, for example, to show how "The Emperor of Ice-Cream," one of his most well-known poems from the collection, may even indicate his siding with Rochelle Gurstein's "party of exposure."[22] Stripped of funereal costume, the poem's dead woman lies wholly subject, "horny feet" and all, to the gaze of everyone, here including anonymous "boys" and "wenches," too. The poem's speaker, an ersatz funeral director, himself calls for this wholesale brand of exposé. True, he would have others "cover her face," but less to preserve the corpse's vulnerable privacy per se than to violate the public's version of it as propagated by the period's middle-class proprieties for waking the dead. He therefore notably omits any directive to alter the corpse's "facial expression with cosmetics," the social function of which, according to Karen Halttunen, was to make "certain that, even in death, the respectable Victorian remained genteel."[23]

Yet as I maintain in Chapter 5, "The Emperor of Ice-Cream," not to mention other poems in *Harmonium,* also disrupts its flirtation with exposing the shame of conventionally understood private matters like death and love. Similarly, if Stevens acknowledges the inescapably public face of his poetry, he does it with a private twist not unlike the kind I argue Poe exercises in his tales. Before and after his poetic career took hold, Stevens insulated his family life from public intrusions. He also rigorously separated his writing poetry from his work as an insurance company lawyer. He even appears to have consigned the domestic sphere itself to a kind of quasi-public one, thus relegating the "private" entirely to his poetic ruminations. Stuart M. Sperry refers to how one of Stevens' visiting nieces noted the separation of the Stevens household into private spaces: " 'Uncle Wallace said, "This side of the house is mine." He had this Spartan bedroom. On the left side of the house were the women's quarters, [his wife] Aunt Elsie's and [his daughter] Holly's. It was such a shock. But this was their understanding of life. He needed to have his separateness, his privacy, very much so.' "[24]

I agree with Sperry that Stevens' conspicuous demarcation of private and public spheres infiltrates his poetry, but I think nowhere more pervasively and deliberately than in his first collection of poems. Occurring in relation to social and literary values knottily tied to a well-established impersonal and invasive public environment, Stevens' inscribed pursuits of privacy in *Harmonium* differ from Poe's only in their less combative inflections. Stevens imaginatively evades rather than ambivalently resists a public he in any case can entertain no illusion of banishing. Whether or not partially motivated by his early lack of authorial self-confidence, he nonetheless practices a poetic privacy that, however elusively inscribed, one can at minimum take as a kind of symbolic stand of bourgeois privacy in a modern world essentially opposed to it.

Other ways exist to frame Poe's and Stevens' respective pursuits of literary privacy in historical and cultural terms, and I attempt to rehearse some of them later. Such formulations no doubt raise an obvious methodological question. Why not equally apply the American public-private issue to a host of other American writers? Regarding Poe's peers, for example, Emerson, as Richard Poirier remarks, "tries to define . . . literature . . . as something prior to publication." Hawthorne sequesters himself in the Old Manse to begin his public, literary career; he also writes about and rhetorically exemplifies his authorial reserve in the prefaces to his published romances. Thoreau goes to Walden, a secluded zone immediately proximate to Concord, "to transact some private business." There he not only writes a draft of the work readers are now reading, but attempts to secure a "higher," private life next to the site par excellence where a promised, American-Revolutionary public sphere historically originated. Abstaining from social protest (" 'I would prefer not to' "), Melville's Bartleby doubly withdraws in words, spirit, and act from the public sphere as defined by mid-nineteenth-century American capitalism.

Given the twentieth century's publicity zeitgeist, not a few later American writers besides Stevens also worry the public-private fault-line in their works.[25] So on what critical grounds can I justify examining a restricted set of works by Poe and Stevens, themselves an odd, literary-historical couple to begin with, as paradigmatic models for discussing the privacy issue within different periods of American cultural history?

3

In the present book, I propose to examine how cultural formations of the privacy issue, itself possessing a certain public cachet, only incidentally affect Poe's and Stevens' respective pursuits of it. Generally speaking, American writers who engage the issue at all do so indirectly, and then in ways readily reducible to a representative defense of "the right to privacy"—to the perceived sense, as Robert Post's contemporary, legal argument has it, that privacy's violation "is *intrinsically* harmful because it is defined as that which injures social personality."[26] In contrast, Poe's and Stevens' works manifest a sustained, radical "write to privacy." Both writers, that is, ply private codes that exceed the perquisites for any socially representative defense of privacy. Like Poe's narrator in his tale "The Man of the Crowd," they look for, want, perversely seek to produce the unreadable text or, to be more precise, a radically private position in writing it. Because they push the issue to such extremes, they also set the parameters, so for me exhibit a "poetics," by which to discuss the private practices of other American literary works.

Thus construed, privacy clearly beggars critical as well as social depictions. To speak critically about privacy is already to endow it with a negotiable or debatable significance within the public realm. As the Warren and Brandeis locus classicus illustrates, in United States culture that almost always means subsuming privacy within ideological constructions like self-autonomy, personal freedom, or an inviolate individualism. But in relation to the privacy Poe and Stevens pursue within their compositional acts, those constructions themselves perforce simulate a "public."

How, then, can criticism at all get at the private? Relentlessly figured as a non-public gestalt, the kind of privacy I attribute to Poe's and Stevens' works poses a methodological conundrum even for an arch-individualist critical paradigm like Harold Bloom's. The problem goes beyond his likely rejection of any ephebe-precursor linkage especially between these two particular writers. Bloom, of course, everywhere extols Stevens' canonical merits while relegating Poe's works to "atrocious" status. In principle, however, the general American aesthetic Bloom finds Stevens exemplifying, namely that it "always exists as a lonely, idiosyncratic, isolated stance," surely applies to Poe, too. As I read them in the present book, Poe's tales also appear to exhibit what Bloom claims for Stevens' poems: a visionary "solitude" that resists mass appropriation, and instead requests equivalent, solitary readings.[27] Moreover, one feature of Bloom's well-known theory of literary influence resembles the method I use to argue for the two writers' respective disaffections from cultural formations of both the public and the private. After all, his theory not only itself focuses on what might pass for writers' private scenes of writing, but also maintains that texts register them alongside the visions they signify for less theoretically inquisitive readers.

Formulated primarily in anxious, literary-competitive or oedipal terms, Bloom's critical paradigm nonetheless replaces a mass public readership with one composed of the poet's internalized literary precursors. For him, in essence, Stevens writes to forge his poetic identity in relation to still another literary public. I argue something different in Chapter 6. Far from anxiously repressing his most proximate, American literary precursors, Stevens' *Harmonium* poems construct scenarios in which he consciously invokes them primarily to distinguish his art from the canonical monuments theirs have become *in the literary public's mind at large*. In that respect, Stevens effectively privatizes Bloom's notion of a writer's (quasi-)private scene of writing.

Examining "The Public Square," a 1923 poem not included in the first *Harmonium* volume, may help illustrate what I mean:

> A slash of angular blacks
> Like a fractured edifice
> That was buttressed by blue slants
> In a coma of the moon.
>
> A slash and the edifice fell,
> Pylon and pier fell down.
> A mountain-blue cloud arose
> Like a thing in which they fell,
>
> Fell slowly as when at night
> A languid janitor bears

His lantern through colonnades
And the architecture swoons.

It turned cold and silent. Then
The square began to clear.
The bijou of Atlas, the moon,
Was last with its porcelain leer.
(*CP* 108–109)

To adopt Bloom's paradigm, Stevens' poetic imagination (the moon) "slants" Emerson's famous, transcendental vision on the "bare common," a public space, as expressed in his essay *Nature*. Crossing the common at twilight, Emerson imagines a scene for the moment bare or absent others. The private scene yet inspires a "transparent" vision of Nature, on principle accessible to any American willing to eschew the conformist pressures of mass-cultural perception. Like Poe's *Eureka* as I discuss it in Chapter 3, Stevens' poem transforms Emerson's visionary use of an empty public space into a monumental "edifice," that is, into a vision having become a renowned and established artifact blocking imaginative efforts by modern American poets like himself.[28] In effect, Stevens right now apprehends his "public square" as an all-too-occupied *literary* public square.

Bloom's theory of literary anxiety can easily enough account for the above scenario's particulars as well. Stevens' "coma" refers to his paralysis of imagination due to the Emersonian precedent. The poem thus enacts his wish to perceive cracks in Emerson's dominating literary-public stature or "edifice." Stevens conjures up its most monumental ("mountain-blue") appearance, the better to imagine its self-destructive metamorphosis. He wants to witness the Emersonian monument's transformation into something "Like a thing," a thing fixed outside of him—a cold (another connotation of "blue") or impersonal public art, now wholly irrelevant to himself. The poem frames that art as tentatively ("as when") giving way ("architecture swooning") to Stevens' own janitorial "lantern"—to the poetic lights of his apparently smaller or lower-literary-class lyrics in *Harmonium*. Written by a poetic novitiate at the time, his privatized literary fantasy seems motivated to mark his own poetic place in the American literary-public square. From a Bloomian viewpoint, the poem wholly consists of its becoming-a-poem: a wish per se to remove the Emersonian canonical edifice from Stevens' scene of writing.[29] "Emerson," we might say, has taken "dominion everywhere" (*CP* 76). His work commands reverential attention from an educated literary public, and not least from a would-be American poet.

But that's the point. Like the internalized, public scenario defining Bloom's own theoretical postulations, Emerson's monument-like American vision exists solely through Stevens' imaginary reading of others reading it.[30] Consequently, he not only stages the older vision's modern breakdown, but also situates it in a nighttime setting or, figuratively speaking, when a sleeping public might no longer perceive the impressive, literary-historical aura marking Emerson's *twilight* vision. Fantasizing the occlusion of public witnesses (the square "turned cold and silent"), Stevens, as it were, makes the edifice disappear entirely from sight. His poem would void Emerson's *public,* his works' readers alias viewers, thus clearing the way ("The square began to clear") for Stevens to write in private the poem he *is* writing. Only by that means can he traverse a truly "bare common" of imagination, which otherwise calls up a public scene rife with the pressures endemic to literary performance.

Stevens' desideratum clearly remains a viable poetic fantasy only if he aborts any wish to construct publicly conspicuous poetic monuments of his own. Constantly becoming a reader to his own work, how can he not embrace that ever-returning motivation, for surely it marks his poetic act both before and after its occurrence, however subliminally registered.[31] Stevens' "private" fantasy therefore hinges on his keeping a public medium (literature) anonymous, an edifice in flux, its notable exemplars, whether Emerson or visionary doubles like Whitman and Dickinson—

> A slash of Blue —
> A sweep of Gray —
> Some scarlet patches on the way,
> Compose an Evening Sky
> (#204)

—made unrecognizable to himself and others. Maintaining its private locus of composition here matters more than his poem's literary-competitive incitements or canonical ambitions, which "The Public Square" precisely seeks to abjure. That is why, in a move equally licensed by Bloom's paradigm, the poem additionally evokes Hawthorne's (moonlit) "Actual" and "Imaginary" scene of writing (in) *The Scarlet Letter.* Doesn't this novel/romance proper itself stage pivotal social meetings in a public square, and not least the private, familial one at nighttime with Hester, Dimmesdale, and Pearl? Evoking the reclusive Hawthorne's offstage scenarios and scene of writing, Stevens' poem averts at least two pressures: the literary-public impress of Emerson's as if oracularly intoned "common" vision in Nature; and the actual public agon, the "Blue" and "Gray" Civil War, that defines Dickinson's at once ironically reserved and "transparent" union with imaginary "scarlet" revision of Emerson's Nature in *Nature*.

Yet *The Scarlet Letter* self-evidently possesses its own canonical cachet in the American literary-public domain. Moreover, given Dimmesdale's public confession and Hester's resolve to turn private deed into social good, Hawthorne's main characters hint at his parallel concession of reclusive, compositional scenes to public mandates. For such reasons, Stevens' "The Public Square" glosses Hawthorne's work only as an en passant trope, and further opts for an even more private, less canonically respected American literary precedent: the catastrophic implosion at the end of Poe's "The Fall of the House of Usher." Poe, himself an avowed anti-Emersonian, there empties the most proximate formulations of a public realm of all content:

> Suddenly there shot along the path a wild light, and I turned to see whence a gleam so unusual could have issued; for the vast house and its shadows were alone behind me. The radiance was that of the full, setting, and blood-red moon, which now shone vividly through that once barely discernible fissure, of which I have before spoken as extending from the roof of the building, in a zigzag direction, to the base. (*P&T* 335)

In Stevens' poem, Poe's wild light appears as a lunar "coma"; the house with its shadows and fissure turn into "blacks" melded into a "fractured edifice"; the zigzag fissure gets figured as "slash" and "slants." And just as Stevens' speaker witnesses the public square turning "cold and silent" after the "edifice fell" in a "mountain-blue cloud," so the "Usher" narrator experiences "the deep and dank tarn at my feet clos[ing] sullenly and silently over the fragments of the '*House of Usher*'" (336). Poe's tale, literally designated as such in quotation marks but also elided by the narrative's representational momentum, in effect mocks its readers by its sudden withdrawal from further public inspection. Besides its final line suggesting much the same, Stevens' poem refers to its own moon-like status, but in the sense of a small, intricate, jewel-like figure: "The bijou of Atlas." Poe's tale flirts with and aborts "deep and dank" meaning; "The Public Square" analogously regards itself as only *possibly* rife with Atlas-like, i.e., demonstrably authoritative, poetic significance in the public realm.

The entire episode also occurs within an imaginary, nighttime *mise en scène* on more than one level. First, as the poem's own private self-designation, the de-capitalized "bijou" differentiates it from public art by punning on the ubiquitous "Bijou" burlesque houses and movie theaters common during the period.[32] Second, hardly noticeable *as* a self-reference and so bound to be overlooked, "The Public Square" defines itself as an *off-stage*, self-referential event or "bijou" poem. As such, it enacts its own withdrawal from any valorized, public setting, in other words from critical and conventional readings alike. In the poem's terms, publics willy-nilly generate the desire for massive, literary monuments, the imagined visibility of which a daylight setting would only accentuate further.

More important, through its barely perceptible yet violent, poetic withdrawal, "The Public Square" ends on a Poe-like note by its own last-minute refusal to justify, even to itself, its fantasy of private writing before its imaginary audience. The poem abruptly registers a reversal from Stevens' former comatose imagination to a simply declared, imaginative élan: a lunar vigor "with . . . porcelain *leer*." To be sure, even in meta-literary terms his self-imaged leer need not express his privately mocking public, literary-canonical standards. For example, in his verse-drama "Three Travelers Watch a Sunrise" (1916), Stevens had written, "There is a seclusion of porcelain"—the artwork—"[t]hat humanity never invades" (*OP* 151). According to James Longenbach, the play arguably goes on to qualify any full-fledged resistance to invasions of its own hermetic privacy.[33] One can also hold that "The Public Square" resists becoming public art not to instantiate a private poiesis, but precisely to recover or redeem Emerson's more "self"-promising public common from Stevens' onerously restrictive, modern-American "public *square*."

These qualifications only testify to what I have stated and reiterate throughout the present work. In pursuing literary privacy, neither Stevens nor Poe, as if gripped by some precipitous, anti-social pathology or literary anxiety, denies the public fate of private writing. Poe ironically frames that pathology in his well-known tale "William Wilson." Similarly, one can read Stevens' "porcelain leer" as imaging how others might apprehend and judge his poem's disaffection from literary-public venues, rather than as expressing his wish to assault them per se. Neither writer naively presumes to foreclose his text's communicative impulses or residual effects, and not only because each wants to publish his works for others to read and appreciate. Both writers eschew an either-public-or-private binary. As I construe it in the present book, their "write to privacy" *begins* in variously defined literary-public squares. It is therefore irreducible to their fetishizing the solitude one normally associates with writing, let alone the kind of reserve that defines ordinary social interactions and acts of communication.[34] For both writers, the private quite literally but innocuously means always something *more*.

4

I have already suggested that that *more* also means more than privacy's usual social formations in American cultural contexts. In my formulation, Poe and Stevens do not pursue any quasi-secure or determinable social state of privacy (autonomous selfhood, for example), which one might peremptorily assume, hope to arrive at, or, conversely, criticize for its conservative political effects. Instead, both writers continually strive to elicit an "other" privacy that in principle finesses all such identitarian concerns.

In literary-critical terms, this thesis inevitably runs counter to both formalist and ideological as well as Bloomian modes of artistic surveillance. I make no claim, for instance, that either Poe's tales or Stevens' 1923 *Harmonium* poems ever realize a private, aesthetic cache in and through the kind of metatextual troping traceable in poems like "The Public Square." Such a claim, after all, traffics in public squares of its own. Among other things, it echoes, if only from the viewpoint of what I consider the dominant paradigm governing current American criticism, the political quietism attributable to the old New Criticism. The ideal New Critical work resists social praxis and otherwise figures an isolated, self-referential artifact. It appears in exact counterpoint to the debased, utilitarian discourse of modern, capitalist life, to historically worn-out literary figures, and to stereotypes mass-produced by the "culture industry." "Private" in a social sense, literary art so formulated not only seeks solace in itself, but also requires specialized exegetes to demonstrate its uniqueness. As Frank Lentricchia asks, how "can the rest of us break into it, so that we, too, can cherish its special meanings . . . which by definition are clearly disconnected from common human experience?"[35]

Lentricchia's brand of ideological critique insists on the inescapable, political motivation that permeates what he reductively terms the "aesthetic isolationism" of New Critical desiderata. How might a thesis that valorizes literary privacy fare any different, and all the more for its illustrative use of two writers whom one might more viably link—if at all—on the basis of their avowed aestheticism or elitist withdrawal from cultural concerns? Who wants "to be let alone" (Warren and Brandeis' axiomatic definition of privacy) but the "haves," always at the expense of the "have-nots"? Do not cultural discourses of New Critical ilk propagandize such quasi-ontological, quasi-autonomous, social privilege?

To a certain extent, the New Criticism, at least as now popularly understood, invited political deconstructions of this kind. Even as it promoted an art at odds with the modern commodity, its practitioners both arguably propagated a consumerist methodology for understanding literary texts, and appeared to propose an idealist experience of literature that would leave the alienated marketplace more or less untouched. Nonetheless, New Critical tenets also insinuated a privileged, literary model for a better if theoretically delimited public world.[36] For most New Critics, the artwork actually entailed a public enterprise from first to last, whatever the specialized if also reproducible methodology required to explain it. What else characterizes "the intentional fallacy" if not an effort to dismiss the writer's private cum privileged authority regarding his or her text? In W. K. Wimsatt's words, "[t]he poem is not the critic's own and not the author's. . . . The poem belongs to the public. It is embodied in language, the peculiar possession of the public, and it is about the human being, an object of public knowledge."[37]

Along with its well-known criterion of the literary work's "sacramental," i.e., publicly shareable, value, the New Critical ethos and aesthetic clearly fall outside my theorizing of the private in the present book. In line with its promotion of the artwork's self-referential autonomy, New Criticism at best promulgates a liberal notion of individualist privacy, which is to say a literary-institutionalized defense of its beleaguered state in the modern public sphere. As I maintain in the following work, Poe and Stevens transgress that notion as much as they do other understandings of their public environments. In the works I discuss, they pursue a privacy, "radical" in this context, predicated on its perpetually insecure, unstable, and especially idiosyncratic status. In pursuing it, both writers produce texts that resist becoming fetishized correlatives of some privacy *accompli*.

For that reason, one might suppose that a poststructuralist conception of Poe's and Stevens' works provides a better way to articulate their "private" pursuits. It is not simply the case, to adopt Murray Krieger's more sophisticated version of New Critical theory, that these works somehow acknowledge their fictionality, and so their "own insufficiency as no more than an aesthetic reduction" of the real. Seeking to elicit their compositional act's radically private ground, the two writers instead fashion their works as pre-textual occurrences, or as if they were *yet* to become public.[38]

Nevertheless, this deferral only superficially resembles commonly understood, poststructuralist conceptions of "texts." Having no outside, the poststructuralist text, subject to persistently unstable or iterative signifiers and contexts of reception, functions as a model for all cultural activities. Post-structuralist frameworks, that is, posit an omnitextualism that manifestly expands the public sphere to the point of denying the public-private binary altogether. Since one can never outwit the "always already" reception of one's written composition by others *or* oneself, any "private" disclosed by *différance* inescapably reduces to a logocentric illusion. The "public" conversely comprises a non-locatable, self-perpetuating project, a semiotic process in which human reference-points remain forever unfixed and problematic. At the same time, if Derridean *écriture* undermines the truth-claims of both private and public positions, its primary cachet lies in the public effects it conceptually proposes, which is why it itself can incur charges of ideological irresponsibility. Louis Montrose argues, for example, that poststructuralist thought dissolves lived history "into . . . an antinomy of objectivist determinism and subjectivist free-play," thus disallowing the "possibility for historical agency on the part of individual or collective human subjects."[39]

With respect to the privacy issue, ideological critique, of course, propagates an omnipublic positionality of its own. The current practice of literary-political criticism consistently deploys public alternatives to what it regards as discursive, public hegemonies, and in that sense, as Mark Bauerlein argues, itself allows for no outside. Like its mostly discredited conservative opposition in the academy, such criticism, aggressively suspicious of formalist recidivism,[40] focuses entirely on the cultural effects literary texts (might) have with respect to one or another social polity. Politically motivated criticism configures all texts as unavoidably public, whether or not it also insists, as do Ernesto Laclau and Chantal Mouffe, on the public sphere's multiple compositions: "What we are witnessing [today] is a politicization far more radical than any we have known in the past, because it tends to dissolve the distinction between the public and the private, not in terms of the encroachment on the private by a unified public space, but in terms of a proliferation of radically new and different political spaces."[41]

Certain kinds of political critique can no doubt sometimes balk at instead of applaud the co-option of private spheres into mini-public ones enlisted to deny dominance to one or another First World variety. In principle, for instance, neo-historical criticism is not averse to working out the public-private complications within specific literary texts.[42] Yet even when one acknowledges its intra-disciplinary diversity and diverse social agendas, the project of ideological critiques aims to effect an implicit or explicit reformation of the regnant public sphere, and "the advancement of freedom" at large.[43] Accordingly, literature might better heed the example of more notably public-oriented arts like sculpture and movies, which at their best, as W. J. T. Mitchell argues, propagate "a utopian venture," or possess the heft of "a *critical* public art that . . . dares to awaken a public sphere of resistance, struggle, and dialogue."[44]

That is exactly what a poem like Stevens' "The Public Square" does not do. Contrary to staging a scene in which "[n]othing more than a clear space . . . serves as . . . the point at which all privacies converge,"[45] Stevens' poem resists its own tendency to become public art, condenses in poetic shorthand its doing so, and inscribes the desire for a scene of private monologue. But none of this occurs *in* public. Stevens' art deliberately abjures its public effects without any self-satisfied aesthetic conviction. His poem therefore cannot even function as some interpellative cultural emissary for bourgeois privacy, say by intentionally corralling reading subjects to adopt positions compatible with its dominant, United States formation. The same situation, and not merely a complex of social, economic, and sectionalist pressures, complicates allegations about the racist scenarios that supposedly mark Poe's fiction.[46]

What interpellative affects Poe's and Stevens' texts do produce happen incidentally to their respective literary pursuits of privacy. Their private enterprises internally stage their culture's extant reading conventions at once to isolate "the public" and to imagine private countermoves in relation to it. Strictly speaking, then, their aestheticism lies not in withdrawal from cultural concerns, but in engaging culture on private poetic grounds. If for both writers the aesthetic disclosure of privacy is irreducible to the contents of those concerns, it yet allows privacy to speak through cultural readings by holding them off from totalization. So at least indirectly, Poe and Stevens do do cultural work in the ways they pursue literary privacy, provided that one values privacy to begin with.

Needless to say, today's critical blame-games run deep. Ideological arguments can always insist that (my depictions of) Poe's and Stevens' abstentions from wholly committing to a public art unconsciously manifest a desire recalcitrantly synonymous with bourgeois individualism or autonomous selfhood. But to what political end, since the goal is precisely to contracept privacy's public attraction? Besides, no critical position can forfend second-guessing as to its own quasi-private public agendas. Many neo-historicists, for example, acknowledge their antidotal relation to and lurking complicity with bourgeois-cultural scripts. As one critic states it, "every act of unmasking, critique, and opposition, uses the tools it condemns and risks falling prey to the practice it exposes."[47]

At best, ideological critique can provide only provisional, discursive exposés of bourgeois values like privacy, were that at all the kind for which I argue Poe and Stevens seek in writing. No matter its particular social agenda, political criticism at bottom stands committed to its own public orientation as well as to a wholly public art, and so ineluctably elides the private as I mean to discuss it in Poe's and Stevens' works. I hold that both writers deploy meta-literary tropes—plots and images referring to their reception—to uncover provisionally viable zones of compositional privacy, the effect of which recasts the artwork more as an ongoing memo of that disclosure than what it signifies for others in social *or* aesthetic terms.

Several corollaries follow from my configuration. First, Poe's and Stevens' meta-literary efforts to postpone their texts' posterior reception entail a subject-position without content. The privacy both writers pursue occurs only in the act of writing, and so cannot secure a private self beyond it. Second, the desideratum of subjective vacancy necessarily forfeits their making public truth-claims, ultimately including about privacy itself, whatever its inevitable social imbrications. Third and not least, the two writers' efforts to abort psychic investment in the resulting text neutralize without attempting to negate the by-definition-public issue of literary evaluation.

From an ideological perspective, to privatize the value of one's work patently falsifies how writers write texts and readers read them. We may think that writing and reading occur in private, but in fact we premise them on a set of social-literary protocols, learned generic expectations, and the like.[48] Both activities methodologically presuppose an axiom on which historicist and other cultural criticism generally relies: all objects, persons, events, and thoughts are constituted by shared or shareable collective experience, observation, and subsequent interpretation. Everything not only takes place in culturally specific public fields, but also becomes nameable and so communicable by means of them in the first place.

Stated bluntly, for any reader, the *public* text always comes first, from which one might only then if at all deduce the private. Indeed, committed to producing knowledge about texts for others, critical readers are less inclined to make any like deduction. The "critical and scholarly world," as James M. Cox puts it, particularly "involves us in helplessly repressing our own secrets in writing" about literary works.[49] Even when I think so-called private thoughts about a text, a self-other communicational paradigm determines their impulse and trajectory, whether I publicly record them or keep them to myself. Nor does this situation change if one grants the contingent aspects of the codes governing literary experience. For example, from the reader's vantage point, writers write in relation to what Stanley Fish terms shifting "interpretive communities." Discursive publics generate strategies of reading that inevitably can get "forgotten or supplanted, or complicated or dropped from favor"; in that case, "there is a corresponding change in texts, not because they are being read differently, but because they are being written differently."[50]

Fish's line of reasoning may just exemplify an instance of *post hoc, ergo propter hoc*. Does public effect (a readable, public text) necessarily cause its only comparatively more private cause (a text's indeterminate process of composition)? Fish's apparently reasonable depiction, I think, rests on a pragmatic fiction that writers address relatively stable, homogeneous, and discrete interpretive publics, tradition-bound or newly emergent, within specific acts of writing. Why not press the formulation further? If these communities ineluctably shift, surely a writer's relation to them can do the same, even with respect to his or her particular, interpretive environment at a given personal or historical moment. It makes no less sense to argue that nothing ever happens without the possibility of one's idiosyncratic relation to it, so that "the public" (and not exclusively its dominant guise) itself consists of a fiction.[51] As Barbara Herrnstein Smith suggests, we never perceive the same thing or read the same text or agree on its significance in the same way. We come to them in different moods, from different experiences, with different needs, and at different stages of our personal histories. Communication thus consists of "a *differentially consequential interaction* . . . in which each party acts in relation to the other . . . in different, asymmetric ways and in accord with different specific motives."[52]

Smith remains tied to uncovering the problematic of negotiating our evaluations of texts and other events in the public realm. But in theory, her argument recursively pivots around how private experience, at least the kind I find Poe and Stevens exemplifying, poses the *other* to all public regimes of literary evaluation and knowledge. From that standpoint, the question finally comes down not to how, given its dependence on social-historical constructions, the private at all exists or appears, but to how the public does, given its constant vulnerability to the idiosyncrasies of private experience.

5

To argue for going private with Poe's and Stevens' works is to encounter a recurring obstacle that, besides its ideologically motivated spin, shifts interchangeably between the contexts of commonsense, critical understanding and epistemological abstraction. Literature self-evidently constitutes a public medium for personal acts of imagining the real. Especially with Poe, writing literary texts noticeably prompts the writer's psychic investments in his work's public reception. An interior if inchoate public unavoidably attaches itself to the work's very process of composition. It makes little sense to deny the general Bakhtinian proposition that "even the most primitive human utterance produced by the individual organism is, from the point of view of its content, import, and meaning, organized outside the organism, in the extraorganismic conditions of the social milieu. Utterance as such is wholly a product of social interaction."[53]

Using language, in short, means to want to go public. Privacy here at most comprises the minor marginalia or whatever appears irrelevant or unsuitable to one's making linguistic "common" sense regarding particular, interlocutory situations. What makes sense is public, actual or de facto; by default, what doesn't is marginally public—or residually private—which, if one willfully withholds it, one can call private in the way we normally use the term. To claim differently, say that the private is primary or at least a positive something in the sense/non-sense dyad, is simply to make the private public.

An observation in Wittgenstein's *Philosophical Investigations* helps illustrate the last point. In proposition 280, he suggests that artists either represent what they imagine or they do not. That is, we have no grounds to believe that a work's imaginative representations include its artist's "private impression" of them, and so mean something different for us than for the artist.[54] To insist further on the radical referentiality of the private—that it refers, say, to an irreducible "other" in human experience—is to indulge the epistemological fantasy Wittgenstein imputes to notions of a "private language," a grammatically correct but semantically nonsensical set of utterances.

Doesn't the present book's thesis, that the Poe and Stevens' works discussed represent a virtually interminable, rhetorical process of going private, exemplify the same fantasy? For that matter, insofar as my thesis makes sense, it contradicts any such thing as a radical privacy. Here, it does no good for me to appeal to the radical contingency of cognitive acts, or the inability of others to duplicate theirs or mine with each other. Its means and ends being thoroughly linguistic, criticism, to apply Wittgenstein's proposition, can only consist of a communicable "representation or piece of information" about literary texts.[55] No experience can escape the public language-game. Even "the relatively private extreme of [idiosyncratic] nuances with which we approach language and people," as Henry Sussman remarks, incurs linguistic-cultural limits, dictating that "we can never fully go over [the edge]" or go utterly private.[56]

Yet there exists at least one phenomenological conundrum for this post-factum analysis of linguistic experience, namely what Geoffrey Madell terms "the unanalysability of 'I', the fact that 'I' cannot be known 'by description'. If 'I' cannot be thus known, it follows that there is no description, the satisfaction of which will entail or imply that what is thus described is mine." For example, trained on bodily experience, any descriptive act leaves "a gap between" itself and "what is in fact my body and my situation . . . [or] the assertion that it is *myself* which is thus described."[57] A residual privacy thus haunts verbal representations of so-called private, personal experience. By extension, objections to a criticism pointing toward radical privacy similarly require a decisive adoption of a third-person perspective. One of course might ask whether the same perspective does not also apply to the preceding observation. But much as Poe's first-person narrators or Stevens' poetic speakers invite a reader's "ironic" contextualizations, the last epistemological disclosure may only *mimic* third-person accounts of one's unanalyzably private (here not merely "subjective") experience, and by that intimate their explanatory inadequacy.

Wittgenstein himself cannot quite dispel the allure of private experience, for why does he, as do many of his subsequent commentators, concern himself at great length in *Philosophical Investigations* with imagining others imagining its possibility? Doubtless he wants to dispel the stubborn illusion of any incommunicable, human experience. By grammatical law, he would proscribe one important ramification of that illusion: the invasion of the public and its discursive support systems by the private. To be sure, he indulges the possibility at least in one instance: "The essential thing about private experience is really not that each person possesses his own exemplar, but that nobody knows whether other people also have *this* or something else. The assumption would thus be possible—though unverifiable—that one section of mankind had one sensation of red and another section another."[58] Using Wittgenstein's own schema, one might argue that his one qualification itself is not exactly private, for wouldn't that other sector of mankind still be understanding "red" in concert? As envisioned here, private experience arguably abides captivated within the network of one or another linguistic grammar—that of a card-game, say, to use another of his observations: "The proposition 'Sensations are private' is comparable to: 'One plays [solitaire] by oneself'."[59]

In other words, were I to invent my own game-rules for playing, so to speak, a truly solitary solitaire, they of necessity still permit duplication, i.e., public representation. However, one need not fully equate solitary with private experience, and not simply because one can feel alone in a crowd and call that private. The disjunction between personal experience and its linguistic depictions transforms conventional and subtler synonyms of privacy (e.g., solitude, reticence, a sense of shame, preference for anonymity, even critical disquisitions on private language—or a poetics of American privacy) into tropes all pointing toward a self-inducible, noetic space devoid of specific content. Properly speaking, such a space does not exist. It has no thereness, no representational status. It appears as a contingent and quickly dissipating aftereffect of the inability to represent to oneself one's therefore unanalyzable, impersonal, and private experience. That is so regardless if one disputes the totality of communication. To justify private, phenomenological experience, one may instead resort to tropes of privacy available within one's particular historical-cultural-discursive environment. But as with the present discussion, these tropes, too, fail to signify the private "it" except, if at all, in passing. They themselves at best turn into linguistic figures as such, or into meta-tropes evoking and tracing "its" disappearance.

To me, the tales and poems I discuss pursue radical privacy by enacting just that kind of processual troping, which as if perpetually trumps the lure of long-term, public significations. It follows, I think, that only in poetic terms does it make sense to play a game of private solitaire. Simply to entertain playing it requires an imaginary and yet real state of mind, which Stevens in fact imagines in a seldom-discussed poem from *Harmonium*, "The Place of the Solitaires":

> Let the place of the solitaires
> Be a place of perpetual undulation.
>
> Whether it be in mid-sea
> On the dark, green water-wheel,
> Or on the beaches,
> There must be no cessation

> Of motion, or of the noise of motion,
> The renewal of noise
> And manifold continuation;
>
> And, most, of the motion of thought
> And its restless iteration,
>
> In the place of the solitaires,
> Which is to be a place of perpetual undulation.
>
> (*CP* 60)

With its trebled "And" and extended second stanza, Stevens' poem, like Poe's "The Bells," mimics its topical, purely sensory theme, here of "undulation."[60] More important, "The Place of the Solitaires" evinces his desire to abort communication in "perpetual" or radical fashion. In "mid-sea," or in the midst of visionary activity—of a mid-*seeing* enabled by the prosodic rhythms of poetry, "the dark, green water-wheel"—communicable, Wittgenstein-like information becomes less important to the poet than "the noise of motion" or language's sub-informational yield. The poem embodies Stevens' wish for poetic rumination absent communicational imperatives. "Let" it remain solely a "perpetual undulation" or rhythmic "motion," in other words a poetic thought going nowhere, addressing nothing, remaining only a "restless iteration" within his own mind.

Why wish to suspend the referential direction of language? Does Stevens' imaginary effort ironically confess, this time in a linguistic-epistemological context, his actual desire to escape the social charge, the communicational use-value, endemic to literary activity especially? The poem, no doubt, might very well reflect an ideological reaction, whether that of capitulation or resistance to the utilitarian ethos of the American marketplace with which he was all too familiar in his own daily work. Perhaps, too, as in "The Public Square," Stevens conflates his "public" with a more interior one composed of literary precedents. One way or another, these publics press him to write meaningful verse, to compete in a poetic agon, to seek distinction before peers or canonical judges. Maybe the wish to float to no end in poetic waters additionally entails an imaginary, neo-Romantic defense of poetry specifically in reaction to the modern, scientific episteme, such as Wittgenstein exemplifies in his disquisitions on language.

"The Place of the Solitaires," in short, may only express a longing for what his alienated public sphere, construed in exterior or interior terms, will not permit except *as* a fantasy: an inevitably losing because unrealistic defense of poetic privacy. Yet true to its imagined, vacation-like setting, the poem, I think, would vacate making meaning only if it could. It never pretends to express more than its poet's wish for a sustained state of poetic self-hypnosis.[61] About itself, the poem means exactly its subjunctive desire, and as such leaves room for—does not resist or itself seek to alienate—the various registers of "public" meanings it no doubt presupposes or may possess for others.

In point of fact, Stevens does not imagine playing poetic solitaire alone. Anyone can play his game, so that it remains social at least to the extent of allowing for other "solitaires." For the poem expresses the wish that the same wish for suspension of the referential would hold true for those of us "on the beaches." If not fully immersed in poetic activity as the poem's speaker right now, nothing prevents even its vacationing or casual readers from becoming so. Stevens should know, since through his poem he in effect concurrently proposes to read or internalize other poets apart from their specific, anxious precedents. He, too, would immerse himself in their lyrics, but with their undulating rhythms dominating their meaning, and so, as noted with "The Public Square," only as if emanating from anonymously authored—private—sources.

Once again, far from engaging a private-public binary where he insists on the former at the expense of the latter, Stevens imagines for his poem a peripheral, public interface deriving from multiple private spheres. "The Place of the Solitaires" entertains a kind of poetic *cogito ergo sum* from which, unlike the Cartesian variety, the private just happens, without determinate ego-concerns as well as contents, even as the poem's "meaning" remains accessible to others. Necessary, of course, within the human economy, the public projects underwritten by linguistic meaning risk assuming totalizing proportions. They therefore require a poetic *vacation,* lest they elide not simply the idiosyncratic aspect of private desires, but the desire for privacy itself. In poetry, at least as Stevens construes it in the present poem, meaning gets vacated, becomes a pretext for "The renewal of noise," and the private, else at the mercy of its public constructions, for the once comes first. No covert defense of liberal individualism or bourgeois privacy, the private subject of his poem eschews the public individual, most notably as defined by Stevens' American social complex. In its place, he imagines a "manifold continuation" of his I's perpetually unstable, formless, undulating, unanalyzable, irrepressibly private source.

There if anywhere lies the literary "place of the solitaires" that I argue Poe and Stevens continually seek to uncover although can never definitively realize in the works I discuss. To repeat, pursuing literary privacy for them does not mean repressing social interaction (the prerequisite premise of writing), or regressing to a myth of utter non-sense. Neither does their pursuit reflect some anxious ideological reaction to or complicit support of their respective social environments. It instead consists of both writers' efforts to figure the inevitable congealment and amplification of social including semiotic interaction into one or another "public," so as continually to disclose a "private" surplus—a "place" where one becomes other to oneself, but by extension, also to others *as* others.

Framed that way, privacy need not be anti-ethical in principle, let alone opposed to the social effects literature can produce. On such an account, if the public is to be, quite literally, an ongoing construction of social interaction, it paradoxically requires each person's pursuit of a radical mode of privacy, as the particular idiom of his or her interaction would provisionally define the project.[62] Compromised versions of privacy, regardless of their good or bad faith intentions, leave their obverse public spheres intact, whether in a state of status quo, reform, or revolution. The "public" then becomes all the more primed to capture one's full, imaginative allegiance for its promise of identitarian fulfillments. In the following work, to answer my earlier question, I claim that Poe and Stevens indeed want matters "other"-wise.

1   Poe's Secret Autobiography

Suddenly I was attracted by Bartleby's closed desk, the key in open sight left in the lock.
    —Herman Melville, "Bartleby the Scrivener" (1853)

I have written to keep the over curious out of the secret places of my mind, both in my verse and in my letters to such as you.
    —Robert Frost, *Letters* #299 (1932)

It is not good for man to cherish a solitary ambition. Unless there be those around him, by whose example he may regulate himself, his thoughts, desires, and hopes will become extravagant, and he the semblance, perhaps the reality, of a madman.
    —Nathaniel Hawthorne, "The Prophetic Pictures" (1837)

1

At certain junctures, Edgar Allan Poe's fiction often takes what look like perverse, private turns, yet paradoxically all but announces in public its doing so. Certainly, Poe's tales always seem fictions motivated in the direction of their imagined reception. For one thing, they impishly advertise their literary seams. The more outré the topic—mad narrators, premature burials, doubles, dying, beautiful women, the conundrum of enigmatic ciphers or written "characters"—the greater its public cachet. Because they promise the frisson of the unknown, of the idiosyncratic, or of "some never-to-be-imparted secret," as he terms it in one of his earliest tales (*P&T* 198), events normally allocated to the private sphere impel Poe's narratives from first to last. A similar tactic occurs in his criticism as well. If he likes to expose alleged plagiarisms by other writers, he always leaves us suspecting his own, which twentieth-century critics have detected in some detail.[1]

The problem is that Poe also frequently privatizes his public exposures of his private maneuvers. He does more than simply bare literary devices or, say, all but advertise his exploiting popular literary genres and pilfering materials from *Blackwood's Magazine*. I also mean that Poe stages the public's interest in the private per se. For example, called by a "letter," an apt analogue for the tale, the narrator in "The Fall of the House of Usher" stands for the reading public's surrogate. As such, he becomes increasingly drawn and draws us with him into private domains. He moves into the interior recesses of an unconventional house already far from town; then figuratively into its namesake's self-sequestered persona: his incestuous relationship with his sister, and Usher's idiosyncratic mind via his conversations and art. At the story's end, the narrator witnesses the house's literal implosion, and the reader the abrupt withdrawal of "The House" from semiotic view. Since no one but the narrator can corroborate the above occurrences, the entire narrative assumes the ambience of a private, dream-like experience, all of which inevitably redounds to Poe's construction of the tale itself.

Even the public-becoming-private narrator's reading of "The Mad Trist" represents, in exaggerated fashion, the way Poe would have us read *his* tale, and so can momentarily distract us from doing so. The scene seems too much or, to use one of his own locutions, "supererogatory." On one hand, the narrative of "The Fall of the House of Usher" enacts Poe's poetics of fiction generally, namely, as he remarks in "The Philosophy of Composition," for the reader to experience its "unity of impression" in "one sitting" (*E&R* 15). On the other, in overexposing that poetics, the tale within the tale threatens to illustrate or signify his literary desideratum as such.

In short, private topics of public interest turn into less detectable or more recalcitrantly enigmatic private performances. Why bother to mystify audiences at a second-degree, contextually gratuitous level? Poe's very words sometimes drift from their sense-making or communicational function to non-semantic sound, or to the sheer materiality of the signifier. Consider the animal sounds mistaken for a foreign language in "The Murders in the Rue Morgue"; or more notoriously, the "nevermore" mimicking of human speech by the bird in "The Raven." The guttural sounds and teeth-gnashing by the dwarf-protagonist in "Hop-Frog" underscore the same drift, given that "teeth" doubles as a metonym for articulate speech itself. Compounding their already hoaxy aura, Poe's tales also devolve on numerous verbal jokes, particularly in the form of submerged puns and commonplace maxims. Hans Phaall dropping a letter to townspeople below from a balloon in the sky translates as a text appearing "out of the blue" and "full of hot air." The narrator in "Berenice" extracting teeth (*sic*) from his dead female cousin puts himself, to use the colloquial expression, "in the jaws of death." Detecting an orangutan as the killer of two women in "The Murders in the Rue Morgue," the "duping" Dupin dabbles in "monkey business." Or perhaps, like the eponymous character in "Hop-Frog," he here "makes a monkey out of" the social establishment represented by the Parisian police. The same applies to reading "The Masque of the Red Death," where we—what else?—"read death."

These trompe l'oeil verbal surprises, ready to spring on the reader at a moment's notice, can deflate a Poe tale's already bizarre yet still compelling story line into a mere language-game that signifies nothing but exhibitionist irrelevance, as it were "Only this and nothing more." Supposing one notices it at all, a Poe fiction that cites its own fictionality disturbs rather than bolsters the reader's conventional expectation of fiction's illusionary facticity. *This* fact accounts for the hoaxy aspect of Poe's tales, and not just those in which, like *The Narrative of Arthur Gordon Pym* or "Mesmeric Revelation," he self-evidently exploits the public's tendency to take fictional narratives for rendering actual events. At most, Poe's meta-literary allusions signify his authorial manipulation as such, or the immanent presence of an authorial "I" in willful control of his text's production. A literary hoax too, after all, shows its writer's awareness of the fiction of his fiction's reception.

Of course, one can view Poe's disruptive, rhetorical acts as evidence for something other than perverse manipulation or self-indulgent exhibitionism. Perhaps they express his "supererogatory" animus toward his mid-nineteenth-century mass-cultural, democratic audience. If nothing else, they unsettle the literary contract whereby readers agree to suspend their disbelief on the assumption that writers attempt to represent shareably imagined and imaginative worlds. Or perhaps, in poststructuralist fashion, Poe's disruptions exemplify an unconscious enactment of "writing" as a constant slippage of signifiers. Surely the forged (in both senses of the word) as opposed to meta-fictional aspect of literary hoaxes suggests a Derridean iterability of fiction at large. Any tale is a hoax, in the sense that it lacks a sure ground from which one might apprehend it as a totally self-present mode of representation.

Yet the verbal static emanating from Poe's tales may strike one as at once too contrived, too repetitive, and too subtle to construe as mere exhibitionism, or as an expression of ideological grievance, or as a sign of an unconscious, semiotic praxis. Quite the contrary, his rhetorical noise mostly calls attention to *his* making it without further point. That is, it refers the tale's imagined reader to the word-mediated traces of its author, the man in the text, and for no apparent reason other than to confront that reader with Poe's terminal, autobiographical presence—or his present absence.

Indeed, the "self" suddenly uncovered by our awareness of hoaxy elements in Poe's tales occasionally leads us to the cul-de-sac of his subliminally inscribed signature. This is the case, for instance, with "Siope," an early brief fable (1832), which he later retitled "Silence." Appropriately enough, the first title includes the caption "in the manner of the Psychological Autobiographists," probably alluding, according to Thomas O. Mabbott (2:199), to Edward Lytton Bulwer and Thomas De Quincey. The full title coats the ensuing fable with a parodic veneer; it encourages us to take it as a fantasy anything *but* autobiographical, at least until one notices that the letters of "Siope" also anagrammatically spell "is Poe."

"Siope" is not the only time Poe resorts to signatorial ambushes. Casually traced in passing as a synonym for the tale's "Ourang-Outang," what to make of the anagrammatic pun "E.A.P.," which doubles the "ape" killer in "The Murders in the Rue Morgue" (*P&T* 430)? Like Poe's rhetorical jokes, his literal self-references occur in subliminal fashion, and so suggest something other than authorial braggadocio or his setting off some attention-getting, rhetorical firecracker. Neither do they cue us to read the tale as if it were a full-fledged literary hoax. At the same time, the suddenly disclosed hidden signature seems to epitomize more acrostic word-play than, say, some symbolically charged, unconscious inscription of a specular name, such as Ferdinand de Saussure argues freighted certain incunabula with mythopoeic significance.[2] Poe's "Here I am" signifiers refer only to themselves. They strike one as too arbitrary to fit back into the fictional story line in which they unexpectedly appear, or else too wayward to add ambiguous density to the tale in question. The same applies to his at best grimly humorous one-liners: they distract a reader's attention from the tale's narrative spell, the very aesthetic that defines the kind of public literary effect for which he presumably aims.

Put another way, enfolded within Poe's tales lie rhetorical gambits that mimic the odd-even game defining Dupin's method of detection in "The Murders in the Rue Morgue": "I know that you know I know that I am in the process of writing this fiction of a fiction." The authorial performative itself "is Poe." At most, it hints at a subtext that, whether understood as hoax or not, appears sealed off from its fictional context. This is a game, so to speak, out of narrative reach, its rules and motive withheld, and in that sense private. At the very least, one can plausibly maintain that Poe constructs his texts in the mode of expanded cryptograms, first to the extent that they elude instant notice, and second, that *when* detected, they express nothing narrationally relevant.

Poe lends credence to the last surmise in an oft-cited passage from one of his *Literati* essays: "the book of an author" doubles as "the author's self. . . . The soul is a cipher, in the sense of a cryptograph; and the shorter a cryptograph is [e.g., like his own brief tales], the more difficulty there is in its comprehension."[3] His 1841 article on "Secret Writing" shows not only a desire to produce but also his ability to decipher encrypted messages. There was never, he claims, "a time when there did not exist a necessity, *or at least a desire,* of transmitting information from one individual to another . . . as to elude comprehension [by others]" (*E&R* 1277; Poe's emphasis). Poe further contends that all cryptographs are decipherable, in other words, that there exists no such thing as a radically private language. Yet he also displays his interest in the latter possibility by reprinting a lengthy response to his contention from a correspondent named W. B. Tyler.[4] Providing his own example, "Tyler" insists that one might indeed produce a cryptographic text that would "be perfectly 'hidden' " and appear "an impenetrable mystery" to others. One can even register Poe's own impulse toward "secret writing" in his later alteration of the title "Siope" to "Silence," which doubly silences his already concealed signature. To someone convinced that a writer's autograph could express his "moral biography" (*E&R* 1323), simply the print-mediated or published tromp l'oeil signature, now sublate in "Silence," might easily instantiate a form of autographic concealment.

All this suggests that a Poe tale's *mise en scène* includes his imagination of its misreading. *In* writing, his "secret" writing serves to delay any full reading of his text. The tale others read, its immediately apprehensible or aesthetic reading, coterminously encodes the very same reading, and so produces the sense that they have not yet really read it. A similar effect occurs from a Poe text's planted anagrams. Once serendipitously discovered, as, fastidious detector that he was, he surely expected they might be, their decodified significance can refer one to yet another "impenetrable mystery." For example, the anagram "nevar" in "The *Raven*" tautologically repeats the poem's "nevermore" refrain, i.e., the reader never gets more. With other anagrams and cryptogrammatic fare, Poe can rely on the future absence of the contingent, personal, or historical illocutionary context in which he wrote them to reinforce the zero semantic value of their already fragmentary, semiotic appearance.[5]

Reading Poe's texts, one incessantly encounters the dead end of his performing, autobiographical self in one form or another. By "autobiographical," I do not mean that he at all reveals his (possible) motives for encrypting anagrammatic variants, let alone his making his private life public in any conventional sense. Nor do I quite hold to Paul de Man's notion of autobiography as a figure of reading as opposed to genre of writing.[6] With Poe, self-referential writing consists of his reading his own texts through their imagined misreading by others. In that sense, the Poe tale only incidentally contains semiotic crypts or subterranean levels of meaning putatively withheld from readers. Nothing prevents those meanings from eventually finding their way to public light. Poe's encryptions do something more: they constitute acts that signify nothing, or more precisely work to defer further access to his act of writing by readings that it itself incites. Even when one apprehends his tales *as* a mode of secret writing, they simply reveal a prematurely buried subtext, the self-referential significance of which requires one to adopt a purely speculative, and therefore alienated, aesthetic relation to them.

Poe's tales thus practice a mode of doubling always greater than their own frequent recourse to doppelgänger themes, characters, and anagrammatic fissions, as in "William Wilson," where the narrator-double's name breaks down into "I am Will, son of Will." Poe's doubling also defines his very construction of texts, a good case in point being "The Gold-Bug," which in fact was first published as a two-part weekly serial in the *Dollar Newspaper* (Mabbott 3:806). Everything about the tale concerns money. The tale's plot obviously devolves on finding a buried treasure. Also doubled by the "dollar" newspaper in which he published "The Gold-Bug," there exists the synonymy between treasure and the likely commodity-value Poe places on his tale within his literary-journalistic marketplace. For that matter, its serial mode of publication arguably redoubles the tale's narrative suspense, thereby overtly soliciting public interest to increase its market value.[7]

Strangely enough, however, "The Gold-Bug" makes its reader pay an unexpected price for its suspense-primed doublings. The tale's first part concerns William Legrand, the narrator, and the slave Jupiter, who together do discover the treasure. At least according to textual precedents on which the tale was based (Mabbott 3:800–803), the first section would otherwise have held greater melodramatic interest for Poe's reading public. But the second section proceeds to abstract or fray conventional, narrative expectations by having readers focus at length on Legrand's mode of deciphering Captain Kidd's cryptographic treasure-map. Literally taking precedence over the first part, Legrand's methodological disquisition, whatever interest it might have held for some readers, serves to displace the tale's "first" or aesthetic reading.

In name and deed, the protagonist occasions a similar deflation within the tale. A pun on "the great Will," "William Legrand" stands for Poe's surrogate in writing tales generally. In his 1842 review of Hawthorne's *Twice-Told Tales,* Poe states that the writer strives to make "the soul of the reader [be] at the writer's control" or will (*E&R* 572). Legrand attempts to do just that with both the narrator and the slave Jupiter, whom I take to be surrogates for the tale's aesthetically enslaved reader and the more critically skeptical one. Legrand's ruse of distracting his cohort treasure-seekers with a literal gold bug metaphorically doubles the desired aesthetic mystification Poe's "The Gold-Bug" would perpetrate on its readers generally. More important, in confessing his "just-kidding" chicanery while narrating his solution of the Kidd-cryptograph, Legrand/Poe would doubly distract the narrator/reader. As author in control of the text or cryptogram that he has withheld and first interprets, he willfully positions the tale's surrogate reader into a reflective relation to it. At this meta-confessional point, the tale's emplotted reader confronts a text the sheer aesthetic effect of which has become retroactively and irrecoverably lost. As with the wine Fortunato never gets to taste in "The Cask of Amontillado," the reader's forfeited aesthetic relation to "The Gold-Bug" effectively reproduces its absent or *still* buried treasure.

Toward the end of his career, Poe states: "To see distinctly the machinery . . . of any work of Art is . . . of itself, a pleasure, but one which we are able to enjoy only just in proportion as we do *not* enjoy the legitimate effect designed by the artist" (*E&R* 1464; Poe's emphasis). From his viewpoint, aesthetic readings ought to forestall theoretical ones, whereas his tales self-evidently prompt both. The aesthetic or "legitimate effect" of a Poe tale no doubt initially distracts readers from recognizing his acts of authorial self-inscription. His fiction also proposes some "truth" about the world it depicts, by which he means the aesthetic impression of "ratiocinative" understanding. With that qualification, he can assert that, unlike the Beauty elicited in poetry, "[t]ruth is often, and in very great degree, the aim of the tale" (*E&R* 573).

Yet Poe's auto-rhetorical games double-cross his fiction's quasi-truth-claims; more precisely, they lead readers to focus on the indeterminable "truth" of his storytelling motives as opposed to its determinate fit with his fictional plots and themes. If a Poe tale's aesthetic effect captivates readers only within a delimited, single sitting, critical readings arrive at the same aesthetic limbo more definitively. To discern hoaxes, signatorial anagrams, terminal puns, repetitive motifs, and other "autobiographical" rumblings deflects attention away from the tale's immediate references to its act of encoding them. He himself demonstrates the principle in his early exposé of Maelzel's chess-player hoax (1836), where he focuses on the creator's "machinery" in lieu of the mechanism's intended effect on its audience.

Poe's own man-in-the-machine devices similarly instigate the reader's *an*-esthetic relation to his fictional narratives, all as if to confirm the public's virtual absence from his act of composing them. And of what do his compositional acts consist if not the "legitimate effect" of art that by inference he then reserves for himself? In his "Marginalia," Poe associates that effect with poetic rhymes that suspend cognition and elicit the "element of strangeness—of unexpectedness—of novelty—of originality . . . all that is *ethereal* . . . the unknown—the vague—the uncomprehended"(*E&R* 1381; Poe's emphasis). More private than literally secret, his own strange scene of writing devolves on (from public viewpoints) a prematurely buried beautiful premise. In another "Marginalia" entry, he equates novel beauty with a special "class of fancies of exquisite delicacy, which are *not* thoughts, and to which, *as yet,* I have found it absolutely impossible to adapt language" (*E&R* 1383; Poe's emphasis). Such delicate, pre-linguistic fancies finally define his desired relation to "Poesy"—the other anagrammatic pun of "Siope."[8]

In line with Dupin's view of truth in "The Murders in the Rue Morgue," Poe, one can say, constructs his stories as all surface, all there for us to read, decipher, and interpret. Whether read for their surface design *or* suspicions of withheld, authorial conundrums, his tales invite rather than resist closed readings. Either way, however, a Poe narrative merely courts a public reading that inversely hints at his private relation to the tale's scene of writing. It is as if he intentionally contrives ways for all types of readers to miss-apprehend any particular tale precisely by thinking they have not, the purpose being to apprehend its "ethereal" status on his own terms. Only by occluding others while writing them can his tales appear *to himself* "uncomprehended," strange, unexpected, that is to say, altogether original.

2

Poe's tales often allegorize the preceding scenario as their private, palimpsest double. To be sure, he airs his distaste for allegory throughout his career, usually because it interrupts a poem or tale's unified, aesthetic impression on readers. Yet the kind of allegory Poe criticizes hardly resembles even a decipherable secret writing. The term etymologically refers to a discourse at once veiled from (*allos*: other to) and embedded within that spoken in the marketplace or before a public assembly (*agora*).[9] Presumably, though, the meanings of ancient allegories remained accessible to elite interlocutors privy to their esoteric code. Poe likely understood current allegorical practices differently. In much pre-twentieth-century British and American verse (Poe's own "Sonnet—To Science," for instance), or in prose works like Hawthorne's early tales, allegory announces its presence by unmistakable personifications.

Modern allegory, that is, seldom attempts to conceal the ideational code to which a lyric or narrative refers, and in that sense traffics more in public than in private discursive venues. Modern allegory's targeted audience consists of not a select few but a literate many. In contrast, Poe finds allegory tolerable only when "the suggested meaning runs through the obvious one in a *very* profound under-current . . . so as never to show itself unless *called* to the surface, [and] there only, for the proper uses of fictitious narrative, is it available at all" (*E&R* 582–83; Poe's emphasis). Poesque allegory promotes a narrative's symbolic truth claims or "obvious" meaning "only" to append to it an indefinite or "suggestive" aura. Allegory thus comes down to a privative figure ("unless") that suspends both its own incipient truth claims and the narrative's topical, aesthetically rendered ones. Regarding both the tale's effect on readers and its writer's deployment, a private reserve clause, so to speak, clings to the tale's illusionary totality and publicly accessible meanings.

Poe constructs his meta-literary subtexts in just that way, as for example in one of his briefer-than-usual tales, "Life in Death" (1842), which he later retitled "The Oval Portrait." Arthur Hobson Quinn succinctly paraphrases the tale's narrator as

> a desperately wounded man who seeks refuge in an unoccupied chateau, and
> seeks the portrait of a young and beautiful girl, which startles him by its like-

ness to life. Finding an old volume that describes the paintings, he learns . . . [that she] had given her life to please her husband, an artist, who, as he painted into his picture her marvelous beauty, drained from her her health and spirits. Finally, when he gazed on his completed work and cried out, "This is indeed Life itself," he beheld his bride dead.[10]

In the tale's earlier version, the narrator informs us that he had just taken opium before he saw the portrait, whereas in the revised version he was merely drifting off to sleep. The recovered excision has led formalist critics to focus on the narrator's ironic function in the tale as much as on the material he narrates, an option for which most of Poe's other tales allow.[11]

But by inviting an ironic reading, the story turns the reader's attention away precisely from what Poe later maintains personifies " 'the most poetical topic in the world' ": a beautiful woman's death (*E&R* 19). In addition, "The Oval Portrait" concerns the theme of art's vampirization of the very effect—"*life-likeliness*" (*P&T* 482; Poe's emphasis)—that the narrative no less than the portrait purports to convey. And the text within the text does the same thing. Abstracting the immediate object of his initial aesthetic response, the narrator's reading of the volume perforce makes him avert his gaze from the else self-present portrait of the beautiful woman. Bereft of both the portrait *and* the text, from which the narrator (only) quotes, the narrative *we* read doubly refers to a virtually absent text, itself in the process of absenting its pictorial referent that had already displaced its living model.

In short, what we read is the narrator's misprision of the picture, a metaphor of aesthetic objects per se. On one hand, the artist, more concerned with his artistic representation of life than with life itself, effectively kills his wife in painting her picture. On the other, the narrator's reading figuratively kills the representational impress of the artistic portrait. Poe's tale leads readers to repeat the same process, since our reading of "The Oval Portrait" will surely double the narrator's own curiosity to know more about what he terms the pictorial "*vignette*," which so affects him that he at first closes his eyes, not knowing "Why I did this" (482). Moreover, his explanation for that reaction, "to make sure that my vision had not deceived me—to calm and subdue my fancy for a more sober and more certain gaze," mimics the reader's desire to maintain a more aesthetically reserved relation to the narrator's tale about the artist's to his wife. Just as the narrator goes on to read the portrait's commentary from "a small volume" (481) that literally distracts him from looking at the picture, so his remarks before citing the commentary force him into the *narrative* picture for us.

Such repetitive de-compositions of, first, the woman by the artist, next the portrait by the volume, then the latter by the tale's narrative, suggest an as if endless or provisional sequence of misreadings, another of which might include how its seeming circularity figuratively mimics an "*oval* portrait." Nor does this plausibly reconstructible sequence end here. Resembling what Poe later perpetrates on the public with "The Raven" through "The Philosophy of Composition," the tale's allegorically staged misreadings outline a scenario in which the reader becomes ever more incognizant of the narrative's self-imagined site of production. Everything leads to an eventual reading of the story that distracts our focus from its affective, poetic source: Poe's own "most poetical topic" of a dying, beautiful woman. Through a series of refractive mediations that literally absent her, the tale positions its readers to reenact the artist's killing of a beautiful woman. One can infer, however, that Poe's scripted misreadings at once increasingly occlude his tale's inspirational source from others and keep "her" *in the process* of dying. What readers perforce regard in past-tense terms, the woman's death, turns out to possess a lingering, aesthetic life ("life in death") for him in writing the tale.

Still, if Poe emplots misreadings to bury prematurely his aesthetic raison d'être, at least two aspects of his project can interrupt its imaginative execution. First, from his viewpoint, such emplotments necessarily dissipate, without any neat demarcation between them, both aesthetic and critical readings of his tales by others. As allegories of their process of misreading, his tales never quite exist except as "ghost" stories. Since for Poe they essentially concern the possibility of stories never read in their published versions, they inversely promote his own aesthetically privy relation to them, but without any sustainable basis for believing in it. At most, his allegorized subtexts point to a private scene of writing from which its public, textual effects derive. Yet for the same reason, Poe's "beautiful" topos may itself appear to him only in absentia.

More literal obstacles also complicate what one might here term his "bad faith" auto-literary project. One of them almost goes without saying: his project's dependence on the sheer contingency of his texts' material, literary-historical survival in the public sphere. Minus his conviction of others literally reading them, he could never entertain encrypting their misreadings in the first place. More important, nothing prevents Poe from imagining *some* reader or double from as if observing his reading-emplotments and their "beautiful" point, thus negating any illusion about his having realized the idiosyncratic "strangeness" defining the aesthetic relation to his tales that they recursively work to effect.

Since either complication can threaten to reintroduce public perspectives into his would-be private scene of writing, Poe sometimes resorts to other allegorical means to circumvent them. Such defines the meta-literary scenario that he smuggles into "The Oblong Box" (1844). The tale's narrator finds himself on a ship with a young artist named Wyatt and his reputedly beautiful wife, whom the narrator nevertheless judges to be plain-looking. He also notices that Wyatt, a pictorial artist of some renown, has brought an oblong box to his stateroom. Wyatt never speaks about the box's malodorous contents, although the narrator can hear him opening it at night and emitting a suppressed "low sobbing" (*P&T* 650). At first merely curious about what the box contains, the narrator soon becomes convinced that it "*could* possibly contain nothing in the world but a copy of Leonardo's 'Last Supper'. . . done by Rubini the younger" (645; Poe's emphasis). He had formerly assumed "feelings of warm friendship" for Wyatt (643). Thus, the artist's present silence, felt to be rife with a Judas-like betrayal as per *The Last Supper* allusion, provokes the narrator to anger, convincing him more than ever that the box contains "artistical secrets" (646) like Rubini's valuable counterfeit.

The tale's scenario already shows the Poe tale's proleptic instincts. Against obvious evidence to the contrary (e.g., the six-foot box's "disgusting odor" and Wyatt's "*morose*" spirits), the narrator stubbornly regards the box as a "mystification" by his erstwhile friend to conceal and "smuggle a fine picture to New York, under my very nose; expecting me to know nothing of the matter" (646; Poe's emphasis). "The Oblong Box," that is, invites us to suspect the narrator's suspicions. As if mocking its own excavations by critical readers who think they can know its author's intention, the tale allegorically stages a surrogate reader determined to find a specific, Captain Kidd–like treasure of meaning amid the intertextual sources that suspiciously mark almost any Poe tale.[12]

However, Poe's mind-games know no end. In the present case, the staged misreading also happens to include its very staging. At the simplest level, the narrator, wanting, as it were, a deep reading of things—here to discover and make public a concealed masterpiece—gets duped after all, since what Wyatt has secreted turns out to lack any public, artistic value. During a storm when the ship begins to sink, he refuses to remain on a lifeboat unless he can take the box with him, which, he exclaims, weighs " 'but a trifle' " or " 'mere nothing' " (652). After the captain rejects Wyatt's request as " '*mad*' "

(Poe's emphasis), the artist returns to the ship, retrieves the box, jumps overboard, and quickly sinks with it. In a postscript to these events, the narrator wonders why the box sank so quickly, to which the ship's captain "Hardy" responds that he himself had packed it with salt, and that once it melts, the box and its contents " 'will soon rise again' " (653). The captain also exposes the narrator's misreading of the box's contents: it did not contain an art treasure in the narrator's sense at all, but rather the artist's dead wife who, unlike her plain-looking maid, "was, indeed . . . a most lovely, and most accomplished woman."

"The Oblong Box" bears most of the previously discussed features of Poe's "secret writing." The tale flirts with one of those proverbial maxims mentioned earlier, this time the artist determined to "sink or swim" with his artistic ideal. The narrator also initially appears to stand for a naive if critically credentialed reader. Misled by the artist, he wrongly assumes that the box contains a publicly valuable artwork as opposed to its utterly contingent content: Wyatt's a.k.a. Poe's private, autobiographical relation to a figure synonymous with ideal, poetical beauty. In brief, Poe's tale allegorizes his wish to provoke the most elementary mode of misreading on unwitting and here pseudo-sophisticated readers like the narrator.

"The Oblong Box" nonetheless simultaneously complicates this apparent rhetorical dupery. First, it is not altogether certain that Poe simply frames the narrator as a representative figure for pretentious art-connoisseurs. For example, the latter's obsession with an artistic copy arguably accords with Poe's own view that artistic originals consist of "novel combinations" of previous artistic materials (*E&R* 570). Since originals themselves constitute only copies of other extant works with a difference, why cannot copies be originals, too? The one differs from the other only in degree, no doubt dependent on the experience one brings to art, or as if the art-object were itself secondary to one's relation to it.[13] So if not Poe's likely surrogate, neither does the narrator definitively spell his ironic dupe.

Equally important, in remaining silent about the box's secret content, Wyatt never provokes the narrator's aggressive desire to know it. In other words, emplotting misreadings here looks like an unnecessary or redundant strategy, and all the more so since, just as the box contains only a lifeless simulacrum of Wyatt's wife, the tale's staging of an egregious misreading of its private contents fails to elicit for Wyatt/Poe a living or *vital* relation to his "beautiful," inspirational source. On the contrary, the tale suggests how his private relation has congealed into a representable secret that additionally refers to something dead, remembered, or absent even for him. "The Oblong Box" allegorically insinuates that its own "most poetical" origin must die or, the same thing, that its origin has already become sealed off from the artist/ writer himself. Like his narrator in the 1841 article "The Island of the Fay," all an Usher-like Poe can do is try to postpone "her" final, entropic disintegration through a text that doubles its story and, as the title of "The Oblong Box" allows, becomes "her" meta-literary coffin.[14]

If nothing else, the tale shows Poe's capacity to recognize the finite materiality haunting his own scene of writing. "The Oblong Box" intimates that, no matter his plotted misreadings, his entire house of fiction will disintegrate. Moreover, the fall of his fictional family will occur not merely because the mesmeric-like control he wants to exert on his (mis)reader in and through brief tales clearly devolves on the limited duration—the impending dissipation—of their reading. No less crucially, Poe's conception of artistic entropy includes the possibility of runaway or historically unimaginable readings that he can never hope to control. To be sure, on occasion he can wonder whether that fate need occur, at least "with certain classes of intellect" who develop "an instinctive and seemingly magnetic appreciation of a thing written." With readers like these, he can think it a "legitimate cause for wonder . . . that, syllable by syllable, men [will] comprehend what, letter by letter, I now trace upon this page" (*E&R* 1319).

Yet Poe can question such idealism, too, as he does in his comic-satiric tale "Some Words with a Mummy" (1845). Notably revivified by material means (a galvanic battery), the Mummy pointedly maintains that only the writer can read a text the way he intentionally composed it. After the writer dies, his " 'great work' " gets decomposed, along with the historical context in which he wrote it, so that his work " 'invariably' " becomes " 'converted into a species of haphazard notebook . . . for the conflicting guesses, riddles, and personal squabbles of whole herds of exasperated commentators' " (*P&T* 816). Far from requiring Poe's intervention, then, misreadings of his texts would seem virtually guaranteed to occur.

Just the same, the Mummy's theory of misreading pertains to texts after the fact, and so inexactly accords with Poe's compositional practice of it. More to the point, the theory presupposes one's having already adopted an objective or public purview on private matters, or the same thing, having assumed that communication ought to match an author's private intention. If one of course can never verify semiotic synchrony like that, at least one ought not to seek its breakdown ahead of time, which is what Poe does by reversing the usual private-to-public trajectory in communication. Provoking misreadings, his writing becomes virtually invisible, its primary focus off-stage vis-à-vis on-staged representative figures of reading who stand for his literary-public environment. It doesn't matter that the specific literary environment varies in form in different tales. For example, "Some Words with a Mummy" conjures the pressures of literary taste exerted by the democratic mob; "The Oblong Box," those of critical peers bent on judging his works by "masterpiece" standards. What finally matters is Poe's ability to envisage converting any and all codes of literary reception into metaphorical foils in relation to which his writing simply appears to him more private.

Sometimes he configures the conversion by staging what he perceives to be culturally dominant modes of writing instead of reception. One notable example occurs in "Ligeia" (1838), a tale that he later considered one of his best, and which initially invites the kind of aesthetic reading mentioned earlier. The story concerns a narrator's abject dependence on the eponymous female hero. Her most notable characteristics consist of her dark, feminine beauty crossed with a masculine-inflected "*intensity* of thought," "abstruse . . . erudition," and "gigantic volition" (*P&T* 265, 266; Poe's emphasis). The narrative particularly stresses her willfulness, bringing it front and center in the tale's epigraph, the words of which Ligeia and later the narrator literally repeat. Putatively written by "Joseph Glanvill," the epigraph asserts that individual will can overcome death.

Despite her willfulness, Ligeia, needless to say, in fact dies, and the aggrieved narrator subsequently marries the Lady Rowena, who only ends up reminding him how she lacks his former wife's "wisdom" and "lofty . . . ethereal nature" (272). Subject to an opium-addicted spouse, Rowena quickly becomes loveless. He abusively imprisons her in his English abbey, which includes a bizarrely decorated room where a wind-machine artificially makes pictures on the tapestries seem "phantasmagoric . . . hideous and uneasy" shapes (271). Not surprisingly, Rowena herself dies, but only after a series of periodic resuscitations. In the "mad disorder" (277) of the final scene, the grave-clothed corpse fully revives, although now the narrator finds to his and the reader's horror that Ligeia has apparently—or is it his delusion?—repossessed the body of Rowena.

Poe later remarked that he should have let Ligeia die one last time (Mabbott 2:307), but doing so surely would have disabled the tale's self-evident theme. "Ligeia" effectively illustrates Ligeia's willful thesis, and not only by her macabre vampirization of Rowena. The narrator figuratively resuscitates his first wife through the very writing of his narrative, showing that her pa-thology of will has infectiously vampirized his own soul as well. But the tale thematizes something more than a psychological truism such as the abyssal narcissism of love. Relentlessly verging on meta-narrative, "Ligeia" also exer-cises *its* will by traducing its reader into a self-referential maze that, like those wind-machined pictures on the room's tapestries, contrives to disable outside perspectives. First, one encounters Poe's persistent fudging of literary-generic contract. If not exactly parodic, the tale's own rhetorical heavy breathing, for instance its use of the dark and light lady convention and exaggerated staging of Gothic literary machinery, surely prompts readers to suspect its meta-liter-ary hijinks. Written around the time of Poe's satirical demonstration of Gothic formulas in "How to Write a Blackwood Article" and "The Predica-ment," "Ligeia" manifestly foregrounds the process of writing a Gothic tale.

Second and more important, Poe endows his eponymous protagonist with characteristics that justify Daniel Hoffman's view of her as a muse-figure,[15] a prevalent topos in Romantic poetry. The narrator himself explicitly associates Ligeia with "*Romance*" (*P&T* 261; Poe's emphasis). With her theory of will and her "airy and spirit-lifting vision more wildly divine than the phantasies which hovered about the slumbering souls of the daughters of Delos," she more tellingly personifies Romantic-Transcendentalist ideology, and not nec-essarily its Continental as opposed to British variety.[16] Given what happens to its hero, "Ligeia" allusively concerns nothing less than the death and resur-rection of Coleridgean Imagination at the expense of Fancy, the faculty of verbal association to which the narrator himself calls attention when designat-ing Rowena as "the fair-haired and blue-eyed Lady Rowena Trevanion, of Tremaine" (270).

Poe also draws a finer if still related allegorical distinction related to the staged contrast between the "dark lady" Ligeia and the "light lady" Rowena, a self-evident allusion to a character from Sir Walter Scott's popular romance-fiction *Ivanhoe*. As the two distinct and oppositional female figures in the nar-rator's life, Ligeia and Rowena compound the Imagination-Fancy binary with the literary-generic one of poetry and prose per se. Ligeia's resurrection at the expense of Rowena thus further points to Poe's privileging the former over the latter, and I would argue in a very specific way. The narrator at once endows Rowena with attributes indicative of conventional, spousal docility, yet also confers on her a full name rife with social authority: the "*Lady* Ro-wena Trevanion, of Tremaine." Rowena, in other words, masks an allegorical figure of literary-domestic writing. Thematically docile yet dominant in Poe's

American cultural marketplace, such fiction played to an audience who "prized the domestic and valued the didactic for its utility," values against which he elsewhere adopts an aggressive stance.[17] As if Poe were addressing "sentimental" fiction in contrast with his Gothic-sensationalist kind, the narrator manifests the same aggression toward Rowena: "That my wife dreaded the fierce moodiness of my temper—that she shunned me and loved me but little—I could not help perceiving; but it gave me rather pleasure than otherwise" (272).

And why shouldn't it, since Ligeia would appear to represent something more private for Poe than a figure for Romantic poesy generally? Combined with "the dear music of her low sweet voice" (263), a Ligeian figure appears in one of Poe's earliest poems, "Al Aaraff" (*P&T* 47), there referring to a spirit who personifies music (Mabbott 2:331). In short, "Ligeia" allegorically figures Poe's most preferred poetical genre and topic, which, through his narrator, he conceals under the representational ruse of *another* dying, beautiful woman. The subterfuge shows his ambivalence toward the honorific status the period's writers and critics still assign to certain Romantic shibboleths. What with its increasing eclipse at the time, the Romantic ethos, like Ligeia herself, looks dead, but Poe here sees to it that it portends resurrection. Conversely, in "The Philosophy of Composition," he himself undercuts the very notion of Romantic originality or genius by insisting on the non-spontaneous, mechanical-deductive construction of "The Raven."[18]

So perhaps Poe's ambition to claim the Romantic ethos for himself, at least in private, explains why he makes his narrator's devotion to Ligeia itself seem perverse. Her power over him clearly exemplifies a master-slave relationship and instigates an aggression toward her, too, which if he represses, his narrative willy-nilly confesses: "I was sufficiently aware of her infinite supremacy to resign myself, with a child-like confidence, to her guidance through the chaotic world of metaphysical investigation" (*P&T* 266). Beyond the tale's otherwise misogynist intimations of women usurping dominant venues of writing, Ligeia's status as the narrator's metaphysical guide argues Poe's own onerous relation to Romantic-Transcendentalist ideology. *Both* literary publics, proponents of a domesticated, American prose fiction threatening to eclipse Poe's own Romantic-Gothic trailer, *and* those subscribing to a Romantic ethos continuing to hold him in its poetic grip, require fantastic elimination via an ambivalent act of allegorical homicide.[19] "Ligeia" traces his imaginary, literary disaffection from both of them by indulging a fugitive, meta-literary allegory in which he has each collapse into the other.

Maybe he was right, then, when stating years later that Ligeia ought to have died one last time, something we suspect anyway from the narrator's emphatic past-tense posture in the tale's opening paragraph. With both women dead, neither represents Poe's most poetical topic, not even in the manner of Wyatt's steadfast memory of his dead wife in "The Oblong Box." Instead, Ligeia represents a residual signifier of his literary desideratum, a figure, like the woman in "The Oval Portrait," becoming less and less representable, less and less accessible to communication, whether by allusive *or* allegorical means. At best, she exists as Poe's muse figure only within a specific moment of signification. And just as he positions readers to envision Ligeia at the tale's end—in raven-like "masses of long and dishevelled hair . . . *blacker than the wings of midnight!*" (277; Poe's emphasis)—so he blacks out the one literary-autobiographical moment of her passing, muse-like significance for himself.

Already headed toward literary privacy with respect to its melodramatic, Gothic facade, "Ligeia" appears always about to become bereft of any social-literary identity whatever. To the narrator, Ligeia the character remains a figure whose "paternal name" he confesses right from the beginning that he has "*never known*" (262; Poe's emphasis). That is, Poe's deliberately "entombed" hero (272) embodies a sui generis or fatherless figure of Romantic Imagination. Stripped of any firm reference point, Coleridgean or other, Ligeia comes to represent an unprecedented, i.e., an American, Romantic vision of Imagination, to which Poe for the moment lays exclusive claim in private.

3

The covert, Americanist gambit of "Ligeia" is no idiosyncratic happenstance in Poe's canon. It appears as well in "The Oblong Box," where the artist's death results from a wreck to a ship named " 'Independence' " (*P&T* 643). The ship's survivors also "landed . . . more dead than alive . . . upon the beach opposite Roanoke Island" (653)—site of the lost colony (1585) that historically inaugurated English settlement in what would become the United States. Both events intimate the American experiment's failure, if not for the captain's namesake, the "hardy" many, then for the artistic few. But Poe inscribes more than some general complaint about his American public's inability to appreciate serious artists like himself. Just as Wyatt's "hysterical laugh," heard from his stateroom before he died, "haunts" the narrator long afterwards (654), so Poe traces a fantasy of the unforgettable impression that, occluded or not, his literary works' axiomatic, most poetical topic will continue to make on future American readers.

Whatever its private trajectory, Poe's tale apparently tries to smuggle *public* contraband after all. At the very least, the subliminal, Americanist motifs of both "Ligeia" and "The Oblong Box" suggest that, despite their increasingly inwrought nature, none of the previously discussed strategies can definitively fend off the impingement of public perspectives on his acts of writing. On one hand, Poe emplots naive or else judgmental readers to fashion a private relation to his work. On the other, his staging simultaneously instigates elitist longings, or his own "hysterical" wish for approbation from more sophisticated readers. Like his pop-up anagrams, Poe's "private" gambits always include a public counter. "The Oblong Box" privatizes his literary scene, yet also hints that it matters to do so in public. "Ligeia" withholds his relation to his most poetical topic; but what he withholds ineluctably triggers his ambition for recognition of his literary originality, and no doubt specifically in relation to American-Romantic peers like Emerson and Longfellow.

Poe himself intuits all this, since he sometimes ironically frames the elitist pretensions that his literary ambition curries, for example in an early tale, "Mystification" (1837). The story centers around a Hungarian nobleman whose name, "Baron Ritzner Von Jung," hints at a transatlantic pun, specifically, aside from the cognate "Jung," the German word *Ritz,* for "scratch." Some German-to-English dictionaries further define the word by the plausible synonym "scribe." Taking into account the *-er* suffix, one can easily jimmy "Ritzner" into *Ritzer:* a scribe or "writer." Moreover, "Ritzner" would refer to the active process of writing, since Poe's *-n-* supplement also phonetically evokes a verb form of *Ritz: ritzen,* meaning "to scratch."[20] Poe barely conceals his sleight-of-hand connections here: a Hungarian character possessing a German proper name that most Anglophone readers will not second-guess or find suspiciously laden with semantic significance; and a German proper noun evoking a common one and its (only) allusive English reference to "writer." Whatever gets lost in these slippery translations, the name "Baron Ritzner Von Jung" suggests Poe's casting *himself* as a quasi-aristocratic "young writer." But the tale in fact traces how the Baron—Poe as "barren" poseur—dupes or un-mans Hermann—"her man"—a literal-minded, pseudo-intelligent reader of texts on dueling—literary competition. In other words, Ritzner/Poe sets up his would-be elitist reader for ridicule before a putatively intellectual, student public, i.e., Poe's more sophisticated readers, as if to display his own elitist credentials regarding texts.

Poe's notorious literary competitiveness nonetheless makes one question the extent of his self-directed irony here and elsewhere. Why not just accept the view that he barely ever muzzles a frustrated wish for public acclaim or, conversely, his private envy of other writers' having it? Suppressed ambition surely characterizes Poe's complaints about how his literary marketplace consists of "little people . . . who succeed in creating for themselves an absolutely positive [literary] reputation by mere dint of the continuity and perpetuality of their appeals to the public" (*E&R* 1313–14). With its mass disseminations of texts, the marketplace even contaminates the premise on which he relies to emplot misreadings for private *or* public reasons. For then the aesthetic attractions "the new," the strange, the unexpected narrative configuration might have for readers are "worn away by the frequent perusal of similar things . . . the frequent inception of similar fancies" (1359).[21] Aiming at all to have his tales capture public interest inevitably sets a premium on their public reception. Indeed, Poe insists that the very venue in which they appear marks their originality, as when he argues that American writers (doubtless excepting himself) presently lag behind their British peers in not recognizing how magazine writing is "a *very* important branch of literature."[22]

Yet expository protests of his literary originality just as often shift into fictional frameworks that equally arrest his impulsive ambition for public, literary recognition. Framed as illusory simply by its disguised occurrence, willful ambition comes to lack any real, i.e., public, meaning in "Ligeia." A similar public dead end defines the fate of "The Fall of the House of Usher," where Poe's surrogate artist would insulate the "House of Usher" from public venues paradoxically by inviting them. Usher wants to keep his "house" far from any intercourse with others, which for him mandates prematurely burying his relation with "Madeline" at least to hallucinate having "made" his own family "line."[23] Guaranteed to offend public scrutiny, his project's means and end inevitably exhibit a scandalous instance of incestuous desire or an irredeemable narcissism.

Then again, just as Usher explicitly calls the quasi-intimate "public" narrator to witness the scandal, Poe's fictional project does much the same. His tale blatantly exploits public interest in private matters, especially those that deviate from "normal" social behavior and so are bound to provoke the reading public's similar judgment about his private project. In imaginary terms, Poe evinces his desire to neutralize his work's public appeal, which simultaneously means preserving his "most poetical" muse identified with his private scene of writing. In the guise of Roderick's already secreted twin sister (the narrator has never heard of her existence before now), Poe doubly buries her via an aesthetically secondary, allegorical narrative that results in her appearing dead to the world but still alive to him. As the tale's events indicate, neither artist can sustain his private project, yet its disintegration, experienced in horrific, representational terms by readers, still allows that for Poe the house-tale has disappeared from public jurisdictions. Readers only read "the fragments of the 'House of Usher' " (*P&T* 336) or the tale here designated as such. Whatever his ambition to write an original fiction, his tale right now becomes an insubstantial artifice that effectively destroys any public evidence of its originality.

In "The Domain of Arnheim" (1847), Poe resorts to a different and more transparent tack to withdraw his act of writing from the contexts of public acclaim. An expanded version of an earlier tale entitled "The Landscape Garden" (1842), the later narrative arguably defines his vision of literary art throughout the 1840s. In a subsequent letter, for instance, Poe remarks that it "expresses *much of my soul.*"[24] More precisely, the tale's spiritual enterprise concerns his imagined voiding of his own public, artistic success.

"The Domain of Arnheim" devolves on the ostensibly minor literary topos of landscape gardening. The tale's unnamed narrator states that he still stands in awe of a dead man named Ellison, who possessed both artistic genius and the economic resources to have realized it in any artistic medium he wished. Despite his option, he chose to become "neither musician nor poet," but instead to traffic in the non-honorific, artistic medium of "materialism" (*P&T* 858): constructing a landscape garden. Significantly, one of Ellison's "elementary principles" as an artist "was the contempt of ambition" (856), but his artistic success in landscape gardening leads the narrator to wonder whether "it is not indeed possible that, while a high order of genius is necessarily ambitious, the highest is above that which is termed ambition[.] And may it not thus happen that many far greater than Milton have contentedly remained 'mute and inglorious'?" (858).

To the narrator, Ellison's garden manifests such genius, for it expresses a beauty "true throughout all the domains of art" (860), a phrase alluding to the (revised) title of the tale itself. The garden intimates the supernumerary labor of an artist who takes nature and so " 'imbue[s] his designs at once with extent and novelty of beauty, as to convey the sentiment of spiritual interference' "; the garden conveys, that is, " 'the *art* of the creator . . . apparent to reflection only' " (863). Ellison considers nature, and in particular American nature—" 'the original beauty of the country' " (862)—as a pretext or textual field in which as artist he can inscribe *his* own originality or "spiritual interference."

Straightaway, we sense the tale's competitive edge. Is "Ellison" Poe's revision of "Emerson" and *his* vision of Nature?[25] In any case, the tale's narrator testifies to the success of Ellison's ghostly self-inscription by commemorating his posthumous identification with an otherwise anonymously authored "natural" artifact. Giving us a verbal tour of the finished garden, the narrator accordingly tries to imagine how others will perceive it for the first time. Ellison's garden requests this detailed response, for his construction clearly entails his and, by inference, Poe's imaginary effort to control the reception of their respective "landscape" works. In particular, the seriatim experience of the imagined spectator/reader through the maze of the garden/narrative seems to lead one to an original if controlled experience of the Romantic Sublime. He and we culminate his tour at some gated Paradise of "Tall slender Eastern trees" and, "upspringing confusedly amid all, a mass of semi-Gothic, semi-Saracenic architecture, sustaining itself by miracle in mid-air . . . [and] seeming the phantom handiwork . . . of the Fairies" (870).

The narrator's imagined experience of others' experience of Ellison's sublime, scenic script suspiciously echoes the experience Poe desires readers to have with his own "semi-Gothic, semi-Saracenic" tales to which, in an earlier collection, he had assigned the terms "grotesque and arabesque." Yet we need to remind ourselves that the tale concerns the narrator's critical "Fair[y]" tale about Ellison's anonymous, material art, the goal of which, "other things being equal," is "attainable happiness" for observers "in proportion to the spirituality of this object" (858). In essence, Ellison's garden, which easily enough stands for Poe's own tale(s), represents public art. With Ellison's blessing, the value of his art lies beyond his control, and so might have gone unappreciated. Even the narrator/reader's reciting the garden-tale's step-by-step effect on readers inadequately renders its original value: "I despair of conveying to the reader any distinct conception of the marvels which my friend did actually accomplish" (864).

Public through and through, landscape-construction (or writing) thus carries a proviso that trumps anyone's reverential (or canonical) insistence on the work's artistic originality. The tale itself, and not simply its sequential, narrative effect on its implicitly evoked reader, conspicuously insists on its originality on its own *covert* terms. For example, the narrator's rendition of Ellison's garden ends by echoing and perhaps attempting to transnationalize Coleridge's "Kubla Khan." Poe, however, does not necessarily endorse the Romantic Sublime in the same unequivocal terms as the narrator appears to do. Personified first by him and then by *his* imagined spectator of Ellison's

Arnheim in the tale, "The Domain of Arnheim" figuratively moves us away from the artist's original act of constructing his landscape work. The narrator's relation to Ellison's garden equally applies to the garden-tale's most perspicuous reader: whoever becomes aware of *its* paradigmatic artistic originality, its being "true throughout *all* the domains of art," also tends to elide "the art of the *creator*." One cannot recover Ellison/Poe in "The Domain of Arnheim" except by "reflection only," that is, retrospectively, and only then as the tale's *now become* anonymous cause.

It therefore seems fitting that the tale's projected, ideal reader will likely miss—and only discover via post factum reflection—anagrams in the tale's self-identifying proper names: "Ellison" and "Arnheim" for "Eli's son" and "near Him." Both anagrams further testify to the tale's act of premature self-burial, premature because to readers it must seem as if it has already occurred before the tale's artistic congealment *into* a tale. And what it buries consists of Poe's radical, god-like ambition to produce a textual "domain near Him," the ultimate Origin. In one last effort to recover the public longing behind Poe's art, one might claim that his submerged anagrams inversely express his defensive self-pity, his psychological sense of crucifixion at the hands of an unappreciative public and, who knows, perhaps his wish for redemption for having been orphaned twice over. At best, the anagrams show how Poe programs his texts to defer the recognition of his own original, "spiritual interference" to the future. The surmise becomes all the more probable if, in accord with his proclivity for punning (e.g., "Siope"), one substitutes the French homonym "demain" for the English "domain" in the tale's title: "Tomorrow near Him"!

Poe had informed James Russell Lowell in 1844 that he lived and wrote in terms of a "longing for solitude" and "continually in a reverie of the future."[26] Perhaps, however, "solitude" means something other than his longing for what he feels that he presently lacks, namely the public's appreciation of his literary originality. Just the once, Poe, no overt religious writer and certainly no moral one, at least within the socially mandated, Christian idioms of his period,[27] means what his provisionally concealed anagrams imply in English: that his sense of original genius comes down exclusively to a private matter between himself and God. In writing "The Domain of Arnheim," he intends to exclude the intrusive perspective of others, which in principle means any internalized "public" sensibility primed to deny this radically private desideratum.[28] Jesus, after all, invokes his Father "Eli" during the crucifixion scene in Matthew 27:46, a Gospel that also happens to inaugurate a radically private mode of spiritual discourse:

> And when thou prayest, thou shalt not be as the hypocrites are: for they love to pray standing in the synagogues and in the corners of the streets, that they may be seen of men. Verily I say unto you, They have their reward. But thou, when thou prayest, enter into thy closet, and when thou hast shut thy door, pray to thy Father which is in secret; and thy Father which seeth in secret shall reward thee openly. (Matthew 6:5–6; Old King James Version)

So when all is said and done, Poe's private language games, his "Kilroy was here" legerdemain in "The Domain of Arnheim" and elsewhere, may very well indicate his effort to write a kind of secret *spiritual* autobiography. He writes fiction a core aspect of which always includes his effort to finesse seeking recognition for it, as it were, on public street-corners. Still, later if not now, going private can always accrue a certain public value, for which another passage from Matthew equally allows: "Fear . . . not [public disapprobation] . . . for there is nothing covered, that shall not be revealed; and hid, that shall not be known. What I tell you in darkness, that speak ye in light: and what ye hear in the ear, that preach ye upon the housetops" (Matthew 10:26–27). In the discipleship manner of Eli's son, Poe like Ellison would construct a material oeuvre intimating " 'the handiwork of the angels that hover between man and God' " (*P&T* 864). Two years later, Poe comes out of the fictional closet and ventures the same project in *Eureka,* a work, as I interpret it in Chapter 3, which bespeaks God's Universe for all, even as it insists on the spiritual élan of utterly idiosyncratic matters for himself.

4

To claim that a spiritual motivation permeates Poe's embedded, rhetorical games obviously underplays their prima facie meretricious appearance. Since his works never address or "speak . . . in light" conventional, Christian matters, who but ultra-inquisitive readers can "hear" his intimations, presuming they at all exist, of a visionary gambit compelling a spiritual apologetics? Absent that context, little if anything about Poe's private, self-referential hijinks appears to possess redeeming social value. At most, they manifest, as I have suggested, an ideologically coerced reaction to his mass-cultural marketplace: an inverted wish not for privacy but *for* literary attention from his imagined, mass-public audience. Jonathan Auerbach maintains, for example, that the typical Poe narrator "exposes his plotting as a fiction in order to verify his identity for the reader," or for the reason that his "ingenuity has meaning only when it is displayed in public."[29]

My argument instead holds that throughout his fiction, Poe undermines the public's sundry incarnations in ad infinitum fashion, which also includes its authority to verify his literary identity to himself. If he actively seeks literary fame, achieving it paradoxically requires more than public confirmation. Among other reasons, this is so because, given the publishing industry's competitive proliferation of texts and the overall fluidity of the United States cultural scene during his period, plagiarized materials may just constitute the primary data readers use to determine a writer's literary reputation. Plagiarism undoubtedly concerns an economic issue, such as of American writers not receiving credit for their work, monetary or honorific, due to the lack of international copyright protections. But in an 1845 editorial for the *Broadway Journal*, Poe casts the problem in more radical terms as the equivalent of some original literary sin: "It is the purity, the nobility, the ethereality of just fame—it is the contrast between this ethereality and the grossness of the crime of [literary] theft, which places the sin of plagiarism in so detestable a light."[30]

For Poe, literary fame finally spells a platonic matter, beyond the practice of regnant literary publics to determine. However much one might plausibly regard it as a defensive reaction to his journalistic circumstance, Poe's nonnegotiable ideal of literary "ethereality" ties fame to textual evidence that simply might never get recognized as the original author's. Other ways exist to frame his idealistic stance here. One can infer that Poe seeks to justify his detections of other writers' plagiarisms as performing a socially responsible service for the American literary public. Conversely, the public notoriety he gains by exposing plagiarisms argues a wish to knock down the literary reputations of others, the better to promote his own. Yet both types of explanation elide one important point: Poe's acts of detection effectively underscore the public's final inability to decide a written work's originality, or, alternatively, how determining it reduces to an utterly private matter.

That position, I think, defines the allegorical tenor of "The Imp of the Perverse," a tale published the same year as his cited editorial remark about plagiarism. Everyone in the tale is anonymous, but in a way that blocks rather than facilitates the possibility of private relations. An unnamed narrator confesses having murdered an unnamed victim to an unspecified, interlocutory "you." The narrative occurs after he has already blurted out his "long imprisoned secret" in "the crowded thoroughfares" (*P&T* 831), or before an abstract public of strangers. But to what does the narrator "*imp*ulsively" confess (my emphasis), his mortal crime or its unnecessary confession? Initially, one tends to assume the former. Occupying more than half his narrative, his periphrastic exposition on the "perverse" as an unmotivated, "radical, primitive, irreducible sentiment" (826) simply protests too much.[31] The narrator clearly aims to deny his deed's social perversion by attributing its perversity to his confession alone. This displacement no doubt accounts for his calling our attention to his own verbosity: "Had I not been thus prolix, you might either have misunderstood me altogether, or with the rabble, you might have fancied me mad. As it is . . . I am one of the many uncounted victims of the Imp of the Perverse" (830).

It all seems patently transparent to us. On a literal level, the narrator's disquisition on the perverse exists only to explain "why I am here," or to provide "at least the faint aspect of a cause for my wearing these fetters" in "this cell of the condemned." Yet his recourse to some motiveless impulse explains nothing. In effect, the narrator's rhetorical periphrases only work to postpone a confession of guilt that he never inwardly made or, undermining the explanatory significance of his "perverse" thesis, for that matter does not make now. Similar to the methodical way he plotted his deed with "thorough deliberation"—"For weeks, for months, I pondered upon the means of the murder" (830)—his present narrative plots not to confess by confessing. Nonetheless, doesn't the tale, in any case, seal his confession and tell all? Nothing remains concealed, whether to the people on the streets who first hear his "shriek aloud" (831) or to "you," the reading public's later surrogate. The internalized, public imp makes the narrator confess his crime, and we all witness his sociopathic motivation in doing it.

Like his confession, however, the tale's fictionally sealed exposé may itself comprise an alibi for a different kind of social violation. Just as he resists making a *full* confession—at most he expresses guilt for having violated a social instead of a moral law—so "The Imp of the Perverse" obfuscates the confessional motivation that the public wants to hear and, in fact, judges *as* heard. Admissions of guilt function much the way proper as opposed to periphrastic language-use does: they validate the public sphere as the guarantor of social order and self-other relations.[32] But as always with Poe's tales, the present one contains its own impish loopholes. After committing his crime, the narrator's "pleasurable feeling" and sense of "absolute security" quickly lead to his "haunting" sense of dissatisfaction (830). As much as denied guilt, "this nightmare of the soul" (831) refers to his urge simply to have his perfect crime made public—to have others recognize its perfection as such.

From the vantage of the public "you," the narrator thus himself personifies "the imp of the perverse." Far from verifying the "absolute" perfection of his absolute deed (murder), the "you" can only regard the narrator's "pregnant sentences" as evidence either of moral guilt or sociopathic madness, both of which confirm the public's authority to "consign[ ]" him to "the hangman and hell" (831). Murder, after all, entails a radically singular, self-other relation in a non-iterable moment of time. A *perfectly* executed murder perversely underscores its singularity as long as no one else knows of it, else it will not have been perfect. From one angle, the narrator's confessing to his "radical, primitive, irreducible" crime might appear to qualify that singularity. From another, confessing before an anonymous or merely grammatical "you" effectively repeats the crime's perverse nature, and as if with the same "thorough deliberation" (830).

This time, though, the crime's perversity lies in the victim's happening to be the "you" itself. From the narrator's viewpoint, the public cannot verify let alone recognize his perfect crime because his motivated, confessional "shriek aloud" on the street only ends up disclosing the public's own artifice. Once the "public," as modern demographics perforce dictate, no longer consists of face-to-face human encounters, it becomes a social fiction, an abstract extrusion of the idiosyncratic surplus endemic to personal acts, including of communication. To sustain itself, the "public" thus needs to suppress all hints of inaccessible private experiences that might expose its fictionality. This is why, whatever its particular disciplinary mechanisms, public ideology, in Edward Shils' terms, at bottom hates "the very idea of privacy."[33]

In "The Imp of the Perverse," Poe, an allegorical excrescence of his narrator, inscribes a private hatred of the very idea of the public. Violating his period's accepted understandings of the literary compact between writer and reader, he returns us to the point before public exposure captured him and his narrator with *its*—to them—perverse attractions. Poe returns us, that is, to when the narrator could still conceive of executing a perfect-because-private crime. Even afterwards, that crime, like a literary text's originality and the meaning of "just fame" for Poe, will likely go unperceived by others, since the tale all but entraps them to pass judgment on the narrator's confession. Others can only perceive the crime's *im*perfection, which in turn recasts the present confessional narrative as all the more private.

On this, to be sure, perverse account of "The Imp of the Perverse," the narrator's final utterance is "pregnant" with an ambivalent and still perverse wish to transgress all extant, public registers of meaning: "To-day I wear these chains, and am *here*! To-morrow I shall be fetterless!—*but where?*" (832; Poe's emphasis). If the narrator's anguished ending refers to his idiosyncratic circumstance, it also calls attention to our own private ones. No matter his horrific deed, we, too, can feel fettered within one or another abstract, public complex, any imaginable release from which anxiously seems equivalent to self-oblivion. But within Poe's "secret autobiography," his narrator's exclaimed, deictic *"here!"* at once signifies both his sense of entrapment within a "chain" of social meanings, and an insistent appeal, a "shriek" overwhelming its accompanying, public message, to be found out instead in his utter particularity. That particularity could only occur some "where," or in some ideal public able to corroborate the haecceity of his perfect crime. But as only a utopian conception of the private, this ideal public possesses no "where."

2 Furniture and Murder in Poe's Private Rooms

> From childhood's hour I have not been
> As others were—I have not seen
> As others saw—I could not bring
> My passions from a common spring.
>
> . . . .
> And all I lov'd—*I* lov'd alone—
> Then—in my childhood—in the dawn
> Of a most stormy life—was drawn
> From ev'ry depth of good and ill
> The mystery which binds me still:
>
> . . . .
> Of a demon in my view.
> —Edgar Allan Poe, "Alone" (1829)
>
> All men are murderers.
> —Wallace Stevens, "Adagia" (*OP*)

1

Why push matters as far as I have? If Poe plays private games, they surely need not purvey the kind of anti-public sentiment that I attribute to "The Imp of the Perverse." On the contrary, some critics may balk at even a minimal concession to Poe's general privacy concerns. After all, he self-evidently wrote his tales and essays in terms of a public, literary stage. At bottom, simply by writing works that have afforded him a certain if also continually vexed canonization within American literary history, Poe manifests a desire to go public with them. In his 1836 Drake-Halleck review, for example, he writes "that *the world* is the true theatre of the biblical histrio" (*E&R* 506; Poe's emphasis).

Common, critical sense also dictates our acknowledging that Poe sought literary fame, recognition, and, at minimum, economic subsistence from his works. These truisms seem to account for the way many of his tales cater to the baser interests of the American literary public in the macabre-Gothic-sensational, or what one might term the dark side of the period's coterminous taste for sentimental literature.[1] For the most part, Poe's works are highly accessible, their emplotted misreadings or no. They play to, even when they spoof or hoax, the American literary-public marketplace. On occasion, he himself was not above appealing to mass public taste, if only to contest that of the period's publishing industry and of literary cliques with which he carried on his well-known literary battles.[2]

Like the old man in his tale "The Man of the Crowd," Poe appears to partake of rather than criticize the new public ethos, never mind promote personal privacy at public expense. And why not, since, as Tocqueville observed of the United States democratic experiment, "public opinion presses with enormous weight upon the minds of each individual"?[3] The democratic culture of which Tocqueville spoke made mass political participation a distinctive and unavoidable feature of American life in the Jacksonian era.[4] Similarly, in the name of an egalitarian ethos, the mass press, doubtless impelled by commercial as well as "republican" considerations, appeared intent on uncovering the private lives of public figures—of transforming public opinion into a new species of publicity. In Tocqueville's words, contemporary American journalists coarsely "appeal[ed] to the passion of [their] readers" and "abandon[ed] principles to assail the characters of individuals, to track them into private life and disclose all their weaknesses and vices."[5]

Yet if Poe ineluctably felt pulled by and himself exploited his culture's mass public scene, his "private" rhetorical moves at least arguably manifest the harassed aspect of social privacy within it. The surmise gains credence when one registers the contemporary upsurge of an amorphous, public sphere resulting from multiple factors besides cultural ones, the composite force of which framed the conventionally understood private sphere in distinctly defensive if also critically restive terms. Certain general comparisons come to mind here. For example, in the United States during the early nineteenth century, "private" and "public" had referred to different realms of social experience, but less as oppositional than uneasily coexisting ones. Federalist and Republican leaders acknowledged the attraction of private domestic life, although as "gentlemen" they conceded the compelling importance of, and so felt obliged to give greater attention to, constructing a new, post-Revolutionary American public sphere.[6]

Writing in 1835, Tocqueville also implied the two spheres' essential compatibility within the American realm. The country's geo-political isolation itself represented a kind of private-public figure: "The policy of Americans in relation to the whole world is exceedingly simple; and it may almost be said that [no other nation] stands in need of them, nor do they stand in need of anybody." Not threatened by other countries on its borders, the Union government's structure appositely underwrote or provided a public sanction for American citizens' pursuits of private affairs. In some European nation-states, Tocqueville noted, "the watchfulness of society penetrates everywhere, and a desire for improvement pervades the smallest details." By contrast, the United States' location, size, and constitutional government all worked to preclude invasive social surveillance. If a similar surveillance had once characterized earlier American-Puritan life, such practice appeared much less the case in post-Revolutionary America.[7]

Furthermore, while pursuing privacy for its own sake scarcely earmarked early American-Republican communitarian values, the country's geographical circumstances, especially as experienced by settlers on the rural frontier, had all along engendered a constitutional assumption of privacy rights. According to Richard Hixson, "the case of access to ownership or possession of land in the New World furnished a secure base for the enjoyment of privacy. Because of the increasing distance between farm homes especially, physical privacy became a characteristic of everyday life." For Hixson, that social-behaviorist pattern helps explain why "American courts and legislatures had for some time recognized the home, confidential communications, and public records as private domains."[8]

Nor was the presumption of privacy necessarily impeded by the growth of urban-commercial centers during the pre-industrial period of United States culture. In Hixson's view, these, too, "provided the 'protective anonymity' that could less readily be found in smaller towns," thus additionally contributing to the notion of "personal privacy at least, if not spatial seclusion." Even as it in effect displaced them, urbanization helped propagate rather than contradicted rural presumptions of privacy. Transposing Richard Sennett's characterization of eighteenth-century London city squares, one might infer that early nineteenth-century, American urban settings, most notably in the northeastern corridor, consisted of "a free zone of crowds," which allowed people to act out different public roles without exposing their private selves.[9]

By the time Poe began writing his tales, however, privacy was becoming anything but what Hixson judges as "taken for granted" or "not seriously threatened."[10] With its abstract inflection of things and people, the competitive market economy made moot would-be urban maskers, not to mention any cooperative construction of a person-oriented public sphere. Advanced for commercial use, bureaucratic and "industrial innovations" also diluted dependence on the private family as the primary venue of entrepreneurial ventures.[11] The general effect was to produce an impersonal public sphere that altered what social privacy formerly meant, for example by breeding suspicions about strangers' private motivations. To alleviate the resulting social anxieties, a new ethos of "sincerity" arose and notably introduced special social-interactional codes and quasi-quarantined zones—most prominently, the domestic realm—by which one could think to know the other's true motivations.[12] "Privacy," in short, became a reactionary category of social experience. Milette Shamir argues that American privacy concerns during the period set the stage for the later 1890 Warren and Brandeis legal defense of "the right to privacy." Expressing such concerns meant "precisely . . . to counter the problem of the alienability of personhood that emerged with modern capitalism, . . . to keep stories about the self from circulating in the market and hence to resist the risk of appropriation by the market."[13]

The market economy represented just one among other aspects of an increasingly ubiquitous public realm. Transportation changes, in particular railroad expansion after 1830, and telegraph linkages between cities (begun around 1844) reduced people's perceived sense of private versus public spaces. Sponsored by the federal government, new infrastructural connections between cities and rural communities even emphasized public spaces at the expense of private ones: "The process of building public thruways, bridges, wharfs, and even parks involved the public expropriation and extinguishment of preexisting rights, usages, and expectations. The invention of public space was contested terrain in the early nineteenth century, requiring a full deployment of the rhetorics and techniques of the well-regulated society."[14] Major cities in effect highlighted the same kinds of division. Philadelphia, to take one, had developed into sectored micro-communities, each subject to their own organizational networks for the most part based on class and ethnic identity. Yet if social groups in effect appeared private to each other, the mass-market economy and its infrastructural support-systems at once increased and promised relief from certain social problems (e.g., epidemics of disease) requiring common urban solutions. So urban culture equally fostered the social sense of an abstract "public," an aspect of which Poe took notice in his allusion to the public waterworks system and public parks of Philadelphia around the time he wrote his 1844 article "Morning on the Wissahiccon."[15]

More immediately relevant to Poe's vocational situation, technological innovations in printing and cheaper postal rates for newspapers and personal letters afforded quicker ways for distributing information. These options inevitably affected how people generally construed writing, namely more as a public flow of information and less as a medium instantiating personal interaction. Even letter-writing by private citizens, let alone by public and especially political figures, accrued an unexpected, public ambience. Personal letters, according to Richard Brown, had functioned as "vital sources of [public] information on events beyond one's locality" in early America. In one sense, letters now became "almost exclusively devoted to personal concerns"; in another, they also retained a kind of "quasi-public quality since they might be opened and read as they passed from hand to hand," a possibility real enough to require federal law to prevent their unwanted scrutiny by third parties.[16]

The entire situation allows for a different reading of Poe's "private" gambits. One can plausibly claim that, far from manifesting a defense of privacy per se, they better protest "the illiberality . . . of the demagogue-ridden public" traduced by the magazine industry's commodification of "literature" cum information (*E&R* 1037). At worst, Poe himself practices what he here criticizes. For example, the relative popularity of his "secret writing" articles for *Alexander's Weekly Messenger* perhaps testifies to more than their having struck a social nerve. They also exploit contemporary American concerns about keeping personal letters private—the "desire," to recall, "of transmitting information from one individual to another, in such manner as to elude general comprehension." As a full-fledged participant in the period's mass-cultural milieu, Poe himself often engages in journalistic practices that verge on outright violations of others' literary privacy. In his notorious "Outis" articles, he "outs" Longfellow for alleged plagiarisms; or in his *Literati* pieces, Poe purportedly conveys the opinions of "private [literary] society" about contemporary writers (*E&R* 1120).

Whether or not one insists on their competitive motivation, his literary detections easily enough accord with his society's newly invested interest in actual criminal detections. With Dupin as their social hero, Poe's three "ratiocinative" tales advertise methods to ferret out secrets dangerous to mid-nineteenth-century public order. The tales all occur in Paris, an impersonal urban setting that figures an abstract public sphere. In large cities particularly, anonymous strangers achieve a critical mass, a situation that Richard Sennett argues in actual fact led to the popularity of "the detective and the mystery novel. . . . Detectives are what every man and woman must be when they want to make sense of the street."[17]

Just as important, to make sense of urban strangers requires instant processing of information primarily based on visual evidence. Helping reinforce an already visually inflected public field, new technological modes of entertainment increasingly became popular with American middle-class audiences. Poe, too, hardly shies away from verbally mimicking the visual impact of devices like the diorama, panorama, stereoscopes, phantasmagoria (ghostly illusions via magic lanterns), and especially the daguerreotype. For example, many of his tales, as Terry Castle argues, stage phantasmagoric effects. These include the "spectacle," complete with "bizarre, claustrophobic surroundings, the mood of Gothic strangeness and terror, the rapid phantom-train of images, the disorientation and powerlessness of the spectator" or reader.[18] In accord with middle-class preferences for new techno-theatrical renditions of reality, by 1840 Poe himself would undercut the representational value of pictorial art compared with the daguerreotype's. He terms the latter "perhaps the most extraordinary triumph of modern science," "*infinitely* more accurate in its representation than any painting by human hands," and he prophetically opines that the daguerreotype's "consequences" would "exceed, by very much, the wildest expectations of the most imaginative."[19]

On the ambiguous evidence of his duped narrator in "The Oblong Box," it remains in doubt whether Poe presciently endorses something akin to "the work of art in the age of mechanical reproduction." Nevertheless, many of his tales register how a socially emergent visual gestalt at once works to define the public realm as such and affects individual perceptions of self and others alike. At the very least, the visual media available by Poe's time helped inaugurate the illusion of access by "almost anyone" to "people at an inaccessible distance," including those "long dead," as in fact Poe became for biographers later deploying his well-known *Ultimate Thule* daguerreotype to get at his real "character."[20] More important, one now tends to see oneself in the same manner. It becomes less and less possible to observe not only other persons and events but also one's personal, spatio-temporal experience of them sans their technological reproducibility. Situated alongside an imaginary, internalized public as if capable of visualizing it, even the formerly private fiat of Romantic self-consciousness no longer makes phenomenological sense.

In short, as with the narrator's double in Poe's tale "William Wilson," the public now represents the capacity to witness one's previously designated "private" actions and thoughts. More, its range goes beyond making, as Richard Sennett has it, "[p]ublic behavior . . . a matter of observation, of passive participation, of a certain kind of voyeurism."[21] Predicating private experience on the possibility of its reversible public observation, the period's visual ethos ends up haunting voyeurism itself in allowing for the voyeur's own vulnerability to other voyeurs. If I can regard strangers without their knowledge, this only means that they can do the same with me.

Poe's 1840 "The Man of the Crowd" concerns exactly that situation, but with the entire American public complex grounding it. Initially, the tale seems simply to register "his generation's shock at realizing that the urban stranger cannot be known."[22] From evening until daybreak, the tale's narrator pursues an old man rushing aimlessly through the crowds of London, whom he ultimately identifies with a book that "does not permit itself to be read" (*P&T* 388). Readers have little recourse but to agree. Through the narrator, we focus on the old man's apparently pointless, urban meanderings, and feel compelled to resolve the inscrutable motives for his actions, which at once suggest "solitude and sociality."[23]

Then again, the narrator resembles a little too much the typical bourgeois voyeur. Before his pursuit, he sits in a hotel, having recently been "ill in health," and amuses himself "in poring over advertisements, now in observing the promiscuous company in the room, and now in peering through the smoky panes into the street" (*P&T* 388). In effect, he regards others "through a glass darkly." Given his secular rather than spiritual focus, his unwitting biblical allusion seems hyperbolic, just as will his later complaint about being "wearied unto death" by the demonic old man's as if interminable peregrinations (396). The narrator, in any case, best befits the role of a budding, bourgeois sociologist. He thinks he can categorize people by class stereotypes, "[d]escending" from higher to lower, socially definable groups like the gamblers, "Jew pedlars," beggars, prostitutes, and the indigent (391). So what to do when he comes upon an old man who to him fits no known type, or whose "absolute idiosyncrasy" (*sic*) he cannot read (392)? Rambling amid the urban crowds "without apparent object," the man finally exhausts the narrator, leading him to judge that the figure possesses " 'the genius of deep crime' " because he " 'refuses to be alone. *He is the man of the crowd*' " (396; Poe's emphasis).

It becomes clear, however, that his "crime" is all too *un*clear. If the old man at first seems to represent the effects of an impersonal, urban public realm gone amok, the narrator only adds to instead of relieves the situation. Needless to say, his assessment of the old man's purposeless wandering redounds to himself. The narrator, too, is "the man of the crowd," reacting to how the man resists as much as accedes to transparent, public codifications. In this sense, "The Man of the Crowd" lends itself to the social-critical interpretations it has received. Robert Byer, for example, argues that, far from reflecting the Republican ideal of an interactive public sphere, the narrator and old man both personify the alienation from public life identified with the capitalist marketplace. Despite the London setting, they together figure the " 'double life' of community and privacy in America's republic" where "[t]he mutually isolating anonymity of the crowd, expressed in the exchange of gazes to which all seems equally and freely visible, conceals the privacy of self-interest."[24]

The problem is that Poe's narrator need not represent a figure unequivocally harboring notions of bourgeois self-interest. For one thing, the tale's scenario allows that the crime imputed to the old man might just as easily evince the narrator's displaced guilt over his own obsessive voyeurism. If the old man's actions appear singularly unusual to the narrator, his pursuit of the old man seems no less conspicuous to us. Moreover, the entire situation hints at a familiar Poe "put on." It remains perfectly feasible, for instance, to regard the old man as a kind of agent provocateur of public ideology. As if he were entrapping the narrator himself into enacting the role of a voyeuristic *object,* the old man's frenetic movements provocatively, i.e., intentionally, stoke the curiosity of his all-too-noticeable pursuer. And in depicting the narrator quite specifically as a reader of an unreadable text, Poe analogously positions us readers as the observed because predictable objects of his own tale.

Where does it all end? The public lies in wait everywhere, infinite, or at least ad infinitum. "The Man of the Crowd" both registers and enacts this ubiquity. No one, least of all Poe constructing his tale in a mass-cultural, public milieu, can escape possible public scrutiny for very long. His narrator's public malaise affects him, too, preventing any imaginative counter to the tale's epigraph from La Bruyère: "*Ce grand malheur, de ne pouvoir être seul*" (388). Like his fictional narrator William Wilson, Poe can never quite kill his public double (here his mass readership) "to be alone." From the imaginary reader's perspective that he adopts in "The Man of the Crowd," the impersonal marketplace inescapably inflects and infects any and all plotted ruses by which he might work to arrive at some private scene of writing.

2

Even as Poe's journalistic practices, critical remarks about literature generally, and the thematic purport of his tales acknowledge the as if totalizing reach of American public ideology, they just as often set it up for a fall. His designation of the "magazine prison-house" doubtless shows his alienation from it. In "The Imp of the Perverse," the narrator's long disquisition of the perverse as a universal, psychic truth manifestly assaults the patience of his representative public "you": "There lives no man who at some period, has not been tormented, for example, by an earnest desire to tantalize a listener by circumlocution" (*P&T* 828). More emphatically, the virtually infinite repetition of public-ideological positions in "The Man of the Crowd" suggests Poe's restless, critical reaction toward what amounts to a "public" juggernaut.

In each case, Poe, although not directly proposing a less omnivorous public sphere, insinuates the perdurable desire for a private one that would effect just such an alternative. From its opening lines, for example, "The Man of the Crowd" frames *itself* as a text that "does not permit itself to be read." Personifying the tale's position, the narrator's frantic pursuit of the old man in fact suggests his unconscious wish not to negate or judge but *precisely to find* a stranger—anyone—who embodies "absolute idiosyncrasy." From his too-public indoctrination, his reflexive impulse to categorize everyone in socially recognizable terms inversely directs him all the more toward some sublime or fantastic conception of an absolute privacy. The narrator's recent illness thus consists of his having repressed his own private spirit, or of himself having surrendered it to public categorizations and characterizations.

Consonant with the narrator's "private" wish—private even to himself— the old man, to whom he arbitrarily imputes a " 'wild . . . history' " (*P&T* 392), stands for the narrator's repressed, idealized figure of redemption. The tale figures the man as old because, as an unconscious political trope, he possesses the authoritative aura of an older mode of social privacy that still haunts the present American scene, if now entirely out of place in it. The narrator's repression also accounts for his aforementioned biblical locutions. A neurotically maimed, all-public man, he can only acknowledge the embodiment of his desired "private" redemption in anxious, i.e., demonic, terms. To him, the old man, on nothing more than the ambiguous, visual evidence provided by the modern public field, evokes "the ideas of vast mental power, of caution, of penuriousness, of avarice, of coolness, of malice, of blood-thirstiness, of triumph, of merriment, of excessive terror . . . of supreme despair" (392)— all unresolvable contradictions from commonsense, public viewpoints.

From one angle, the narrator cannot accept the totalizing, public significance of the man of the crowd, any more than as the tale's surrogate mass reader he can rest content with the infinite public positions of "The Man of the Crowd." From another, neither can he acknowledge its private alternative, for if anything, the anguish at the heart of Poe's tale spells the *loss* of "private" self-interest, or the inability to be let alone. Faced with this unreadable contradiction, the narrator/reader ends on a note suggesting *his* "supreme" or spiritual "despair": "I grew wearied unto death."

Contextualizing all this, Poe's restless representation of the public-private stalemate suggests less his own resignation over *or* public exploitation of privacy's demise than his determination to keep privacy a volatile category of social experience. The same critical edge inflects his "secret writing" generally, and even one of his most popular tales, "The Pit and the Pendulum" (1842), which at first glance simply smacks of unabashed Gothic melodrama. Far from resisting its mass-cultural, public milieu, the tale self-evidently caters to the American marketplace's taste for literary sensationalism. Indeed, what with General Lasalle's last-minute deliverance of the narrator from his interminable near-death encounters via the pit and the pendulum at the hands of faceless Inquisition judges, the plot would appear to request its own literary-critical rescue operation. At best, the tale's prolonged near-death motif earnestly stages in condensed form early Victorian anxieties about death, which Poe elsewhere exploits in his theme of premature burials.[25] The narrator initially protests that "even in the grave all *is not* lost. Else there is no immortality for man" (*P&T* 492; Poe's emphasis). Like the narrator in "The Man of the Crowd," the narrator in "The Pit and the Pendulum" glosses his physical condition in biblical-spiritual idiom, as with the seven apocalyptic candles that he hallucinates as charitable angels. Right from the beginning, he religiously intones that "I was sick—sick unto death" (491).

Yet "The Pit and the Pendulum" also perplexes its accommodating gesture toward a religious public. For example, a self-evident heretic in American-Protestant terms, the narrator never acts or thinks in a way that would link his imminent sense of death with the period's religious-sentimentalist propaganda about an afterlife. It seems easy enough to conclude that, if at all discerned by contemporary readers, the story's proto-Modernist theme of hope quite literally colliding with a "no exit" hopelessness would scarcely play well in mid-nineteenth-century Peoria. Neither does the narrator's abrupt and brief last-paragraph salvation appear anything but secular and arbitrary to boot, then or now.[26]

Other social-oriented justifications fare much the same way, whether or not one takes more sophisticated critical views of the tale. For example, David Reynolds stresses its deviations from and critique of the kinds of literary sensationalism commonly practiced in both the contemporary mass press and more respectable middle-class journals. In particular, Reynolds maintains that the narrator's "terrified but scrupulously detailed responses" to his situation "show Poe consciously using a firm rationalism" to counteract "the themes and images" of "mere violence and murderousness" that he "saw treated more loosely in popular culture."[27]

Poe's tale, however, conspicuously breaks literary as well as religious faith with his contemporary readership. For one thing, his blatant melodramatic tactics here again strut and come close to parodying literary-Gothic conventions like those comically rehearsed earlier in his 1838 "How to Write a Blackwood Article" (1838).[28] For another, "The Pit and the Pendulum" all but advertises the means by which it intends to propagate a singularly *irratio*nal effect on its readers. Poe's melodramatic plot obviously hinges on the protagonist's moment-to-moment encounters with the perils of the pit and those of the pendulum, a movement thematically doubled by his back-and-forth sense of impending death and its respite. So "the pictured image of a huge pendulum" (498) on the chamber's ceiling constitutes an ekphrastic image of the tale's own performative movement. Nor does the tale dabble in mere traditional self-reference. In conveying the impression that it could go on indefinitely were it not for the exigencies of time mandated by the brief tale, the narrative's oscillating motion mimics mesmeric "passes," the goal of which was precisely to *nullify* a person's conscious or rational thought.[29]

Why does Poe subliminally expose in trompe l'oeil fashion the effect he wants his tale to have on its reader? Moreover, if it refers to the effect it wants to purvey on a reader not privy to this reading, the tale uses more bizarre means than usual to undermine its self-referential spell. As I argued in Chapter 1, Poe's narrators often figure readings that simultaneously conceal different ones. In "The Pit and the Pendulum," the fictive narrator represents not so much the tale's would-be reader as a fictional character *as such*, by which means the tale displays its own interior process of narrative construction. Again resorting to one of his subliminal, verbal maxims, Poe redundantly personifies his "character" as if watching readers putting "him" through his paces, that is, being forced to perform with "my teeth . . . on edge" (501) for a thrill-seeking audience that itself wishes to be kept "on the edge of its seats." The sensation-bound reader no doubt also prefers the full effect of fiction without noticing its fictionality, for which reason the narrator obligingly differentiates his situation from fictional ones: "Yet not for a moment did I suppose myself actually dead. Such a supposition, notwithstanding what we read in fiction, is altogether inconsistent with real existence" (494).

Unlike the usual Poe tale, though, the present one internally stages a reading of its reading all as if the aesthetic illusion it would have on readers were too precarious to sustain. As the tale's self-conscious personification before a literary public, the narrator, returning to consciousness from a swoon, states that he can only retain a shadowy recollection of his former "mental or spiritual" experience. Ostensibly, this is the effect Poe wants his tale to have on its inscribed, mesmerized reader: for him or her to experience "sad visions," such as of "the perfume of some novel flower," which "the many may not view" (492). But in "The Pit and the Pendulum," these visions never come to pass. The narrator/tale instead feels haunted by ghostly "black-robed judges" whose "inquisitorial voices seemed merged in one dreamy indeterminate hum," and whose "lips" appear to him "white—whiter than the sheet upon which I trace these words. . . . I saw them fashion the syllables of my name; and I shuddered because no sound succeeded" (491).

I take the narrator's paranoid scenario to refer to the tale's private register, or to its own meta-literary, allegorical "under-current." While writing his tale, Poe thematizes his inability to escape its fate as an already written and published text in effect being read not merely by enthralled or as if mesmerized common readers. In other words, the tale exists in the process of becoming fixed with a public, literary identity ("the syllables of my name"), this time captivated by the anti-sensationalist criteria specifically associated with Inquisitorial, black-robed judges. Cultural emissaries of an amorphous and alienating literary-public sphere, these critically judgmental readers subject each compositional moment to one or another ("indeterminate") critical "sentence" emanating from "lips . . . thin even to grotesqueness," and with the "expression of firmness—of immoveable resolution."

Poe himself oversees the entire *mise en scène,* since he remains allegorically positioned one step removed from his narrator/tale's abject, self-conscious performance for a popular *and* critical public. With its overdone Gothicisms, mesmeric mimicry, and allusive self-allegorization, "The Pit and the Pendulum" finally resists by mimicking total captivation by its public environment. More than that, the tale plays at captivating its now fictively configured public, a reversal marked by the narrator's last-minute deliverance. In aesthetic terms, Lasalle's rescue signals Poe's *auctor ex machina* intervention, his transgression of fictional illusion; in social-symbolic terms, it represents the rescue of his tale from mid-nineteenth-century abstract modes of communal surveillance.

For whether in fact or effect, Poe's prison tale, I want to suggest, revises Jeremy Bentham's 1787 "Panopticon" speculations about a prison structured to allow a supervising "inspector" to see the prisoners "*without being seen,*" thus leading them "always [to] feel as if under inspection." Bentham's Panopticon would install total publicity in the guise of one-sided visibility, and at the expense of any automatically suspect desire for privacy: "public establishments ought to be . . . thrown wide open to the body of the curious at large—the great *open committee* of the tribunal of the world. And who ever objects to such publicity, where it is practicable, but those whose motives for objection afford the strongest reasons for it?"[30] Michel Foucault regards Bentham's architectural apparatus as symptomatic of bourgeois society's ideological dream of controlling all forms of deviant social behavior. As a kind of secular conscience, the Panopticon would instill in people the disciplinary illusion of a faceless and invisible bureaucracy. Bentham's bureaucratic mechanism would perpetually monitor not only one's activities but also thoughts: "the Panopticon must not be understood as a dream building . . . [but] a figure of political technology that may and must be detached from any specific use."[31]

All the same, it does possess one crucial, social-political use for Foucault: to produce market-productive citizens. A similar use of omnivisual publicity characterizes Poe's environment, and not least when dressed up in civic-republican values. A 1826 American legal treatise on defamation, for example, argues in Benthamite fashion that "[t]he dread of public censure and disgrace is not only the most effectual, and therefore the most important, but in numberless instances the only security which society possesses for the preservation of decency and the performance of the private duties of life."[32] Besides the threat of literal death, Poe's narrator in "The Pit and the Pendulum" clearly suffers the power of public censure. He experiences the sensation of being watched—his "every motion was undoubtedly watched"—without being able to identify clearly his controllers, who in any case soon "vanished" (*P&T* 503, 491). In each instance, these "demons . . . took note of my swoon," even as at any time they "could have arrested" his pitiless torture (500). And as if the tale were particularly referring to Bentham's Panopticon structure, the narrator, after escaping death by the pendulum, "beheld it drawn up, by some invisible force, through the ceiling" (503).

Poe was no advocate of Bentham's utilitarian philosophy, the use of whatever means to effect the greatest social good.[33] So it is no surprise that, obliquely referring to his visual-oriented public milieu, Poe's tale reverses Bentham's omnivisual, utilitarian Panopticon into a darkened dungeon, which Foucault argues was precisely what the "panoptic mechanism" was designed to eliminate: "[This mechanism] reverses the [dungeon's] three functions—to enclose, to deprive of light and to hide—it preserves only the first. . . . Full lighting and the eye of a supervisor capture better than darkness."[34] Along with an overt as opposed to invisibly censorious mode of punishment, Poe's reversion to a dark, dungeon-like chamber points to a situation in which at least an old-style if still coerced mode of privacy still obtains. Darkness allows the narrator to happen upon improbable, last-minute escapes from his judges' intentional design to execute their death-sentence in one or the other manner. Reminiscent of "The Man of the Crowd," the tale's biblical intimations, Spanish Inquisitorial setting, and unmentioned heretical crime again suggest Poe's desire to regard the new, indeterminately styled public incarceration of privacy in spiritual as opposed to secular-bourgeois terms. Unlike Foucault, Poe intuits the purpose of Bentham's publicity-figure not to be political control over or power within the public realm, but the expansion of this realm for its own sake—or for the total evisceration of privacy.

As I have already stated, the significance of Lasalle's otherwise arbitrary rescue of the narrator analogously devolves on Poe's own literary privacy as a writer. In social-symbolic terms, the rescue also applies to the privacy of the very American readers ironically supporting public surveillance practices in the venue of literary reception. On one level, of course, Lasalle's figure simply adds plausibility to the tale's plot. As Mabbott notes, a "General Antoine-Chevalier-Louis Colbert, Comte de Lasalle" invaded Toledo in 1808, and was said to have immediately entered the palace where the Inquisition took place. Poe derived these facts from reprinted British magazines and two histories of the Inquisition that he undoubtedly knew.[35] But this Lasalle, likely a specialized allusion at least for the period's average reader, resonates with further historical allusions that better fit Poe's ad hoc deliverance of his tale's character-as-such from literary "public establishments." Just as important, his fudging of historical reference makes "Lasalle" an even more telling trope for Poe's fantasized rescue of a threatened social privacy in mid-nineteenth-century United States culture.

Admittedly speculative, my surmise is nonetheless consistent with his practice of homonymic puns, as discussed in the preceding chapter.[36] Lasalle's name, not to mince matters, also conjures up that of Robert La Salle, the French seventeenth-century explorer of the Mississippi region. *That* La Salle had contested Spanish territorial claims over the region. He also suspected Jesuit missionaries, inevitably identified with Spanish Inquisitors, about their designs on the New World. Alluding to the American wilderness at large, Lasalle's last-minute rescue of Poe's narrator figures nothing less than the American nation's revolutionary escape (also supported by French allies) from claustrophobic, Old World societies—from "the sound of inquisitorial voices" that "conveyed to my soul the idea of *revolution*" (*P&T* 491; Poe's emphasis).

If only in an immediate chain of associations, however, Poe, hardly a supporter of Jackson and his Manifest Destiny policy, might well have regarded the "frontier" La Salle in a negative light. At this point, "Lasalle" elusively segues from historical to contemporary, social significance; or what amounts to the same thing, he becomes more and more a private figure or trope, especially by means of a word-play apt to go unnoticed by American Anglophones. Covertly relevant to the tale, Lasalle's name literally if ambiguously mimes the French word for "the room."[37] The semiotic slippage toward indeterminate reference itself subtly instantiates a symbolic defense of privacy over against a populist and popular Jacksonian policy synonymous with an expanding American public sphere. Snuggled within the tale's verbal sedimentations, "Lasalle" thus more precisely signifies a *private* room. The "room" at once alludes to the actual interior space where Poe writes, and, as culled from "Lasalle's" semantic affiliation with the frontier, to its "giving Poe room"—freeing him from pressing social concerns—to imagine a different, less publicly hectored mode of composing his present tales and others. Small as it is, Poe's tale additionally intimates larger public significance. Screened by his narrator, Poe fantasizes his own Lasalle-like rescue of one important feature of the original American Revolutionary ideal: both to protect and promote each citizen's private pursuit of happiness. In its present state, the American public sphere seems to do anything but that, given its own apparent captivation by literary, commercial, social, and political mandates.

Although only in private terms, Poe's enactment of literary privacy thus imaginatively evokes a reformable public sphere for his American readers.

Like his narrator, he, too, hears the plural "discordant hum of human voices" supporting the rescue of his tale from the perdition of a demonic, abstract public: "The Inquisition was in the hands of its enemies" (505). His fantasy, then, turns on the inimical presence only of a specific yet ominously inchoate public's inquisition and ideological imprisonment of private freedoms in the American social realm. Here again, Poe's literary moves function as social-symbolic tropes, especially since one might associate them with the various means by which his middle-class contemporaries were attempting to construct private, domestic havens—as it were, rooms of their own—in reaction to an increasingly impersonal, American marketplace.

For that matter, Poe's performative analogue to domestic private havens happens to echo yet another eponymic avatar of "Lasalle," this one a notable seventeenth-century writer of manuals on etiquette and interior decoration.[38] Poe's theory that tales like "The Pit and the Pendulum" ought ideally to mesmerize their readers in a single sitting would effect at least one desideratum of domesticity. Lasalle-like, doesn't the tale quite literally deliver its readers back to the private rooms in which, supposedly having given their spellbound attention to it, they have all the while shut out invasive, public distractions? In that sense, Poe's tale would rescue its own captivated readers from submission to the inquisitorial pressures governing and alienating the American public-cultural realm at large as well as his literary-public one in particular.

3

"The Pit and the Pendulum" at best offers tenuous evidence for Poe's socially inflected privacy concerns. Why, for example, do his works seldom engage frontier or domestic topoi, either of which might have provided him with an explicit avenue for airing these concerns? Two minor exceptions to the pattern exist in Poe's canon, both of them appearing in 1840 when he served as editor for *Burton's Gentleman's Magazine*. One was the serialized fiction entitled *The Journal of Julius Rodman*, which fictionalizes a Lewis and Clark–like expedition into a yet unexplored American West. For whatever reason, perhaps his inability to sustain imagining an alternative to his social-economic-cultural milieu, Poe soon aborted the project.[39] The other work was "The Philosophy of Furniture," a brief article in which Poe sketches his ideal for decorating American apartments.

Of the two topics, domesticity most clearly engaged the issue of social privacy, if only "as a retirement or retreat from the larger world."[40] During Poe's period, "[t]he home . . . became an island of stability in an increasingly restless society," in response to which contemporary architectural reformers, for example, adopted eighteenth-century aesthetic theories to justify "the creation of a new, private, domestic lifestyle for the middle class." In one sense, domestic privacy referred to a gendered, feminine domain arguably at odds with the kinds of private retreats males associated with frontier scenes.[41] Yet Hawthorne, too, whose *Twice-Told Tales* Poe reviewed in positive terms more than once, expressed similar privacy concerns. Milette Shamir maintains that in "The Minister's Black Veil," the protagonist's terminal refusal to take off his veil protests his "absolute privacy" as household head from "the intrusions of official authorities . . . from the inquisitive gossip of the congregation (the 'multitudes'), and even from the sympathetic queries of his fiancée." Compatible with literary-domestic writers in this one instance, Hawthorne never quite ventures extreme privacy claims, perhaps lest they result in something akin to the Minister's "unpardonable sin." He simply attempts to strike a liberal-individualist balance by resisting public intrusions into private household matters.[42]

Poe's "The Philosophy of Furniture" purports to do neither. It scarcely appears some daring, critically motivated picture of the domestic realm, whether as a besieged site of American social privacy, or else a pressing alternative to an impersonal public one. At most, as Kenneth Silverman plausibly surmises, Poe implicitly criticizes, perhaps with the intention to reform, the American public's "lack of aesthetic discrimination" due to corrupting material pursuits and the pressures of mass production.[43] Poe himself asserts that, thanks to "an evil growing out of our republican institutions," Americans mistake "the *display of wealth*" in decorating rooms for "the heraldic display in monarchical countries" (*P&T* 382; Poe's emphasis). If anything, in upholding the English model of interior decoration, the article frames its domestic topic in terms of a worldwide public stage, just as Poe does with his view of American literature.

"The Philosophy of Furniture" in fact plays down its social-critical intimations. As the article's ostensible speaker, Poe not only assumes the persona or "We" of an inquisitive, middle-class public, but specifically writes as if he were one more contemporary journalist contributing to what Shamir terms the "immense growth of [and modes of arriving at] information about the domestic sphere."[44] In his criticism of American designs, Poe also adopts the role of aesthetic expert, say of an American-styled John Claudius Loudon, the period's influential Scottish authority on matters of interior design. Loudon's 1833 work *An Encyclopedia of Cottage, Farm, and Villa Architecture and Furniture* was both widely circulated in the United States and often cited in *Godey's Lady's Book*.[45]

The gist of Poe's argument is that emphasis on "cost" too often leads to an "inartistical arrangement" of furniture in American rooms. The impulse to display wealth leads to "a want of keeping. We speak of the keeping of a room as we would of the keeping of a picture." In his view, all primary decorative items—curtains, carpets, wallpaper—ought to remain modest and uniform in quantity, color, and in their floral or other representational designs, for which he notably prefers "rigidly Arabesque" ones (*P&T* 384). In short, Poe espouses the same aesthetic principle for interior decor that he does for his tales. No one part should stand out. Loudon's principle further maintains that a room's unified effect results from "the cooperation of different subordinate parts with one principal part," which for Poe as for Loudon redounds to the room's "soul," or carpet.[46] For both decorists, clearly, "[t]he harmony of the colouring of a room . . . can only be produced by the same kind of knowledge which guides an artist in painting a picture."[47]

A similar aesthetic principle guides Poe's most severe criticism of American interior decorations, namely their reliance on "gas" lighting and glassy accouterments. Poe dislikes "strong *steady* lights" (his emphasis), glittering ones as well, and so lampshades that effuse light in an "unequal, broken, and painful" manner. Similarly, the frequent use of "four or five mirrors arranged at random" on the walls result in "a perfect farrago of discordant and displeasing effects." Instead, he asserts that, as occurs from "the astral lamp proper—the lamp of Argand, with its original plain ground-glass shade" emitting "tempered and uniform moonlight rays," a "mild, or what artists term a cool light, with its consequent warm shadows, will do wonders for even an ill-furnished apartment," and best frame "Female loveliness, in especial" (*P&T* 384, 385).

Shifting from his criticism of typical middle-class interiors, Poe proceeds to cite an anecdotal instance of what an ideal room would resemble, and which might compete with "the spirituality of the British *boudoir*": "Even *now* [not emphasized in the 1840 version], there is present to our mind's eye a small and not ostentatious chamber with whose decorations no fault can be found. The proprietor lies asleep on a sofa—the weather is cool—the time near midnight" (386). The writer takes notice of the "oblong" room's crimson color-scheme, which "appear[s] everywhere in profusion, and determine[s] the *character* of the room" (Poe's emphasis), especially because framed by a silvery wallpaper marked by "fainter" Arabesque designs. Besides landscape paintings "of an imaginative cast" and portraits of "three or four female heads, of an ethereal beauty," the walls include only one small mirror, "hung so that" one cannot receive "a reflection" from any "of the ordinary sitting-places of the room" (387). Sparsely furnished, the room accommodates only two "large low sofas," two "conversation chairs," one bare "octagonal table," an uncovered pianoforte, and four "gorgeous Sèvres vases" by "the sofas." Finally, in accord with Poe's concern about lighting, "[a] tall candelabrum, bearing a small antique lamp with highly perfumed oil, is standing near the head of my sleeping friend." Other than "two or three hundred magnificently bound books" placed in elaborately decorated, hanging shelves, "there is no [other] furniture, if we except an Argand lamp . . . which depends from the lofty vaulted ceiling by a single slender gold chain, and throws a tranquil but magical radiance over all."

Nothing about Poe's sketched, ideal room in "The Philosophy of Furniture" significantly deviates from what one might expect to find in magazine fillers of the period. The article's conventionality becomes more apparent if one compares his room with its idiosyncratic, Romantic predecessor six years earlier, the sensory-promiscuous private apartment furnished by the Byronic protagonist in "The Assignation": "In the architecture and embellishments of the chamber, the evident design had been to dazzle and astound. Little attention had been paid to the *decora* of what is technically called the *keeping*, or to the proprieties of nationality. The eye wandered from object to object, and rested upon none" (*P&T* 205; Poe's emphasis).

The bizarrely decorated room proposes to please or be seen by no one except its occupant and perhaps his select confidants, and thus stands in marked contrast to the ideal and more economically designed middle-class room in "The Philosophy of Furniture."[48] Poe turns from a patently aristocratic aesthetic to a more prosaic "republican" one, specifically charged with the nationalistic goal of bringing middle-class Americans up to interior-architectural snuff. More important, the essay evokes a room likely intended to impress a public composed of unknown strangers, presumably including anyone reading the present essay. Poe's room accordingly resembles his period's middle-class conception of the household parlor as a mini-public stage. The parlor's main function, according to Katherine Grier, was "to retain the identity of a family sitting room even as it also served more public and formal uses." Located in the ostensibly private domicile, this quasi-formal room symbolically proffered a cultural alternative to the threat posed by anonymous strangers in large American cities, such as Poe addresses directly in

"The Man of the Crowd" six months later. In Karen Halttunen's view, the mid-nineteenth-century American parlor, to recall, served to screen persons whose "sincerity" one could not readily determine. It essentially provided an intermediate public stage for meeting them in situations different from "the private family circle where the sincere ideal was virtually meaningless."[49]

From that viewpoint, Poe's article seems more intent on reconfiguring the domestic realm as an interface with his impersonal, marketplace milieu, than with posing a critical alternative to it. The household interior, a synecdoche of domestic privacy rife with larger social significance, not only possesses a general "public" orientation, but also devolves on small-scale materialistic symbols like Poe's books. Ronald and Mary Zboray argue that people of the period "charged their literary possessions with meanings in ways that countered the natural depersonalizing effects of mass production." Poe's books, moreover, quite literally double as literary figures for the room's social function of entertaining "groups" rather than "selves." Displayed in ornate, hanging shelves, don't these "magnificently bound books" appear intended more for show than for any private, professional use?[50] Everything in Poe's room seems to propagate a kind of intermediate, public-private space. With its straightforward exposition and topical orientation toward American middle-class consumers, the illustrative anecdote of his friend's private abode additionally points to the article's *own* publicity-oriented status.

Nevertheless, Poe's cited furnishings deceptively abstain from the idea of an abstract public to which such rhetorical publicity might lead. For example, to rid "glare" from his ideal room, Poe rejects the household use of gas lighting, which he would replace with the Argand lamp. As it happens, his distaste for gas lighting and preference for the Argand lamp, essentially an oil lamp commonly used throughout the nineteenth century, involves more than the issue of glaring light. "With a public gas supply," according to Wolfgang Schivelbusch, "domestic lighting entered its industrial—and dependent—stage. No longer self-sufficiently producing its own heat and light, each house was inextricably tied to an industrial energy producer," in other words to an abstract public source.[51]

By inference, other features of Poe's room keenly deviate from contemporary norms of decoration and otherwise spell the domestic realm as a distinctively private space. For instance, his recommended use of the Argand lamp and double window curtains might well entail a reversion to turn-of-the-century decorative practices. According to William Seale, "the innovative oil lamp of the late eighteenth and early nineteenth centuries" led to an "increasing number of curtains for windows," at once allowing people "to stay up longer into the night"—aren't we inspecting Poe's ideal room at "midnight"?—and blocking "peering eyes from the outside."[52] Likewise, Poe's endorsement of only one small mirror counters in miniature the period's previously mentioned fascination with large-scale visual staging. The single mirror aborts both the room's amplitude, its refracted expansion, and, since one would not see oneself reflected in it from any "ordinary" seating position, the visual display of self, or the sense of one's publicly accessible appearance before others. For the same reason, perhaps, Poe disparages Bentham and his followers, "who, to spare thought and economize fancy, first cruelly invented the Kaleidoscope, and then established joint-stock companies to twirl it by steam" (*P&T* 384). Even Poe's minimalist setting of two small sofas and "conversation" chairs reinforces a specific aspect of domestic ideology, that of informal and intimate social interaction.[53]

Who, however, would notice or care to look for such "private" rhetorical intimations in a brief journalistic article, itself pitched toward a consumerist audience? Like his furniture items, Poe's already oblique tropes of domestic privacy at best constitute token defenses against a more powerful public complex. They also refer to things (carpets, wallpaper, etc.) that depend on materials deriving from it. Domestic ideology, to repeat, proposed to fashion a mini-public sphere of its own—at most, then, a *quasi*-private sphere—especially associated with American middle-class women to whom magazine fillers on domestic topics typically catered. That is why, depending on one's critical motivation, one can charge domesticity with an array of public-oriented meanings. For some critics, it figures a social space where the period's males sought respite from the competitive public marketplace's threats to "manhood." For others, it represents a social setting in which women exercised freedoms else denied them in patriarchal culture. Or was the white middle-class domestic haven a site more generally indicative of class and racial privilege, fostering ideological quiescence vis-à-vis antebellum social issues? Then again, as some feminist-revisionist frameworks have it, perhaps domesticity stood for an ideological metonym, a symbolic zone in which the period's women and some men attempted to construct a more egalitarian model for the American public sphere at large.[54]

Measured against these options, Poe's apartment tropes at most protest the fragility of domestic privacy, as he perhaps indicates with his passing thought to construct a setting for "Female loveliness in especial." Yet "The Philosophy of Furniture" also contains a reserve clause that veers more toward the privacy practiced by Hawthorne's Minister than that of literary domestics. Poe himself felt he knew the Minister's secret, a crime of passion that the "rabble" was bound to miss (*E&R* 574–75). In his merely decorative article, Poe's secret goes Hawthorne's one better, first by remaining inconspicuous, and second by having it refer only to a figure of privacy no one *can* observe except as a sign that effectively says nothing.

The generic ambiguity of "The Philosophy of Furniture" provides a glimmer of his concealment. Poe's article borders on a latent satirization of domestic advice manuals that it too purports to be, if only in miniature form. Nor is the self-reference incidental when one considers that in 1845, Poe removed his 1840 title's definite article. This minor and virtually non-existent revision yet conceals his having earlier left room for others to construe his article as referring to itself as much as to interior decoration per se. "Philosophy of Furniture," the 1845 title, modestly connotes Poe's views about decoration, whereas "The" in the first title denotes a more authoritative stance regarding the article's topic. The last point becomes more viable when one reinserts the 1840 version's later omitted first paragraph:

> "Philosophy," says Hegel, "is utterly useless and fruitless, and, *for this very reason,* is the sublimest of all pursuits, the most deserving of our attention, and the most worthy of our zeal"—a somewhat Coleridegy [*sic*] assertion, with a rivulet of deep meaning in a meadow of words. . . . Philosophy has its merits, and is applicable to an infinity of purposes. There is reason, it is said, in the roasting of eggs, and there is philosophy even in furniture. (Mabbott 2:495; Poe's emphasis)

Good stylistic reasons exist for Poe's later excision of the passage. Cutting Romantic-rhetorical excesses obviously better focuses the reader's attention on the essay's useful as opposed to "useless" propositions about improving the decor of American apartments. At the same time, a contrary motive seems no less feasible to entertain. The passage subtly suggests how the essay itself possibly includes an "under-current" of "deep meaning . . . in a meadow of words." More than once, Poe elsewhere charges small or relatively commonplace rhetorical matters—say the "brief tale," poetic prosody, even punctuation—with hints of their formerly unappreciated but for him significant import.[55]

Why, then, does he excise "The" Hegelian introduction? Leaving it, I think, would call attention to how "*The* Philosophy of Furniture" pushes its speaker to possible fictional status. Like many of Poe's middle-to-late-period tales, such as "Mesmeric Revelation" and "The Imp of the Perverse," Poe's article segues from exposition to fiction, although here the transition never demonstrably occurs. Absent actual "fictional" cues, the article encourages readers to accept its expository utterances as solely the author's. However, if not fully turned into fictional narrative (no story line exists), it swerves into a barely discernible or withheld fiction that effectively reverses the usual private-becoming-public tables. For it is his "we" persona, not Poe himself, who assumes the role of authoritative, aesthetic expert and, as if some tour-guide, sets up the putatively private domestic room and sleeping male figure for our complicit, public viewing.

If anything, one can infer that, if only to Poe himself, "The Philosophy of Furniture" literally stages the public and puts *its* intrusive inclinations on display. Those reading the article as an "essay" therefore serve as an imaginary, "public" reference point against which he can determine its "private," already allusive fictional ambience, and in that way imaginatively occupy a space more private than social notions of a separate and private domestic sphere would ever allow for. Even on a topical level, "The Philosophy of Furniture" arguably dispossesses the domestic realm of its gendered association. The article appears in *Burton's Gentleman's Magazine,* thus ostensibly addressing a male audience as opposed to middle-class women. As if to emphasize the point, a male figure, observed "during his slumber," alone occupies the article's room.

These are arguable surmises, but not the fact that, maneuvered by Poe's narrative into adopting an impersonal, voyeuristic public gaze, we ourselves invade a domestic scene supposedly synonymous with the central site of American privacy. And what we see when we do invade it comes down to his outright violation of domestic privacy. In posing as an essay, "The Philosophy of Furniture" promotes a conventional response that mutes and so keeps private its veering off into a "useless" fictional anecdote. The article thereby *becomes* a truly interior, *literary*-decorative item for Poe alone, a form of writing by which he not only privately resists his period's appetite for information and growing specialization in modes of production and consumption, but also figuratively disappears from the informal private sphere of the home. That the room belongs to a *single* man underscores all this. As Jack Larkin points out, domestic ideology purveyed norms such that a person's "living alone" during the period "was customarily seen as a sign of eccentricity or even madness."[56] Who else is the article's midnight-slumbering figure but

Poe's mad projection of himself, as if entirely oblivious to his narrator or public persona, to the latter's interlocutors, and to us later readers as well?

"The Philosophy of Furniture" does not deploy the private to contest some burgeoning, hegemonic American marketplace. Neither does it worry the boundary between what later in the century would become known as the right to privacy against the public's right to know. Least of all, and despite its conventional topic, does Poe's article settle for some comfortable, middle-class domestic privacy, which at bottom constitutes a coerced or compromised substitute for an abstract public realm that supervises privacy's very social identity. Rather, with his audience of readers inveigled, as it were, to look on, a self-imagined slumbering Poe instigates their misprision of his literary dreaming. His article positions its public never to know what he *is* dreaming while sleeping/writing. The article's internalized readers only encounter a figure sans any interior at all, a vacant exteriority—a public self aptly figured by those anonymous, already objectified "magnificently bound books" that Poe emplots in his ideal room.

4

Sleep as a trope for private writing inevitably carries its own limitations for Poe, a problem that goes beyond the trope's referential extension. As with other bodily functions, sleep leaves one vulnerable to others, or simply unable to suppress the waking thought of how one appears in public.[57] Still, if writing is never sufficiently oneiric to banish his cognizance of a "public," Poe can continually write to make it so.

The real problem lies elsewhere. By using a trope like sleeping to evoke private scenes of writing, he himself perforce adopts a public perspective on writing, suggesting that no other might possibly exist. His dilemma, that is, and one he never underestimates, stems from how writing persistently regenerates a different public ultimately identical with himself observing himself trying to stage the public so as to be let alone in his scene of writing. Robert Gerstein notes that whether "[w]e watch ourselves to see what sort of point our actions appear to be making" with others, or even "'intend [such actions] only to be observed by ourselves,'" we still perform them "to be seen," and in that sense internalize the role of public "observers."[58] Emplotting alien publics only leads Poe to here. How can he eradicate *intimate* public doubles too—or at least stand-ins for himself—to imagine a convincing scene of private writing?

Almost a year after "The Philosophy of Furniture," Poe tries out one solution in "The Murders in the Rue Morgue," (1841) where, first of all, the public most prominently appears in the guise of the media. Through newspapers, Dupin and his narrator-friend initially gather information about the murders of a mother and daughter, Madame and Mademoiselle L'Espanaye. The media also report how a variety of persons heard " 'voices in contention' " during the homicide's occurrence (*P&T* 415). Known only by their vocations, these nondescript figures not only evoke an impersonal public sphere, but also stand for the tale's emplotted readers, who reductively translate the sounds of the murdering ape into their different linguistic codes—islands of cultural privacy, so to speak. Not surprisingly, the tale suggests that foreign publics will literally miss the "ape" solution altogether.

Neither the perplexed media nor the essentially anonymous witnesses exhaust the duped misreaders of the solution or of the tale itself. Based on his personal relationship with Dupin, the narrator would appear to have privileged access to the crime's solution. *Some* reader, some proxy of Poe's, must have the same. After all, Dupin and the narrator live together in a decidedly private retreat, "a time-eaten and grotesque mansion, long deserted," where they indulge themselves in "reading, writing, or conversing" (400). As if to reinforce the privacy defining his already private relation with Dupin, the narrator cites their common separation from public affairs of all kinds: "Our seclusion was perfect. We admitted no visitors. Indeed the locality of our retirement had been carefully kept a secret from my own former associates; and it had been many years since Dupin had ceased to know or be known in Paris. We existed within ourselves alone" (401). No female domesticity exists here, no parlor games or temptation to display one's room to anyone else, just a secured place for masculine, literary interaction.

Clearly, though, the relationship between the two is a one-sided affair, and since the relation consists of literary affairs, Dupin plays the same *authori*tative role with an intimate friend cum reader. By extension, Poe through Dupin apparently has no scruple in bursting the illusion of social privacy, here understood strictly in terms of male interpersonal relationships. The narrator remains totally subject to Dupin's narrative. In the tale's famous street scene, he duplicates the narrator's " 'meditations' " (403), illustrating how he can read the narrator's mind without the reverse being also true. As his name inevitably suggests, Dupin also dupes his supposedly trusted friend, the tale's otherwise privy, surrogate reader, from whom he withholds his solution of the crime until the last moment.

So Dupin plays a by now familiar Poe rhetorical trump card, only this time with a "reading, writing, or conversing" self, an apparently intimate social and literary equal shadowing a de facto author's acts of imagination. In "The Murders in the Rue Morgue," the rhetorical maneuver means more than Poe's using an air of ratiocination to mystify his interlocutors, for he also deploys the ruse of perversely forfeiting literary privacy to an impersonal public sphere he elsewhere criticizes. Dupin comes out of retirement or complete withdrawal from public affairs to solve a publicity-amplified crime. His solution rests on his becoming the voyeur's voyeur, just as he will do again in Poe's other two "ratiocinative" tales. Laura Saltz, for example, argues that in "The Mystery of Marie Rogêt," published a year or so after "The Murders in the Rue Morgue," Dupin/Poe exemplifies "his interest in staging" the female victim's "violation—in reproducing and reviewing it—as a private spectacle."[59]

In "The Murders in the Rue Morgue," Dupin's voyeurism further happens to coincide with public interest and interests. He performs, that is, the nineteenth-century detective's function, as Richard Sennett defines it, of demystifying for others an anonymous urban-public environment. Dupin notably personifies the kind of non-institutional surveillance Tocqueville saw operating in mid-nineteenth-century American society. Lacking a "state police," American officials had "few" means for discovering crimes and arresting criminals; absent that official police force, "everyone conceives himself to be interested in furnishing evidence of the crime and in seizing the delinquent."[60] In Poe's tale, only Dupin, not "everyone," can solve its "locked-room mystery," which as John T. Irwin defines it "confronts us with an enclosure that appears, from both inside and outside, to be . . . unopenable, without there being left some physical trace of its having been opened."[61]

Dupin, of course, discovers how the "Ourang-Outang" or "ape" (*P&T* 430) entered and exited the women's apartment. He imaginatively reconstructs and makes public the private scene of the ape's breaching a central but noticeably fragile conventional symbol—a window—synonymous with the period's demarcation between public and private, i.e., domestic, spaces. The tale's primary emphasis on Dupin's method of solving the crime invites *us* to do much the same. By drawing attention to his method, the narrative fosters the reader's non-intimate or impersonal relation to the two victims, as it were anesthetizing us to the gruesomeness of the ape's deed.[62] In effect, we violate them too, and all the more so since neither we nor Dupin can assign guilt to a non-human ape. For that matter, the ape's killing of the women (one mutilated with a razor) only indirectly results from its sailor-owner's threat to whip it after seeing how it mimicked the way he shaved. Who can blame the owner, whose own privacy, not unlike the narrator's in his former "[perfect] seclusion," Dupin disturbs, although as " 'hav[ing] done nothing . . . culpable' " (428)? Even the sailor could not keep the ape "carefully secluded" in his apartment to let it heal from a foot-wound; and after pursuing it when it escaped, he helplessly witnessed the animal's deed in "the interior of the room" through the window (429).

In a tale putatively touting reason, the L'Espanaye women die for no apparent reason, the victims of a guiltless homicide. What comes to public light turns out morally meaningless. The narrated events occur as if solely to give Dupin an opportunity to display his powers of detection to his narrator-friend and us. The same meretricious motive pertains to Poe himself. The events furnish him as their author with an "ape" tale he intends to sell to the public from first to last, just as the sailor does with the tale's ape: "His ultimate design was to sell it" (428). Still, and despite what Dupin claims about truth's superficial locus, "The Murders in the Rue Morgue" contains one "undercurrent" of "deep meaning," for it concerns a subject (murder) and method of solution that literally and figuratively entail the violation of everyone's personal privacy. Locked rooms get opened on all levels of the tale: not just the two women's, but the sailor's, that of the narrator and Dupin's home, and by implication the domestic security assumed by Poe's emplotted public.

Only one interior room remains sealed, and it refers to where Poe imagines the tale's violent yet also innocuous crime. If Dupin exposes private domains to the public's impersonal gaze, the tale as a whole, much as "The Philosophy of Furniture," uses its summoned public doubly to conceal Poe's own authorial privacy. The game he plays resembles the one Dupin refers to in "The Purloined Letter": concealing words on a map that "stretch, in large characters, from one end of the chart to the other" (*P&T* 694). In "The Murders in the Rue Morgue," Dupin makes a method out of the ape's slavish mimesis of the other, a figure for a poetics Poe consistently disparages for its nullifying a literary work's mesmerizing "under-current." Like Poe's method of writing, Dupin himself relies on aping for his method of detection, as his explanation to the narrator about how to win at "draughts" surely indicates: "Deprived of ordinary resources, the analyst throws himself into the spirit of his opponent, identifies himself therewith," to "seduce [him] into error or hurry into miscalculation" (*P&T* 398). Of course, in reading the tale, we no less than the narrator surrender to the logic of Poe/Dupin's narrative, and so "ape" him in its duration.

The Poe/Dupin equation, however, leads us to underestimate the significance of Poe's signatorial anagram ("ape" = "E.A.P."), assuming we notice it at all. He himself doubles as the murdering ape. Linguistically mute, the ape represents the instinctual or private other to Dupin, Poe's analytical or publicizing double. Poe, then, only mimics, i.e., apes, rational discourse—a mimicry that defines literature itself—by which he covers up or privatizes a more intolerable act of imagination: his killing a mother and daughter, in other words Maria and Virginia Clemm, the two beloved centers of his own domestic hearth.[63] Everywhere one turns, the tale similarly mimics the authority of linguistic communication, the fundamental cornerstone of public understanding. If Poe occasionally "borrows words from other languages, and Englishes them,"[64] he does it here with a vengeance. The name "L'Espanaye" traffics in the same muddle of cultural-linguistic codes that the arbitrary witnesses do in conveying what they heard during the murders. Apparently French, "L'Espanaye" invokes not merely "Spain," but specifically the Spanish word *espantar,* that is, to frighten away; *espantado,* meaning frightened, scared; *espanto,* or fright, horror, scare, a ghost, a phantom.[65] Coupled with his anagram and combined with the English homophone "aye," "L'Espanaye" in the tale's context translates into something like: "I, E.A.P., fear or frighten away the female ghosts of the domestic-public realm haunting my private imaginative domain."

Poe's crypto-confession at least reflects what one might term his own "close shave" with guilt in imagining his literary-homicidal act. After all, through Dupin, his fictional double, he can surely anticipate his detection as the criminal "ape" or (the pun holds) bête noire of fiction-writing. Needless to say, however, Poe does not literally imagine killing Maria and Virginia Clemm, let alone cater to the period's rabid interest in actual domestic homicides.[66] Within his act of writing, the women function as phantom tropes, allegorically aimed at exposing the vulnerability of female-domestic formations of social privacy to the very impersonal public they would forfend. That one inadequacy accounts for and privately justifies his private, performative violation of them. With its own sub-linguistic signifiers, Poe's tale leaves behind a *dumb* "ape" tale in which "E.A.P." inscribes a mode of privacy more radical than domestic havens could ever hope to realize.

His offense thus consists precisely of his *offensive* assertion of privacy, his ersatz terrorism of the public realm that in principle extends to any domesticated formation of privacy. Poe's target also includes alternative domestic havens such as the narrator and Dupin's forfeited one of masculine, non-familial friendship. Friendship, in fact, serves as an apt figure for the period's conventions about writer-reader relationships. Allan Silver notes that the impersonality of modern societies "creates the possibility of personal relations valued as expressions of inner intention and commitment, apart from practical agendas and formal obligations."[67] In contrast, Poe's tale represents the public at large not just unable to resolve but programmed to misread the ape's quasi-articulate sounds at the murderous domestic scene in the even more private if still publicly vulnerable apartment.

The sounds themselves mimic the linguistic mimicry pervading "The Murders in the Rue Morgue," the further implication of which points to Poe's violation of antebellum social protocols for "fiction-reading." As Barbara Hochman argues, sentimental literary-domestic fiction in particular devolved on the model of "a reciprocal exchange between friends,"[68] one that Poe violates twice over in the meta-fictional sanctum of his tale. Not only does he eliminate the two women, but just as important he privately counters Dupin, the tale's surrogate author, who himself transgresses any two-way exchange with the friend who, also the tale's surrogate reader, traces the Poe/Dupin narrative that we are reading.

In all the above ways, Poe strives to become his own private other in the act of imagining or writing his fiction. Rendered more fully, the passage cited in the previous chapter from his 1846 "Marginalia" isolates his literary desideratum as "fancies" at the threshold of eluding his own "power of words":

> There is, however, a class of fancies, of exquisite delicacy, which are *not* thoughts, and to which, *as yet,* I have found it absolutely impossible to adapt language. I use the word *fancies* at random, and merely because I must use *some* word; but the idea commonly attached to the term is not even remotely applicable to the shadows of shadows in question. They seem to me rather psychal than intellectual. . . . I am aware of these "fancies" only when I am upon the very brink of sleep, with the consciousness that I am so. I have satisfied myself that this condition exists but for an inappreciable *point* of time. (*E&R* 1383; Poe's emphasis)

What else but some such inchoate, dream-like state of imagination likely dominates the slumbering Poe's attention at the end of "The Philosophy of Furniture," even as he retains "the consciousness" of constructing a decorative text for public eyes? The same Poe lurks in the margins of "The Murders in the Rue Morgue." Regardless of his intention to sell his "ape" tale to the public, his narrative act continually moves toward "the very brink" of an ever more interior room, a figure for the tale's own scene of writing.

Poe would keep *that* room locked and private, itself a mystery impervious to solution even by his own power of words. Keeping it so requires mimicking his ape's "crime," which at bottom tracks how he violates various discursive codes that, as evoked by his writing, signify the "public" per se, and so not simply those identifiable with perceived social norms of moral or literary behavior. Also like his ape-killer, he need not justify his attraction to literary privacy, let alone fear the public's invasion of it. At best, his "private" pursuit occurs only en passant, or "for an inappreciable *point* of time" in writing. It comes down to a purely fanciful state in which he can momentarily suspend his literary-public longings and "hurry[] onwards . . . to some never-to-be-imparted secret," as his narrator puts it in "MS. Found in a Bottle" (*P&T* 198). Since this secret's "attainment" would amount to "destruction," or the utter disappearance of public writing into private dream, who among Poe's readers would care to follow him there supposing they at all could? Besides, detectable or not, whatever public crime he commits by going private would anyway seem to him no crime at all.

3   Falling Stars: The Private Matter of Poe's *Eureka* and Wallace Stevens' *Harmonium*

If a man would be alone, let him look at the stars.
—Ralph Waldo Emerson, *Nature* (1836)

He considered that he would one day accomplish some quiet subtle thing that the elect would deem worthy and, passing on, would join the dimmer stars in a nebulous, indeterminate heaven half-way between death and immortality.
—F. Scott Fitzgerald, *The Beautiful and the Damned* (1922)

1

Poe's *Eureka* (1848) concerns anything but private interiors. The cosmos remarks the one unavoidable public stage or backdrop—and impersonal to the core—against which all human activities take place. For Poe, cosmological nature consists of heterogeneous matter, the result, he claims, of Divine volition that originally dispersed Its "irrelative" Oneness (*Eureka, P&T* 1277, 1278, 1289). Captivated by a meta-gravitational force, of which Newton's version comes down to a secondary effect or signifier, the atomic dispersal of matter always exists in the process of returning to the Divine "*Matter no more*" (1280; Poe's emphasis).[1] That return is only temporarily deferred by the equally meta-physical principle of repulsion, "electricity" being *its* physico-semiotic manifestation (1281). Everything partakes of "another creation and radiation, returning into itself" ad infinitum (1356). Nothing escapes this eternally recurring process, from atomic minutiae, " *Thought*" or "Conscious Intelligence" (1354), to what Poe designates as "the Universe of Stars," actual cosmic formations, the evolution of which he here rehearses with fastidious narrative attention.

By its own internal references, *Eureka*'s theory comprises a syncretistic composite of different past and current cosmological theories, most notably those of Johannes Kepler, Pierre Laplace, Sir John Herschel, John Nichol, and especially Alexander von Humboldt, the person to whom Poe dedicates his work. For some Poe critics, *Eureka*'s syncretism devolves on other disciplinary sources, which further indicate his theory's derivative status and perhaps suspicious textual credentials. Kenneth Silverman argues that *Eureka* "blends [Poe's] fantasies about the nature of physical reality with traditional pantheism, popularized versions of nineteenth-century astronomical thought, and related nineteenth-century bunkum like Mesmerism, Spiritualism, and Phrenology."[2] Not least, Poe's disquisition flirts with Christian-eschatological prophecy, the fact, as he claims, that "Man . . . will at length attain that awfully triumphant epoch when he shall recognize his existence as that of Jehovah" (*Eureka* 1358).

Other critics deem the work's primary concern in more honorific modern terms. Deploying Humean and Lockean ideas about ideas, Poe, according to Joan Dayan, "uses our ignorance . . . to suggest God's power" and our inability "to transcend [the] human limitation" of knowledge. *Eureka* dramatizes epistemological finitude, the impossibility of our being able to conceive not only the Universe's extent, but also what Poe terms God's "plot" immanent within it (*Eureka* 1342). From a different viewpoint, *Eureka*'s narrative of "universal" collapse presciently outlines Freud's notion of the death instinct. Sensing no such master ideational narrative at work, Jonathan Elmer surmises that *Eureka* traces an ideological allegory of Poe's "mass-ochism," that is, his inability to imagine a way out of his Jacksonian, mass-cultural milieu's final "Attraction."[3]

No matter their different interpretations, critics of *Eureka*, whether minimizing or stressing its originality, tend to accept Poe's own serious investment in the work's vision. As Edward Davidson maintains, "despite its strange mélange of science, pseudo-science, and plain wishful thinking, Poe expended a great deal of effort" on *Eureka* and regarded it "as offering a *summa* of human thought in his own time."[4] Some critics even consider it a kind of master code-book for deciphering his entire oeuvre,[5] and not just tales like "Mesmeric Revelation" and "Mellonta Tauta" that refer to similar themes in similar quasi-scientific idiom. Critical arguments like these propose that, whatever its intellectual caliber and rhetorical excesses, *Eureka* reveals the philosophical ground on which Poe's other writings rest.

Above all, however, he clearly invests both his topic and work with the power of establishing his public literary reputation, if not in the present, then in the future.[6] Poe all but states as much in a letter he wrote after the work's publication: "I have no desire to live since I have done *Eureka;* my final success is certain or I abandon all claim to the title of *Vates*."[7] His comedic surrogate at the beginning of *Eureka* already suggests the same in his "remarkable letter, which appears to have been found corked in a bottle . . . floating on the Mare Tenebrarum." As if endorsing its tenor, Poe adds emphasis to the letter-writer's putative quotation from Kepler: "*I care not whether my work be read now or by posterity. I can afford to wait a century for readers when God himself has waited six thousand years for an observer. . . . I will indulge my sacred fury*" (*Eureka* 1263, 1270).

Poe's protest, a loose paraphrase of Kepler's words, of course shows he does care. Unlike his dual identity in "The Philosophy of Furniture," this time he wholly adopts a tour-guide role with *Eureka*'s readers, in effect outsubliming their expectations of the "Sublime" literary experience.[8] For example, in what reads like a fictional re-creation of the Universe's own process of creation, he would have us try to apprehend the otherwise inconceivable notion of " 'Infinity' . . . [a word] representative but of the *thought of a thought*" (1272). Through "graduated steps," his narrative would "*startle the mind*" by leading us to experience "the infinitely sublime," the paradox of witnessing past star-formations in "the awful Present" and "still more awful Future."[9] Words and conventional exposition thus figure a glass darkly that Poe's *emphasized* words and narrative work to shatter. By sheer typographical means like italicized words, he would paradoxically instantiate the sublime experience.

Whatever "private" intimations exist in his briefer tales, *Eureka* thus apparently proclaims the "public" Poe on all levels. Still, a certain self-referential animus simultaneously pervades Poe's narrative from first to last. His Preface, for instance, defensively protests that *Eureka*'s thesis applies to the work itself: " *What I here propound is true:*—therefore it cannot die—or if by any means it be now trodden down so that it die, it will rise again to the Life Everlasting" (1259). Similarly, his concluding peroration effectively transforms the preceding cosmological argument into an *apologia pro sua vita*: "no one soul *is* inferior to another," he claims, since "each soul is, in part, its own God" (1357).[10]

So it hardly surprises one to find that the contingent, "autobiographical," and especially literary-competitive investment evident in Poe's other works marks *Eureka*'s literary "under-current" as well. Going beyond what Silverman terms "slighting" competing theorists like the "widely-praised" Dr. John Nichol,[11] Poe has his anonymous letter-writer satirically dispose of traditional scientific methodologies, both Aristotelian deduction and the inductive method of "Hog," or Francis Bacon (1263–64). More important, *Eureka*'s ideational edge applies to the Romantic-Transcendentalist pretensions of his own thesis. As John Limon persuasively argues, Poe duplicitously constructs an apparently scientifically grounded, counter-Transcendentalist treatise expressly directed against the then influential *Naturphilosophie* of German Idealist philosophers.[12]

My guess is that *Eureka* covertly counters a specific, homegrown version of *Naturphilosophie,* namely the precedent of Emerson's American-Transcendentalist theory of Nature as expressed in his 1836 essay. Poe's competitive response to *Nature* particularly concerns how Emerson there proposes to replace the mass-conformist American public sphere with Nature as an ideal site where individuals might realize a unique, self-reliant citizenry. Already suggested by his tales' conspicuous focus on interior settings, Poe's animus toward Emerson's vision of Nature bypasses the latter's own displacement of an older American public "common." In *Nature,* Emerson would revise it into a "*bare* common," where, *as if* in private, he could enjoy "a perfect exhilaration" of self.[13]

Emerson's "bare common" in fact etches a space where he can continually transform private experience into public contexts and vice versa. In "Experience," for instance, he concedes that in theory nothing can escape knowledge, scientific or philosophical. When we become "impatient of so public a life and planet," we futilely "run hither and thither for nooks and secrets" that turn out to be "superficial": "Then the new molecular philosophy shows astronomical interspaces betwixt atom and atom, shows that the world is all outside; it has no inside." Emerson would concede to neither extreme. For example, if our knowledge of Nature can explain our private experiences, so our private "temperament" in turn "shuts us in a prison of glass which we cannot see" and determines the very Nature generating our explanations. Emerson thus holds that "[t]he mid-world is best" for living life. Whatever public or quasi-private stage on which we think we act—small or large, personal, domestic, historical or natural—finally amounts to a wash: "How long before our masquerade will end its noise of tamborines [*sic*], laughter, and shouting, and we shall find it was a solitary performance? . . . What imports it whether it is Kepler and the sphere; Columbus and America; a reader and his book; or puss with her tail?"[14]

This is not Poe's Keplerian vision of Nature in *Eureka,* which among other things vetoes the ideological impulse to convert Nature into a Columbian, revisionary trope: into a means for discovering (Eureka!) the unique potential of American experience at large. *Eureka* both expands Emerson's topos of Nature to misrecognition, and unmasks his presupposing a cosmic perspective to make his claims. In *his* work, Poe assigns that perspective to the exclusive provenance of God: "That Nature and the God of Nature are distinct, no thinking being can long doubt" (*Eureka* 1313). For Poe, moreover, cosmic "magnitude," along with Keplerian expositions of it, minimizes the significance of individual human experience. Transforming Emersonian Nature into a wholly abstract field of atoms, Poe argues that everything possesses a physical disposition toward "coalescences"; themselves subject to an equally abstract, gravitational force, these too, in turn, are pulled toward a "centre unknown" (1395, 1347). In essence, Poe's atomic argument effectively negates Emerson's along with regnant American notions of "individualism." From the perspective of an utterly impersonal and sublime because invisible cosmic sphere, Nature represents a public "common" out of reach to anyone's immediate personal experience.

Poe's redaction of Emerson's vision resists any "mid-world" solution of the extreme binary possibilities to which the public-private dilemma might lead. Poe conceives of a Public Sphere radically impervious to any of its actual *or* idealized versions in human society.[15] When viewed as an agglomeration of Poesque atoms, a social public grounded in Emerson's model of Nature lacks any normal meaning. If the "irrelative particle primarily created by the volition of God" identifies "a condition of positive *normality,* or rightfulness," then "wrongfulness implies *relation*" (1297), the very definition of any socially defined public sphere. Obversely, Poe's cosmic sphere appears to cancel Emerson's most viable social manifestation of individual privacy. For Emerson, self-reliance entails a withdrawal from public affairs, which one can realize by retiring not "as much from his chamber" or "society" as by "look-[ing] at the stars" or Nature. By focusing on cosmic processes, Poe removes Nature from sight (looking), Emerson's non-negotiable sensory relation to Nature: "In the woods . . . I feel that nothing can befall me in life,—no disgrace, no calamity, (leaving me my eyes)."[16]

For Emerson, Nature can serve as a refuge from shame or "disgrace," or from one's usual surrender to public determinations of self-identity. For Poe, no such refuge exists. True, his radicalized impersonal Nature, a primordial cosmic force of Unity the attractive force of which no single atom can escape, allows that "the infinitude of division refer[s] to the utterness of individuality." However, the fact "[t]hat *no* two bodies are absolutely alike" constitutes a temporary aberration, to be canceled by the Divine Unity (*Eureka* 1287, 1282). Poe also negates the privilege accorded "consciousness" or "self" in Transcendentalist credos from a different angle. Both finally consist of nothing more than the residue of the two forces, attraction and repulsion, which govern the Universe's composition. Distinguishing itself from Emerson's vision of Nature, Poe's abstract, cosmic version of it shrinks not just socially defined public spheres, but private ones, too, to patently finite signifiers within God's "plot."

If its remorselessly *"objectless"* (1354) Public Nature reduces social notions of public and private experience to cosmic fictions, Poe's Eurekan vision yet legitimates a privacy as, in the two senses of these words, a repulsive, abnormal, even perverse truth in its own right. Like everything else in Poe's imaginary universe, truths gain credence from a public consensus always in the process of collapse, and so are necessarily partial and arbitrary. Logical axioms, for instance, accrue their "'indisputable'" cachet only from the radically relative or contingent public contexts—social, cultural, and historical—in which they inescapably appear: "what is obvious to one mind may not be obvious to another," and "what is obvious to one mind at one epoch, may be anything but obvious, at another epoch, to the same mind. . . . [T]he *axiomatic principle* itself is susceptible of variation" (1303). Thus, the sole criterion for truth is aesthetic: *"a perfect consistency"* alone constitutes *"an absolute truth"* for Poe (1349). His own relativistic thesis need only possess a rhetorically persuasive consistency, which no doubt applies to his representation of the Universe right now. And relative or not, its truth is not only as good as but, since it recognizes its status as a truth-*effect,* also better than most claimants of it.

Poe's view of things explains why art, as he states at *Eureka*'s very beginning, *is* truth, and why his present artistic rendition of the Universe is *"beautifully true"* (1312). A self-serving proposition or not, *this* truth lies on the surface for all to verify. His discourse exists on a par with those "stellar bodies" that will "finally be merged in one . . . *already existing* [central orb]," but which, if only for now, are accessible to "a superficial observation of [their] cyclic and seemingly . . . *vortical* movements." (1349). Yet because its truth also reduces to a contingent truth, Poe's theory, precisely as he writes it, remains true for himself alone. In effect, it does what his narrator in "William Wilson" could not do. At least *in theory,* his theory negates any would-be public double, and not merely because he rejects outright public regimes of judgment, moral or other. Each reader can grasp *Eureka*'s truth only from his or her equally contingent perspective, not to mention within a specific act of reading itself subject to change vis-à-vis future readings. That fact alone makes *Eureka* appear abnormal, emphatically heterogeneous, an aberration in Poe's own canon of work. Citing Dupin's method of detection in "The Murders in the Rue Morgue," Poe underscores his work's self-referential aberration when he asserts that "it is just by . . . such protuberances above the plane of the ordinary . . . that Reason feels her way, if at all, in her search for the True" (1293).

Eureka's argument at bottom suggests that even his motivated, literary redaction of Emerson smacks of a purely accidental collision of atoms. These are but two alone among "an infinity of local deviations," and could just as well metaphorically figure any other text covertly impinging on *Eureka*'s composition. In Poe's schema, every human truth is "wrong"; therefore different visions of it concern not truth per se, but rhetorical positionings, themselves subject to purely atomistic relations. They too traffic in "continuous differences of relative position among the multitudinous masses, as each proceeds on its own proper journey to the End" (1347). To be sure, as if a proto-proponent of cosmic "chaos theory," Poe allows that persons or texts undetectably influence each other: "That each atom attracts—sympathizes with the most delicate movements of every other atom, and with each and with all at the same time, and forever, and according to a determinate law of which the complexity, even considered by itself solely, is utterly beyond the grasp of the imagination" (1286).[17] But these influences occur unconsciously, in the sense of the complex posed by sheer spatio-temporal proximity and the attractive force of mass, as opposed to willed or repressed human desires.

So here again, Poe's "unconscious" and private quarrel with the more massive literary and cultural presence of Emerson in *Eureka* reduces to only one among many other possible ones. Like each different universe that exists "apart and independently, *in the bosom of its proper and particular God*" (1330), the Poe-Emerson literary collision is at once existentially absolute, with "its own proper journey," and of passing critical moment in relation to *Eureka*'s envisaged "End." Nothing escapes Poe's obliterative ending. All are subject to it: personal and social projects alike, whether progressive, egalitarian, transcendental, or, as I will argue, even his own local literary pursuits of privacy.

That defines Poe's true tale of terror. *Eureka*'s cosmological fantasy would metaphorically void any commonly understood public sphere, which by definition generates homogeneous—not just conformist but also contestatory—beliefs, practices, and ideal values.[18] In propagating the latter, social publics repress each person's heterogeneous conditions and his or her inescapably heterogeneous relation to them. For Poe, in short, everyone is alone and will never not be, and not least when, perversely pushing the meaning of democratic culture to its limit, his cosmic figuration of Unity eventually annuls heterogeneity.

2

Whatever its social intimations, *Eureka* proposes no covert politics of revenge on Poe's mass-cultural or democratic milieu, but instead a poetics of art as private practice. His thesis applies to "All Things," including to how "the Universe . . . is but the most sublime of *poems*" (1348, 1349; my emphasis). Moreover, as do Poe's tales, *Eureka*'s central, cosmological topic cavorts with suspicious tropes and verbal puns that nip at its expository postulations. For example, the work reduces not simply to a "Poem" (1259), but to a Uni-*verse*. In line with the colloquial maxims that perplex Poe's tales, *Eureka* at bottom asserts that few of us appreciate "the gravity" of our situations. No doubt a seriously intended, theoretical exposition of the Universe, his treatise yet plays literary games, some with prima facie small, semiotic import. Aside from its redaction of Emerson's and other Transcendentalist visions, not to mention its paraphrases and likely plagiarisms of scientific texts, *Eureka* also plies a spoofing, epistolary introduction and trompe l'oeil puns. The small, however, here ends up looming large. *Eureka*'s "notoriously unstable, maddeningly transformable, and . . . dubious generic status" confesses its imperfect composition,[19] but in performative accord with a thesis that collapses its own narrative postulations into "Matter no longer" (1354).

The last pun suggests that, since Poe's vision unavoidably defines itself as just one among other heterogeneous truths, "nothing matters," so to speak, including the personal or socially definable, self-destructive nihilism to which his apocalyptic vision else appears reducible. *Eureka* inscribes its own helpless pull or "return to [Divine] Unity"; in other words, its own generic makeup self-referentially collapses into a "Book of Truths" *and* an "Art-Product" (1259), which Poe elsewhere considers to be incompatible poetic principles.

Likewise, God's Creation of the Universe exhibits "an absolute reciprocity of adaptation" between cause and effect, "so that we can never absolutely decide which is which" (1342, 1341). In comparison, *Eureka* perforce exemplifies an "imperfect *plot*," as occurs "in a romance" (1352), another designation that Poe uses to depict his treatise.

Nonetheless, his work's self-ordained fate at least allows him to mimic the "reciprocity" of a Divine plot, which by inference also intimates his assent to radical privacy. If God's Universal Plot is perfect in its "complete mutuality" of cause and effect, Its purpose remains sealed from human inquiry, and all the more so for Its purposeless repetition. No one can divine "the idiosyncrasy of the Divine Art" (1354). In theory if not fully via his present narrative mimicry of it, Poe can state that the "Heart Divine . . . *is our own*" (1356). As the effect of language's virtual infinity of associations, *Eureka*'s implosive self-references, like God's cosmic bodies, appear right there for all to see, in symmetrical accord with his meta-physical thesis, rather than idiosyncratic or private in any conventional sense. Yet when positioned against the more gravitationally attractive import of the work's universalistic (*sic*) thesis, Poe's rhetorical self-references increasingly lack relevance for readers; or the same thing, they accrue more and more referential significance for himself in private.

Poe begins *Eureka* by claiming that all things hold "*the Germ of their Inevitable Annihilation*" (1261), a postulation pertaining not only to the text's own collapsing of heterogeneous genres, but also to its concussive unfolding of condensed modes of literary self-reference. The work's allegorical substratum even marks Poe's narration of nebular formations evolving from their initial appearance "not [of] true spheres, but oblate bodies," such that, drawn evermore closely to a "central orb," their "orbit becomes a circle" (1330, 1351). His principle of consistency allows that the same process allegorically traces how, thanks to the gravitational force of *Eureka* within his particular literary universe, his own past works now appear to him more a matter of *formal* or objectified "matter" than texts expressing some immortal artistic vision. Just so, Poe introduces his cosmic disquisition with the "remarkable letter" that happens to internalize or re-collect one of his first published tales, "MS. Found in a Bottle" (1833). Germinal within his career, the tale also concerns a ship, the sail-inscribed name of which is "*Discovery*," or a synonym for "Eureka."

Eureka's intimations of a parallel, literary universe license further surmises of the same kind. As suggested, its narrative of nebular rings condensing into stars and planets (1307–11) metaphorically doubles for Poe's as if telescopic perception of his own earlier literary works now condensing into non-signifying, materially mute, physical particles. The vision realizes in extreme the materialist configuration of art he had envisaged through his surrogate Ellison in "The Domain of Arnheim" (see Chapter 1). From *Eureka*'s purely physico-cosmic perspective, his poems, too, the literary genre in which he originally invested his literary ambition, perhaps dub as comets, effervescent "*lightning-flashes of the cosmical Heaven*" (1351). Something similar applies to stars forming as if they were just-occurring nebulae, "this instant whispering in our ears [of] the secrets of *a million of ages* by-gone" (1340). Readers cannot help *but* misread Poe's tales simply because fiction traffics in a preterit present, whereas from his Eurekan perspective they instead consist of entirely past-tense affairs.[20]

Literature here becomes subject to the formalism of an extraordinary geometry in which all objects not only ideally but also literally coalesce into an infinite, self-enclosed "circle" (1344). With their fictional characters already intimating the same fate, Poe's past tales, framed by his Eurekan discovery, mime the appearance of reified, heterogeneous entities that were always already coalescing or dying from their individuated literary identities. Through the astronomical formalism of *Eureka*, they come to resemble "every atom," each one "proceeding inwardly, and finally attaching itself to the condensed centre"—to *Eureka* itself—thereby "add[ing] something to the original velocity of that centre." (1307).

Distracted by "stars," who will discern any of this? Poe can plausibly assume that his readers will bypass *Eureka*'s implosive, self-referential moves, for which his occluded redaction of Emerson's *Nature* figures as but one. Although the text's thesis and rhetorical emissions bring his allegory front and center, only by deduction or post factum guesswork might readers at all surmise that his Universe of Stars parallels the literary universe of his own former works. Like God's utterly idiosyncratic Plot, Poe's Eurekan plot produces its own literary privacy in a medium and thematic métier that seem to deny any inward subjectivity, the last bastion of privacy within a fading Romantic ethos. In short, *Eureka*'s evermore elusive, self-referential condensations processually shut doors to all hermeneutic, i.e., public, inquiries.

Quite literally, then, Poe doubly discovers the "Germ" of his own literary career's annihilation, which he here imaginatively enacts executing at last. Privately transforming them into all outside, evacuated of any content, *Eureka* more perfectly seals off his previous works' respective scenes of writing, something their rhetorical sleights-of-hand and allegorized, self-referential undercurrents had only imperfectly realized. Formerly, for example, he could never quite renounce his wish for public approval, as through the artistic surrogacy of Ellison in "The Domain of Arnheim." Writing poems and tales meant competing with other writers for such approval. Like Ellison, Poe tried to effect "the contempt of ambition," the "most difficult" artistic stance to realize (*P&T* 856). He had therefore sought to frame his art using non-discursive models like landscape-gardening, or to construe original writing as reducible to "novel combinations" within an elementally anonymous, literary langue.

But preparing for literary anonymity is one thing; embracing it as a primary, imaginative desideratum is another. Poe himself had already played out the conundrum through the allegorical purport of "A Descent into the Maelström" (1841), a tale that invokes and tries to avert his Coleridgean-large ambitions. The narrative regales us with an "Ancient Mariner" motif of survival, complete with Coleridge's surrogate reader-narrator. Poe's mariner presumably survives his fishing-boat's pull toward an abyssal, oceanic vortex by having earlier constructed the right kind of boat: "When a boat is well built, properly trimmed, and not deep laden, the waves in a strong gale, when she is going large, seem always to slip from beneath her—which appears very strange to a landsman—and this is what is called *riding*, in sea phrase" (*P& T* 441–42; Poe's emphasis).

"A Descent into the Maelström" allegorizes Poe's anxiety of literary annihilation in the face of an elemental maelstrom, a sea of words, the meaninglessness of which his invoking precedents like Coleridge in fact serves to postpone. The tale outlines his pre-Eurekan method to "slip" the abyssal thought of literary oblivion, with its capacity to nullify his desire to write at all. Both well-built boat and the cylindrical cask that eventually saves the mariner metaphorically refer to Poe's ideal conception of the "brief tale"—to a "riding"/writing that, to "landsmen"/readers, "very" strangely might just survive life-threatening matters, understood in a literary-performative sense. Those matters weigh down other writers, whose thematically "deep laden" works bespeak their large literary ambitions. Novels and Coleridgean poems sink into the literary vortex faster, their gambits for survival and public fame more deluded. To use *Eureka*'s language, they more easily disappear within the gravitational "agglomerations" of greater visionary precedents ("waves in a strong gale") than Poe wants to think his more modest, self-referentially or cylindrically constructed tales will do.

But the shipshape seams of "A Descent into the Maelström" finally don't hold, and not only in the tale's actual story line. After all, the narrative consists of the mariner's twice-told tale, doubled by the narrator's, all the while evincing a latent allegory of writing that dis-figures the story itself. If through writing tales Poe would finesse his ambition to become a publicly acknowledged, Coleridgean "Vates," like the mariner he still nostalgically clings to a public readership (e.g., the narrator) to confirm his having avoided the abyssal vortex. At best, the latter intimates Poe's prescience of the Ur-text he later thinks to write in *Eureka*. In "A Descent into the Maelström," he descends into but swerves from what attracts him: a radical private imaginary, or a vision of writing that lacks any social-literary supports, literary-competitive ones among them.

In *Eureka*, however, he willingly entertains and *ascends* toward that starry imaginary. Privately forecasting a kind of literary self-annihilation, *Eureka* itself becomes the irreducibly private Ur-text attracting and eclipsing his former works' inability, because of their heterogeneous circumstances, to elude the continually intrusive pressures of his social and literary milieu on his scenes of writing. In the last analysis, matters of any kind, literary, too, don't matter, since for Poe they all occur in an immaterial medium: "the ether thus conceived is radically distinct from the ether of the astronomers; inasmuch as theirs is *matter* and mine *not*" (*Eureka* 1352). For that matter, regarding material-literary influences as well, "*no two* stellar bodies in the Universe . . . are particularly, while *all* are generally, similar" (1323). Except in general and genre, Poe's past works thus reduce to eccentric particularity.

In *Eureka*, Poe indeed writes the summa of his previous works, but with all of them reducible to a "Unity" become "Nothingness" (1355). Through his cosmological trope, he scans his past works in private *as* private, and in retrospect redeems their imperfect plots. For no matter his allegorical efforts to ward off the possibility, his tales inescapably got written in the grip of a "repulsive" if self-consciously suppressed ambition for overt or more subtle kinds of public literary performance.

3

In the same month and year that he first delivered his lecture on "The Universe," Poe proposes in his "Marginalia" for *Graham's Magazine* the one kind of literary ambition he endorses:

> If any ambitious man have a fancy to revolutionize, at one effort, the universal world of human thought, human opinion, and human sentiment, the

opportunity is his own. . . . All that he has to do is write and publish a very little book. Its title should be simple . . . "My Heart Laid Bare." But—this little book must be *true to its title*.

Now, is it not very singular that, with the rabid thirst for notoriety which distinguishes so many of mankind—so many, too, who care not a fig what is thought of them after death, there should not be found one man having sufficient hardihood to write this little book? To *write*, I say. There are ten thousand men who, if the book were once written, would laugh at the notion of being disturbed by its publication during their life, and who could not even conceive *why* they should object to its being published after their death. But to write it—*there* is the rub. No man dare write it. No man ever will dare write it. No man *could* write it, even if he dared. (*E&R* 1423; Poe's emphasis)

The resistance to one's writing that "very little book" has little to do with its contents, since writers would not find its publication disturbing "during their life." Poe makes clear that writing one's secret autobiography concerns more than the issue of publication or otherwise making one's private thoughts and deeds public. People with a "rabid thirst for notoriety" *and* people who do not "care a fig" about what others think of them would equally find the book difficult to conceive and impossible to write.

The resistance to baring one's heart through writing lies in the scandal it would pose to human public spheres as such. *Eureka*'s implicit theory of language, the primary foundation of any public sphere, already advances that very scandal. One can communicate one's experiences generally, realigning them with those of others, but because they occur in an ongoing state of idiosyncratic heterogeneity, they simultaneously refer to their incommunicable and therefore private particularity. Just as in God's Cosmic Plot, the private *is*, although, as in a photographic negative, one can apprehend it only in terms of its disappearing from ever-coalescing public scenes, themselves destined to concede their mass yet individuated formations to even more massive ones. By emplotting misreadings and the like, Poe had earlier tried to outwit discursive capture. Now he recasts public discourses, the various codes of reception, as media through which the private approaches ontological as opposed to ontic or merely representational status.

Bluntly put: as formulated by Poe, the private scandalizes the public as authoritative arbiter of human knowledge, which is why, to refer to my earlier citation of Edward Shils (see Chapter 1), the public hates the private. Poe previously ventured just that *mise en scène* in "The Cask of Amontillado" (1846). Simply in conventional terms, the tale consists of private scenes and perspectives. Not only does Montresor lure Fortunato into a catacomb, literally hidden from public concourses above ground, the tale's events also occur during carnival when people mask their public identities. Montresor ultimately seals Fortunato within a wall within the catacomb, a murder itself having gone undetected for fifty years before Montresor's apparent deathbed confession in the present narrative. In addition, both characters dabble in private social agendas. Fortunato belongs to the secret society of Masons, and Montresor's confession conjures the privacies protected by social sanctions, here underscored by ecclesiastical ones. Given how he once disingenuously used language in the most serious of circumstances, his present confession also incurs the charge of a privately motivated performance. Montresor himself states, "neither by word nor deed had I given Fortunato cause to doubt my good will" (*P&T* 848). The tale allegorically traces a similar game: if Montresor entraps his unwitting victim via his taste for amontillado (hardly a special wine), so would Poe lure certain readers to misread his tale for their "taste" in popular literature.

But just as occurs in other Poe tales, language converts these different privacies into public matters. Like the "You, who so well know the nature of [Montresor's] soul," we readers get to know all of the above and more. If not moral guilt, then an unrepentant and unmitigated desire for exacting revenge, frustrated in the first instance, still motivates Montresor's confession. Despite its apparent success, his deed necessarily fails to satisfy his negative criterion for true revenge: that insults go "unredressed when the avenger fails to make himself felt as such to him who has done the wrong" (848). Timothy Scherman has noted how the cave's "nitre," to which Montresor repeatedly refers (850–51), instances an anagram for "inter," the project he executed then and continues to execute now by rehearsing its particular details.[21]

"The Cask of Amontillado" thus entices *us* to seal Montresor's character by judging or knowing his motivation. On one hand, the tale positions *its* "You," the anonymous and as if carnival-masked reader, to (want to) confirm its codes of knowing others. On the other, Poe induces these variant codes to miscarry. For example, the tale tempts us to regard Montresor and Fortunato—their names are synonymous—as doubles. Moreover, by trusting Montresor's confession, the "You" in the tale also adopts and doubles his perspective. In case we suspect that Montresor represents Poe's effort to memorialize a perceived insult done to *him,* personal or literary, we, of course, do the same. But no less than his unspecified insult, Montresor's motive remains stubbornly ambiguous, on a par with how he himself can never occupy

Fortunato's position to know if he fully experiences the intended revenge. The same predicament confronts the reader. Specifically concerning him and Fortunato, Montresor's failed project to know the other exists in particular form, whereas for us his failure dissipates into generic truisms, such as that guilt will out, or else that "the perfect crime cannot be committed."[22]

Poe's tale also stages more than a contextually self-enfolding series of epistemological mishaps that invite moral tags or hermeneutic tangles. Whichever "double" relation we focus on confirms not public knowledge *or* its problems, but the ineluctably recessive particularity of private experience, the most important being Poe's final encryption of his own literary privacy. At the center of this Poe tale, too, "is Poe" himself, self-entombed, as if dead or incommunicado by choice. Jonathan Elmer surmises that even by his "furious encrypting of meaning," Montresor, a provisional double of Poe, cannot contain his traumatic memory of Fortunato's last self-signifier—"only a jingling of bells" (*P&T* 854). That sonorous finale finally "figures Poe for us," poet of "The Bells," whom Emerson would later term "the jingle man."[23] Montresor's "nitre" resonates with a similar, self-referential echo, something more (or less) than an anagram for what we might say he already unconsciously desires. "Inter," that is, further breaks down into an abbreviated anagram for "w*ritten*," by which Poe's text arguably inscribes its own entropic, about-to-become past-tense status.

With its cold, cosmic carapace, both rhetorical and thematic, *Eureka* analogously anticipates its future " 'Life Everlasting,' " with Poe its anonymous or as-if-dead author. This is what it means for him to express in public his private "Heart Laid Bare," or rather, because it specifically pertains to his poetics of literary art, his secret *Biographia Literaria*. *Eureka* is a text that would consist entirely of material signifiers, like the bricks and mortar used to en-crypt Fortunato. However much they wall in a secret(ed) "Poe" by reductive, verbal materials, Poe's tales still engage a complex of meaning and competitive urges within a literarily defined public field. Poe's cosmological allegory transcends the problem by enacting the motion of interchangeable genres and a thesis that posits the gradual but inevitable voiding of public meaning, social, literary, or "autobiographical." Literally concerned with spheres, Poe's Uni-verse configures human public spheres—*any* abstract relation of selves that achieves the figural impress or mass of quasi-visibility—in a framework that dictates their nihilistic recession into an All-Public Sphere. *Eureka*'s visionary "End" essentially spells a Nothingness in which no other comparative point will then exist to confirm anything *as* public.

One might contend that Poe here reveals himself as a cultural Montresor. The vision, after all, exists at odds with a United States culture that constantly enlists various social and economic means in an ongoing project to construct a socially self-conscious public sphere. Yet Poe's Eurekan stance aims to transcend critical edge, insisting on a poetics of privacy that in principle underwrites an *E pluribus unum* ethos. As an End that Poe tries to hallucinate before the End, his cosmic Public Sphere or, the same thing, God's Private Plot, will leave in Its wake an infinity of private lives for their each being abnormal, heterogeneous, and transitory. For Poe, this will finally be to be let alone, a final private state formulated through rather than against public milieus and media. His vision, then, is no wish for death, whether of his literary career or of his actual life, but more accurately a wish to imagine it. In that "dying" imaginary lies the beauty he essentially argues any person can experience on his or her terms alone.

Poe, of course, recognizes that from public viewpoints, his vision would look mad to anyone but "dreamers and those who put faith in dreams as in the only realities" (*Eureka* 1259). He all but courts this judgment when he adopts a volcanic perspective at the very beginning of *Eureka*: "He who from the top of Aetna casts his eyes leisurely around, is affected chiefly by the *extent* and *diversity* of the scene. Only by a rapid whirling on his heel could he hope to comprehend the panorama in the sublimity of its *oneness*" (1261). Poe requests readers to adopt the same view of *Eureka*. They, too, must take in its extent and diversity—its disquisition not just on stars, but also on "*all things, spiritual and material, that can be imagined to exist*" (1262). As I have argued, these things perforce include his text's subliminal, fleeting references to former, disappearing scenes of writing along with their condensations into "written" texts, none of which could sustain their private stardom. On one level, Poe makes *Eureka* methodologically accessible to everyone. On another, the fact that he insists on an already fantastic perspective to imagine the death of semiosis makes his text unreadable, not to mention frames as preposterous anyone's likely adoption of his perspective in practice.

Mad though it may appear to readers, Poe's pursuit of radical privacy in and through his apocalyptic fantasy of God's many cosmic mansions appears anything but that to Wallace Stevens, who would write his own poetic postcard from a volcano years later. *Eureka*'s resistance to reading raises a problem that he would interrogate from a no less dizzying array of lyrical perspectives: if the public exists to confirm the private, the private yet requires such confirmation lest it appear merely hallucinatory to oneself. With that one qualification, it takes little to imagine (madly, of course) that Stevens' volcanic poem in essence aligns itself with not only Poe's *Eureka* but also his entire Usher-like house of fiction. In the cold light of earth's star—or modern visions of reality rabid to make public and to demystify all private fantasies— non-dreamers who merely read Poe's words in the way we "speak our speech" likely will "never know,"

> Will say of the mansion that it seems
> As if he that lived there left behind
> A spirit storming in blank walls,
>
> A dirty house in a gutted world,
> A tatter of shadows peaked to white,
> Smeared with the gold of the opulent sun.
> ("A Postcard from the Volcano," *CP* 159)

4

As it happens, Poe, in the sense of his pursuit of privacy, makes unexpected cameo appearances throughout Stevens' first published collection of poems in 1923. To be sure, even in the most general literary-historical sense, establishing the Poe-Stevens linkage must rely on tenuous objective evidence and scattered critical precedents. Stevens passingly refers to Poe, if always in a favorable light, only in a handful of letters. There exists, of course, the loose French connection between the two writers. Thanks to Baudelaire's sponsorship, Poe helped inspire the late-nineteenth-century Symbolistes; they in turn influenced some of Stevens' earliest poetic efforts. To certain critics, however, he had overcome that influence by the time he came to write his later *Harmonium* poems, many of which undercut the movement's notable quest for "transcendent" meaning along with "the absolute authority" accorded poets purporting to reveal it.[24]

So exit Poe chez Stevens (early or late), except for the occasional and brief associations made by critics during or following the *Harmonium* period. These connections break down, as they do in criticism of Stevens' work generally, into what Melita Schaum terms "the polemical confrontation between tenets of 'humanism' and 'aestheticism.' "[25] In 1924, for example, Llewelyn Powys noted Poesque "shades and tinctures" haunting "the visible world" of Stevens' poetic representations. In 1943, Yvor Winters regarded the two's association as anti-humanist to the core. Mostly focusing on the *Harmonium* poems, he found Poe and Stevens continually striving for "the new" poetic experience. This "quest . . . [was] devoid of hope and of significance," since the new inevitably becomes "familiar" and thus keeps requiring newer "degrees of intensity and of strangeness." For Winters, the only difference between the two "hedonist" writers lay in Stevens' Modernist, ironic awareness of the quest's "futility."[26]

In pressing language to its limit, Poe and Stevens also complicate their conscriptions into traditionally humanist and aestheticist critical paradigms. At the very least, they attempt to elicit the linguistic new at the expense of constructing either a mimetically productive humanistic vision *or* an autotelic, ontologically formal art. Supporting that view, a few critics regard both writers' works as exemplifying deconstructive practices. Joseph Riddel argues that in his early and later poems, Stevens "reflects upon the motives of metaphor," just as Poe risked literary madness in reflecting "so much upon language."[27] Poe and Stevens' works therefore have no humanist message to convey and no aesthetic closures to proffer. Because its language doubles up on itself, nothing a Stevens poem says ever gets said, but only, as his speaker states in "The Snow Man," "the nothing that is." What Eleanor Cook discerns in Stevens' "Notes toward a Supreme Fiction" analogously applies to his *Harmonium* poems. For him, the one "incarnate Word which he could accept" instances "the human imagination reentering and being wounded by a world of language that it has itself created," a vision that Cook sees also occurring "in Poe's story, 'The Power of Words' . . . [which] Stevens admired."[28]

Beyond such heuristic asides, however, the Poe-Stevens critical trail runs cold. Interpreters of Stevens' poems, and not only Harold Bloom, generally prefer to see them preoccupied by Whitman's literary precedent more than with any other American writer's, regardless that in his letters Stevens mentions Whitman less than Poe. Many *Harmonium* poems undoubtedly echo with Whitmanian allusions, such as the very title of "Last Looks at the Lilacs." More explicitly, Stevens refers to his "Song of Myself" phase during his surrogate Crispin's poetic development in "The Comedian as the Letter C":

> His violence was for aggrandizement
> And not for stupor, such as music makes
> For sleepers halfway waking. He perceived
> That coolness for his heat came suddenly,
> And only, in the fables that he scrawled,

> With his own quill, in its indigenous dew,
> Of an aesthetic tough, diverse, untamed,
> Incredible to prudes, the mint of dirt,
> Green barbarism turning paradigm.
>
>   (*CP* 31)

Stevens' poetic engagement with Whitman's precedent, though, here includes a conscious awareness of it, so not ostensibly its unconscious repression and consequently pervasive influence. For that matter, the passage also inscribes Poe, whose violent tales and poems of death, at least as conventionally understood, thrive on narrative "stupor," or dwell in Gothic dreamworlds. Crispin/Stevens looks to abandon Poe's "halfway" métier of dream-coated reality for Whitman's "green barbarism," a vision of reality grounded by an energizing chain of poetic metaphors like those exercised in "Song of Myself": common grass/leaves/people/poems. Why does Crispin, then, eventually find his Whitmanian "aggrandizement" inadequate in the following sections of "The Comedian as the Letter C"?

From a Freudian viewpoint, of course, acknowledging repressed material can strategically serve to repress it at a deeper psychological level, in the present case, for example, to aggrandize Stevens' desire to establish his own poetic voice. Yet in "The Comedian as the Letter C," what he moves beyond concerns less his consciously desired or unconsciously anxious mimicking of Whitman's poetics than the "paradigm" that "Whitman" or "Poe" has become from the angle of how Stevens reads others reading their works. To Crispin/Stevens, those works now assume a more or less consolidated status in American literary history. They have become parts of a discursive system that accelerates and short-circuits the transformation of particular poetic process into public product.

As I argue in the following chapters, Stevens' efforts to disclose and preserve the privacy endemic to his poetic process from its public fate defines the issue that he specifically addresses in his *Harmonium* poems. "The Comedian as the Letter C" manifestly presents a condensed summation of various means by which he tries to effect this poetic charge. There, Crispin first focuses on his poems as objects coldly unrelated to human life:

> The myrtle, if the myrtle ever bloomed,
> Was like a glacial pink upon the air.
>
>   (*CP* 34)

Art divorced from life attenuates life's beauty for himself, so he attempts to deny the poem-making impulse altogether, as if the idiom of lived experienced without written expression could satisfy his imaginative desires:

> How many poems he denied himself
> In his observant progress, lesser things
> Than the relentless contact he desired;
>
> . . . .
>
> Perhaps the Arctic moonlight really gave
> The liaison, the blissful liaison,
> Between himself and his environment
> Which was, and is, chief motive, first delight,
> For him, and not for him alone.

But absent poetic expression, his "Arctic" or aesthetic sangfroid turns out "Wrong as a divagation to Peking"; it stunts the imaginative perception of "his environment," and so gives way to Crispin's recognition that "It was a flourishing tropic he required" (*CP* 35). Unable to suppress his desire for imaginatively vivified experience, he would build a new "colony," a modern, poetic vision of reality focused entirely on the "prose" of his immediate experience. This bears comparison with Whitman's comprehensive, spiritual vision for an American public commensurate with the country's political promise. Crispin's modestly private enterprise still devolves on its not being "for him alone." Poems that valorize the particular contingency of places and their different imaginative yields ("Abhorring Turk as Esquimau, the lute / As the marimba." [*CP* 38]) nonetheless aim to articulate "man's intelligence" at large (*CP* 36). In Crispin's project, poetry can do that by finding the "comprehensive" within heterogeneous cultural situations:

> Upon these premises propounding, he
> Projected a colony that should extend
> To the dusk of a whistling south below the south,
> A comprehensive island hemisphere.
>
> (*CP* 38)

Contrary to Winters' view that Stevens fetishizes the new, Crispin comes to regard his modern project as old, or as merely "bland excursions into time to come" (*CP* 39). Not unlike Ezra Pound's, Crispin's theorizing the contingent American-cultural experience resists official public versions of it, and in effect updates the Whitmanian "paradigm":

> The responsive man
> Planting his pristine cores in Florida,
> Should prick thereof, not on the psaltery,
> But on the banjo's categorical gut.

"Life Is Motion" from *Harmonium* exemplifies the new Americanist poetics: even "In Oklahoma," any dancing "Bonnie and Josie" can celebrate "the marriage of flesh and air" (*CP* 83). Still, the neo-Whitmanian poem soon induces formulaic behavior for Crispin, or the presumption that real places, contingent or local, already possess poetic value, as if an all-but-a-done-deal. In Whitman's poetry, for example, particular and out-of-the-way private métiers often get subsumed by their abstract public outcomes ahead of time: "All these [cultural-geographical] separations and gaps shall be taken up and hook'd and link'd together."[29]

Just that public-poetic fait accompli, the precipitous conversion of the local into the universal, defines Crispin's proto-reading of his own work. In response, he attempts to formulate a more private mode of writing—to write as if his work might have poetic relevance for others only by chance:

> Preferring text to gloss, he humbly served
> Grotesque apprenticeship to chance event,
> A clown, perhaps, but an aspiring clown.
>
> (*CP* 39)

In one sense, Crispin/Stevens, like other poet "dreamers," still cannot help but construe his poetic "dreams" in relation to major literary precedents or "babbling" like Whitman's. Yet he can "gingerly" try to revise them, and so constantly regenerate his wish to imagine the new:

> There is a monotonous babbling in our dreams
> That makes them our dependent heirs, the heirs
> Of dreamers buried in our sleep, and not
> The oncoming fantasies of better birth.
> The apprentice knew these dreamers. If he dreamed
> Their dreams, he did it in a gingerly way.

Revisions of others' "dreams," however, inevitably breed competitive comparisons, which he would prefer not to consider:

> All dreams are vexing. Let them be expunged.
> But let the rabbit run, the cock declaim.

Cocky or no, his new wish, too, turns fatuous, a heady fantasy simultaneously subject to judgments. Crispin cannot avoid the thought that others will read his work, assess its impact, and so measure its value vis-à-vis literary precedents anyway. In the event, his work will perforce appear not serious but comic or minor—a "Trinket pasticcio, flaunting skyey sheets" (*CP* 40).

Need he write in terms of literary (self-)judgments at all? Why not, as he goes on to do, try to become a "hermit" in his "Nice Shady Home," alone with his "prismy blonde" muse (*CP* 40, 42)? Crispin's vocational shift transpires not, as before, by self-consciously abstaining from writing, but by writing only up to the point (*scriptio interrupta*) where it serves to engorge his immediate, perceptual experiences of the real. Thus,

> Whoever hunts a matinal continent
> May, after all, stop short before a plum
> And be content and still be realist.
>
> (*CP* 41)

Write, yes, but do so as if not to publish it; try, that is, not to become concerned about its wider public value:

> Should he lay by the personal and make
> Of his own fate an instance of all fate?

His new goal, to maintain the private contingency of poetic acts, pervades the tenor of the poem's final two sections.

Crispin's former efforts to find a poetics suited to his unorthodox vocational desire eventually required his outright avoidance or denial of internalized literary publics. Now he simply tries to displace or buffer himself from them by resorting to conventional tropes of privacy, specifically his domestic scene of four daughters. Appearing in the final section of "The Comedian as the Letter C," they figure Stevens' newly preferred poetic practices. Allegorically understood, each daughter variously comes to the fore here and in his other *Harmonium* poems: serious, high-minded intention and tone ("Attentive to a coronal of things"); suspension of quotidian modes of thinking ("not yet awake"); an endless troping of nature's materials ("A creeper under jaunty leaves"); and, not least, an impish, socially irresponsible play,

> Mere blusteriness that gewgaws jollified,
> All din and gobble, blasphemously pink.
>
> (*CP* 44)

Taken together, Crispin's "daughters" compose an energizing ("strident") poetics ("compendium"), at once rife with a private "doctrinal . . . design" and an ad hoc "form" or unity: "Crispin concocted doctrine from the rout." "Disguised" *by definition,* his late-found ("Autumn's") poetics nevertheless must forgo any investment in public approval for his poems:

> The fatalist
> Stepped in and dropped the chuckling down his craw,
> Without grace or grumble. Score this anecdote
> Invented for its pith, not doctrinal
> In form though in design, as Crispin's willed,
> Disguised pronunciamento, summary,
> Autumn's compendium, strident in itself
> But muted, mused, and perfectly resolved.
>
> (*CP* 45)

Early and later critics of "The Comedian as the Letter C" have argued that its conclusion forecasts Stevens' resigned retreat from writing poetry altogether, since between *Harmonium*'s 1923 publication and republication in 1931 (with added poems), he turned his attention to actual private affairs.[30] But as we have seen, Crispin had previously rejected the option of not writing. More important, the "Disguised," disheveled poetics at which he arrives is, if it may appear unsatisfactory to readers, "perfectly resolved" in "muted" or private fashion to himself. It matters not whether others find exemplary the poem's efforts to discharge *his* particular imaginative desires to reconfigure reality, or

> if Crispin is a profitless
> Philosopher, beginning with green brag,
> Concluding fadedly.
>
> (*CP* 45–46)

Profitless as to known poetic values, he concludes "fadedly" only according to literary-public criteria. Crispin's end also echoes Poe's End in *Eureka*. For Crispin/Stevens, it finally doesn't "matter" if "what he proves / Is nothing," or if what he writes seems to readers "All din and gobble, blasphemously pink." Still, this is because—here without Poe's apocalyptic edge—"The relation" they have with his poem(s) simply "comes, benignly, to its end." In other words, the Stevens poem eschews making important public claims. The same applies to everyone, for each person's imagination of reality ends similarly, expressed, though it may be, in idioms other than literary: "So may the relation of each man be clipped."

Stevens' poetic quest thus results in an aesthetic epistemology that should matter to anyone, poet or not. But *to* express it also requires that he forgo the "should matter" corollary; else, like the speaker in the *Harmonium* poem following "The Comedian," he would truly despair and write nothing. The no less comic, Quixote-like figure in "From the Misery of Don Joost" has jousted (*sic*) "with the sun" and lost. Like Don Quixote, he has lost his "combat" for imagining reality on his own if also would-be humanly representative terms, so that now, an "old animal," he "Knows nothing more" (*CP* 46). Like Crispin, the present poem's quester alludes to the "Song of Myself" Whitman whose poetic I-become-you stance purports to convey the transcendental real to others, as when he ups the ante of perceiving the empirical "sun" in that poem's concluding peroration: "I shake my white locks at the runaway sun."[31] From the viewpoint of Stevens' persona, Whitman, too, may appear a white-locked "old animal," yet he remains an influential poetic *vivant* of the physical world whom Joost has failed to emulate. However outmoded his stance appears to modern readers, in vision and style Whitman still embodies the poet par excellence of and for a pervasive American public sphere.

Whereas Joost fails because he cannot envision an alternative poetic stance, Crispin/Stevens deliberately eschews Whitman's audience-oriented American poetics. To pursue it would only enlist him in trying to revise or best Whitman at his game, and turn Stevens into his Joostian double. Adhering at all to Whitman's poetic gambit would further make Crispin/Stevens forfeit his enabling resolve not to think beyond the *mere chance* of his poetry's communicative effects. In *Harmonium,* "Whitman" thus serves as an internalized foil against which Stevens pursues poetic privacy by meta-poetic means. The strategy and goal more accurately resemble Poe's in his tales and *Eureka,* as opposed to the literary-historical, i.e., the publicly received, *poet* "Poe," whom Crispin rejects early on. Attempting to finesse social-literary relations, Stevens like Poe *actively* seeks "nothing more" than to write apart from them. The conspicuous play on Poe's famous refrain from "The Raven" evades its fatalistic significance there, but rather holds out for its "private" Eurekan echo in Crispin's final "what can all this matter" regarding *his* meta-poetic quest.

The connection between the *Eureka* Poe and the *Harmonium* Stevens therefore sidesteps general intuitions about the two writers' aesthetic hedonism or proto-deconstructive proclivities. Poe's "Poem" on the "Universe of

Stars" in fact explicitly defines the "private" visionary trajectory of one poem in Stevens' 1923 collection. Published the same year as "The Comedian as the Letter C," "Stars at Tallapoosa" at first pointedly invokes Whitman's "Out of the Cradle Endlessly Rocking" and other Whitmanian tropes to purvey its cosmic meditation:

> The lines are straight and swift between the stars.
> The night is not the cradle that they cry,
> The criers, undulating the deep-oceaned phrase.
>
> . . . .
>
> Let these be your delight, secretive hunter,
> Wading the sea-lines, moist and ever-mingling,
> Mounting the earth-lines, long and lax, lethargic.
>
> . . . .
>
> The melon-flower nor dew nor web of either
> Is like to these. But in yourself is like.
>
> (*CP* 71–72)

Harold Bloom thinks that Stevens here anxiously acknowledges his inability to live up to Whitman's transcendental trumping of death. For Stevens, the stars are cold, indifferent objects, their relations among themselves and him "straight and swift" and unavailable for troping. In Eleanor Cook's view, Stevens' universe simply falls short of "what Whitman found, a generating erotic muse of this earth." Disagreeing with those judgments, James Longenbach argues that Stevens resists any naturalistic resignation or narrow-minded literary anxiety. In lines like "The body is no body to be seen / But is an eye that studies its black lid," he fastens on the "dead-end" to which such thinking leads. Stevens instead seeks, in Longenbach's words, to "become the 'secretive hunter,' not following the lines of the mind's eye" or "retreating into the rarefied world of the self." In that sense, Stevens takes his cue precisely from Whitman's "final word" of "death" in "Out of the Cradle," "turning outward . . . to mediate between [earth and sky], conscious of the limitations of the mind."[32]

But the Stevens speaker's wish to become the "secretive hunter" ("Let these be your delight") folds Whitman's invoked precedent into a more secretive allusion to Poe's *Eureka*. The poem necessarily manifests "outward," i.e., public, longings, whether these mean expressing a human-wrought vision of death, or else an anxiety at falling short of Whitman's poetic power to do so. Yet referentially and self-referentially, literally and figuratively, topically and thematically, "Stars at Tallapoosa" concerns a Poesque uni-verse of "Stars." Beneath the poem's Whitmanian cover lies the sort of rumination defining Poe's depiction of cosmic objects throughout *Eureka*. For example, Poe straight out discusses

> the paths through which . . . different spheroids move. . . . In the longer diameter [of an ellipse] are two points, equidistant from the middle of the line, and so situated otherwise that if, from each of them a straight line be drawn to any one point of the curve, the two lines, taken together, will be equal to the longer diameter itself. (*P&T* 1330–31)

In passing, Poe also happens to mention "the great 'nebula' in the constellation Orion" (1319), associable with the mythological hunter Stevens prefers to designate in "secretive" terms.

The most telling connection between Poe's and Stevens' two works lies in their both existing as projects to displace human discourse with cosmic monologue.[33] In comparison, one can read "Stars at Tallapoosa" as finding *Whitman's* vision wanting or still all-too-human, and Poe's Eurekan one the Stevens poem's agglomerative double. As if he himself were yet unable to believe in a "straight" naturalistic credo, the speaker in "Stars at Tallapoosa" *wants* and writes *to* reconfigure the body into a "black lid." He aims to shed the "melon-flower" tropes or human "webs"—the anthropomorphic impulse evident in Whitman's cosmic references[34]—by which Stevens as poet knows "stars." So he asks himself to know them ("But in yourself is like:") in terms of pure geometry, or as

> A sheaf of brilliant arrows flying straight,
> Flying and falling straightway for their pleasure.
>   (*CP* 72)

Burdened by human-mythological encrustations, even these figurative arrows, like the putative "pleasure" of stars, connote human purpose. The speaker would thus expunge any lingering human discursive habit ("Or, if not arrows, then the nimblest motions"), the better to experience nature, even his own "body," from a non-human, cosmic perspective—as the

> young nakedness
> And the lost vehemence the midnights hold.

Referring to a desired and definitive state of mind, Stevens' cosmic erasure of self, the drive toward a midnight psychic "vehemence," evokes not death wish but Poe's imaginary materialist crash of selves and things into *Eureka*'s final "Unity." As with Poe, focusing on catastrophic cosmic "truth" enables Stevens to conceive the obliteration of others within his acts of imagination, which here means to entertain the possibility of arriving at an absolute sense of poetic privacy.

Outlining a poetics that defines the "private" trajectory of Stevens' other *Harmonium* poems, "Stars at Tallapoosa" is no mere Eurekan coincidence. The same intention complicates credible readings of the extended, subjunctive sentence defining "The Snow Man." In trying

> not to think
> Of any misery in the sound of the wind,
> In the sound of a few leaves
>
> (*CP* 10),

"The Snow Man" is often understood for Stevens' Modernist rejection of the "nineteenth-century pathetic fallacy."[35] With its "listener" who

> beholds
> Nothing that is not there and the nothing that is,

the poem, in keeping with its "January" scene, also proposes a quite chilling "hopelessly materialistic" vision, "devoid of human meaning," and perhaps ironically exposes the consequences of an unchecked empiricist mind-set.[36]

Whatever its thematic meanings—its "nothing" arguably abjects the preceding irony, too—"The Snow Man" redundantly concerns its own poetic authority to make them. Lines like

> the same wind
> That is blowing in the same bare place

noticeably point to the poem's intertextual locus, specifically its evocation of Emerson's aforementioned "transparent eyeball" experience on "a bare common" as recorded in *Nature*. Noting the allusion, Harold Bloom argues that Stevens' poem attempts to best Emerson, the premise being that Stevens feels himself "stripped of delusions . . . and illusions . . . whereas Emerson was obsessed with Transcendental" ones.[37] However, Bloom's reading denies the poem's subjunctive raison d'être, its self-evident effort—a plausible, illocutionary meaning for "One *must* have a mind of winter / To . . ."—precisely to imagine itself free from "common" literary contests.

Expressing its poetic motivation per se, "The Snow Man," very much in line with Poe's *Eureka,* openly evokes Emerson to differentiate its desired vision from *Nature*'s. And like *Eureka*'s, Stevens' evocation moves beyond any attempt to gain unique literary-public distinction at the expense of Emerson, or in relation to any literary public unavoidably if unconsciously convoked to witness the effort's success. Even as Stevens acknowledges the enduring and onerous visionary attraction of the "transparent eyeball" experience for modern American poets like himself, he stresses its radically contingent or private occurrence on a *"bare* common"—on a public space stripped of public use-value. Emerson also writes about his experience on, as it were, the "common" that defines the essay genre itself. Stevens, in contrast, would write his self-annihilating poem in and as a permanently "bare place."

"The Snow Man" consists of a prolonged wish *to become* "the nothing that is," which in writing Stevens cannot quite secure its (not) being. His poem suggests more than that he "is moving against the community and the commonalty of [literary] topoi," which the poem supposedly makes "no longer common."[38] Stevens seeks a "bare" or totally private scene of writing where he would feel free "not to think," or at least to think only as a discursively dumb—an opaque rather than a transparent—Snow Man, utterly incognizant of others. Blocking its reader, "The Snow Man" personifies its wish through a figure that doubles the notoriously ambiguous snowman appearing at the end of Poe's *The Narrative of Arthur Gordon Pym*: "But there arose in our pathway a shrouded human figure, very far larger in its proportions than any dweller among men. And the hue of the skin of the figure was of the perfect whiteness of the snow" (*P&T* 1179).

5

Like many Poe tales, "The Snow Man" is a poem about a poem it itself is not, and so not, then, quite the "nothing that is." And like *Eureka,* Stevens' poem enlists Emerson's vision of Nature in *Nature* to condense and disappear from a public scene, which by Stevens' time also includes an established, American-cultural tradition. Neither writer supposes that absolute literary privacy exists in social-empirical terms. Only as a *poetic* truth, a perpetually exercised imaginary project, can privacy become irreducible to the way any "public" generates its own contingent, quasi-private modifications.

Poe's and Stevens' works entertain these, of course, but the private for them primarily devolves on textual acts understood as metonyms of conscious human experience generally, and which induce the sense of communicative exchange in relation to a constantly variable literary milieu. To go private, both writers at least try to baffle the exchange, Poe most often by emplotted misreadings, and Stevens by a host of pirouetting verbal gestures. A surety claims lawyer, Stevens was surely aware of contractual liability, which in matters of poetry appertains to the poet's implicit semiotic contract with readers to communicate something of shareable value. In that case, he pointedly breaks his contract, since like Poe he persistently writes to preserve his writing over against possible claims by its readers.

For openers, under Stevens' directed arrangement, *Harmonium* begins and ends with poems that in Poesque fashion emplot as if explicitly to block their full accessibility to readers. In the collection's first poem, "Earthy Anecdote,"

> The bucks clattered.
> The firecat went leaping,
> To the right, to the left,
> And
> Bristled in the way.
>
> (*CP* 3)

According to Eleanor Cook, the poem "blocks the reader in more ways than one: it blocks ready paraphrase, ready generic classifying, and especially ready answers to the question, what is the point of this poem. . . . Nor does it invite an allegorical reading."[39] Stevens himself stated that the poem lacks any "symbolism" (*L* 216; 1918), and his firecat image self-evidently does not appear in any lexicon, mythological or other. At best, one can argue that the image "draws attention to itself, partly because it is a neologism, but more important because it constitutes a striking image in a single word," as if it itself were "a miniature poem."[40]

Yet the firecat image arguably derives from and makes allegorical use of Poe's well-known tale "The Black Cat" (1843). Having already plucked out its eye with a "pen-knife," Poe's narrator, bound to "the Fiend Intemperance," hangs his pet cat Pluto "in cool blood . . . *because* I knew that it had loved me, and *because* I felt I had given me no reason of offence . . . *because* I knew that in so doing I was committing a sin . . . that would jeopardize my immortal soul" (*P&T* 598, 599; Poe's emphasis). That same night, his house burns down.

> On the day succeeding the fire, I visited the ruins. The walls, with one exception, had fallen in. This exception was found in a compartment wall, not very

thick, which stood about the middle of the house, and against which had
rested the head of my bed. . . . About this wall a dense crowd were
collected. . . . The words "strange!" "singular!" and other similar expressions, excited my curiosity. I approached and saw, as if graven in *bas relief*
upon the white surface, the figure of a gigantic *cat*. (600; Poe's emphasis)

Subsequent events—a second cat doubling the first; in a moment's anger at
the second cat, the narrator's killing his wife instead; this cat's exposing his
having walled up her corpse—clearly invite us to assume the self-exculpatory
motive governing his present narrative. In brief, the narrator associates both
cats with his wife, the real object of his animus.[41]

This reading would suffice were it not that a by-now-familiar allegorical
alternative underpins Poe's tale and marks the first cat as the prototype for
Stevens' firecat in "Earthy Anecdote." "The Black Cat" traces the wish and
its own failure to get away with a *fictional* equivalent of murder. The tale,
that is, assaults both the claustrophobia and compromised privacy endemic
to domestic ideology, here evoked by pets and wife. Accordingly, the narrator
acts intemperately in two senses. He drinks to escape a claustrophobic domesticity, for otherwise his wife's "disposition [was] not uncongenial with
my own. Observing my partiality for domestic pets, she lost no opportunity
of procuring those of the most agreeable kind" (*P&T* 597). His drinking also
signifies an aggressive reaction to contemporary social Temperance norms, or
to the penetration of public mores into his putatively private domicile and
self.

Still, the narrator's resistance is inexplicable, or rather too explainable, vis-
à-vis such mores. As suggested, "The Black Cat" positions its readers to acti-
vate normative, social standards in guessing at the narrator's displaced, i.e.,
repressed, misogynist motivation and guilt. After all, he notably feels worse
about killing Pluto than his wife.[42] Handmaiden of the domestic *and* patriarchal public sphere, Pluto's double helps expose all this, most obviously by
instigating the narrator's act and turning his private wish into public deed.
Moreover, the second cat not only reveals where the narrator has concealed
his wife's corpse, but also makes him subject to legal punishment: to the
"hangman" (*P&T* 606) or figure for the public's inescapable authority.

Unlike its substitute, Poe's first (fire-)cat functions as the narrator's preferred double and represents the tale's effort to fancy an impenetrable privacy. Cutting out Pluto's one "eye," Poe, using *his* "pen-knife," in effect
aggressively inscribes his wish to keep one aspect of *his "black" tale's* "I" radi-

cally inaccessible to public scrutiny and interpretive judgments. So the first cat figures the heart of the tale. If killing it must occur for the tale to get written at all—as I have argued, Poe never denies his resurgent literary ambition for public attention—the actual execution yet constitutes the tale's primary crime (a "sin"). The story dramatizes the return of the repressed, but of the "private" cat, not of the killed spouse who, here a substitute for *her* supposed substitute, represents the fallacious privacy of domesticity. To the same effect, the cat revealed in the house's wall after the fire exists "as if graven in *bas relief*" in the "figure of a gigantic *cat.*" The figurative desideratum of "The Black Cat," the first cat therefore appears in public ("a dense crowd") only as some " 'strange' " or enigmatically fictive cat. As a "*base* relief," it at once signifies Poe's *fundamental* effort to elude, and, were it at all known, his "Black Cat" tale's *offensive* significance to the public represented by his imagined readers.

In "Earthy Anecdote," Stevens as poet occupies the position of Poe's firecat, but with a different if no less public bête noire in mind. Stevens' firecat parades the same enigmatic status as Poe's:

> Every time the bucks went clattering
> Over Oklahoma
> A firecat bristled in the way.

Milton Bates notes that, "like the bucks, one's clattering, discursive mind swerves left or right whenever it approaches the firecat, thus duplicating the pattern of bafflement and evasion in the anecdote."[43] If the bucks represent the poem's inquisitive interpreters, why conspicuously situate them in Oklahoma? Eleanor Cook offers one explanation. Oklahoma, she helpfully observes, "is America in its raw state," having become an actual "state only eleven years before this poem was written." By extension, Stevens imagines blocking not just culturally sophisticated readers, those whom he associates with urban-American settings, but anyone who attempts to transgress the frontier state of mind by which he would define his act of writing this and his other *Harmonium* poems. Wishing to preserve the public-private interface as such, firecat-Stevens, very like Poe, would obstruct appropriations of his work by a critically persistent as well as cosmopolitan literary public. Put another way, even as Stevens imagines a public relentlessly pursuing his work to make it make sense, he also envisions a place that figuratively evokes a private, geopoetic topos: an imaginary "Oklahoma" where no established American public as yet exists.[44]

"Earthy Anecdote" allegorizes its resistance to allegorical meanings formulated "left" and "right" by a quasi-private, i.e., a specialized or uncommon, coterie of critical frontiersmen. The poem hinges on the oxymoron of
an already non-existent firecat that verbally enacts saying nothing. Unlike
Poe's prose tale and *its* figural firecat, Stevens' lyrical firecat would escape the
need to make final public sense at all. Yet like Poe's interminably staged resus-
citation of public pressures, Stevens never underestimates the way his inscribed readers perpetually "buck" his efforts to protect the private poetic
space he desires. Writing poems like the present one require an exhausting,
ever-alert tropological "leaping" with "bright eyes" to guard against his own
anticipated understandings of his poem's critical understandings. For that
reason, only in some imaginary future will his poem be the poem it still is not:

> Later, the firecat closed his bright eyes
> And slept.

A preface to Stevens' ensuing *Harmonium* poems,[45] "Earthy Anecdote"
suggests that they, too, practice "firecat" designs. In a less ambivalent way
than Poe's tales, Stevens' lyrics singlemindedly focus on suppressing the pressure of public relevance. Interchangeable "public" pressures impinge on each
poem's respective moments of composition and define the contingent form
or spin that his scene of writing must assume to defuse their force. As he
writes in *Harmonium*'s second poem, "Invective against Swans" (*CP* 4), his
poetic "soul, O ganders, flies beyond the parks"—beyond publicly designated private spaces; "*And* far beyond the discords of the wind" (my emphasis)—beyond conflicts or thematic matters that attract him and define *any*
public sphere.

Forming bookends with *Harmonium*'s first two poems, its final two
poems, "Tea" and "To the Roaring Wind," also distance themselves from
"ganders," a pun for public onlookers internalized in Stevens' acts of writing.
Cook terms both poems "envoi," and thinks they figuratively "hand his
book over to the reader." One might suppose, after all, that taking tea, a
beverage associated with civil interaction, occurs between at least two persons, as it does in another *Harmonium* poem, "Tea at the Palaz of Hoon."
So it makes perfect sense to argue that "Tea" reflects "elegance, order, ritual,
and civilization."[46] If the poem has self-referential significance at all, it addresses a reader scanning Stevens' poems with their unfamiliar topoi and
tropes (in this one, the non-northern caladium plant, or "elephant's-ear") in
"Your" private room:

When the elephant's-ear in the park
Shrivelled in frost,
And the leaves on the paths
Ran like rats,
Your lamp-light fell
On shining pillows,
Of sea-shades and sky-shades,
Like umbrellas in Java.
                    (*CP* 112–13)

For Cook, the topos of "Tea" evokes "a common domestic habit," the way by which Stevens regards his other *Harmonium* poems. If the poem refers to "other worlds," it does it to "nourish us"; here especially, it proffers an invitational, social message: "Take my [tea or poetic] leaves . . . preserve them, but do not let them grow stale; try them as you prefer."[47]

But even as it scripts a courteous scene of reading, "Tea" traffics in less civil and I would claim Poesque contraband, if nothing else underscoring the "firecat" poetic reserve of "Earthy Anecdote." For instance, whatever its tropical and other tropological allusions, the "elephant's-ear in the park" puns on an inquisitive public. Already connoting being nosy, Stevens' large-ear image suggests people in public spaces, i.e., readers of his poems, trying hard to overhear other people's private conversations, or in his case trying to fix the content of his private poetic musings. It is these readers—all of us—whom the present poem would coldly shut out in the "frost" and aggressively shrivel. As he construes them, "Tea" and his other *Harmonium* poems leave behind only "leaves on the path" running away "like rats": poetic images definitively avoiding civil expectations that they (ought to) make *common* sense, as when two take tea.

Stevens thus ends up addressing himself alone ("Your") in a Poe-like interior room, at odds with the critical view that, even with its musing about "sea-shades and sky-shades," the poem presents an "extramural" and shareably "appealing alternative to" any "artificial, indoor world."[48] Quite the contrary, once they become filtered through his poems—call them the loci or "pillows" associable with dreams and waking, or simply the site of imaginative activity—the poem's nature images suggest a further shading out of the external world. By inference, American readers predominantly occupy Stevens' world, and he configures them here as a public that inversely situates his act of taking "tea" in private. For those readers, his poems might as well refer to Java, what with their strange images and as if foreign because private scenes of composing them. Moreover, self-imaged as "umbrellas," his poems protect him from the sun, which "Tea" does not specify and, given its night-time ("lamp-light") setting, in fact literally absents from *its* scene. In "Tea," the sun does not represent unmitigated reality, the cold but privately beautiful real of "The Snow Man," for example. Instead, it refers to reality as perceived through the glaring light of publicity, such as in American parks and other venues where "elephant's-ear" leaves abound.

Situating its readers on the outside looking in, "Tea" takes back its invitation to readers of *Harmonium* as a whole. What about the subsequent and volume-ending poem, "To the Roaring Wind"? There, according to Cook, "Stevens seems to call on a spirit or genius loci (why of sleep?), who will speak, and thereby make his book speak, to the reader."[49]

> What syllable are you seeking,
> Vocalissimus,
> In the distances of sleep?
> Speak it.
> (*CP* 113)

The move in "Tea" to private, dreamy musing helps provide one answer to Cook's parenthetical question, but it again shows how one needs to read the fine-print reserve clauses in Stevens' poetic contract. "To the Roaring Wind" loudly evokes visionary spirits, Shelley's in particular, but also other precedents that would link Stevens' *Harmonium* poems to a recognizable Western poetic tradition. An ephebe poet in Harold Bloom's sense, Stevens thus asks himself what place he might have in this tradition, or what poems he might write to become a major ("Vocalissimus") part of it.

The reading seems plausible enough—except that the poem includes a *caveat lector* addendum suggesting how Stevens also adopts a viewpoint similar to Poe's figure of privacy in "The Philosophy of Furniture": the sleeping man finally shielded from public scrutiny. The poem's "you" is its *reader,* imagined through the distancing perspective of Stevens' own private poetic scene. It is as if, with the preceding poems now having been read, the reader were being asked to articulate his or her sense of them. More precisely, it is as if a bemused Stevens were figuring his poems' reader as in a perplexed state of making them make sense: "What syllable are you seeking . . . ?" Having finished taking "tea" in his private poetic room, Stevens, from a still more private position, hears faint words "In the distances of [his poetic] sleep." Even as he writes, he imagines hearing responses to his work, the total metaphorical impression of which resembles an inchoate sound ("the Roaring Wind") synonymous with a public clamor. Stevens *wants* to hear that clamor ("Speak it"), whatever contributes to it: high-cultural or visionary interpretations, casual readings—outright dismissals of his poems, too. Let them all speak their most ("Vocalissimus") about his poems. That way, the inchoate sounds, critical noise included, of imagined public responses to *Harmonium* will leave in their wake the contrasting silence of his written utterances, or of their having become an entirely private matter to himself.

Poe also invokes public reception to score private points, but in *Eureka* his public-become-private project turns into a pro tem means to a Starry-eyed end. Focusing on stars, he finds ("Eureka!") his work and "private I" congealing into things, then those into larger wholes, until the former's private effects disappear, as it were, from each other and himself. On one hand, this End gives the lie to any meaningful human union with others—to any public sphere—although not the ineradicable desire for it. On the other, Poe pursues privacy to the point where its final Public remainder ("Matter no longer") prevents even him from witnessing his desired "private" finale.

Promising only loss on elegiac par with his "most poetical topic," the metaphysical extremity of Poe's private End-game is sure to enervate imaginative élan, exactly what Stevens wants to effect by his own heterogeneous lyrical pursuits of privacy in *Harmonium*. He therefore would turn Poe's Eurekan conclusion into poetic license for perpetually beginning a "private" literary project as an end in itself. Poe's tales in particular gauge the private by at once inviting and slipping public codes. First and last, Stevens' poems enact and theorize the private by wholly reneging on that invitation, as if to nullify others' readings *and* misreadings of them: "Later, the firecat closed his bright eyes / And slept."

What can it mean to aim to take "tea" wholly in private? What then actually gets written? And despite what I claimed earlier in discussing "The Comedian as the Letter C," can any of what does get written really matter to anyone else?

4   *Harmonium:* Private Man, Public Stage

> People do not know what they lose when they make way with the reserve,
> the separateness, the sanctity of the front yard of their grandmothers. It is
> like writing down the family secrets . . . ; we Americans had better build
> more fences than take any away from our lives.
> —Sarah Orne Jewett, "From a Mournful Villager" (1881)

> There's something strange going on, you cant even be alone any more in
> the primitive wilderness ("primitive areas" so-called), there's always a heli-
> copter comes and snoops around, you need camouflage. . . . I have no ax
> to grind: I'm simply going to another world.
> —Jack Kerouac, "The Vanishing American Hobo" (1959)

1

No one would deny that Wallace Stevens was a notoriously private person,
and that to a certain extent the same characteristic carries over into his *Harmonium* poems. Right from the beginning of his career, he appears drawn to
a rather bourgeois notion of personal privacy: "Personality must be kept secret before the world; . . . for young men etc. it is most decidedly well-
enough to be left alone" (*SP* 82; 1900).[1] But to claim that privacy somehow
dominates the tenor of his first collection, especially of the radical sort for
which I am arguing, surely merits skeptical dissent.

True, many critics of the period suspected the same tenor, although mostly
in response to Stevens' (for them) crypto-poetic style. Louis Untermeyer, for
instance, judged Stevens perversely obscure, and wondered "whether [he]

even cares to communicate in a tongue familiar to the reader." Stevens' critical supporters also "perceived in [these poems] a disturbing or threatening quality of radical otherness, to the extent that the poems seemed to be written in a completely different language." Such reactions persist today, and not just with inexperienced readers. One hears more critically sophisticated echoes of Untermeyer's complaints, often pertaining to Stevens' subsequent poetry as well. Thomas Byers sees him deploying poetic "strategies" that one can "consider . . . [examples of] a sort of perverse secretiveness." C. Roland Wagner states that "Stevens' separation from others pervades all aspects of his life" and writings. Mark Halliday examines his poetry's content and style in light of how they suggest Stevens' "profound aversion to the demands of interpersonal relationships."[2]

But in *Harmonium,* Stevens' stylistic obscurity and apparent aversion to self-other relationships clearly register his poems' public effects rather than denote his determined effort to secure literary privacy through his act of writing them. Besides, anyone who cares can conditionally appreciate their effervescent beauty, a criterion to which Stevens himself alludes when claiming that all poetry "is a pheasant disappearing in the bush" (*OP* 198). Beyond that, his reticence, personal or poetic, occurs within a specific social-historical complex. In the period when he wrote his *Harmonium* poems, the social instability of the public-private dichotomy in United States culture had arguably reached crisis proportions. A conspicuous feature of his environment was its increasing denial of any real separation between public and private spheres, which an American liberal-individualist ethos had ideologically endorsed throughout the nineteenth century.[3]

Put another way, the "public" was now, as it were, itself going public with increasing notice, constructing and dominating definitions of an ever more compressed private sphere in distinctively manifest ways. Above all, social mechanisms used to construct a public medium largely for commercial interests had begun to penetrate all phases of American culture. James Beniger documents how new "control" technologies not only serviced but also transformed the earlier American capitalist marketplace. These technologies—among others, home telephone systems, electrical and other public utilities, mechanized food-processing, and a public world made vividly accessible via radio, cinema, tabloid newspapers, and the mass-produced automobile—gave rise to modern commercial enterprises that dramatically skewed the already attenuated meaning of domestic privacy.[4]

For example, "American courts and legislatures" during the nineteenth century "had recognized the home" along with "confidential communications . . . and public records as private domains."[5] By the turn of the century, however, the capitalist marketplace was making the so-called private home itself a public myth, in good measure because the American household no longer depended upon itself for many of life's common needs. According to Thomas Schlereth, "[f]orces beyond its domestic circle now dictated the quantity and quality, cost and availability of several of its vital life-support systems." One result of "the introduction of new utilities for daily life was their gradual but increasingly widespread homogenization of the domestic environment." Other factors, of course, also contributed to microsocial homogenization. Smaller ones like the popularization of etiquette books (Emily Post's in the 1920s, for instance) and insurance company tips on health helped standardize social interaction, hygienic behavior, and the like.[6]

The era's reliance on mass-market advertising and the side effects from certain political events effected analogous changes in the macro public sphere. Beginning in the 1880s and "accomplished by the 1920s," advertising in mass-circulated newspapers served "as a means to stimulate and control consumption." Amplified by the press and other media, political events fostered a highly visible and centralized public common, whatever particular political disagreements within it. Woodrow Wilson used advertising "to shape public opinion during World War I." The war itself worked to "strengthen [America's] moral consciousness," giving "new life [to] the myth of the Puritans' mission," most notably in the "passing of a Prohibition amendment." And just as the post-war depression had justified efforts to control the economy by government-originated statistical data, so political policies like Prohibition and the 1919 Palmer raids effectively endorsed official intervention into the private affairs of average Americans.[7]

In short, a host of new social venues worked to enervate the import of private life, most of them adverting normative measures by which to evaluate personal behavior. Even the quasi-private workplace was unable to maintain a firewall between itself and the expanding American public realm. "Private" business enterprises promoted the compilation of information on people's personal "needs"—surely a prominent feature of Stevens' insurance world—which themselves necessitated the creation of more impersonal bureaucracies to control the new data. Alternatively, these bureaucracies destabilized the security of owners' private businesses, not to mention of workers' private affairs.

At least regarding the last issue, one might argue that the breakdown of public and private life applied to all classes. On one hand, businessmen sought to establish norms of behavior by mass-cultural, political, and economic means, the better to exploit workers' labor. On the other, capitalists themselves were surrendering their own modes of private self-determination both to the ideology of a national public stage and to new technological-bureaucratic forces that, if only potentially, structured private business decisions as matters of public record. The same private-public breakdown crossed gender lines. In earlier times, American males had arguably construed the workplace as a site of private, homosocial fraternization, or as an alternative to the feminized domestic sphere of American-Victorian culture. Now the workplace "itself was seen as increasingly feminized with more women employed in increasingly feminine offices—hardly the world of real men at all. The enactment of women's suffrage in 1920 accelerated women's entry into the public sphere."[8]

In brief, by Stevens' time, privacy had already become public, notwithstanding legal attempts to protect it, the most important of which had appeared in Samuel Warren and Louis Brandeis' *Harvard Law Review* article of 1890, "The Right to Privacy." As I suggested in the Introduction, given the fluidity of a capitalist marketplace fueled by "[r]ecent [technological] inventions and business methods," Warren and Brandeis no longer could defend privacy by invoking the liberal-individualist sanction of private property. They instead tried to defend privacy, "the right to be let alone," on the ersatz legal ground of one's "inviolate personality."[9] In his previously cited journal entry, Stevens himself echoes the same defense of his personal privacy when stating "it is most decidedly well-enough to be left alone."

The Warren-Brandeis defense, however, was too little too late. First, the disappearance of the American frontier by 1890 cut into American ideological myths about escaping established social milieus, owning one's homestead, and otherwise leading lives less subject to the pressures of conformity and public scrutiny associated with urban life. Four years after the Warren-Brandeis article, Frederick Jackson Turner wrote his famous elegiac thesis about the frontier's formative influence on the country. Indeed, the Oklahoma territory, the last area within United States boundaries to remain unsettled, became open for settlement in 1890, the same year that "The Right to Privacy" appeared. Before but more so after that date, the "Western" became public-cultural myth: more consumerist material than viable existential option.

Second, despite their disclaimers, Warren and Brandeis's defense of privacy, as some commentators have maintained, effectively "produces person-hood as a new class of property in whose ownership . . . one holds legally protected rights."[10] The argument, that is, converts privacy into a species of information always *potentially* public. Moreover, if the turn-of-the-century household was becoming a site of homogenized goods and communication, what could "the right to be let alone" mean except a wish, perpetually ex-posed as imaginary, to deny a "public" fait accompli? One might even char-acterize the Harding administration's policy of national isolationism, set in place around the time Stevens published *Harmonium*, as a political substitute for an American personal privacy now become more ideological myth than real option.

Third and most compelling, the idea of a "public," whether liberal myth or working hypothesis, was becoming indistinguishable from the "publicity" that Warren and Brandeis targeted as their primary social concern. So contex-tualized, "The Right to Privacy" more accurately defends a "right" privacy. In principle, it devolves on conceptually identifiable, socially circumscribed privacies, such as in areas like morality, gendered divisions of labor, and fam-ily life generally.[11] In practice, the article would defend them essentially to stall a threatening quantum segue from a "right" public to a newly disclosed, social publicity-impulse subject to the promiscuous whims of a consumerist marketplace. The danger of publicity lay not primarily in its invasion of pre-viously private domains. Exposing conventionally understood private events in public might result in a person's sense of shame or embarrassment, but that merely exposes how moral and familial matters always possess a latent public aspect. Nor does the article really concern protecting "individualism" in the face of an ever more efficient publicity-machine's capacity to propagan-dize homogenous norms of social behavior. Those norms, too, are subject to publicity's random or unpredictable whims. At bottom, "The Right to Pri-vacy" responds to the modern anxiety over how publicity infiltrates the pri-vate sphere and transforms the public into the primary site of the real. Privacy, the psychological and often physical space everyone inhabits, here becomes no more than an embryonic preliminary to a public life seldom realized but constantly fantasized.

One might therefore recharacterize Richard Sennett's thesis about the pri-vatization of modern public life, which he terms "the fall of public man," as the publicization of modern private life.[12] This was so even for social critics in Stevens' time who reckoned with the epistemological losses in personal perception effected by the new publicity's collusion with an American consumerist ethos. For example, stoked by new technologies and "oriented entirely toward public life,"[13] the modern mass media, especially newspapers, generated the craving for "news." As Walter Lippmann argued in 1922 that the media also exploited people's otherwise benign tendencies to stereotype or process information about events occurring in distant places, or what amounted to "an invisible world." All the while shaping "public opinion," the news media inevitably emphasized the sensational over the truthful aspects of that world: "Where there is no constitutional procedure in industry, and no expert sifting of evidence and the claims, the fact that is sensational to the reader is the fact that almost every journalist will seek."[14] Among their other social effects, the media had helped create what now appeared a bewilderingly abstract, yet centripetally protean public arena defining American social life. As if in accord with Henry Adams' thesis about modern "multiplicity," John Dewey remarked that there were now "*too many* publics."[15]

In his 1922 work, Lippmann could only hope "that we shall develop more and more men who are expert in keeping these pictures [of distant public events] realistic." In his 1927 work on the same subject, he had given up even that hope. Perhaps in reaction to the twentieth century's abstract environment, "a public," Lippmann argued, "will not be well informed . . . since it . . . personalizes whatever it considers, and is interested only when events have been melodramatized as a conflict."[16] Dewey, too, could only think of public solutions to such "problems" in similar terms. Less and less concerned with acting as an informed, community-oriented public, people now appeared interested in "personal clashes and conflicts . . . the element of shock which is the strictest meaning of sensation . . . the *new* par excellence." Only Dewey's faith that private desires "are reflections into the singular human being of customs and institutions," and not "natural . . . organic propensities," afforded him hope that multiple, personalized publics might still come "together in an integrated whole."[17] For both critics, in other words, a mock-private or "personalized" mode of "public opinion" was as much the problem as were the notable social manifestations of cultural, economic, and technological surveillance-practices. Nevertheless, all of these factors threatened the Warren and Brandeis notion of an inviolable private life.

2

Lippmann and Dewey hold out for a "good" public, the loss of which they at once mourn and struggle against. For them, the private sphere remains a secondary, social problem, and to that extent they ironically add fuel to contemporary "public" fires. It is a good question whether Stevens' private poetic turns in *Harmonium* symbolically resist the public juggernaut in a more dialectically responsible way. One can at least plausibly maintain that they manifest representative reactions to, and at best socially responsive criticisms of, a progressively abstract public environment. James Longenbach essentially argues for the second option: Stevens' poetry, along with much post-Romantic literature, gains its "power not by avoiding the confrontation of public and private, retreating to one extreme or the other, but by dramatizing their tension and complicating their opposition."[18]

Ample evidence exists to support Longenbach's contention. In working for an insurance company, Stevens surely experienced firsthand the sociological blurring of the private and public realms. Well before writing his *Harmonium* poems, he shows little difficulty in wanting to keep the two areas separate in his personal life, as when he playfully but critically juxtaposes his preference for his private relationship with his future wife to newspaper advertisements and news events: "The newspapers, with their . . . tedious messages from earth to a blazing inhabitant . . . of some planetary *Terra Incognita*, where only Elsie lives always" (*L* 140; 1909). As if enacting the analytical thrust of Lippmann's or Dewey's arguments, Stevens' poems sometimes appear actively to criticize an omnivorous consumerist public.[19] That critical edge qualifies his allusion to Whitman's visionary sense of an American-democratic public in "Last Looks at the Lilacs." In social context, the poem ironically reflects the extent to which the modern public world's commodity-orientation has infiltrated a would-be suitor of the muse:

> And tell the divine ingénue, your companion,
> That this bloom is the bloom of soap
> And this fragrance the fragrance of vegetal.
>
> (*CP* 48)

The commodity-world burrows into one's very perceptions, so that "you see / Nothing but trash" (*CP* 49). The Stevens speaker's evident mockery of this "you" suggests how he, too, can trash others, including his own poem in the very process.

It is as if nothing he writes can halt the contamination of perceiving things, including his own poetic acts, in terms of their objectification into mass-public commodities. The same ethos also invades former tropological sites of American privacy, giving the lie to any Warren-Brandeis sentiments Stevens may have harbored in non-poetic moments. The oft-discussed "Anecdote of the Jar" provides a condensed example of his critical stance toward American commodity-culture's runaway invasion of the private realm, if not in the sense that some recent critics have asked the poem to perform some heavier, geopolitical lifting. In Frank Lentricchia's view, Stevens' "gray and bare" jar (*CP* 76) pointedly criticizes the social-imperialist assumptions underlying the poem's most obvious precursors, the burial figures in Thomas Gray's "Elegy" and Keats' "Grecian Urn" poems. With its Tennessee setting and placement on a hill (an ideologically elided burial-site?), "Anecdote of the Jar" also dredges up associations with nineteenth-century American Indian removals and the like. Stevens' poem devolves on "an American jar, plain, bare, and gray," that finally targets not "Grecian urns and Thomas Gray's poetry but . . . plain old democratic American jars which he insists we see as figuring a work of oppression that cannot be explained in classic European terms of class relations."[20]

Lentricchia's politicized criticism throws out the baby with the bathwater, no doubt in haste to trump an old-style criticism's treatment of "the poem as a formalist icon: a written equivalent of the hermetic, purely self-referential vessel."[21] Self-consciously dodging its making any important thematic claims (hence the jar's non-ekphrastic plainness), the poem more simply sketches (in an "anecdote") the potential social trajectory of any artwork, and Stevens' in particular, once it takes on a public life of its own. The speaker's famous initial statement, "I placed a jar in Tennessee" (*CP* 76), allusively refers to his writing a poem about an out-of-the-way topic "in" a rural place. Put more pointedly, he means to eschew literary work apt to attract notice by cultural elites and commercial publishers from major urban centers.

The round jar, however, ineluctably elides its localist scene, soon making all things around it round, not the least being the poem's own linguistic resonance: "Surround," "around," "The jar was round upon the ground." As if a miniature version of Poe's Primordial Orb in *Eureka,* the jar-image uncontrollably annexes the style, theme, and other images of its own poetic setting: "It took dominion everywhere." In effect, the jar destroys the very heterogeneity that would make it a distinctively vivid image in its own right and particular locale. "Anecdote of the Jar" thus seems to inscribe *its* own fate, the eventual annulment of its own poetic vitality either in human or natural terms, for the jar

> did not give of bird or bush,
> Like nothing else in Tennessee.

In outlining the jar's fate, though, the *poem* clearly has yet to arrive at it. At the same time, if the expansionist jar is not quite identical with the poem in which it appears, neither does it merely stand for the poem's ironic foil. Rather, the jar exists in the process of taming the poem as much as it does the Tennessee wilderness:

> The wilderness rose up to it,
> And sprawled around, no longer wild.

Stevens' poem equally alludes to the fate of his past poetic efforts, in particular their now lacking imaginative vitality ("did not give of bird or bush") to himself. One can infer that a Stevens poem originates in "Tennessee," a trope for a "wild" and anonymous, free-to-go-anywhere private scene of writing. It begins, as it were, in a regionalist place, far from urban settings where mainstream cultural pressures and pretensions abound. Stevens writes on the assumption that his resulting poem will likely go unnoticed. But despite beginning in the spirit of whimsical play (his bizarre placement of a jar on a hill in Tennessee) or without serious poetic ambition ("The jar was gray and bare"), writing this or any poem soon quickens his desire to overcome "the slovenly wilderness" of a literary langue. *In* writing, Stevens' writing sooner or later assumes the equivalent, imaginative form of a plastic self-image, an ersatz visible object, in short of a published artifact that makes him want it to have important status in public eyes: "tall and of a port in air."

"Anecdote of the Jar" fully justifies his wish. The poem has notably led to critical views that, whether construing it as a formalist *or* an anti-imperialist icon, helplessly become an extension of the poem's round semantic orbit, as much as does the Tennessee world within the poem's jarring double. Yet for Stevens in writing it, the poem's possible success in the literary-public realm comes down to private failure. Imagining poetry as to its ever-expanding public profile ("upon a hill" for all to see) destroys the contingent singularity (placing a jar in a specific Tennessee) of his *Harmonium* poetry's own recessive or "Tennessee" scenes of writing. In becoming "Like nothing else in Tennessee," Stevens' poetry becomes everything elsewhere for everyone else.

If anywhere, this is where "Anecdote of the Jar" accrues a political inflection. Propagating the sense of its public value, his writing figuratively congeals into a kind of commodity against his will: a "good" for Stevens to profit by in the American cultural marketplace. The jar image alone reinforces the metamorphosis. Referring at once to commodities and their efficient medium, the jar is a metonym of commodity culture per se. In a visit to Tennessee before writing the poem, Stevens undoubtedly encountered a ubiquitous fruit-jar labeled "Dominion" from Canada.[22] The mass-reproduced jar surely lends a special connotative twist to the poem's jar taking "dominion everywhere." Just as the jar exploits nature in the poem—one usually thinks of "wilderness" as overcoming man-made things—so commodity-culture homogenizes everything, from actual jars to poetic ones. It also exports the process as if everywhere in America: urban centers, rural Tennessee margins, even Canada. Commodity-culture's pervasive reach explains why the poem eventuates in a poetic "anecdote," a condensed tale tracing a transgressed moment when Stevens' poetic act might have been aesthetically intricate instead of only "gray and bare."

Isn't the poem's narrative therefore a de facto political critique, with Stevens resisting his poetry's becoming a "gray" or non-visionary commodity? If commodity-culture governs Stevens' public world, his private poetic proclivities would resist its social alienation—the very "tension" that James Longenbach notices in the *Harmonium* poems. In the present case, Stevens' "private" moves implicitly criticize a "bad" public, not *any* public. So his poems *do* possess the political charge for which some of his recent critical apologists have tried to argue. Do Stevens' *Harmonium* poems go so far as to mask, as Lentricchia wants to believe about his poetry generally, a "utopian urge toward classless society"?[23]

3

Why, then, does Stevens express social grievance in private, or in a way that requires specialized hermeneutic excavation? If "Anecdote of the Jar" allegorizes how commodification takes dominion everywhere, the poem's anomalous manner runs counter to how the issue might or should possess an urgent, political cachet for others. The speaker states his already elusive point matter-of-factly. He scarcely complains or otherwise signals any resistance to a ubiquitously invasive, commodity-culture world. If anything, the poem more tenably bespeaks Stevens' fatalism regarding his capitalist environment, not some dormant let alone energized, public charge for himself or others to contest it.

His period's most notable capitalist rationale poses the same problem for him. Competition for consumption of goods or monetary profit comes down to a social Darwinian world in which "Frogs Eat Butterflies. Snakes Eat Frogs. Hogs Eat Snakes. Men Eat Hogs" (*CP* 78). No one can reform "the man" who, though perhaps once capable of more—

> the man who erected this cabin, planted
> This field, and tended it awhile

—eventually ends up regarding everything around him in terms of appetitive needs, so that "the rivers went nosing like swine" and the "air was heavy with [their] breath." The Stevens speaker hardly expects that his fellow man will care more for "the quirks of imagery" (say like those in "Anecdote of the Jar") than for how things will "suckle themselves on his arid being." The speaker's viewpoint, of course, looks elitist, and in a politically generous reading may just be the poem's ironic point. Yet well before referring to him in the third stanza, the poem demonstrates how "the man" also "hogs" reality, that is, has infected the speaker's own vision of it by the time the poem has begun: "It is true that the rivers . . ."

An extreme version of "Anecdote of the Jar," "Frogs Eat Butterflies" outlines human behavior permeated by an omnivorous, animalistic expansionism, the intractability of which belies any effort to halt it. What social alternative *can* the "quirks" of poetry ever really proffer? Whatever critical complaints they seem primed to make, Stevens' *Harmonium* poems more often bear on his wish to write them without feeling compelled to make significant social points. In "Infanta Marina" (*CP* 7–8), for example, he metaphorically absolves his poetry from making the socially affective insights associated with "major" literature. Stevens considers his muse an "infanta marina," a "minor" or "infant" figure compared with any time-tested, traditional muse who could inspire poetic thoughts potent with import for others. The comparison makes his poetic utterances seem child-like or "out to sea," so to speak. The Stevens muse's greatest intentions—

> She made of the motions of her wrist
> The grandiose gestures
> Of her thought

—result in nothing of general human consequence. "Partaking of the sea" or as if occurring away from land, his verse appears ephemeral: it lacks any important social and literary ground.[24] Stevens' poetic writing, here figured in his muse's "rumpling of the plumes" and "roamings of her fan," metaphorically resembles sailing nowhere in particular. It

> Came to be sleights of sails
> Over the sea.

Moving without ideologically invested or "grandiose" direction, his poetic "roamings" only end without having made any momentous point:

> they flowed around
> And uttered their subsiding sound.

"Infanta Marina" suggests that Stevens subtly invokes the pervasive reach of capitalist culture in other poems not to criticize it, but to steer his poetic "sails" clear from how it invades the private errantry by which he more consistently tries to define his acts of writing. In truth, American commodity-culture stands for merely one version among others in *Harmonium* of social imperatives associated with "the people" or public at large. A quite different public appears in "Architecture," a poem Stevens later excluded from the re-published *Harmonium* volume in 1931.[25] Far from inscribing political critique, progressivist or reactionary, "Architecture" assigns an inverted aestheticism to socially engaged art, this time alluding to the period's exact political antithesis to capitalist culture. The poem embodies the utopian urge per se, and not simply to reform but to revolutionize the entire public realm through art.

"Architecture" (1918) specifically associates its political-artistic charge with the fairly recent Bolshevik Revolution. Its speaker envisions an eminently public art like architecture that will effect an equivalent cultural revolution. Repeatedly denying self for "we," he assumes the role of the people's dictatorship possessing an unequivocal carte blanche to deploy imagination entirely for constructing a new social reality.[26] Right from the start, however, he slips into an elitist cultural idiom when attempting to imagine an ideal socialist art:

> What manner of building shall we build?
> Let us design a chastel de chasteté.
> De pensée.
> (*CP&P* 66–67)

For the speaker, moreover, the new art should encourage high-toned modes of "utterance," on a par with "heavenly dithyramb / And cantilene." Against bringing art down to the level of the people, the speaker wonders if the people shouldn't shed their politically aggressive pre-Revolutionary identities—"their ugly reminders"—and instead dress "gaudy as tulips"

> As they climb the stairs
> To the group of Flora Coddling Hecuba.

Revolutionary scenes here willy-nilly metamorphose into aesthetic ones. In traversing the building, the people will encounter paintings that represent the people's Trojan War–like victory over a capitalist world, along with those depicting the Communist annihilation of history: "Overlooking whole seasons." On one hand, the speaker rhetorically adheres to a Marxist-ideological script that would glorify "the commonplace." On the other, he practices an art that imagines an ideal proletarian art constantly lurching toward aesthetic diversity and non-teleological ebullience. His imagined "edifice," for example, will socialize nature, but he asserts this in language that, rife with verbal excess, contradicts nature's mere social use-value:

> How shall we hew the sun,
> Split it and make blocks,
> To build a ruddy palace?
> How carve the violet moon
> To set in nicks?
>   .   .   .   .   .   .
> Pierce the interior with pouring shafts,
> In diverse chambers.
> Pierce, too, with buttresses of coral air
> And purple timbers,
> Various argentines,
> Embossings of the sky.

None of what he imagines is for the mundane eye or political propagandist of a classless society. The would-be social architect of "Architecture" in fact comes to regard his imagined "kremlin" as akin to a private space ("the interior") that will limit public access, and use grim commissars of political correctness to enforce the charge:

> And, finally, set guardians in the grounds,
> Gray, gruesome grumblers.
> For no one proud, nor stiff,
> No solemn one . . .
>   . . . may come
> To sully the begonias, nor vex
> With holy or sublime ado
> The kremlin of kermess.

"Architecture" represents less Stevens' "Red Scare" or reactionary critique of a Marxist utopian aesthetic, than his effort to imagine a socially effective art that does not fully subscribe to a fervent belief in "holy or sublime" ideologically scripted publics.[27] Even as he articulates a revisionist social aesthetic, the speaker inadvertently bespeaks the limitations in realizing it. To transpose such scripts into poetic truths leads straight to an aesthetic politics—to another public script that seduces his imagination with an equivalent, utopian fervor. Regardless that he deviates from "solemn" political designs for "the people," the speaker still converts private aesthetic impulse into a public imaginary, now coincident with restrictive privilege:

> Only the lusty and the plenteous
> Shall walk
> The bronze-filled plazas
> And the nut-shell esplanades.

Writing to re-form the public scene in *any* way—to protest commodification, for example, or to offer its ideological alternative—risks turning a politicized aesthetic into an aesthetic politics.[28] Writing then fixes on "the people" as an abstract end and entity, as opposed to promoting each person's and especially the Stevens poet's imaginative acts.

From his viewpoint, however, "the people" resist conceptual capture altogether, and thus reveal the essential fictionality of a socially motivated art's "public" foundation. A speaker observes in "The Wind Shifts" that "a human" is this, is that; at times multiple, at others singular. Comprising an amorphous amalgam of persons that finally figures *in*human motion, "human" comes down to a social trope—a fictional truth—always slipping its referents:

> Like humans approaching proudly,
> Like humans approaching angrily.
> This is how the wind shifts:
> Like a human, heavy and heavy,
> Who does not care.
> (*CP* 83–84)

Nonetheless, the abstract "human" public's "heavy" tread self-evidently weighs down the speaker's imagination, so that by itself the public scarcely registers as an airy or insubstantial "Wind." To grasp its fictionality instead requires his present extended poetic rehearsal. As "Anecdote of the Jar" and "Frogs Eat Butterflies" illustrate, Stevens can never quite dismiss the public's affective pressure, or simply declare his poetic privacy with blithe bourgeois self-assurance.

On the contrary, an amorphous public, as if it were too much with him, constantly tests his "private" poetic resolve. The poem "Gubbinal" simulates what happens when a poet cares about his work's public import as he writes it, in this case without either reformist or revolutionary inclinations. An epistemological fatalism then makes *his* imagination (not the public) seem the fiction by prematurely denying the possibility of particular "strange" disclosures of the real:

> That strange flower, the sun,
> Is just what you say.
> Have it your way.
>
> The world is ugly,
> And the people are sad.
>
> (*CP* 85)

Conceding ahead of time to common ("ugly") denominations of reality, the poet becomes an atheist of poetry, himself all public man, with the private pursuit of beauty forsaken as a possible poetic option.

4

Pressed by all manner of "people" agendas, Stevens' *Harmonium* poems yet consistently interpose a wider perspective in which poetic privacy actively redefines rather than passively assumes or accedes to one or another conceivable public. Whatever its concessions to them, his private codicil looks to resist rigorous social-critical readings. At first glance, it also shows Stevens' adherence to certain "Modernist" artistic agendas, many of which subscribe to an ideological zeitgeist that propagates the politically obdurate, bourgeois desiderata of artistic "elitism, isolationism, and [political] inactivity."[29]

His *Harmonium* poems clearly traffic in familiar Modernist themes such as the death of God ("Sunday Morning"), the inability of imagination to transcend the real ("Domination of Black"), or the reduction of modern love to sex ("Le Monocle de Mon Oncle"). They also employ techniques of aesthetic estrangement prominently associated with Modernist visual arts and their resistance to narrative formulations. For example, placing a jar on a Tennessee hillside mimics the outrageous tactics of Marcel Duchamp's famous *Fountain,* with its "porcelain urinal [placed] on its side atop a pedestal." Like much Modernist art generally, Stevens' bizarre images and style cultivate a kind of "private code that simply [does] not admit world or reader."[30] Little about his themes or style abets "Complacencies of the peignoir" ("Sunday Morning," *CP* 66), or otherwise endorses the values one supposes middle-class readers would want to find confirmed in reading poetry.

In short, Stevens at least dallies with the Modernist, ideological practice of *épater les bourgeois.*[31] Some of his *Harmonium* poems appear actively to mock middle-class panaceas, religious or social, to "the domination of black." The educated bourgeois doctor in "The Doctor of Geneva," for instance, encounters the unexpected, earth-shattering real—"long-rolling opulent cataracts" of "the Pacific swell" (*CP* 24)—through sophisticated literary lenses. He perceives the oceanic swell mediated by "Racine or Bossuet," and so "did not quail" or "felt no awe" before it. In spite of his armed knowledge, the doctor still experiences poetic-apocalyptic intimations before "these visible, voluble delugings"; for these

> set his simmering mind
> Spinning and hissing with oracular
> Notations of the wild, the ruinous waste.

Just the same, if the experience momentarily flushes his senses with "unburgherly" vitality, it quickly gets absorbed by traditional religious forms (his locale reminds us of Calvin's) when he returns to "his city" and sees its familiar "steeples."

The doctor's excursion all but inscribes a poetics of artistic Modernism. Bent on urging their bourgeois spectators to face a "ruinous" reality, Modernist poets often adopt the speaker's position with the middle-class woman in "Sunday Morning." Like T. S. Eliot in his post–World War I poetry, they write to make a "Pacific" or presumably settled reality "swell" with apocalyptic impact. At the same time, they anticipate and resist dilutions of their poetic revelations by readers, and not least by knowledgeable middle-class ones like the Swiss doctor. Stevens' "private" tactics here arguably reduce to similar Modernist aggressions against "the people," in elitist relation to whom he confirms the truth of his visions and (an American bonus) his unique individualism. Others may inhabit "The houses [that] are haunted" by colorless lives and commonplace dreams in "Disillusionment of Ten O'Clock" (*CP* 66), but Stevens identifies with the drunk social misfit, a sleeping "old sailor" to whom he imputes poetic dreams of catching "tigers / In red weather."

So why does Stevens hold back from outright, aggressive assertions of poetic self contra bourgeois others? The old sailor harms no one with his private dreams, perhaps matching Stevens' own "hard-to-get reticence" in publishing the poems he would collect (also not without reticence) in *Harmonium*. The poems themselves balk at the Modernist movement's heady agenda, sometimes openly espoused but always ideologically assumed, of an ersatz artistic coup d'état. At the very least, Modernist artists exhibit an ambition to make a public impact. William Carlos Williams, for example, "pleaded in a letter of June 8, 1916, to an unresponsive Stevens: 'For Christ's sake yield to me, become great and famous!' "[32]

Stevens doubtless avails himself of the Modernist artistic smorgasbord. "Six Significant Landscapes" (*CP* 73–75) reads like a primer for poetic adaptations of Imagism (I), Surrealism (II), and the Modernist break from past literary monuments, such as Whitman's:

> I measure myself
> Against a tall tree.
> I find that I am much taller.
>
> (III)

On the other hand, his *Harmonium* poems just as often set themselves apart from identifiable Modernist programs.[33] "The Doctor of Geneva" not only targets the religious or social pacifier (*sic*), but also contemporary poetic dabblers in apocalyptic matters, such as Eliot and Stevens himself. Elsewhere in *Harmonium*, he eschews by ironically framing the epistemological conundrum Modernist poets tend to engage. In "Metaphors of a Magnifico," the speaker's potentially infinite constructions of reality, here concerning an illustrative incident of men crossing a bridge into a village, result not in clarity but virtually endless confusion:

> Of what was it I was thinking?
> So the meaning escapes.
>
> The first white wall of the village . . .
> (*CP* 19; Stevens' ellipsis)

Stevens also indirectly questions Modernist poetic theories and practices as well as themes. "Anecdote of the Jar," as I have argued, traces a self-referential allegory that undermines claims for his own poetry's ontological status. Lentricchia maintains that the poem specifically critiques the "artifice . . . at the center of the imagist movement" and of Modernist poetry generally.[34] If not outright critique, then a deconstructive impulse marks Stevens' William Carlos Williams-like Imagist gambit in "Nuances of a Theme by Williams." À la Williams, the poem would separate the art-object from its utilitarian appropriations by a consumerist, middle-class readership. Stevens asks the "*ancient star*" (his emphasis), an erstwhile symbol of poetic inspiration, to "Shine alone," that is, to shed its traditional poetic associations and

> Lend no part to any humanity that suffuses
> you in its own light.
> (*CP* 18)

But the brief poem's repetitive requests for this to happen ("Shine . . . shine . . . shine," "Lend," "Be not," "Be not") testify to the star-image's resistance to evading human meaning, or to its *just being* an unmediated shining star-image—a shimmering poetic object and nothing more.

Stevens's *Harmonium* poems also demur at Modernist artistic shibboleths and their "public" contrariness.[35] He never appears dead set to damn the public as Pound had done in his well-known comment to Harriet Monroe. On the contrary, one senses Stevens' disaffection from pro and contra views of his literary public at large, as when he informs Monroe that, "having elected to regard poetry as a form of retreat, the judgment of people is neither here nor there" (*L* 253; 1922). Indeed, figures like the underclass sailor in "Disillusionment," the Oklahoman couple in "Life Is Motion," or "the roller of big cigars" in "The Emperor of Ice-Cream" intimate that "people" not locked into middle-class habits of perception can grasp the poetic élan on a par with poets.

And of course it seems foolish to think that Stevens was unaware of his own bourgeois proclivities, whether concerning his personal tastes (his liking fine meals, cigars, the private life) or his chosen legal profession at an insurance firm. How these proclivities problematically affect the poetic imagination—the unresolved standoff between them—forms the topic of five poems in *Harmonium,* which he arranged into a rough sequential cluster. As do "Six Significant Landscapes" and "Thirteen Ways of Looking at a Blackbird," Stevens' textual clusters mimic the destabilizing perspectivism of Modernist art, but less to represent or incarnate a poetic "life is motion" than to enable private visions of the real. Taken in clustered relation, each poem overlaps with the others to forestall the ever-lurking transformation of private insight into public truth. The present sequence begins with "A High-Toned Old Christian Woman," a declamation about poetry's cultural potency, and ends in "Banal Sojourn," where Stevens appears to express his poetic impotence or bourgeois anomie vis-à-vis the "fat beast" of nature, which otherwise ought to inspire his imagination.

Exemplifying a version of the Modernist poet's aggressive anti-bourgeois credo, the speaker in "A High-Toned Old Christian Woman" discursively assaults not so much religious belief as the woman's conservative ("old") or unimaginative mode of apprehending it. As the new "supreme fiction" (*CP* 59), poetry, which he regards as a master cultural code, converts or reinterprets religious forms

> into palms,
> Like windy citherns hankering for hymns.

If the poetic impulse once generated religious-ontological metaphors, now it comes to redeem their dead metaphoricity by stripping them entirely of their former referential meaning. "Unpurged by epitaph, indulged at last" by the poet who makes beauty and truth synonymous, religion can be made to express "novelties of the sublime" that result in

> A jovial hullabaloo among the spheres.
> This will make widows wince. But fictive things
> Wink as they will. Wink most when widows wince.

Milton Bates thinks that the speaker intends "to elicit from the woman—and those readers who share her outlook—the 'wince' that concludes the poem."[36] The speaker, however, protests too much for "ironic" readers not to notice. *His* formal posture is "high-toned" ("Madame, we are where we began"), and his thesis smacks of preachy harangue. To intone that poetic imagination defines religion's essential value, else it is dead, practiced only by *its* "widows," would treat poetry itself as a religion, or

> Take the moral law and make a nave of it
> And from the nave build haunted heaven.

Taken to that extreme, poetry becomes subject to the same imaginative bankruptcy the speaker imputes to religion and its Victorian, middle-class practitioner. Signaled by the speaker's posturing, his Modernist thesis (to some extent Stevens' own in "Sunday Morning") becomes indistinguishable from the bourgeois shibboleths that it apparently assaults. Both poem and thesis derive their imaginative cachet, the energy of shock-effect, from the very public that Modernist poetic credos seek to baffle and abjure.

Since Stevens frames this poetics ironically, it fails to account for his own practice. He therefore entertains a quite different poetics in the next poem, "The Place of the Solitaires," where he appears to hold to rather than aggressively deny or mock the poetic placidity afforded by bourgeois living. There he indulges imagination precisely as a respite ("poetry as a form of retreat") from thinking about its public effects at all. Instead, as I noted in my Introduction, he would imagine (or write) as if on perpetual vacation from such thinking,

> In the place of the solitaires,
> Which is to be a place of perpetual undulation.
>
> (*CP* 60)

Imaginative self-indulgence, however, can lead to its own unhappy consequences, which Stevens records in "The Curtains in the House of the Metaphysician" as a metaphorical

> drifting . . .
> . . . full of long motions; as the ponderous
> Deflations of distance; or as clouds
> Inseparable from their afternoons;
> Or . . .
>
> (*CP* 62)

Like its interior setting, the poem's "curtains" become tropes for other things and finally, as the above ellipses suggest, of everything and therefore of nothing:

> Of night, in which all motion
> Is beyond us, as the firmament,
> Up-rising and down-falling, bares
> The last largeness, bold to see.

In a Modernist move like Gertrude Stein's "A rose is a rose is a rose . . . ," troping without check—without trying to make a point to others—results in ad infinitum motion ("or . . . / Or . . . / Of . . . / Of . . . / Up-rising and down-falling"). Metaphorical movement goes nowhere or, the same thing, ends up troping tropes. Yet writing cannot help *but* make a point, which in the present poem consists not only *of* directionless poetic motion, but also its ironic implication: "It's curtains" or death ("night") to muse poetically while relying on bourgeois sanctions, especially those that require a quite literal private or curtained "room" as the primary social condition for imaginative acts to occur free from pressures to mean for others. Cruising the real can only turn imaginative desire into a "banal sojourn," an unsatisfying because sequestered subjectivity, the modern equivalent of Coleridge's Fancy absent Imagination: "One has a malady, here, a malady. One feels a malady" (*CP* 63).

For Stevens, bourgeois retreat disguised as High Modernist strategy remains tethered to public prerogatives. Traced in "A High-Toned Old Christian Woman," the disguise entails pompous self-certainty, an unconscious attachment to public life. In "The Weeping Burgher," the midway poem of the present *Harmonium* cluster, that attachment at first assumes the form of a bourgeois poet's uneasy, self-conscious critique of his bourgeois readers' *weltanschauung*:

> It is with a strange malice
> That I distort the world.
> (*CP* 61)

Though he prefers social accommodation to self-isolating critical edge, neither can he quite adopt a join-the-bourgeois-enemy poetic policy. Identifying with his middle-class audience merely forces the Modernist speaker to express his "ill humors" by "mask[ing]" them "as white girls," an image of laundered poetic figures as such that only serve to *suppress* his anti-public stance. At best, then, his unconventional imaginative activity can minister a therapeutic function for himself and others. For example, in taking "The sorry verities" to

> excess, continual,
> There is cure of sorrow.

But the burgher-poet's apologia for writing any which way he desires incurs the nagging suspicion that others may still regard its idiosyncratic poetic idiom to be more affronting than therapeutic. So he moves to justify his writing on other grounds. He writes, he tries to think, for "the people," but without their knowing it, i.e., privately, or in a style that, although it might appear nonsensical or aesthetically elitist, has serious intent:

> Permit that if as ghost I come
> Among the people burning in me still,
> I come as belle design
> Of foppish line.

In the end, his would-be justification doesn't work either; it still leaves him

> tortured for old speech,
> A white of wildly woven rings.

Apposite "speech," "white" as a noun evokes the background of traditional tropes. The Modernist speaker thus feels guilty ("tortured") for *not* using familiar modes of poetic expression, except, again, as a linguistically laundered ("white") background for the "wildly woven" verbal intricacies more commensurate with his sense of reality. This leaves him, a poet wanting to be neither for nor against "the people," *bitterly* private—"weeping in a calcined heart." His former "malice" toward the public has returned, but in an irresolvably displaced form. Lacking both critical animus and a willingness to work with conventional visions of "the world," he now regards his writing as at bottom an aggressive weapon without purpose: "My hands such sharp, imagined things."

In contrast to his socially chastened but inwardly blocked Modernist speaker in "The Weeping Burgher," Stevens prefers to write his *Harmonium* poetry without any oppositional or "sharp, imagined" relation to his reading public. If generally inaccessible to the public at large, his poems nonetheless acknowledge the crippling effect of Modernist credos that promote aesthetic isolation. For example, "Palace of the Babies" effectively recasts the metaphysical position adopted by the speaker in "Sunday Morning" from certain truth (if only about there being no eschatological truth) into no more than a pro tem fictional musing. The poem proposes that religion as gullibly believed and formally practiced by others, i.e., "babies" in churches, can admit to no doubts. Yet an aggressive skepticism or mockery of conventional religion's followers confesses a no less recalcitrant, religious-congregationalist impulse:

> The walker in the moonlight walked alone,
> And in his heart his disbelief lay cold.
> His broad-brimmed hat came close upon his eyes.
>
> *(CP 77)*

The poem stages a voyeuristic alter-ego poet (he observes life by "moon-light" cum imagination) whose set ("broad-brimmed") "disbelief" preemptively rejects the public's naive faith in religious and other kinds of truth. On the other hand, his ironic vision of "babies" itself reflects a closed-minded ("close upon his eyes") belief—a truth-position rife with suppressed public envy, despite his would-be private or here elitist reserve.

"Palace of the Babies" suggests that Stevens differentiates a poetics of privacy from an isolationist mind-set or any predetermined resistance to mass-public naïfs, although another palatial *Harmonium* poem, "Tea at the Palaz of Hoon," looks as if it expresses exactly the opposite point. Hoon, like some modern aesthete mourning the loss of his Paterian credo, descends "in purple" from a former, transfixed vision wherein "the golden ointment rained" (and reigned) and "I found myself more truly and more strange" (*CP* 65). To confirm his vision requires a sympathetic yet skeptical interlocutor. Carefully selected and socially refined, the poem's "you" will not press Hoon's strange vision to the point of self-estrangement; instead, "you" will take "tea" with him, take Hoon at his word, in some ivory-tower-like isolation far from the public masses.

One can easily infer Stevens' own attraction to Hoon's elitist sensibility, an equation that would confirm Fredric Jameson's judgment that Stevens consistently adopts the "purely epistemological stance of . . . a detached subject contemplating a static object in a suspension of praxis and rootedness." Hoon's vision doubtless appears to epitomize an escapist subjectivism, a world of utter "abstract potentiality."[37] Echoing, to recall, the poetic desideratum that Stevens reserves for himself in "Infanta Marina," the poem provides no external measure by which to verify Hoon's vision, therefore making it seem socially inconsequential.

Of course, one might object that "Tea at the Palaz of Hoon" leaves room for an ironic reading. Stevens quite explicitly stages the social contingency (here the regal privilege) grounding Hoon's melancholic aestheticism, or his would-be universalistic resignation about *temps perdu*. Still, another mock-imperial poem in *Harmonium*, "The Emperor of Ice-Cream," shows how Stevens can venture similar claims about human fate ("The only emperor is the emperor of ice-cream") when adopting the carnivalesque perspective of working-class denizens. More important, Hoon never really proposes the universality of his vision. On the contrary, he refers to his former vision in a way that protests its utter idiosyncrasy and, since it lacks witnesses, in the face of its potential hallucinatory ephemeralness. Hoon, that is, *presupposes* others or, what amounts to the same thing, socially ensconced regimes of knowledge about the world. He insists on his vision's singularity fully aware of how others will regard it:

> and what I saw
> Or heard or felt came not but from myself;
> And there I found myself more truly
> (*CP* 65)

"Tea at the Palaz of Hoon" locates itself at the threshold between public others, never dismissible, and private vision, never securable. The poem traffics in both, resists committing to either, and so represents neither one in detached or static fashion.

No doubt, the last position, too, looks evasive (yet another bourgeois move), even absurd (like Hoon's name) and socially irrelevant (an aristocratic scene in a modern, American poem). But just as occurs in "The Comedian as the Letter C,"[38] the Hoon poem openly acknowledges its comic, i.e., limited, effort to convince others of its particular vision. At the same time, in allowing for only one symbolic, intimate reader, the guest or poem's fictive addressee, "Tea at the Palaz of Hoon" internalizes, anticipates, and deliberately distances readers who will perceive Hoon's vision *only* in a "comic" way. From one view, the poem's regal speaker and invited reader not only ruminate about a now absent, idiosyncratic vision—a synecdoche for any Stevens *Harmonium* poem—but do it as if insulated from the masses. From another, what looks like an elitist effort to protect a royal Hoon/Stevens from "the people" in fact serves to renounce any public critical privilege over them as well. Positioned at a distinct distance from the poem itself, they, i.e., we readers, can yet overhear Hoon's and his invited guest's private discourse. Readers witness *something* (including the poem's elitist overtones), although not the same thing that Hoon's intimate hears, and even less the poetic, "golden ointment" of Hoon/Stevens' recollected and now no less elusive vision to himself.

If anything, the poet's private, *as if* regal space, which in the poem refers back to a more private vision subjectively and temporally understood, exposes the reading public's voyeuristic enactment of the private. "Tea at the Palaz of Hoon" differentiates between conventional determinations of the public-private dichotomy and Stevens' own private configuration of it. Not even Hoon's guest can know his vision; but neither can Hoon *not* attempt to communicate it or we avoid trying to overhear it. In a double irony, Hoon thus may merit his privileged, aristocratic status after all, but precisely *in* the quintessentially American sense of fashioning a *re*-public that would originate from each person's private pursuit of happiness, which for Stevens finally comes down to the pursuit of privacy itself.

5

Hoon turns out to be a strange closet democrat, but Stevens treats private matters stranger still in other *Harmonium* poems. Never denying their private vision's public value, he writes them in terms of although not *for* "the people." And yet he can also write precisely *not* to know the other's either casual or sophisticated knowledge of his work, lest he himself precipitously adopt a public relation to its process of composition. In "Nomad Exquisite," for example, Stevens at once maintains a non-aggressive relation to his reading public, and yet attempts to affirm a radical poetic privatism that sidesteps both Hoon's defensive musings over it and the weeping burgher-poet's guilt-ridden Modernist ones.

The poem's Floridian topos at first appears anything but private. The speaker evokes Florida as if he were a tourist, self-fancied into some romanticized "nomad," there experiencing aesthetically "exquisite" sights. His situation bespeaks nothing less than a travel-episode sanctioned by bourgeois social prerogatives. But since

> the immense dew of Florida
> Brings forth hymn and hymn
> From the beholder
> (*CP* 95),

one also senses the speaker's Romantic-visionary designs on an otherwise traditionless American tableau. At the very least, "Nomad Exquisite" exemplifies a limited "visionary capacity for respon[ding]" to Nature.[39] Traveling in less a tropical than a tropological Florida, Stevens terms himself a "nomad exquisite" in the sense of a poet seeking pretexts for the quintessentially sublime experience. Harold Bloom suspects that Stevens teeters a little too much on Romantic bravado. His speaker's notice of

> The big-finned palm
> And green vine angering for life,

as if with

> the eye of the young alligator,
> And lightning colors

suggests his overdetermination of the scene's poetic value. In other words, he self-consciously attempts to transform the scene into a self-referential analogue:

> So, in me, come flinging
> Forms, flames, and the flakes of flames.

The poem's self-reference, however, concerns more than the persona's, for the figuratively fissioning and alliteratively ebullient flames additionally refer to Stevens' conception of his poetic process both here and elsewhere in *Harmonium*. And in referring exclusively to that process, the poem becomes rife with serious significance for him alone. If he grants that others encountering his poem(s) will regard him a "nomad exquisite" or some fanciful aesthete, in private he regards himself as "no mad exquisite," not even in the apologetic sense of "The Weeping Burgher."

"Nomad Exquisite" aims neither to expunge its actual reception by others (impossible to imagine) nor to deny or duplicate the visionary precedents swelling the ranks of his present poetic effort to infuse a natural scene with inspirational significance. These all unavoidably exist. Stevens primarily writes to prolong his poem's conceptual, which is to say its pre-formative, beginning. Because his writing transpires between poetic nothingness and an inevitable public product that will annul his recursively private poetic process, he writes to immerse himself in the seminal "dew," the inchoate energies "angering for life," released by the birthing of words. *This* experience, already private to the extent that he, let alone we, can never repeat it, only secondarily results in a decipherable poem like "Nomad Exquisite," subject to the preceding interpretations. For Stevens in writing it, the poem's final, public form comprises a fiction, a contingent effervescence or arbitrary tracing of its private process. Readers thus encounter only the residual form of its private process. Moreover, in writing his poem, Stevens can only register its process as a just-happened event, or as a memory image akin to "flakes of flame." He, too, is always becoming his own activity's reader, replete with his literary public's codes of understanding that prompt him to convert poetic process into public performance.

Conceptually aiming to finesse that problem, "The Plot against the Giant" (*CP* 6–7) allegorically rehearses three nodes of interpretation deriving from Stevens' literary-intellectual environment, which he explicitly specifies as "plots against" his acts of writing.[40] More precisely, in the guise of seductive female figures, he identifies his own temptations—not, therefore, merely assignable to some alienated critical public—to make his writing assume recognizable public forms. The first girl would anesthetize the aforementioned "angering" edge of his tropes by

> Diffusing the civilest colors
> Out of geraniums and unsmelled flowers.

The second would make his poems glitter with aesthetic preciosity, an art-for-art's-sake desideratum, for which *Harmonium* was ironically criticized:

> I shall run before him,
> Arching cloths besprinkled with colors
> As small as fish-eggs.

The third temptation would have him reach for sublime, visionary insights, "Heavenly labials," a Modernist revelation of the real beyond the linguistic-stereotypical representations people resort to in daily life or "in a world of gutturals." As in "Nomad Exquisite," all three amount to one "plot." At any given moment, they affectively converge on Stevens' act of writing, and so can be said to mark his *Harmonium* poems individually and as a whole. His flower-tropes are words, themselves finally fictions of smell, say. Many of these poems self-evidently thrive on their uncommon poetic topoi and imagistic clusters (like "fish-eggs"). And doesn't a poem like "Sunday Morning" express the Modernist, i.e., inverted, equivalent of a visionary or "Heavenly" claim?

"The Plot against the Giant" stages these plausible depictions of his work *as* "plots," that is, as fictions that tempt him to read his work in ways he tries to evade as he writes it. Regarded separately, no one of them defines his writing to himself. Stevens converts all three incompatible temptations into a single, interchangeable trope of reading ("*The* Plot") by which he constantly eludes the objectification or final public identity of his compositional process. The same function defines the non-sequential perspectivism that characterizes Stevens' arrangement of poems for his *Harmonium* collection. In one sense, as I noted, his arrangement constitutes a Modernist strategy for representing the multi-real. In another, it reassembles his completed poems—now de facto objects for others' perusal—into tropes of poems as if still within the orbit of his composing them.

Continually oscillating between becoming public product and remaining private process, each *Harmonium* poem inscribes *some* audience for itself, from which it incessantly inclines to withdraw. That is why one can never be certain about a given poem's semiotic locus.[41] For Stevens, pursuing poetic privacy is truly synonymous with a nomadic enterprise. It consists of his effort to avoid settling for poetic principles, Modernist or other, any of which would realign his practice toward *a* public response, whether understood as emanating from literary or social contexts of experience. Construed differently, poetic privacy would amount to a frivolous aestheticism, or else a displaced public fantasy.

Stevens exercises just this fantasy in the figure of "X," "the mighty man" in "Anecdote of Canna," who ponders "mighty thought" (*CP* 55) as he wanders the American nation's capitol area and there observes its canna flowers. Presumably Stevens' image for Woodrow Wilson (*L* 505; 1944), the celebrated figure represents public-political man par excellence. Here, his momentary private respite from wartime public affairs resembles a "dream," the sole content of which—"They fill the terrace of his capitol"—are the conspicuous, tropical canna. Marked by their pervasive appearance and visual draw for observers, they figuratively double the public import or sensational impress of his daily political actions. Like the canna flowers, X's mighty thoughts wholly absorb or provide the content for his so-called private reveries. For political man, in other words, *private* dreams become well nigh impossible. Unlike the old sailor's socially useless tiger-dream in "Disillusionment of Ten O' Clock," X's can never indicate anything "other" to its protean, public translations:

> Yet thought that wakes
> In sleep may never meet another thought
> Or thing. . . .

James Longenbach argues that these lines represent Stevens' criticism of Wilson's "detachment" from his sending men to their deaths, and that his "thoughts ramble unchallenged because in this private world, one thought meets only itself."[42] I think "Anecdote of Canna" instead sketches a political field like the academic public indicted in the following poem, "On the Manner of Addressing Clouds." There, "Gloomy grammarians in golden gowns" care more for public formalities than the intricacies of thought, which Stevens specifically associates with poetic thinking. In "meet resignation," the addressed "philosophers and ponderers" allow public ceremonies, "the speech of clouds," to annex activities of mind or the (Shakespearean) "bare splendors" of imaginative work. More culpably, these public figures redouble ("magnify") thinking's publicization by ceremonial means, those

> still sustaining pomps for you
> To magnify, if in that drifting waste
> You are to be accompanied by more
> Than mute bare splendors of the sun and moon.
>
> (*CP* 55–56)

On one level, "On the Manner of Addressing Clouds" plausibly concerns and criticizes the hollowness of hallowed social ceremonies. On another, it implies that public approbation, whatever the official form it might assume, entails an epistemological effect. The attractions of "pomp" infiltrate and elide the "mute," i.e., the private, conceptual ambience of thinking *in* thinking—precisely that which Stevens tries to effect in "Nomad Exquisite."

Within limits, the public defines the private. But with the public taking dominion everywhere in Stevens' era, the private loses it dialectical legitimacy. "Anecdote of Canna" exposes public man's ineffectual or *privative* wish for a private modality of thinking or dreaming, which X already compromises by his unyielding commitment to public affairs. Even when he wakes up from his somnambulistic "promenades" to "reality" (*L* 504; 1944), X remains fixated on the visual impressions of the showy canna. It is as if for public man, private experience were little more *than* a dream, an insubstantial and meaningless Hoon-like fantasy, which only its affording a restful respite from pressing political issues can justify. Lest the private *become* private or other to public denominations of reality, X anxiously holds to them "in daybreak," in the way he

> Observes the canna with a clinging eye,
> Observes and then continues to observe.

Stevens does the opposite. These canna are not his far less noticeable and more intricate poetic flowers—his *Harmonium* images and tropes—that for him foster ruminations at once engaging and eluding their public substitutes.

He keeps trying, that is, to imagine a kind of privacy that stays other to the vacuous, canna-like configurations of the public-private dichotomy arising from his American environment. "Anecdote of Canna" itself enacts the private by inconspicuously staging its factitious social constructions. One can say that, like his other *Harmonium* poems, this one, too, traces a wish to go private privately.

5   *Harmonium:* Dying to Love (in Private)

That you are innocent
And love her still, still leaves you in the wrong.
Where is that calm and where that ecstasy?
Her words accuse you of adulteries
That sack the sun, though metaphysical.
        —Wallace Stevens, "Red Loves Kit," 1924

And if my thought-dreams could be seen
They'd probably put my head in a guillotine
But it's alright, Ma, it's life and life only.
        —Bob Dylan, "It's Alright, Ma (I'm Only Bleeding)," 1965

1

In writing to go more private than social formations of privacy manifestly allow, Stevens risks undermining the very means by which his project becomes possible in the first place. He perforce encounters, that is, what one might designate a fourth temptation in his write to privacy: to hallucinate its realization *tout court,* as if the public posed little or no obstacle to it at all. In "Colloquy with a Polish Aunt," for example, Stevens frames the dilemma as one that readers of his poems are most apt to experience.

Just as he rehearses the vacuous option of denying privacy's otherness in "Anecdote of Canna," so his colloquy indicates the futility of trying to end-run the public's pervasive influence. Imputing a mysterious life to an Eastern European woman, a New World, presumably American speaker thinks to find the private on the slimmest of evidence.[1] Her strange religious practices and paraphernalia "touch [his] spleen" (*CP* 84). In other words, they incite a precipitous wish to have found an alternative to an all-public world in which mysteries are incessantly subject to exposés. The aunt's final words expose the illusory ground of the speaker's reactionary impulse:

> Imagination is the will of things. . . .
> Thus, on the basis of the common drudge,
> You dream of women, swathed in indigo,
> Holding their books toward the nearer stars,
> To read, in secret, burning secrecies. . . .
>
> (*CP* 84)

These "books" can just as easily stand for Stevens' *Harmonium* poems, given their own strange locutions and images. His Polish aunt therefore speaks for how his works do more than rebuff readers who—the target of Modernist artistic gambits—support or accede to the modern public's machining "of things" into the old and familiar. "Colloquy with a Polish Aunt" equally affronts readers like the speaker. Resisting such reductions, they "will" the private new, or, as here, insist that the poem hold(s) "burning secrecies," an option that Stevens vetoes simply in letting an old cultural figure personify his poem. By extension, she represents a poetic muse whose idiom (e.g., a "colloquy") seems strange in modern contexts paradoxically for its traditional cast ("a common drudge"). Insinuating the patent absurdity of the speaker/reader's hasty equation of private life with mere cultural otherness, Stevens' own poem speaks as a *polish*ed relative of his other *Harmonium* poems, most of which practice Modernist idiosyncrasies. Pertaining to those poems as well, "Colloquy" suggests that, if ever disclosed, the aunt/muse's "burning secrecies" would lose their "private" attraction, or would themselves seem all too "common."

At the same time, "Colloquy with a *Polish* Aunt" personifies a foreign or *distant* relative of Stevens' other *Harmonium* poems, meaning that the aunt's apparent disbelief in the privacy of intimate secrets is not exactly his. Can't *he* refer to his own secrets, particularly those of an erotic ("burning") cast, at least to conjure the kind of privacy he seeks in writing? Even if he can, however, the poem *as* "colloquy" underscores an ever-recurring dilemma: the de facto fore-presence of others, which is to say Stevens' intuition of readers as if already witnessing and even required to notarize his poetic references.

Nothing less haunts the eponymous speaker in "Jasmine's Beautiful

Thoughts underneath the Willow." An ersatz poet, Jasmine wants to assert an utterly private or supposedly incommunicable experience of past "bliss." For her, no existing poetic idiom can convey her experience's stubborn contingency. On the contrary, the available discursive means to express it only end up reinforcing her sense of its incommunicable singularity:

> My titillations have no foot-notes
> And their memorials are the phrases
> Of idiosyncratic music.
>   (*CP* 79)

Reminiscent of Hoon, Jasmine's "thoughts" of recollected "love," of an intimacy that itself represents a conventional topos of privacy, "will not be transported" or otherwise communicated "In an old, frizzled, flambeaued manner." By avoiding stock, sentimental expressions of her love-experience, she instead proposes to convey its resistant idiosyncrasy to herself. Just as her supposedly unique thoughts already frizzle her present manner of phrasing them, so they instigate her musing on her particular experience's "eccentricity," such as its suddenly appearing

> like a vivid apprehension
> Of bliss beyond the mutes of plaster,
> Or paper souvenirs of rapture.

In haste to deny the capacity of "old" yet extant poetic conventions ("the mutes of plaster / Or paper souvenirs") to capture her former experience, Jasmine nevertheless conveniently elides two problems. First, those conventions self-evidently condition her ability to imagine her experience's private singularity. To intuit its singularity at all presupposes her having recognized the expressive inadequacy of what formalist critics from T. E. Hulme to the later New Critics define as public stereotypes or dead, universalistic metaphors. Found wanting, they prompt Jasmine's "flambeaued" imagistic inversions, leaving behind the sense that her experience emanates as if from a private "interior ocean rocking."

Second, her would-be private experience ironically mimics the uncomplicated closures of desire synonymous with the sentimentalist discourse she purports to eschew. The poem's title itself plies tired tropes of sentimental poetry: Jasmine's flowery name, along with the "weeping" sentiment of her unspecified, putatively unverifiable "beautiful thoughts" beneath a willow tree. A similar irony taints her claim that only "long, capricious fugues and chorals" can best express her thoughts. Her chosen meta-images not only move toward oxymoronic imprecision (formless musical form), they also surrender the "capricious" to inescapably vague, musical-sentimental feelings. All things said, Jasmine's insistence on her love's inexpressible beauty acknowledges its illusory, periphrastic essence. Her poem expresses only the clichéd sentiment that it can say nothing about her supposedly inviolate experience.

If "Jasmine's Beautiful Thoughts" tracks Stevens' own desire to find a shortcut route to private poetic ruminations, the poem's self-deprecating title frames the Jasmine rationale and effectively forgoes it. The same applies to how the poem echoes ("an interior ocean rocking") Whitman's "Out of the Cradle" ocean poem, which Harold Bloom attributes to Stevens' "bad" effort at poetic competition.[2] The allusion occurs explicitly, and then only in a hit-and-run or rhetorically delimited manner. Stevens stages the *limitation* of Jasmine's effort to avoid the clichéd aspect of inexpressible love. By resorting to a virile, visionary declaration of idiosyncratic selfhood, she would abort a sentiment stereotypically associated with feminine poetic practice throughout the nineteenth century. Stevens himself makes no such declaration in his *Harmonium* poems, since, as Jasmine's "interior" allusion suggests, it leads straight to Whitman's assertive, "manly" poetics ("what I assume you shall assume"), or to the public transformation of any private poetic principle.

As for the privacy assignable to intimate experiences, Stevens, his attraction to Jasmine's quick solution aside, elsewhere casts them in an erotic light that at once scandalizes sentimentalist views of intimacy and resists obverse transcendentalist revisions. Many *Harmonium* poems clearly engage erotic motifs, sometimes with specific reference to a public-private scenario. Most notably, for example, "Peter Quince at the Clavier" consists of "the story of how a private place is violated."[3] The poem positions puritanical elders into roles of pseudo-private voyeurs witnessing the Apocryphal Susannah's more private bodily ablutions:

> Of a green evening, clear and warm,
> She bathed in her still garden, while
> The red-eyed elders watching, felt
>
> The bases of their beings throb.
>
> (*CP* 90)

A similar scenario concerning "secret, female erotic desire" occurs in "Cy Est Pourtraicte, Madame Ste Ursule, et Les Unze Mille Vierges."[4] There, Ursula presents the "Lord" an "offering . . . / Of radishes and flowers," symbols of physical love, which she makes in "Half prayer and half ditty," and which "He" receives in a mode "That was not heavenly love, / Or pity" (*CP* 21). Unwritten "In any book," this scene and that in "Peter Quince" associate female erotics with privacy in the familiar way of Stevens' early twentieth-century Freudian milieu.

Still, in exposing the repressed sexual origin of moral and religious beliefs, both poems arguably stage a violated private scene the better to violate perceived public norms. Both deploy tropes of sexual privacy to reveal how physical pleasure comes to the only truth in a Godless modern world—an eminently public charge. The same kind of desideratum marks certain feminist dicta that insist on Stevens' gendered duplicity in all this. To be sure, one can second-guess the sexual-liberationist intent behind his erotic poems as masking a male-voyeuristic reduction of female figures.[5] True or false, however, such interpretations forgo the erotic trope's elicitation of the private sphere per se in favor of a Stevens poem's (imagined) public effects, whether reformist or reactionary.

The *Harmonium* poems set out precisely to bypass *any* public gaze that would delimit the privacy associable with erotic intimacies.[6] For one thing, they push erotic-literary proprieties to *their* limits. Some poems hint at scatological references that redundantly stress raw sexual naturalism at the expense of safe, voyeuristic relations to the erotic scene in question. Just so, the name "Peter Quince," as Joan Richardson observes, refers "in veiled slang to both male and female parts"; or in "Cy Est Pourtraicte, Madame Ste Ursule, et Les Unze Mille Vierges," the "roughened radishes dug from the soil, surrounded by wildflowers with curling tendrils" evoke images of male and female "genitalia."[7]

The slanging gets worse if one holds to the period's or even today's culturally correct proprieties. "Exposition of the Contents of a Cab" (later left out of his *Collected Poems*) imagines a "negress" named Victoria Clementina wearing

> a breech-cloth . . .
> Netted of topaz and ruby
> And savage blooms.
> (*CP&P* 52)

Conversely, the speaker addresses a presumably white, middle-class woman who wears less sexually exciting undergarb:

> What breech-cloth might you wear,
> Except linen, embroidered
> By elderly women?

At first glance, "Exposition" makes little more than the ironic, anti-Victorian point signaled by the black woman's very name. Conflated with a brazen sexuality, her racial identity exists in critical contrast with the white woman's concessions to suppressive sexual mores. Victoria's depiction might appear to reflect Stevens' own racist fantasy—the speaker himself is not *in* the cab—about "immigrant and black" sexuality and its "sinful" attraction for WASP Americans like himself.[8] Yet if so, why does he stage that "white" cultural fantasy as such?

> Victoria . . .
> Took seven white dogs
> To ride in a cab.

Referring to the poem itself, the "cab" restricts white readers' prurient curiosity, finally keeping "White dogs at bay." Stevens' "exposition" thus includes an implicit critical exposé of the very racist perspective that present-day cultural criticisms might suppose his poem unwittingly reflects.

More to the point, the poem's scandalous fantasy lies in how *its* "contents" refer to female genitalia as if barely covered by the "breech-cloth" metonym. That is, the poem's own thinly disguised exotic tropes—"Oh-héhé! Fragrant puppets / By the green lake pallors"—tease the speaker, really its surrogate reader, into an erotic fantasy, the literal source for which remains publicly unviewable, whether in moral or representational terms. Nothing gets revealed; and what gets imagined amounts to a bodily commonplace that grounds his fantasy too soon and interrupts any voyeuristic titillation. For at bottom, Victoria Clementina "too is flesh." White *or* black, culturally the same *or* different, women become reducible to their "private parts," a vulgarization that also doubles as a poetic self-reference or trope. Apart from its "sexist" effect, the vulgarizing trope, itself private, evinces a wish to envision an impregnable private spot in and through language. In one sense the thinnest or most transparent of media, poetic language yet can promote the illusion of "burning secrecies" by dissimulating the sexual real.

The present poem nonetheless shows that male voyeurism never delivers the private, poetic goods for Stevens. From its would-be secret but still public purview, what it perceives, female private parts, disappoints the erotic imagination, including the reader's of the poem's feminized scene of writing. A Stevens speaker registers a similar "malady" regarding a sex-drenched nature in "Banal Sojourn":

> Moisture and heat have swollen the garden into a slum of bloom.
> Pardie! Summer is like a fat beast, sleepy in mildew,
> Our old bane, green and bloated, serene, who cries,
> "That bliss of stars, that princox of evening heaven!" reminding of seasons,
> When radiance came running down, slim through the bareness.
>
> (*CP* 62–63)

From one angle, "Banal Sojourn" reflects Stevens' sense of his "diminished aesthetic" generally.[9] For example, the poem banalizes and inverts Milton's sexually charged scene of Satan's temptation of Eve in the Garden of Eden: "For who can care at the wigs despoiling the Satan ear?"

From a different angle, the poem substitutes a scene of reading for one of writing. The intellectualizing sexless "wigs" refer to tradition-bound readers of *Paradise Lost*, an image that redounds to the speaker's own position with a summer's eve (*sic*) or "evening heaven." Mindful "of seasons," Stevens only momentarily adopts the position himself. Like scholarly readers who intellectualize or abstract the permutable (Satan's) force of seduction, the poem's speaker exists in a state of observing other poets' imaginative-sexual energy. Unable to "do it" himself, he can only watch their conceptual-coital embrace with nature's beast-like and as if moist genitalia, with all its "radiance . . . running down" or *coming*. For Stevens, imaginative impotence especially occurs when one writes, say, with Miltonic poetic ambition, or with an eye toward the potent impact a poem might have for a scholarly or judgmental audience ("the wigs") looking on and interpreting it. One then becomes more a voyeur to one's own scene of writing than a "princox," a sexual boy of erotic poetry impelled to act rather than to watch. Itself associated with a Miltonic Fall, premature knowledge of the poem *as* poem elides its primary point, namely to foster unexpected, disparate connections between things, lacking which writing becomes nothing more than a "banal sojourn."

A deliberate yet covert vulgarization of literary-public proprieties designates one way Stevens can try to thwart self-voyeuristic inclinations. The strategy at once includes and goes beyond the shock-tactics of Modernist art, a case in point being the poem "Floral Decorations for Bananas," which likely alludes to Duchamp's *Nude Descending a Staircase*.[10] The speaker would introduce sensual dishevelment into formal social scenes, here doubling for Stevens' sense of conventional poetic ones. Writing the poem in the guise of imagining reading another, the speaker would reject his own formal tendencies, specifically to write poems subject to public ("outdoor") restrictions:

> The table [poetic tableau] was set by an ogre,
> His eye on an outdoor gloom
> And a stiff and noxious place.
> (CP 54)

Instead,

> Pile the bananas [or poetic tropes] on planks.
> The women will be all shanks
> And bangles and slatted eyes.

The poetic scene ought to exude wildly framed bananas and "plums"— disordered, sexual intimations outrageously scandalizing

> the women of primrose and purl,
> Each one in her decent curl.

A Modernist impulse undoubtedly governs the poem's speaker. Although himself off-stage and leaving the present scene untouched, he wants to replace an art serving social forms with one perpetrating sensuous havoc. Immersed in such art, he might then eliminate his current position of merely watching others, although he would still be performing before and for them.

Despite or because of its Modernist revision, however, "Floral Decorations" remains a contained social scene, a poetic repast that only points to a potential Dionysian art. Stevens' vulgarizations in other *Harmonium* poems further direct his vulgarities not only at his feminized inspirational sources, but also at his own desire to write. In the poem that follows "Banal Sojourn," "Depression before Spring," he metaphorically equates pre-poetic ebullience (the non-signifying "Ho! Ho!" of a princox) with a sexual excitation in effect absent a heterosexually figured object. Either woman or muse, her impersonal, sexual arousal (her genitalia depicted as "the spittle of cows") leads to anything but sensual, self-other coition, whether with an actual woman or a figurative one apostrophized as "Spring":

> The cock crows
> But no queen rises.
>
> The hair of my blonde
> Is dazzling
> As the spittle of cows
> Threading the wind.
>
> (*CP* 63)

Like the social occasion and counter-envisaged repast defining "Floral Decorations," "Depression before Spring" (really an aborted *ex*pression) occurs in private *potentia*. It reduces to a poem tracing a poem that doesn't get written and readers thus never see.

Here we begin to approach the autoerotic reflex of Stevens' writing throughout *Harmonium,* the aspect of his work that would forgo becoming erotic tease for others. Of course, both types of sexual tropes may appear indistinguishable to readers, and so in fact provoke hermeneutic excitation. For instance, Stevens later denied that he intended any sexual meaning by that "much crumpled thing" in "Le Monocle de Mon Oncle." But don't the last four lines of the poem's first stanza suggest a masturbatory male fantasy?

> The sea of spuming thought foists up again
> The radiant bubble that she was. And then
> A deep up-pouring from some saltier well
> Within me, bursts its watery syllable.
>
> (*CP* 13)

2

Stevens' autoerotic script of writing poses the same self-defeating promise of poetic privacy as does his sentimentalist gambit in "Jasmine's Beautiful Thoughts." The script hinges on a fantasy that "bursts" erotic self-other relations by means of tropes provisionally designed to evoke the intimate presence of others within his scene of writing. In epistemological terms, Stevens' goal is to negate the other, or, more accurately, to fasten upon an entirely private if inchoate experience of subjectivity itself as other. By definition, however, such tropes lack staying power, for even as he pens them, they continually reinstate the other's figuration of a "public." Like his surrogate poet-figure in "Disillusionment of Ten O'Clock," the drunken sailor (seaman/ semen?) dreaming of catching "tigers / In red [read: sexual] weather," Stevens inevitably awakens to hangovers spelling the hallucinatory status of his just-written autoerotic fantasies. Moreover, since the privacy envisaged requires removing the erotic other from imagination, nothing of the poem's would-be private, compositional auto-*jouissance* remains except its painful absence.

A like depression *after* spring, as it were, defines the allegorical drift of "The Cuban Doctor," where Stevens tries to configure pain, too, as tropological grist in his pursuit of poetic privacy. In more ways than one, the poem vulgarly reduces the male poet to *his* "private parts":

> I went to Egypt to escape
> The Indian, but the Indian struck
> Out of his cloud and from his sky.
>
> This was no worm bred in the moon,
> Wriggling far down the phantom air,
> And on a comfortable sofa dreamed.
>
> The Indian struck and disappeared.
> I knew my enemy was near—I,
> Drowsing in summer's sleepiest horn.
>
> (CP 64–65)

The poem's condensed, bizarre, and disorienting scenario (a Cuban doctor trying to escape an Indian—Western? Eastern?—by going to Egypt) reads like a Poesque cryptogram. Its shorthand figures suggest a private code requiring translation into a coherent narrative, for example as an allegory "of an exotic dreamer who refuses to wake up to reality."[11] If so, the allegory also transpires in a conspicuous cultural idiom. The speaker, presumably the Cuban doctor in the poem's title, plausibly represents a Western-rationalist view of reality, whereas the pursuing Indian, at least according to European American stereotypes, conjures an ahistorical and threatening irrational nature: "the Indian struck / Out of his cloud and from his sky." Supporting the last view, in Stevens' time novels and movies often portrayed Indians as implacably hostile figures who attacked white settlers, disappeared, only to attack again. "The Cuban Doctor" thus looks as if it subscribes to an "Orientalist" ideology, asserting a putatively universal, philosophical truth about civilization continually pressed by its minority discontents. The poem's colonialist doctor futilely tries to repress the irrationality of the real, here made synonymous with a Third World culture.

Nonetheless, the poem's "private language"[12] also permits a contrary reading. Unlike the Indian, the doctor possesses a specific ethnic identity, and his medical vocation, a practical science, hardly suits the role of some Western cognitive imperialist. Precisely as an indexical figure designating an amorphous cultural other whom the doctor feels continually compelled to understand, the "Indian" contrariwise provokes the discursive incentive to codify everything everywhere. As a result, sky, clouds, familiar or unfamiliar places, all become "his." The code's unfixed pervasiveness—the Indian strikes and disappears at will—reflects the indeterminate pressures that proliferate public discourses to account for them, and not least to Stevens seeking "to escape" them in writing his poems. The present *Harmonium* poem's elliptical images and narrative register his effort to find some private haven safe from the need to heed this or that discursive demand (such as endowing the poem with allegorical meaning), which during writing can strike him arbitrarily. Wanting to escape what amounts to public service, the doctor/poet would refrain from practicing medical/literary art altogether.

Why does Stevens use the specific figure of a doctor as a surrogate for his own vocational plight? Strangely enough, the connection bears on how the demonized because public-provoking Indian causes the doctor pain. Physical pain, of course, dovetails with his actual vocational métier. From one viewpoint, his own pain also helps explain why he seeks relief from it by going to Egypt, a place in a season ("summer's sleepiest horn") synonymous with the body perpetually tranquilized or metaphorically mummified. Exactly along these lines, the doctor's pain lends itself to a meta-poetic analogue. Just as brute physical pain disrupts the body as a transparent medium of experience, for the poet pain refers to a hyper-self-conscious sense of meaning. The doctor-as-poet's pain registers his inability to write poems except in the mode of work, in particular because "Indian" cultural obsessions press him to make them mean something *as* he writes them. The reverse of poetic pain, a transparent sense of poetic play marks the speaker's allusively sketched, autoerotic wish in "Ploughing on Sunday":

> The white cock's tail
> Tosses in the wind.
> The turkey-cock's tail
> Glitters in the sun.
>
> .   .   .   .

> Remus, blow your horn!
> I'm ploughing on Sunday,
> Ploughing North America.
> Blow your horn!
> (*CP* 20)

Stevens would write "on Sunday," not on workdays, and in North American byways, not cultural centers. He would strut his words in animal-like pleasure, a mating motion without procreative, i.e., public, outcome, such as the double entendre of a "cock's tail" just tossing in the wind exemplifies. In short, Stevens would write his poems in the manner of an Uncle Remus fable: with blithe unconcern about their significance for a serious adult public, paradoxically the only audience that *could* read them.

"The Cuban Doctor" would "blow" its poetic "horn" in the same manner were it not for the pain that arbitrarily strikes its Cuban speaker. Prevalent ethnic stereotypes of Stevens' period and place allow that the doctor stands for a semi-professional (a Latin- rather than an Anglo-American) practitioner of a vocation the poem makes synonymous with writing.[13] Mimicking the kind of images Stevens himself indulges, the doctor also dabbles in exotic remedies for his pain. Moreover, the poem's own images permit one to surmise that the doctor/poet's pain metaphorically alludes to the sexual site of male creativity. In accord with the stylistic maneuvers to which Stevens occasionally resorts,[14] the poem's allegorical riddle and embedded puns may very well concern the doctor's efforts to escape the pain associated with a venereal disease. A commonplace European-colonialist myth, for example, held that gonorrhea first appeared after Columbus's return from the New World, specifically having derived from Indians located in the Central American region.[15]

Consistent with its already implicit sketch of the Central American doctor's post-colonialist malaise, the poem further allows that he has experienced stabs of pain striking him unpredictably like a lightning-like "clap" from the sky and clouds. Crispin, Stevens' meta-poetic quester in "The Comedian as the Letter C," also encounters "the thunder, lapsing in its clap" in *his* South American venture (*CP* 33).[16] By extension, the poem's typographical "I," otherwise referring to the unidentified doctor, subliminally personifies the penis attacked by venereal pain. Stevens means the "I" to be no ersatz phallus, the bowdlerized "worm" appearing in popularized versions of Freudian symbology, but instead a physically contingent thing, periodically struck by

claps of physical pain. Instinctively attempting to escape it, the penile and pe-
nalized "I" temporarily lapses into its foreskin, "summer's sleepiest horn," a
homonymic pun on an object "consisting of an epidermal sheath growing
about a bony core."[17]

The poem's vulgar literalism finally vexes any thesis about the doctor's exemplifying colonialist guilt—an eminently accessible theme fraught with public relevance. More to the point, the covert and reductive particularity of the
poem's allegorical scenario inescapably includes a meta-poetic addendum
that refers to Stevens' pursuit of poetic privacy. In overdetermined fashion,
the poet's pain, his heightened sense of meaning, stops metaphorical play in
its tracks and underscores his awareness of the limited strategic value that sex-
ual-poetic vulgarizations possess in determining private scenes of writing.
Plausible tropes for each other, sex and writing entail intimate self-other con-
tact, or the drive of two to become one in the moment. In addition, if only
according to sexual-ideological norms in Stevens' time, procreative, i.e., public, outcomes justify both activities. Writing eventuates in texts that others do
or just simply might see and judge as valuable.

As his present poem has it, only by making physical pain its central meta-
poetic trope can Stevens think to deny the public consequences endemic to
playing his poetic "horn" in private, or the same thing: metaphorically
equate his act of writing with a radically private experience. Sexual pleasure is
constitutively social, even if, framed in autoerotic terms, it spells the fantasized presence of others. In contrast, physical pain remains resistantly private,
a single person's singular experience in specific moments, even if others can
help alleviate it, or else imagine its happening to themselves.[18] Similarly, one
can easily imagine that readers will want to apprehend, judge, extend, and
generally share the pleasures of a text, but will just as surely resist a poem's
vulgar contamination of metaphorical protocols, or of textual intercourse
abruptly reduced to the metaphorical equivalent of physical pain.

Stevens practices this very reduction in "The Cuban Doctor." And for
him, there exists no remedial reading for such pain, whether scientific, psychoanalytic, or literary: "This was no worm bred in the moon." He means
the pain to be no mere imaginatively aired one "on a comfortable sofa
dreamed"; neither is it the mourning aftermath of any intimate relationship,
the memory of which might now help rationalize the doctor/poet's pain:
"The Indian struck and *disappeared*." Nor does it stand for a metaphorical
figure of the speaker's or of anyone's anxiety about death, since he denies that
his pain resembles a "worm . . . / Wriggling far down the phantom air." *That*

worm clearly alludes to "The Conqueror Worm," the eponymous character's death-obsessed, Gothically frantic poem in Poe's "Ligeia":[19]

> But see amid the mimic rout,
>   A crawling shape intrude!
> A blood-red thing that writhes from out
>   The scenic solitude!
> It writhes!—it writhes!—with mortal pangs
>   The mimes become its food
> And the seraphs sob at vermin fangs
>   In human gore imbued.

Whereas Poe's "Worm" literally appears to "out" itself "from . . . the scenic solitude" of *his* writing, Stevens cannot use Romantic-exotic remedies for his poetic pain. Doing so would only make of it an airy fantasy ("the phantom air"), or else part of some urgent drama (Poe's "mimic rout") of life and death, which the speaker noticeably eschews by "Drowsing" while his "enemy was near."

Allegorizing the contingent physicality of a particular sexual pain, "The Cuban Doctor" disavows all manner of readings that would disarm its own poetic contingency. Readers, of course, can still adopt a Freudian paradigm, say, to explain the poem's allegorical malady.[20] Stevens simply *wants* to see it otherwise. Consisting of an allegorical resistance to other allegorical decipherments, the wish perforce wholly defines the poem for him. On one hand, like the "Venereal" goddess or genius loci whom he apostrophizes in "O Florida, Venereal Soil," Stevens would have his *Harmonium* poem "Conceal yourself or disclose / Fewest things to the lover" (*CP* 48). He would conceal his poetic goddess/muse from the reader attracted by the present poem's own elliptical narrative. On the other hand, his *Harmonium* poetry's elusive erotics always risk contracting "venereal" disease. Like Poe's narrator in "The Imp of the Perverse," Stevens' poetic doctor cannot help but want to go public, which in his case means that he cannot escape his desire to have *some* singular someone decipher his poem even as he indulges covert sexual allegories. Privately enacted or not, to seek the pleasures of imaginative acts at the expense of fantasized intimate others risks becoming a full-fledged semiotic disease, or the same thing, a means for the ubiquitously public "Indian" to invade his scene of writing.

In "The Philosophy of Furniture," Poe could stage literary privacy in the guise of a sleeping figure decidedly oblivious to public spectators. Poe targets a "public" still in the process of formation for sustained if privately inscribed passive-aggressive assaults. By Stevens' period, the "public" lies everywhere in wait for whatever private poetic scenario he can imagine: intimate or vulgar, passive or aggressive. Unlike Poe's sleeper, the best Stevens' doctor-surrogate can do is drowse "in summer's sleepiest horn." Stevens, that is, can engage the one vocational medium—poetry—least likely to attract public attention, given his understanding of the dominant social and literary values of his American cultural environment.

Still, he can never finally assume that his writing *won't* attract such attention. So he makes spot, pro tem metaphorical visits to exotic, Hoon-like topoi ("Tea at the Palaz of Hoon" immediately follows "The Cuban Doctor"), restlessly attempting to wrest a modicum of poetic privacy there. For the brief moment he can conjure it *while* writing, he writes as if in an Egyptian poetic scene that might dissuade his imagined, inquisitive reader from robbing an empty tomb. For in the end, like some Pharaonic architect's ruse, Stevens' *Harmonium* poems conceal nothing of any real public import or else of private, prurient interest to others.

3

As I have just remarked, a self-referential emptiness characterizes the allegorical tenor of Stevens' *Harmonium* poems, whether construed separately or in relation to each other. However, his poetic desideratum of "the nothing that is" has little to do with Fredric Jameson's criticism of the Stevens poem's "inner hollowness" generally. Jameson claims that Stevens subscribes to an "impersonal" or anti-collective stylistic code inducing him to bypass "one of the key features of the modernist [writer's] will to style . . . the necessity . . . for a painful conquest of the private voice over against the universal alienation of public speech."[21]

Far from forfeiting his private voice, Stevens' rigorous pursuit of it in *Harmonium* allows him to mimic and precisely to alienate speech emanating from the modern public sphere as he intuitively apprehends it. What Jameson rightly senses is that Stevens also writes toward an impersonal poetic privacy resistant to its enlistment in public (read: political) enterprises, be they bourgeois-individualist or some collectivist alternative. Stevens' *Harmonium* poems essentially act like double-agents of the private sphere. They convert the public's protean array of discursive costumes, which perforce include interpersonal intimacies or what we normally associate with "private experience," into tropes continually made to elicit a privacy no longer subject to pressing social-literary imperatives.

Perhaps no *Harmonium* poem illustrates the last point in more condensed and playful fashion than "The Emperor of Ice-Cream," one of Stevens' most well-known poems during his lifetime:

> Call the roller of big cigars,
> The muscular one, and bid him whip
> In kitchen cups concupiscent curds.
> Let the wenches dawdle in such dress
> As they are used to wear, and let the boys
> Bring flowers in last month's newspapers.
> Let be be finale of seem.
> The only emperor is the emperor of ice-cream.
>
> Take from the dresser of deal,
> Lacking the three glass knobs, that sheet
> On which she embroidered fantails once
> And spread it so as to cover her face.
> If her horny feet protrude, they come
> To show how cold she is, and dumb.
> Let the lamp affix its beam.
> The only emperor is the emperor of ice-cream.
>
> (*CP* 64)

Stevens cited the poem as his "favorite" because its "singularity" typified the "peculiarity" of all poetry, and because it "wears a deliberately commonplace costume." (*L* 292 [1933], 546 [1945]). The poem's famous and *un*common ambiguities also define it as a riddle inviting virtually endless hermeneutic speculation. In a poem that to most first readings seems firmly to insist on "finale of seem," we instead encounter a circular series of possible interpretations that seem to express indecision about the finality of seeming. Seventeen years after he wrote "The Emperor of Ice-Cream," Stevens himself showed how difficult it could be to paraphrase the meaning of one of the poem's most memorable, gnomic pronouncements: "the true sense of Let be be finale of seem is let being become the conclusion or denouement of appearing to be: in short, icecream [*sic*], but about being as distinguished from seeming to be" (*L* 387; 1939).[22]

Stevens' depiction translates into the rather knotty philosophical paraphrase that being—what *is*, and what many readers take for the modern sense of life and death starkly stripped of their conventional trappings—exists only in the moment of the disappearance of appearance ("seeming to be"). The circularity of his proposition seems inescapable: being depends on appearance to be being. Moreover, in what sense does the poem itself represent the "denouement" of being's appearing at the expense of mere appearance? The ice-cream synecdoche, after all, is just that: a *verbal* "seeming" of ice-cream. For that matter, in echoing "seems" from *Hamlet*,[23] the poem goes so far as to underscore its literary character as such. Even if one were to miss the poem's fictive mediations, actual ice cream includes not only its transformation from visual object into subjective taste or residue, but the eventual absence of anything by which one might determine being as not nothing.

If nothing else, such philosophical "obfuscation," as W. B. Stein terms it, provokes public inquisitions and endless attempts to resolve it. Indeed, the poem's provocative but elliptical images have led some critics to overspecify its basic scenario. What in the poem leads one to suppose that the "[Freudian] roller of big cigars . . . would seem at least to entitle him to find in the kitchen curds of beer"? Neither does the "The Emperor of Ice-Cream" at all specify the roller as someone "who in smoking rolls his cigars from one side of his mouth to the other," let alone denotes a person "who works in a cigar factory."[24]

The poem's critical history points to other precipitous overspecifications. James Baird equates the cigar-roller with an American business tycoon. Helen Vendler terms him a "big muscular neighbor who work[s] at the cigar-factory," here "called in to crank the ice-cream machine," with the "scullery-girls ["the wenches"] to help out." Robert Haas pinpoints his identity as "no doubt a Cuban or a Puerto Rican . . . set to work in the kitchen." As for the dead woman, William Burney surmises she may have been "murdered," and that the scene therefore represents "not a wake" but "simply a party, perhaps in a brothel." Alan Chavkin more prudently specifies the scene as "the simple funeral of a poor woman in a destitute part of the city"; but Stuart Silverman thinks the scene bespeaks "a carnival or circus," so that the "wenches" are "performers, wives, ticket sellers" at some "informal" wake, with the lamp in the dead woman's room a "spotlight" for the "last act of life, death."

And who, one might pertinently ask, is "the emperor of ice-cream"? Richard Ellmann, Edward Neill, and Shirley Strobel identify him with the invoked cigar-roller. Beverly Coyle and R. Viswanathan view the emperor as a separate figure, synonymous with whatever "ice-cream" symbolizes. Or is he the poem's speaker, and as such, in Joan Piccioto-Richardson's interpretive leap, Stevens' revisionary version of the Romantic tradition's Satanic poet? The "fantails" image on the dead woman's "sheet" produces the same inflated speculation. Lucy Beckett sees them as metonyms of commonplace "pigeons," but W. B. Stein ventures that they blasphemously allude to "the sacred dove." In line with two other notable poems in *Harmonium,* both Baird and Maureen Kravec conjure a different bird, "the peacock," but, at least for Kravec, as a denigrated mythological or religious symbol.[25]

Taken together, these scene-setting surmises suggest that the poem, as if it were a Rorschach text, itself consists of all "seem," with *its* "being" being only ambiguously resolvable. Certain things, however, at first seem certain enough. The scene concerns an informal wake for an older woman's death. The poem's setting exhibits a distinctly lower-class atmosphere, suggested by items like the homemade ice cream and its kitchen-cup containers. Likewise, the speaker refers to socially unpolished wakers in a notably casual idiom: "boys" vulgarly court "wenches" at a death-scene, tritely bringing them flowers in old newspapers. Moreover, who can avoid noting the impoverishment suggested by the woman's broken and cheap pine dresser, not to mention her room's single lamp? Yet pinpointing the poem's sketchily shoddy scenario quickly leads to further unverifiable conjectures. Is the speaker an equally crude funeral director, or perhaps someone pompously playing the role? Is he an ersatz philosopher uttering high-toned dicta that double as double-talk or fancied-up truisms: "Let be be finale of seem" and "The only emperor is the emperor of ice-cream"? In stating that anything said in the face of the "cold . . . and dumb" corpse will only "seem" to mean, these truisms seem to contradict their own apparent meaning.

More noticeably, "The Emperor of Ice-Cream" traffics in a kind of thematic and tonal indeterminacy, low and high comedy both, that primarily evokes a public scene. The speaker seems to fit the bill for modern public man. He calls someone to call someone else to stage a public death-scene. He also shifts our attention from the party-like sociality of the kitchen to the private sanctum of the dead woman's bedroom, but where she literally appears in a state of social de-privation. For him, the corpse *ought* to signify a totally public datum, a body entirely devoid of subjectivity, which he would have its viewers regard in utterly objective terms. Directing others to focus attention ("Let the lamp affix its beam") on the dead body as "only" an object the same as any other, his quasi-philosophical moves figuratively aim to erase its simulacrum of personhood.[26] Like her "dresser of deal / Lacking the three glass knobs," she lacks any private otherness, not even the remnants of a past private life. Formerly hidden away in her dresser, the "sheet / On which she embroidered fantails once" now becomes a means for public viewers "to cover her face," or, as befits the poem's central ice-cream image, have them regard her body in a way not to offend their taste. The speaker's directives, delivered in biblical-oracular tone ("Let be be"), manifest his wish to control and eradicate the private totally: "The *only* emperor. . ."

Or is it the other way around? One can just as easily claim that Stevens' poem at least balks at an all-public perspective. For one thing, the speaker's calling "the roller of big cigars" to whip up "concupiscent curds" bespeaks a sentiment at odds with the pervasive puritanical climate during the *Harmonium* period.[27] For another, his opening call invokes a working-class scene also at odds with Stevens' capitalist marketplace. Deploying an anonymous speaker, generically designated cigar-roller, boys, and wenches, and of course the non-identified "she" peremptorily introduced in the second stanza, the poem exposes that social-economic complex for its effective elimination of personality.

Set in contrast with any gesellschaft world, the poem's scene thus seems a more intimate type of social sphere in which public and private activities occur in interactive rather than oppositional fashion. This surmise accords with the poem's probable sources and the fact that it *stresses* its working-class setting.[28] The speaker's directive for "the muscular one" to whip up ice-cream in a home setting might well argue an assertive ("muscular") populist resistance to the period's mass production and consumption of food and other commodities, which, like the ice-cream and broken dresser, all lack per-durable value.[29] Similarly, his asking the boys to wrap their "flowers in last month's newspapers" frames the news as passé. Stripped of their informational function vis-à-vis a mass-public audience, the poem's newspapers possess a distinctly inessential value. They themselves figure a kind of communicational corpse, or come down to a vestigial public text by which, as John Dewey would claim, "only the date . . . could inform us whether [sensationalist news events] happened last year or this."[30]

More important, the newspaper image deflates the significance of mass-media events straight and simple. Stevens' poem ironically juxtaposes them to its main focus on a socially private scene of death, the delineation of which also suggests a nascent resistance to middle-class funeral procedures.[31] Particular private experiences of life and death here take precedence over events in the mass public sphere, a theme that the poem's title may itself underscore by alluding to the passing importance of a very specific and highly visible public figure in the American marketplace. For in almost the exact metrically synonymous terms as "The Emperor of Ice-Cream," the press had designated J. P. Morgan, himself a well-known smoker of big cigars, as "The Napoleon of Wall Street."[32]

In any case, the motif of death's primacy defines the most prevalent understanding of Stevens' poem. Without any "sense of cheerful hedonism or brave existential defiance," the speaker directs both the poem's funeral witnesses and implicitly us readers to accept "the bleak fact of death." Framing death "as an unavoidable aspect of being" lacking any significance,[33] the poem exemplifies an elegy of elegies. No consolation, religious *or* poetic, including the merely transitory or ice-cream-like tracing of one, can suffice to buffer the fact of death. Replete with plain, everyday denizens and things, Stevens' small, ice-cream-cold poem plays no second to literary precedents like Keats' well-known "Cold Pastoral!" ode, in which universal truth and beauty can yet console us about our urned destinies.

If "The Emperor of Ice-Cream" thereby enacts in miniature Stevens' earlier poetic theme in "Sunday Morning," the poem further inscribes more and less than the same theme, especially when taken in tandem with another *Harmonium* poem, "Cortège for Rosenbloom." In both poems, the dead figures come down to the same material residue, whether the woman's "horny feet" or the dead Rosenbloom, "the wizened one / Of the color of horn" (*CP* 80). According to Richard Ellmann, "horn" signifies "death's color in Stevens' verse." Ellmann, however, thinks "Cortège" contrasts with "The Emperor of Ice-Cream" in the way the first satirically exposes "conventional mourning, its stilted decorum, its figmental afterlife," whereas the ice-cream poem shows "the right way" to mourn death. The contrast also concerns more than formal versus informal mourning practices. In thinking "They are bearing his body into the sky," Rosenbloom's mourners act like "infants of misanthropes" and "of nothingness" (*CP* 80). Like children, they "commit men to a life lived in hope of an empty illusion."[34] Despite the inclusion of "boys" and "wenches," the same is not true for Stevens' "Emperor" poem, which cuts to the bleak chase and would have the woman's mourners follow the speaker's carpe diem directives to enjoy life's ice-cream and erotic pleasures while they can.

Not the least important contrast lies in how both poems frame death and mourning as a public-private issue. In particular, the mourners in "The Emperor of Ice-Cream" are few and unceremoniously "wear ordinary clothes";

Rosenbloom's mourners instead resemble a "buglike" mass,[35] dressed to their formal gills in "turbans" and "boots of fur":

> Now, the wry Rosenbloom is dead
> And his finical carriers tread,
> On a hundred legs, the tread
> Of the dead.
> Rosenbloom is dead.

"Cortège" clearly embodies a mass public at work, calling to mind William Carlos Williams' roughly contemporary poem "Tract" more than it does "The Emperor of Ice-Cream." Williams would Americanize funeral conventions, making them homespun, democratic, i.e., entirely public, affairs:

> Then briefly as to yourselves:
> Walk behind—as they do in France,
> seventh class, or if you ride
> Hell take curtains! Go with some show
> Of inconvenience; sit openly—
> to the weather as to grief.
> Or do you think you can shut grief in?
> What—from us? We who have perhaps
> nothing to lose? Share with us . . .[36]

Intertextually considered, "Cortège" shifts the focus from Williams' assimilating, anyone-can-do-it American culture to an isolated and immigrantist one (East European Jewish) conspicuously inserted into an American setting. So understood, Stevens' poem actively transforms communitarian sharing into communitarian claustrophobia. The poem, in other words, emphasizes the pervasive pull of public sharing per se, and does so by a prosodic rendition that doubles the aural "tread" of Rosenbloom's funeral marchers:

> To a chirr of gongs
> And a chitter of cries
> And the heavy thrum
> Of the endless tread
> That they tread.

His mourners' public march and the orations spoken in his behalf machine down anything unique about Rosenbloom's life, turning it into

a jumble of words
Of the intense poem
Of the strictest prose
Of Rosenbloom.

Above all, the poem's American speaker cannot escape—cannot not hear—the "lamentable tread" of the present funereal moment. We want to say that he stands apart from the scene and judges it critically. In fact, he himself not only becomes part of it, mesmerically repeating its homogenizing acoustic cadences, but in doing so surrenders to its closure or repression of any alternative perception. "Cortège for Rosenbloom" more precisely exhibits the death of its speaker's private mode of perception, a publicly drummed out aesthetic "Of the intense poem" here become "the strictest prose / Of Rosenbloom" and his cortège (*CP* 81).

"The Emperor of Ice-Cream" not only bypasses the issue of "right" mourning or of regarding death in democratic unison, it also inscribes anything but the death of death's privacy. For that matter, the poem arguably drifts away from the prima facie death theme it poses before readers. For example, far from proselytizing a proper public script for mourning, the speaker shifts his own lamp-like focus from a small group of people to a single corpse whose brute thereness resists any attempt to turn it into a symbolic pretext for thanatopsic musings. Along with her uncovered face and feet (both body-parts prominently featured), the dead woman's anonymity, unlike the casketed "Rosenbloom," potentially signifies a radical limit to social intercourse. *This* arrest of the public gaze may better explain the speaker's order to cover her features, either with her own embroidered sheet, or figuratively with his own Modernist shibboleth: "they come / To show how cold she is, and dumb." Why state the truism unless face and feet threaten to mean something else?

The woman's corpse, that is, indeed threatens to evoke a *person's* simulacrum: someone as if still alive, capable of expression, and yet, as "dumb," unable to communicate to others. Both as referent and trope, Stevens' forever mute woman constitutes a figure quite literally dead *to the world*. Contrary to the speaker's public staging ("To show how") of the woman's death, her corpse paradoxically resists discursive capture. No way thus exists to "wake" her properly. Never mind appealing to some religious belief in her particular life beyond death, one cannot propose *any* type of consolation. Not even the poet can convert her contingent corpse into a trope memorably instancing poetic beauty, such as the Stevens speaker dictates doing in "Sunday Morning": "Death is the mother of beauty" (*CP* 69).

Still, if the "Ice-Cream" speaker cannot wake the woman, his directives suggest that he at least tries to awaken us. His calling for shareable "concupiscent" pleasures not only helps mitigate *our* "dumb" reaction to her utterly contingent death, but also counterproduces the importance of enjoying life totally "in the present moment."[37] Who can miss how the poem accents those pleasures in inescapably echoing the famous children's rhyme: "I scream, you scream, we all scream for ice cream"?[38] Read one way, of course, the ironic juxtaposition of cold reality and child-like delight favors the former while consoling us with the latter. The speaker's slip on "I scream" itself appears no ironic accident, since it looks to confirm his vision of death making life seem as enticing as "ice-cream."

Or does it? Given the directorial posture of the speaker, one might just as feasibly claim that, like his truism in the face of the corpse, the "I scream" echo undermines his control over the poetic scene before us, and so indirectly raises the issue of the private poet now screened by his persona. If nothing else, the speaker's *multiple* verbal slips belie his philosophical poise. Suggesting Stevens' own private under-writing of his persona's public poem, they also lead to vulgar extremes that the speaker patently never intends.

To begin with, the poem's "cigars," a synecdoche for a special event in a déclassé setting, includes its own imperial metonym, that of "corona" cum crown. The embedded pun leads to another no less contextually plausible one: "the roller of big cigars" refers to a "coroner," an official representative of the public realm to whom, beginning in the late nineteenth century, people would report a family member's death to certify its occurrence. The poem's overdetermined and subliminal pun at once makes a joke of public officialdom and, in sync with a former American slang term for "cigar," identifies coroner with undertaker, someone who dresses up corpses to make them presentable for public viewing.[39] The undertaker-role also happens to define the speaker's with respect to the dead woman. In a discursive sense, he, too, would convert the corpse into a kind of palatable ice-cream for the scene's viewers and readers, by which I mean into something simple to understand, whatever existential anxiety it initially induces.

Read alongside the speaker's public directives—or directions for a public scene—the poem's submerged semiotic slippages again permit us to infer his wish to eliminate the privacy signified to others by the corpse's anomalous singularity. In addition, his directives invoke roller, boys, and wenches to participate in something metaphorically akin to a sarco-cannibalistic rite, the object of which is to consume the corpse orally and make it disappear. Bronislaw Malinowski has pointed out, for example, that in primitive societies, relatives react ambivalently to a family corpse. They hold reverential respect for "the personality still lingering about the body," yet also "fear . . . the gruesome thing that has been left over." In modern societies, too, "we no longer know how to 'kill the dead' and . . . in the absence of a ceremony to alleviate guilt[,] survivors continue in their fantasies to be obsessed by the deceased."[40]

If "The Emperor of Ice-Cream" would abort such ceremonies, Stevens' speaker nevertheless seems bent on certifying the deadness of the dead. To accomplish it, he performs the role of a latter-day shamanistic funeral director (the reason for his own incantatory tone throughout the poem), resorting to word-magic (his dramatic monologue) to convert the liminal, private body into a publicly confirmed, dead corpse. Otherwise, phenomenologically speaking, she might only *seem* dead. To dispel that possibility, "Let be *be* finale of seem" and "cover her face." And "*If* her horny feet protrude," we should understand how they wholly signify her death, as opposed to the latent motility of her corpse—the illusion of a still-living self.

Figuring her corpse as ice-cream, the speaker also directs the poem's readers to consume her in an "I scream" ritual of reading intended to make disappear what comes down to a Poesque afterimage of death. All images that might provoke our sense of the woman's *revenant* status, for instance her broken dresser and once-embroidered sheet, must be similarly reconfigured, their impoverishment stressed. One should regard them like "last month's newspapers," with their former public or utilitarian value now displaced by a specific, quasi-private function: satisfying the mourners' present, personal desires. All as if the women's death were of secondary importance or had not occurred, the speaker calls for a funeral scene in which "the wenches dawdle" in commonplace dresses, wooed by "boys" using newspapers to bring fresh "flowers" for the sole purpose of no less commonplace rites of seduction.

A subjunctive core, a wish to discharge his anxiety, thus lies behind the speaker's imperative directives. It exposes *him* as the "emperor of ice-cream," an ersatz yea-sayer of life against death, but who himself wears no clothes since his own pun-ridden language takes him beyond where he wants to go. At the very least, his language unwittingly runs at cross-purposes with socially honorific efforts to displace abstract, public formulations of death with gemeinschaft or lower-class communal ones, as if he were calling for something akin to an Irish wake. To make matters worse, the poem's puns drift into an entirely different and less seemly register of signification than death. The relentless ambiguities defining "The Emperor of Ice-Cream" not only undercut both Romantic and its speaker's Modernist metaphysics of death, they also permit a reading out of its sexual innuendoes, the vulgar nature of which further insulates the poem from what Stevens' public would want to hear. Or so it seems.

4

"The Emperor of Ice-Cream" appears within a cluster of two previously discussed poems in *Harmonium*. "The Cuban Doctor," with its masochistic intimations, comes right after, followed, as I have noted, by "Tea at the Palaz of Hoon," which concerns a different kind of emperor. He broods without benefit of any audience, intimate or not, able to confirm his self-satisfying poetic ruminations. An autoerotic element also defines Stevens' later recollection of writing "The Emperor of Ice-Cream": "I do not remember the circumstances under which this poem was written, unless this means the state of mind from which it came. I dislike niggling, and like letting myself go. The poem is an instance of letting myself go" (*L* 293; 1933). If only in passing, certain critics have noticed the poem's sexual innuendoes: "Much of the sexual symbolism is direct: the big cigars, the kitchen cups, the concupiscent curds . . . the wenches. But it is also marginal." Or the kind of pleasure the poem's figures "provide is implicitly sexual. The roller of big cigars calls to mind both carnival strongman and peepshow barker."[41]

Concupiscent images, sketchily drawn seduction-scenes, even the poem's brothel-like atmosphere,[42] still possess a distinctly social cast, however perverse they might appear vis-à-vis the poem's palpably serious topic. Whipping "concupiscent curds" at an old woman's wake echoes the violation of the Victorian religious figure addressed in Stevens' "A High-Toned Old Christian Woman," a poem that appeared in the same year as "The Emperor of Ice-Cream." Calling for indecorous pleasures might be another way to make "widows wince," those "disaffected flagellants" of religion, to elicit Modernist "novelties of the sublime," and so "A jovial hullabaloo among the spheres" (*CP* 59).

More generally, "The Emperor of Ice-Cream" outlines a male homosocial scene in which the speaker invokes a "muscular" man and reduces women to "wenches," not to mention the dead woman to insignificance. One critic thinks that the speaker's depiction of her "horny feet" makes her the butt of masculine "grotesque humor." Is the poem, then, a gender-coded, aggressive riposte to contemporary women's threatening usurpation of American public mores? Stevens, after all, took pleasure in smoking "big cigars," and his speaker's call for a cigar-roller might bespeak a covert assertion of male prerogatives in the face of Prohibition's threat, notably endorsed by women, to ban sales of tobacco along with alcohol.[43]

The conjecture makes sense only up to a point, for the poem's sexual undertow also occurs within its tropological recesses, and so would elude any affective social response, at best ambiguously called for, from a reactionary masculine public. Here I want to risk critical parody and let myself go, fully aware that the following reading traffics in vulgar Freudianism, first of all by vulgarizing the already Freudian image of "big cigars." Cigar as "corona" both puns on "coroner" and doubles as a metonym for a "crown," although not exactly of an emperor. Crown equally doubles as a vulgar idiomatic allusion to the head of the penis. Calling "the roller of big cigars" thus means invoking the biologistic force that results in erections, which, as "The muscular one," the roller personifies. And just as one prepares food to satisfy physical appetites, his whipping up "concupiscent curds" in "kitchen cups" evokes filling testicles with sperm, the goal of which is sheer pleasurable discharge for the male.

Outrageous or not, the preceding gloss helps account for the poem's otherwise cartoonish imagery in the first stanza. The speaker unwittingly asks the "wenches" and "boys," figures that at once suggest the prime of sexual urges and anonymous human types, to play out a dehumanized sexual scenario in which "The only emperor is the emperor of ice-cream." For "cream" doubles as a vulgar idiomatic expression for gism, with "ice-" its icily impersonal, biological discharge and nothing more.[44] The conventional "dress" of seduction accordingly reduces males and females to no more than sexual objects. Letting "the wenches dawdle in such dress / As they are *used* to wear," for example, interchangeably translates into: Let women remain, or else let men focus on women, as no more than objects of male sexual desire.

These reductions provide an alternate and obscene gloss for the putative death-scene in the second stanza. Why "Take" the woman's sheet, conspicuously marked by once embroidered fantails, from a specific dresser specifically lacking three glass knobs? "Take" again spells an aggressive sexual reduction of the woman, once one regards her "dresser of deal" as a pun for the physiological repertoire of women dealing with, i.e., profiting from, their sexual wares, unconsciously or not. In missing its "three glass knobs," the cheap pine ("deal") dresser alludes to female genitalia from a vulgar male viewpoint: a woman's private parts lacking the triune male genitalia, or what lower-class parlance would term the "family jewels," themselves here debased into mere "glass knobs." Supported by the poem's brothel-like atmosphere, the speaker reduces the woman to her cheapened, genital function—to a "dresser of *deal*" in two senses. Her embroidered sheet points to the romantic illusions with which inexperienced women ("once"), at least in vulgar male stereotypes of them, regard the sexual act. But not now and not here. Even the otherwise quaint image of fantails, which some critics regard in idealized religious terms, conjures up cancan burlesque shows, and in that way reduces to a pun on "fanny" and "piece of tail."[45]

And why stop there? The phrase "If her horny feet protrude" suggests another reduction of the woman's romantic illusions to the register of brute lust, with "horny" in this context "an alley word for libidinous."[46] The conditional "If" argues the speaker cum poet's awareness of his own tendency to romanticize the woman's persona. To suppress his impulse, he would "spread [the sheet] so as to cover her face": extinguish any manifestation of her sexual desire or life that might signify her personal or human otherness. His directive also hints at a related vulgar joke, this one about putting a bag over a woman's face to fuck her without regard to her physical appearance. For the woman's facial beauty or lack of it again potentially opens up the issue of her personality and so of self-other relationships. The ventriloquized speaker must reinterpret all indications of her sexual otherness, her own sexual desires or "horny feet," as signs of her being *just* "cold . . . and dumb," in the sense of her mental vacuity. She is to signify no otherness other than dumb, sexual being, a body *solely* there ("Let the lamp affix its beam") for sexual pleasuring. Any appearance to the contrary requires his willful resistance: "Let be be finale of seem."

The only emperor, then, the dominant human desire, comes down to the "I scream" orgasm, a private, impersonal experience, yet, be it said, one that equally applies to the other within the sexual act. In "The Load of Sugar-Cane," a *Harmonium* poem published a year earlier, Stevens shows how he can hear the vocative cry of the other's orgasm as well. Like ice-cream, the sugar-cane image refers to the sweet sexual "load" he intends to deliver via the gliding (and gladding) rhythms of poetic intercourse:

> The going of the glade-boat
> Is like water flowing . . .
>
> . . . .

> Through the green saw-grass,
> Under the rainbows . . .
>
> . . . .
> That are like birds,
> Turning, bedizened,
>
> While the wind still whistles
> As kildeer do.
>   (*CP* 12)

Known for their distinctive cry, the kildeer respond to the crowned (*sic*)
"red" male organ of the speaker steering its poetically inscribed sexual cargo:

> When they rise
> At the red turban
> Of the boatman.

The "Turning, bedizened," ecstatic "whistles" tell of no coerced intimacy
between self and other, whether one understands the duo for male and female or writer and reader. With its aggressive sexual design, one might suppose that "The Emperor of Ice-Cream" whistles a different tune. Yet both
poems inscribe the same strategic point: the desire to expunge any desire to
know the other except through zero semantic, vocative effects.

If only as I render it here, Stevens' sexual allegory no doubt appears vulgar
in two ways, first for its content, second for its crude word-to-referent mode
of allegorization. But in "The Emperor of Ice-Cream," his "horny" allegory
only *seems* vulgar and, of course, sexist in today's public terms. Subject to
ideological deconstruction, "sexism" presupposes a fixed, quasi-ontological
construction of gender, one's own and the other's.[47] Under cover of its
speaker's publicly intoned imperatives directed at a public-becoming-private
scene of death, the poem instead traces its *more* private sexual desideratum
only in subjunctive ("Let" as in "Allow that") terms. Sex primarily serves
Stevens as a trope to instantiate his poem's private scene of writing. Its vul-
garity consists of an entirely privatized fantasy, an "in" male joke without any
male-homosocial group to endorse the interpellations of gendered power
that such jokes rhetorically enact and promote. The "is" in the refrain, "The
only emperor is . . . ," in effect masks the poet's wish *not* to communicate
with others, male *or* female. He would bar absolutely—as by imperial fiat—
anyone bent on intimate knowledge of his work, which like Poe's "is Poe"
moments anyway only expresses a private, "I scream" vocative thereness.

Sooner or later, Stevens eschews erotic intimacies or "burning secrecies" for his model of writing, since they simultaneously invoke scenes of public performance and the literary criteria it entails. Writer-reader intimacies prevent letting himself go *in* writing, which in "Fabliau of Florida" he reckons as a "Move outward into heaven" where "There will never be an end / To this droning of the surf" (*CP* 23). Stevens also acknowledges the distress to imagination coincident with either the public's return or else its sheer absence, in other words the painful aftermath endemic to transitory autoerotic hallucinations like the Cuban doctor's and Hoon's. Only writing in terms of a contentless self-other scenario, one that paradoxically lends the poem content through rhetorically "concupiscent" words, permits his eating ice-cream, i.e., writing, concurrently in public and in private. As "The Load of Sugar-Cane" suggests and as I try to explain in the next chapter, Stevens' pleasure in writing his *Harmonium* poems must finally include transforming imaginary interlocutors into taking pleasure from them in radically private terms like his own.

In a 1928 letter to L. W. Payne, Jr., concerning "Le Monocle de Mon Oncle," Stevens insisted he had nothing to do with exploiting sex for commercial reasons: "it is going to be a long time before I let a commercialism like sex appeal get any farther than the front fence" (*L* 279). One can only suppose that he differentiates his well-recessed vulgar "Emperor" from the period's sex-sublimated romantic fiction that at once disguises and exploits its readers' sexual fantasies. In "The Ordinary Women" (*CP* 10–12), another poem from the same year as "The Emperor of Ice-Cream," "ordinary" readers in sexual "poverty" rise "From dry catarrhs, and to guitars," drawn "Through the palace walls" to an escapist fiction's faraway imperial scenes. These scenes launder the sexual real via figures fancifully dressed in "coiffures" and "civil fans." Mere "Insinuations of desire" homogenize sexual experience. They make its "Puissant speech, alike in each," and thus represent the antithesis to the rhetorically concealed yet blunt orgasmic particularity traced in "The Emperor of Ice-Cream."

In principle, the same judgment applies to sex's more sophisticated modern understandings and public cachet. As "Le Monocle de Mon Oncle" makes clear, the Stevens *Harmonium* poem ultimately abjures the possible sex-appeal that its "much crumpled thing" might have for any public coterie, whether populist, prurient, consumerist, artistic, or psychoanalytic:

> If sex were all, then every trembling hand
> Could make us squeak, like dolls, the wished-for words.

But note the unconscionable treachery of fate,
That makes us weep, laugh, grunt and groan, and shout
Doleful heroics, pinching gestures forth
From madness or delight, without regard
To that first, foremost law.

(*CP* 17)

Abstracted, sex means nothing, although everything for those intellectually pondering it. The *Harmonium* poem instead aims to reduce all sexual matters to a vulgar nothing. Shifting to more private semiotic registers of meaning, they turn into meta-poetic tropes that, because they work to en-chant a private scene of writing, underwrite the contingent particularity of Stevens' aesthetic perceptions. *He* is the "rose"-colored, i.e., poetically risen, "rabbi" at the end of "Le Monocle de Mon Oncle," aching to embroider "fantails" of different ilk from the woman's in "The Emperor of Ice-Cream." His would consist of very particular blue and white pigeons, or pellucid poetic tropes.[48] Their fluttering activity would result not only in beautiful shades of color or meaning for others, but also in nothing less than a definitively shaded—a private—beauty for himself:

until now I never knew
That fluttering things have so distinct a shade.

(*CP* 18)

6   *Harmonium:* A Private Poe-session

Is there one word of sunshine in this plaint?
Do I commend myself to leafy things
Or melancholy crows as shadowing clouds?
   —Wallace Stevens, "Stanzas for 'Le Monocle de Mon Oncle' "

It is necessary to any originality to have the courage to be an amateur.
   —Wallace Stevens, "Adagia"

1

Stevens privately pays a price for indulging his poetics of privacy. For one thing, as I noted in the preceding chapter, he sometimes worries premature assertions of it. The temptation always exists to concede its necessary process, its particular, meta-poetic procedures, to a formulaic poetic principle.

More important, going private can attenuate poetic incentive altogether. As I also argued earlier, certain *Harmonium* poems like "Earthy Anecdote" and "Tea" set out to obstruct the reading public's inquisitions, commonsensical or critically sophisticated. In Poesque fashion, the poems provoke missed readings, which Stevens identifies with a variously defined "public," in particular with codes of reading that he himself tends to adopt during his acts of writing. By itself, this remains a negative design, unable to confirm the poetic élan he seeks in writing privately. Confirmation instead requires a special *quod demonstrandum erat:* Stevens needs to write poems that simultaneously invite aesthetically compelling readings by others, but double as foils for yielding a private surplus to himself. Where the poem ends in public, there, as it were, it ought still to-be-about-to-become-a-poem for him.

Most of the *Harmonium* poems already discussed work to realize his private *mise en scène* in one way or another, but few do it more formatively than, ironically, one of Stevens' earliest successes in publication, "Peter Quince at the Clavier" (*CP* 89–92). To recall, the poem explicitly concerns the issue of the Apocryphal Susanna's violated sexual privacy by morally hypocritical elders.[1] From a formalist viewpoint, certain passages from the four-part poem—for instance "The body dies; the body's beauty lives" (IV)—support claims that it concerns "form as it comes to be imperative in a world of flux."[2] The poem therefore also recursively concerns itself. Like art generally, "Peter Quince at the Clavier," which evokes an instrument synonymous with the title of Stevens' *Harmonium* collection, at once incarnates and transcends transient, human experiences: "So maidens die, to the auroral / Celebration of a maiden's choral." As it did for Poe, music and dying maidens provide the paradigmatic impetus for poetic art. With Quince playing his clavier—or Stevens writing his poem—art captures erotic moments "in their green going." Freezing time through formal embodiments ("in the flesh [beauty] is immortal"), art perpetuates otherwise "going" moments by means of its own "finale of seem" or celebratory "choral."

Just as important, "Peter Quince at the Clavier" not only redeems but would also transform Susanna's violated private scene into a public icon, although one at critical odds with the egregious public figured by "The red-eyed elders watching" her in the moment "She bathed in her still garden" (I). For a feminist critic like Mary Nyquist, the poem unwittingly purveys a masculine pornographic voyeurism beyond that of the elders'.[3] Peter Quince, after all, the poem's putative speaker, performs his "music" and monologue with lustful thoughts ("desiring you") about an unknowing woman "Here in this room." While "Thinking of your blue-shadowed silk," he clearly fantasizes her naked body, since her presence immediately reminds him of Susanna's violated scene of bathing. By extension, isn't that also true for Stevens, who of course imagines both violations in the first place?

Yet such critical exposés willy-nilly participate in the same process. Indeed, the poem appears deliberately to stage and invite its own critical violations, leading us to watch others "watching" Susanna's violation. That is no less true for feminist-revisionary viewpoints. They presuppose the feminist reader's own role in witnessing the male poet's sexist, spectatorial position with a private, feminine scene, ripe for liberation from the last but not the first mode of spectatorship. One way or another, formalist, feminist, and other readings come to duplicate the elders' position. We watch the *poem* doing its thing, for example in the way it calls attention to its blatant deviations from the literary scaffolding it explicitly invokes. Many critics have noted how Susanna represents an itself apocryphal version of the faithful-wife namesake from the Apocrypha. Peter Quince, the speaker, refers to the farcical character who comically directs a play within Shakespeare's *A Midsummer Night's Dream,* provoking us to ask why Stevens enlists a slapstick figure to play the fine music of a clavier. To the same effect, the poem fails to provide narrative logic for Quince's transition from lustful self into the aesthetic sophisticate who beautifully theorizes beauty in the poem's fourth section. How does base, sexual motivation, with art its pimpish go-between, metamorphose into full artistic sensibility, with sex *its* pretext instead?

No doubt, ways exist to account for these apparent discrepancies, but, at the behest of the poem, they too reproduce public violations of its self-staged, private scene.[4] If they miss noticing the above discrepancies, readers cannot avoid the publicly enticing tropes Quince/Stevens uses to depict Susanna's private bathing scene:

> In the green water, clear and warm,
> Susanna lay.
> She searched
> The touch of springs,
> And found
> Concealed imaginings.
> She sighed,
> For so much melody.
>
> (II)

It is her private poetic moment, unconsciously autoerotic through and through, that the elders and we readers come to violate with crashing "cymbal . . . / And roaring horns," in other words with our symbol-hunting or discursive noise. Just the bare thought of public critical inquiry interrupts the moment. In the guise of Susanna's socially compromised Byzantine attendants, Stevens' internalized image of a less moral or ideologically intrusive public does the same. The servants dub for readers attentive chiefly to the poem's aesthetic surface, or who in reading follow and enjoy the graceful, prosodic rhythms that background its beautiful statements about beauty. But after announcing themselves "with a noise like tambourines" (III), the attendants can only whisper and wonder ineffectually about "why Susanna cried," until "Anon, their lamps' uplifted flame / Revealed Susanna and her shame." Socially naive defenses of privacy can never withstand the force of public codes of judgment, however defined. Even when we resist them at first, we inevitably yield to them, must reckon, say, with the various designs—social, political, intellectual—others make on beauty, and not least on the beauty Stevens links to private poetic pursuits.

In his Quince poem, Stevens' insouciant faith in private poetic outcomes dialectically outmaneuvers that obstacle. On one level, the desideratum and praxis of his *Harmonium* poems remain the same: to stage various thematic aspects of the public realm, social to literary, so as to finesse them and recover (in private) the poem's private scene of writing. In staging its public judgments, "Peter Quince at the Clavier" stages their leaving untouched or literally inviolate ("Still quavering") its "Concealed imaginings"—not, that is, the beauty of performed form, but of the "woven," i.e., textual, acts of composition that formerly went unobserved:

> She walked upon the grass,
> Still quavering,
> The winds were like her maids,
> On timid feet,
> Fetching her woven scarves.
>
> (II)

The same scenario applies to Quince. If he performs his musical compositions in a high-cultural social setting (where else would one play a clavier?), he nonetheless practices a formal or an eminently public art in the way Susanna bathes or Stevens likes "letting myself go" in writing his *Harmonium* poems. The goal is to make art beautiful for and by its being private. That is why, like Quince and his claviered music, Stevens exercises sub-semiotic, even sub-phonic lyrics ("Music is feeling, then, not sound"), played in private spaces: the room, the enclosed garden, the poem. He writes lyrics, that is to say, precisely to eschew writing loud, ostentatious ones, whether those apprehensible by public elders, or else for intimate others, like the woman Quince fantasizes while playing his clavier.

In short, Quince, Susanna, and Stevens hold no aggrieved sense of their privacy's inevitable violation. On the contrary, for them poetic privacy comes to *just exist*. The peroration marking the fourth section of "Peter Quince at the Clavier" suggests that what at first looks like the public's spelling death for the private poetic event in fact means quite the opposite. There, Stevens turns his poem's public stagings of the private into private stagings of the public to recover his private "feeling" in composing his poem. Poetic "flesh"—artistic form—immortalizes beauty precisely *because,* from public viewpoints, the formal "body dies." Just as

> Susanna's music touched the bawdy strings
> Of those white elders,

so "Peter Quince at the Clavier" and Stevens' other *Harmonium* poems seduce us by their "bawdy," quasi-intimate, aesthetic doings. Yet the poem's formal residuum, its dead "scraping"—

> but, escaping,
> [She] Left only Death's ironic scraping.

—is all that the public gets, and not least aggressive, elder-like expositors demanding that the poem adhere to literary or ideological norms of behavior.

Quince, Susanna, and Stevens all escape such demands. For Stevens, the poem endures immortally insofar as it comprises a private memo of an unviolated private act, which in his American world of rabid, "red-eyed" publicity amounts to a miracle. Eluding intercourse with public worlds, "Susanna" thus comes to figure her namesake of the holy Apocrypha after all. On the same terms, she figuratively embodies a faithful spouse to Stevens' private poetic principle:

> Now, in its immortality, it plays
> On the clear viol of her memory,
> And makes a constant sacrament of praise.

Each new playing—the poet's reading of his poem or else writing another—testifies to a privacy miraculously preserved. Susanna's requires no last-minute rescue from "white elders" the way Poe's narrator does from *his* white-lipped Inquisitors in "The Pit and the Pendulum." Right at the beginning of Stevens' public poetic career, he imagines a violated scene of privacy that he converts into a harmless, unsensational, i.e., private, violation of the public's right to know.

2

Like "Nomad Exquisite," "Peter Quince at the Clavier" states its private case with self-evident panache. Nevertheless, what privacy gives Stevens, it can just as easily take away and lead him to play a different tune. Others may apprehend the poem's beauty apart from the kind he works to apprehend in and through its meta-poetic process of composition. But without witnesses to its processual means and fugitive aesthetic, the poem's private beauty can also die, that is, come to lack, as it threatens to do for Hoon, the sustaining power of the real for Stevens himself. Always proposing to take back what they pose for others, his *Harmonium* poems thus moot their public accessibility and significance as often as they dally with a desired, privatized éclat.

The poem "Theory" (*CP* 86–87) provides a theorized example of what I mean. It begins with the epistemological truism, "I am what is around me," and so loosely argues that "one's identity varies according to one's surroundings."[5] Nothing can halt the theory's further application to Stevens' own theory of poetry, in which case the truism doubles as his apologetic use of idiosyncratic topoi and other crypto-poetic fare. As such, "Theory" proposes: at any one point, readers can reformulate his eccentric images and whatnot according to whatever makes them make familiar sense.

Why, then, does Stevens add a meta-poetic proviso that in effect reneges on his theoretical apologia? Itself a cryptic self-reference to begin with, "Theory" conspicuously cites only one imaginary environment to illustrate its poetic thesis: "A black vestibule; / A high bed sheltered by curtains." To be sure, the speaker acknowledges the scene as one among other possible "instances" that might illustrate a generic proposition or "theory," theoretically accessible to anyone. But his chosen instance happens to resemble a Poesque interior, moreover one that connotes his poetic isolation from others. Right *now*, Stevens writes *this* poem as if in a dark, curtained scene. Only the "black vestibule," the poem's already shadowy meta-poetic intimation, allows access to its scene of writing, at least until, as if receding further, that scene, too, becomes occluded by curtains—goes private.

In general, Stevens' poetic "theory" inclines to keep readers in the dark, and not simply "in theory." Yet a pretext for saying nothing to them, his poetic act risks becoming a poem that says nothing to himself. If he parallels Poe's privatization of the tale, Stevens does not accept Poe's unquestioned, representative theory of *poetry*. In "The Poetic Principle," Poe depicts poetry's teleological point, however futile its realization, as "the desire of the moth for the star," or for supernal Beauty (*E&R* 77).[6] Stevens uses the same image in "Hibiscus on the Sleeping Shores" (*CP* 22–23)—there "The mind roamed as a moth roams"—to inform a surrogate reader ("Fernando") of his poetry's purpose*less* activity. No matter how much it seeks specific public correlatives, for instance a café's colored flag, the inspired poetic idea

> Rose up besprent and sought the flaming red

> Dabbled with yellow pollen—red as red
> As the flag above the old café—
> And roamed there all the stupid afternoon.

If Stevens were to take Fernando's viewpoint, his poem would merely appear to make no point. It would possess the same (in)significance as an out-of-place public flag, even to himself. Other *Harmonium* poems react to this predicament in different ways. Just as Poe does with his emplotted misreadings in his fiction, Stevens can sometimes formulate a poem's inaccessibility as applying to naive readers alone. His poetic roamings might seem "stupid" or aimless to a "Fernando," an unlikely littérateur, but still "mean" for a more sophisticated reader.

If they do, however, the allowance only turns out to confirm their private ambience more intractably to himself. For as I argued in the case of "Earthy Anecdote" (Chapter 3), Stevens also proposes to block imagined readers who persist in seeking significance in his verse. Not to deny them completely, he can try, among other options, to formulate their desire as an egregious aggression that his poem's quest for beauty would *un*self-consciously finesse. In "The Virgin Carrying a Lantern," the speaker asserts that

> There are no bears among the roses,
> Only a negress who supposes
> Things false and wrong

> About the lantern of the beauty
> Who walks there, as a farewell duty.

> (*CP* 71)

The Stevens poem itself is no bear, no aggressive riposte to its "negress" prying at night (images of the demanding reader kept in the dark twice-over) into the poem's garden of roses, i.e., the meanings of its redolent, sensuous tropes.[7] Though of necessity ("a farewell duty") his writing "walks" or traffics in enshrined literary-canonical idioms, it aims to discern an original ("Virgin") beauty privately. For that reason, it makes its visionary disclosures ("Carrying a Lantern") heedless of frustrated critical readers gripped in a "heat so strong!" to know the disclosed.

Stevens' intention nonetheless remains tenuous. As the poem "Of the Surface of Things" (*CP* 57) demonstrates, it can result in his own adoption of the reading public's position with a former poem that now appears minus *its* private sense-making process. In the present poem, he depicts himself "In my room, the world . . . beyond my understanding." So he goes walking, i.e., imagining/writing, at which point reality appears clear and simple: "it consists of three or four hills and a cloud."[8] But later "From my balcony," or his assuming the position of reader to his own writing—

> Reading where I have written,
> "The spring is like a belle undressing"

—he encounters non-sequiturs, in effect his former imaginative self (a "singer" internalizing the "moon") having become cloaked or private to his present self:

> The gold tree is blue.
> The singer has pulled his cloak over his head.
> The moon is in the folds of the cloak.

In becoming like others who also want to understand "the world" via poetic art, he can no longer make sense, though it still strikes him as beautiful, of what made private sense to him at the time of writing.

Stevens can't keep shutting his eyes to others without sensing his *Harmonium* poem's own ephemeral or moth-like substance, which accounts for why he also plays out the solipsistic implications of denying others access to his work. Such denials at best result in the epistemological indeterminacy traced in the poem "Tattoo." There, the speaker ostensibly argues that nature's otherness doesn't bear scrutiny, for

> The light is like a spider.
> It crawls over the water.
> It crawls over the edges of the snow.
> It crawls under your eyelids
> And spreads its webs there.
>   (*CP* 81)

Light reduces all things made by man and nature, for example "rafters or grass," to the same. Facilitated by light, eyes, too, come to identify the very "flesh and bones of you": one inexorably comes to see one's own "filaments of . . . eyes" when viewing the already I-delimited object-world of water-surfaces and snow-edges.

Reminiscent of Emerson's essay "Experience," "Tattoo" arguably constitutes less an argument for the tattoo-like or "real" impress nature makes on us than a poem expressing the indeterminacy of whether man or nature constructs "reality."[9] Whereas an actual tattoo signifies anything but inscribed impermanence, in Stevens' poem man-made and natural kinds of construction *both* reduce to an ephemeral substance like evanescent spider-webs. As in the poem "Theory," the "tattoo" theory complicates its wider referential point. Since "light" spreads everywhere, right into "your" eyes, it perforce extends to poetic "light": the disclosures of the real made through Stevens' first-person ("I") lyrical perspectives. In *that* light, "Tattoo" leaves unresolved the question of whether his visions, the present one included, will make either a lasting or transitory impression on others.

The question clearly pertains more to him than to the poem's readers, meaning that the "you" referred to throughout the poem in fact figures a self-address. When and if he deliberately attempts to shut out others, a durable poem-as-tattoo—visually accessible, therefore public, in short the desideratum that motivates writing—comes to possess the so-fragile substance of a "filament" to himself. Through imaginative derrings-do, he connects up everything and therefore nothing, in effect abjuring the epistemological paradigm of self-other by which we daily judge and negotiate "reality." It is no accident that "Tattoo" figuratively represents the Stevens speaker as though he had just been sleeping: when the light first registers "under your eyelids." With his eyes still closed, he can keep the light dim, that is, can perceive, imagine, write—tattoo—things without others (or public lights) simultaneously testifying to or endorsing the reality of those things, as constantly happens in quotidian life.

The following *Harmonium* poem exposes the hubris of not questioning private visionary closures like the one Stevens outlines in "Tattoo." At first glance, his mock depiction of the "parakeet of parakeets" in "The Bird with the Coppery, Keen Claws" (*CP* 82) invites a more publicly relevant allegorical reading. According to one critic, the bird stands for an Idealist version of God, or say a Hegelian Absolute making philosophical mincemeat out of human existential particularity—man as mere sublated part in some Transcendental design.[10] Or perhaps the bird more simply represents any absolutist ideologue willing to sacrifice human part for one or another social design. Either way, one can claim that the bird's "lids are white because his eyes are blind" to individual human suffering. The bird appears utterly aloof from it "because he broods there and is still," and

> As his pure intellect applies its laws,
> He moves not on his coppery, keen claws.

At minimum, "The Bird with the Coppery, Keen Claws" ridicules the thinker whose "dry," self-certain vision bears no relation to human life as people really live it:[11]

> He munches a dry shell while he exerts
> His will, yet never ceases, perfect cock,
> To flare, in the sun-pallor of his rock.

The bird trope, though, also borders on satirical caricature. Skewing the poem's apparent ironic point, the rhetorical excess frames the unspecified speaker as himself "keen" on exerting a self-certain judgmental will. Further undermining the poem's putatively "human" import, the trope's specificity resists extended metaphorical translation. Why use a parakeet to illustrate the stance of some abstract and/or absolutist self capable of sacrificing the partic-ular for the universal? Itself particular, the poem's presumably ironic trope ironically drifts away from generic, public significance, human or deific, to the bird's contingent or more private one.

If any targeted figure, the parakeet, a small songbird, more immediately alludes to the poet and his diminished authority in the modern world. Resist-ing minor status, the bird even more specifically represents Stevens' own alter-image as a poet who, "blind" to others in his act of writing, might then fantasize himself a prevailing "parakeet of parakeets." The mock-poet thinks himself alive to reality's disheveled lushness: "The rudiments of the tropics are around." Compared with other poets (and people) subscribing to dead-ening, single-focused visions of reality, he judges himself "A pip of life amid a mort of tails." His poems may seem smaller in scope to others, but they possess much larger, potential significance—"His tip a drop of water full of storms."

"The Bird with the Coppery, Keen Claws" exposes the limitation of any such private poetic fantasy. A parakeet, after all, typifies a caged pet—the would-be imperialistic bird-poet flares his imaginative wings within a re-stricted poetic space. Declaiming poetic truths in private all as if grounded on some unquestioned "rock," he can exert his will over his semiotic domain only on condition of being insulated from others or stripped of public counters. The bravado of Stevens' poetic stand-in thus depends on a fatuous privacy by which, to make private matters worse, he hallucinates his work's public importance. What might have passed for his assertion of poetic privacy *per se* unconsciously manifests his pull toward a serene public pose, the "Panache of panache" of some "perfect cock." In other words, the parakeet adopts the stance of a deluded poet whose poetry possesses no more public *or* private substance than a "dry shell."

Better, then, to assume the anti-elitist bird-role that Stevens sketches for himself in "Bantams in Pine-Woods" (*CP* 75–76), where a bantam cock plays "anti-hero" to the "Damned universal cock," "Chieftain Iffucan of Azcan"—"If you can of As can."[12] Against the Shakespearian-sized "ten-foot poet among inchlings," the small bantam represents "the personal" trying to "halt" the larger cock's pretense to express all of life for everyone. Refusing to have his particular vision of it displaced, the bantam boldly insists on the right to a private poetic life: "Your world is you. I am my world."

If the poem tempts us to identify the bantam's position with Stevens' own, it nevertheless baffles their equation in at least two ways. First, the bantam speaker equally fits the role of some conventional reader reading the *Harmonium* poems. Encountering a Stevens poem, he or she feels belittled (inchling-like) because intimidated by its bizarre lyrical tableaus and other linguistic manifestations of the poet's imaginative brio. "Bantams in Pine-Woods" projects its own writer writing without apparent restraints, or on the reader-affronting premise of "if you can."

Second, the resentful reader doubles as a poet manqué whom Stevens rejects *along with* the public draw imaged by the accomplished poet's sizable reputation with others. The speaker represents the minor poet envious of a self-assured, "ten-foot" poet's as if mythological (Chieftain's) authority in the literary domain. The "bantam" poet's assertion of his private poetic rights ("I am my world") surely smacks of authorial ressentiment, a competitive defensiveness intimated by the puns Eleanor Cook notices in the title, "pining" and "would,"[13] and within the poem by a twofold rebus-like pun. Himself indulging a motivated, poetic fabrication, he identifies Azcan as a "tan" bête noire, insinuating that the latter produces not only texts (etymologically, woven or *fabric*ated things), but also fabricated-as-in-faked ones:

> Chieftain Iffucan of Azcan in caftan
> Of tan with henna hackles.

The bantam figure's poetic-alliterative, i.e., exhibitionist, complaint gets him nowhere, suggesting that his is not Stevens' literary anxiety. More likely, the cocky bird's frustrated tone and manifesto-like postulations mimic the anxiously aggressive stance of Stevens' American-localist peers ("Bantam*s*"), whom he here portrays as self-consciously resisting traditional literary influences:[14]

> An inchling among these pines,
>
> Bristles, and points their Appalachian tangs,
> And fears not portly Azcan nor his hoos.

"Bantams in Pine-Woods" all but reduces the issue of literary influence to a male cock-fight, an internalized, public agon in which Stevens himself feels no inclination to participate. At other times, he quite literally frames influence as a dead issue. Esteemed writers' once publicly impressive "hoos" amount to just that: the equivalent of anonymous sounds now absent their formerly urgent and contingent formulations of poetic truths. More than some "anti-religious" sentiment,[15] meta-poetic pointlessness defines the thrust of the Stevens speaker's rhetorical questions directed at critical readers in "Of Heaven Considered as a Tomb":

> What word have you, interpreters, of men
> Who in the tomb of heaven walk by night,
> The darkened ghosts of our old comedy?
> Do they believe they range the gusty cold,
> With lanterns borne aloft to light the way . . . ?
>
> (*CP* 56)

To the living poet, the literary-historical "burial, pillared up each day," of renowned dead poets, those endowed with monumental or Azcan-like status, only

> Foretell[s] each night the one abysmal night,
> When the host shall no more wander.

From one angle, the speaker's what-does-it-all-matter? metaphysical stance reversibly bespeaks his anxiety over or wish to kill off his literary precedents. From another, his vision concerns his anxiety over their very absence. If the literary public, the addressee of the poem, makes those precedents anxiously matter within the living poet's acts of writing, the resulting poem anyway subsumes his having written it. Since *making* the poem *is* his poem for Stevens, the public comprising the cultural medium through which poems outlive their authors redundantly testifies to the latter's eclipse. Precisely *that* misprision by readers ("What word have you?") foretells the doom not only of former poets' literary-historical ambitions, but also of his own however much already muted ones. With cosmic thoughts like these, nothing he or any poet writes can achieve permanent value, which means that writing poems reduces to an entirely private affair.

3

"Of Heaven Considered as a Tomb" noticeably traffics in the funereal and ghostly tableaus of Poe's tales, for example the cacophonous "tones in the voice of the shadow" in Poe's 1835 "parable" entitled "Shadow" (*P&T* 220). More important, the poem fastens on the fatalism that I have claimed marks *Eureka*'s meta-literary prediction of an "abysmal" materialist implosion bearing on his and other writers' literary works. Yet Poe's vision, "private" for its nullifying the nagging eruption of "public" influences and criteria in writing his tales, requires his rigorously extended exposition. *Eureka* enacts an ascetic poetics of privacy, the goal being to have him finally forgo his continual attraction to one or another kind of literary-public approbation.

In "Of Heaven Considered as a Tomb," Stevens stages how he can write his poems with Poe's "End" already in mind. To begin there, however, prematurely vitiates the incentive or imaginative vitality required to write them. Stevens' willful efforts to suppress the public's virtual co-presence *while* writing his poems provide only delusional "parakeet" or "bantam" alternatives to this situation. If pursuing privacy is to mean not the death but the enabling vigor of Stevens' poetic work, then he must find ways to avoid excluding readers in wholesale fashion. More precisely, he needs to include them lest to himself the private genesis of his poems become wholly identified with their tomb-like public remains. For him, the *Harmonium* poem at most ought to embody what in "Peter Quince at the Clavier" he terms "Death's ironic scraping," or what others read sans the irony.

Stevens' charge accounts for his particular revisionary inscriptions of Whitman's poetic vision throughout *Harmonium*. With its "lilacs" reference, "In the Carolinas" (*CP* 4–5), for instance, at once acknowledges and privatizes Whitman's public poetics:

> The lilacs wither in the Carolinas.
> Already the butterflies flutter above the cabins.
> Already the new-born children interpret love
> In the voices of mothers.

Nature inspires transcendental ("above the cabins") interpretations, in line, as Eleanor Cook notes, with Whitman's ubiquitously "new-born" vision of its "essentially generative" aspects.[16] The poem addresses the Whitman poem as such, alluding to the universal vision of rebirth à la nature found in his well-known "Lilacs" poem. But for Stevens "*in* the Carolinas," the transcendental reach of Whitman's poems "wither[s]," if only because, as "The Comedian as the Letter C" succinctly records, poet and reader fall into expected ("Already") patterns of interpreting nature. The same applies to poems, given the "Carolinas" pun (*carol* and *lines*) also remarked by Cook. For the Stevens speaker, interpretations of either one amount to ephemeral or butterfly-like public responses, in the end reducible to mother tongues—to the literary gestalts, "the voices of mothers," inculcated by "new-born" generations of readers.

"In the Carolinas" particularizes the sentiment of "Of Heaven Considered as a Tomb." Even Whitman's transcendental visions of nature no longer apply, are subject to time, occur but once, or, in essence, constitute residual written effects of *his* private experiences. Shorn of Whitman's communicative optimism, the Stevens speaker acknowledges that this bitter ("aspic") fate presses upon his therefore only momentary, uplifting connection with nature:

> Timeless mother,
> How is it that your aspic nipples
> For once vent honey?

Unlike Whitman's, Stevens' transcendental poem can neither mean nor be for others. Still, in forfeiting communal codifications, it also releases nature's unexpected singular nowness for him. Embodied solely by the deictic tenor, specifically the italicized typography, of the poem's last two lines—

> *The pine-tree sweetens my body*
> *The white iris beautifies me.*

—Stevens' poetic experience just happens ("For once") without rhetorical preparation or any promise of future recurrence.

Whitman's poems, of course, presume to unionize or bring together conflicting American "states" including individual states of mind, past and present. In contrast, "In the Carolinas" alludes to being "in" a region with a historical secessionist past. The poem enacts its own meta-poetic secession by forcing readers to adopt an *outside* relation to itself, one analogous to the speaker's with a venting, people-unfriendly nature in the poem. Tersely communicative, or, more accurately, communicating only its tropological terseness, the poem's "aspic nipples," its privatized, linguistic "carolinas," abjure grand Unions or communally nurturing, poetic schemas. Stevens' risked secessionist disaffection from semiotic communion is exactly what "sweetens my body" or beautifies his experience in writing *Harmonium* poems like the present one.

If Whitman defines one limit for Stevens' impulse to go public in writing these poems, Poe marks the boundary of wishing to go private, with the former constantly turning into the latter. The conversion itself resembles Poe's Ligeian dispossession of Rowena in "Ligeia," an occurrence consonant with what Eleanor Cook characterizes as Stevens' other "sinister-metamorphosis or horrid-metamorphosis poems."[17] In *Harmonium*, though, Stevens resorts to the literary-ancestral switch in a very specific if privately allusive meta-poetic manner. For example, in minimalist fashion, "Whitman," as it were, becomes "Poe" in the two-stanza movement of "The Emperor of Ice-Cream." With its informal, public setting, the first stanza allegorizes a Whitmanesque "muscular" poet, the populist "roller of big cigars," i.e., of large, celebratory poems, whom it invokes to whip up "concupiscent *curds*," i.e., democratically enticing public tropes or *words*. The poem would have its imagined poet present his words in immediately accessible poetic forms ("kitchen cups"), the earthy pleasures of which will attract all stripes of readers, from the philosophically curious to the literarily illiterate "boys" and "wenches."

The second stanza initially evinces more Modernist irony than affiliative intertextual gesture toward Poe. Helen Vendler even thinks that the poem's dead woman represents precisely "a savage refutation of Poe's claim that the death of a beautiful woman is the proper subject for poetry."[18] If anything, however, the woman more accurately evokes Victorian poetic practices, what with her embroidered sheet—a text with bird cum flowery tropes—and "her horny feet," here a meta-poetic pun for conspicuous, metrical prosody. Personified by its coroner-as-speaker, the present Modernist poem in effect certifies the death of an older American poetics.

The private "Poe" appears in a much different guise. As I argued earlier, the speaker's imperatives, or rather his imperial-sounding public performatives, mask a subjunctive anxiety/wish concerning the dead woman's *reve-nant* status. In meta-poetic terms, she conjures up Poe's paradigmatic notion of poetic beauty. For example, the scenario of the speaker with the unbeauti-ful dead woman resembles the misprision staged in Poe's "The Oblong Box." There, to recall, a persistent art-connoisseur mistakes a "plain-looking woman" for the artist Wyatt's dead, beautiful wife, whom he has kept se-cret(ed) in an "oblong pine box" (*P&T* 645). Just as Poe conceals his "most poetical topic" in "The Oblong Box," the tale, in "The Emperor of Ice-Cream" Stevens arguably disguises the death of his "mother of beauty," a revisionary version of Poe's most poetical topic.[19] On one level, both writers convert the topic into a poetic principle possessing a universal aesthetic ca-chet. On another, the topic remains utterly contingent: for Poe because, among other things, of its inwrought, autobiographical association with *his* dead mother; for Stevens because of its would-be abjection of others as the precondition for his particular poetic acts.

Like Stevens' arch–public speaker in "The Emperor of Ice-Cream," others apprehend her death (read: absence) only in the guise of an uncanny (who is she?) Poesque corpus, with her contingent remains held in *her* boxy pine-dresser. Ventriloquizing his speaker, Stevens would "Let" all such readings happen. Their effect is to preserve "Poe" or prematurely bury *him* as Stevens' privatized figure of a poetic figure. *This* "Poe" keeps returning throughout Stevens' *Harmonium* poems as a literary-ancestral trope or itself a *revenant* figure of his private writing. Within Stevens' Modernist literary milieu, Poe's poetic principles and literary-historical reputation else look as passé as the conspicuous, all-too-memorably monotonous and obtrusive prosodic "feet" of poems like "The Bells" and "The Raven."[20]

Purely conjectural, of course, the "private" as opposed to "public," i.e., manifestly literary-historical, affiliation of Poe and Stevens yet makes strange sense when one reckons with how many *Harmonium* poems lend credence to it. For example, the connection appears in the shift between stanzas VII and VIII in "Thirteen Ways of Looking at a Blackbird" (*CP* 92–95). VII rehearses Stevens' initial, Whitmanian poetic impulse:

> O thin men of Haddam,
> Why do you imagine golden birds?
> Do you not see how the blackbird
> Walks around the feet
> Of the women about you?

Why do people, starving ("thin") for visions of life, look for them writ by canonized poets ("golden birds"), when, like Whitman's poetic "leaves," a democratically accessible "blackbird" poem lies "around" their very "feet" right now? And yet Stevens' Whitmanian self-confidence becomes haunted by Poe's shadow in the next stanza:

> I know noble accents
> And lucid, inescapable rhythms;
> But I know, too,
> That the blackbird is involved
> In what I know.

Stevens acknowledges how his poetic visions depend on his imagination's necessary intercourse with things from common reality as nobly accented or transcended by poets like Whitman. Nonetheless, in the same stanza (a mini-*Harmonium* poem in its own right), he qualifies his dependence by suggesting that the "inescapable rhythms" he knows also derive from "the blackbird" poet.[21] Stevens' "But" marks a caesura of "Poe," a coded self-reference that differentiates his private sense of his stanza/poem from its less contingent if still elusive meaning for others. At least from his position, the abrupt "blackbird" insert poses a referential conundrum for them: how *is* the blackbird involved in what he knows, and can it matter for anyone else? Whatever else it means, the blacked-out transition concerns meta-poetic revivification for Stevens alone as he now happens upon it.

The same *mise en scène* occurs more explicitly in "The Worms at Heaven's Gate" (*CP* 49–50), which, along with the following two poems in *Harmonium*, "The Jack-Rabbit" and "Valley Candle," perpetuates Poe's vision of poetic inspiration in almost literal fashion. The "worms" of Stevens' poem "bring Baldroulbadour," body-part by body-part,

> Out of the tomb . . .
> Within our bellies, we her chariot.

"Baldroulbadour," a figure for imagination, refers to a princess who marries Aladdin in *The Arabian Nights*.[22] Yet in an act nothing short of verbal cannibalism and necrophilia combined—

> And, finger after finger, here, the hand,
> The genius of that cheek. Here are the lips,
> The bundle of the body and the feet

—the poem's worms, i.e., "words," quite literally resuscitate Poe's dead muse-figure into vital food for Stevens' imagination. The typographical ellipsis (". . . . . .") appearing between these lines and the poem's last line (which repeats the first), points to the gruesome thought of her literal ingestion. Scheherazade-like, the poem's worms/words metaphorically forestall death. In perverse, meta-poetic terms, they figuratively extend the life of Poe's dead and otherwise forgotten beautiful muse, and do it in a way that out-macabres Poe.

The effect is to repulse rather than entice the poem's imagined readers. What defines poetic life for Stevens means the semiotic equivalent of death (or worse) for them, although the poetic scene need not devolve on macabre matters for that to occur. Stevens can induce an analogous effect in poems the generic cues of which lead readers to expect more lighthearted than deadly serious fare. The "Br'er Rabbit" folk-tale, for example, backgrounds "The Jack-Rabbit":

> In the morning,
> The jack-rabbit sang to the Arkansaw.
> He carolled in caracoles
> On the feat sandbars.
>   (*CP* 50)

The poet begins writing his poem (carolling "caracoles") in a playful, "Uncle Remus" manner. He would celebrate his local scene with earthy, animalistic verve, as if he were some naive or poetically unambitious Whitman using accessible prosaic metrics ("sandbars") and semantic idioms suitable (an archaic meaning of "feat") to its bare-bones American topos. But in preparing readers for easy literary pleasure, the poem's speaker adds a "Raven" twist to it. A "black man" asks a now passé or here old Poesque muse-figure literally to *signify* death:

> The black man said,
> "Now, grandmother,
> Crochet me this buzzard
> On your winding sheet . . ."

Merged with Poe's, Stevens asks his dying muse—a mother of beauty become grotesque grandmother and prefiguring the dead woman in "The Emperor of Ice-Cream"—to help him make or embroider a de-Romanticized raven alias buzzard. He wishes to commemorate "The Raven," an all but dead artifact by his time, its having barely survived the "winter" of an old literary history:

> ". . . And do not forget his wry neck
> After the winter."

No lyric, whether occasional "local color" verse or transcendentalist poem (or the one dubbing for the other), can escape the blackbird's fate, in other words can avoid the intimations of its own eclipse:

> "Look out, O caroller,
> The entrails of the buzzard
> Are rattling."

As in Poe's *Eureka,* poetic death pertains to privately wrought and publicly ambitious poems alike. Still, if neither possesses perdurable value, the first kind anticipates what Poe termed its heterogeneous wrongness, for it will lack even momentary value in the public realm. With its Poesque motif, "Valley Candle" makes clear that while Stevens writes, he knows that

> My candle burned alone in an immense valley.
> Beams of the huge night converged upon it,
> Until the wind blew.
> (*CP* 51)

The wind-image echoes the public figured in "The Wind Shifts" and "To the Roaring Wind," poems discussed in Chapter 3. Construed as modest, singular efforts, Stevens' poems, each one like a "candle," at first attempt to illuminate the "immense" real for him "alone." These efforts self-evidently figure death in its common associations ("Beams of the huge night") and significance for anyone. However, if the Stevens *Harmonium* poem engages real death through condensed, poetic lenses—

> Then beams of the huge night
> Converged upon its image

—it does it only for the nanosecond in compositional time that he can refrain from considering the poem's accretion of public meanings. For the "wind" inevitably ("Until") shifts and roars. Nothing can stop the inchoate aspect of "public" winds from blowing out Stevens' candle-like visions, the enabling premise of which was precisely to elicit the private élan of their compositional genesis.

On one hand, the poem's exoteric tropes frame lived experiences "in their green going," and so mother beauty for us. On the other, Stevens' poetic revelations paradoxically derive from his effort to prolong *their* "going" or death, all as if they had not yet gone public. In "Domination of Black" (*CP* 8–9), he can accordingly ask whether visions by renowned poets, figured as royal peacocks, don't as well residually manifest a zero-semantic "cry" beyond poetic thoughts at first edged by literal death:

> I heard them cry—the peacocks.
> Was it a cry against the twilight
> Or against the leaves themselves
> Turning in the wind . . . ?

Echoing both Whitman's "leaves" and the mournful "heavy hemlocks" themes of Poe's oeuvre, "Domination of Black" is a poem concerning its inability to decide its poetic charge. Alone in a private "room," the speaker-poet, in a mood to write, entertains tropes of reality (the turning leaves and colors) invading his mind. His poetic "leaves" possess a certain derivative quality; they hook up, that is, with past or "fallen" literary tropes:

> At night, by the fire [of imagination],
> The colors of the bushes [nature]
> And of the fallen leaves [past tropes of nature],
> Repeating themselves [via literary conventions],
> Turned in the room [his scene of writing],
> Like the leaves themselves
> Turning in the wind [the literary-public domain].

The poem enacts what it depicts. Turning words turn, "leaves" fall before the speaker and us—everything turns into flickering, literary tropes, themselves troped as colorful fall leaves falling. But if all things, nature and its literary mediations, appear as if they would repeat "themselves" ad infinitum, the very repetition leads the speaker straight to thoughts of actual cum poetic death:

> Yes: but the color of the heavy hemlocks
> Came striding.
> And I remembered the cry of the peacocks.

Brought about by his own initially innocuous yet vibrant poetic musings, the sense of a cosmic real invades the speaker's scene of writing, abruptly reminding him of how other peacock-poets' works have come down to the same terminal import: poetic cries against their own annihilation.

Stevens later remarked that the "sole purpose" of "Domination of Black" was not to purvey "any ideas," but "to fill the mind with the images & sounds it contains. . . . A mind that examines such a poem for its prose contents gets absolutely nothing from it" (*L* 279; 1928). If "black" connotes death, cosmic meaninglessness, or reality radically beyond one's comprehension—

> Out of the window,
> I saw how the planets gathered
> Like the leaves themselves

—the poem's turning images also black out or reduce to non-meaning whatever meaningful meaninglessness we might wish those turnings to signify. The poem is no Modernist word-game intended to bollix readers, whether to mock them or bring them face-to-face with the poem's self-referential presence—with *its* being the only real in a world of appearance. Neither does the semiotic "domination of black" strictly work to keep the poem's readers in the dark, the futile consequences of which poems like "Tattoo" and "The Bird with the Coppery, Keen Claws" exercise ad terminum.

The quasi-infinite swirl of images and sounds existentializes Poe's cosmic, Eurekan vision, and leaves the Stevens speaker himself in the dark. Threatening to annul imaginative activity altogether, it voids everything of referential significance, including his thoughts of death's cosmic externality. The speaker's self-hypnotic ("by the fire") tropings gather both nature *and* its poetic renditions into a self-enclosed verbal universe. But rather than fueling the illusion of self-autonomy *or* its unavoidable if futile quest, verbal self-enclosure ushers in the poet's dread of claustrophobic solipsism. It leads directly to an anxious thought that there might be no outside to poetic thought: "I felt afraid. / And I remembered the cry of the peacocks." Experienced only as perplexity in "Of the Surface of Things" and as fatalist proposition in "Of Heaven Considered as a Tomb," Stevens' anxiety concerns a meta-poetic moment of death: the turning of his own words into sheer sound ("the cry") that says nothing either to others or himself.[23] He thus risks despair in writing *wholly* to fix on private scenes of writing. Without even an illusory public to believe in, the vivid "leaves" and inspiring "cries" of peacock poets and poems he at first thought to emulate turn into merely "remembered" occasions.

Stevens knows that he can take Poe's dying, beautiful aesthetic too far, a point that ultimately fastens "The Curtains in the House of the Metaphysician."[24] While writing, Stevens can drift despairingly (e.g., "It's curtains . . .") from poetic thoughts in and of a curtained interior, to those of "the firmament, / Up-rising and down-falling," finally arriving at "The last largeness, bold to see." The poetic drift of "Curtains" and "Domination of Black" all but retraces Poe's escalating effort from "The Philosophy of Furniture" (interior room) to *Eureka* (the universe) to determine a radically private aesthetic. In "The Silver Plough-Boy," Stevens underscores how it can instantaneously lead to poetic despair. Dancing over "a black field," "A black figure" wraps himself in a commonplace "sheet" that makes him appear silver. Despite his dancing "back of a crazy plough, the green blades following," the figure signifies Stevens' repetitively finite and therefore doomed effort to write a "crazy" poem that might illuminate or "silver" reality for himself:

> How soon the silver fades in the dust! How soon the
> black figure slips from the wrinkled sheet! How
> softly the sheet falls to the ground!
> (*CP&P* 42)

Dramatized all the more by its narrative compactness, the poem bespeaks the limit that Poe's shrouded figure and figure of writing represent in Stevens' own pursuit of poetic privacy.

Holding back from Poe's Eurekan "Nothingness," Stevens nevertheless does not feel compelled to accept the semiotic circuit of self-other-self governing lyric poetry's interlocutory situation: "I" come to know my vision of things by forging it in and against discursive media—language, literary exemplars, cultural constructions, and so on—synonymous with others. Instead, he would retain self-other-self-as-other, the unconscious dynamic of private but not discursive experience generally, as the communicational paradigm for his poetic acts: "I" come not to know that vision again. A later "peacock" poem in *Harmonium,* "Anecdote of the Prince of Peacocks" (*CP* 57–58), allegorizes the paradigm with decisive precision:

> In the moonlight
> I met Berserk,
>
> . . . . . .

> Oh, sharp he was
> As the sleepless.

Milton Bates thinks "Berserk" represents the subversive side of Stevens' imagination; Harold Bloom that the figure figures "the reductive element or First Idea in the imagination,"[25] the myth of discerning reality stripped of myths, as to "see the sun again with an ignorant eye" (*CP* 380). More accurately, the poem sets up a dialogue between "Berserk," or the private Stevens responsible for his poem's "sharp" dictations, and himself as his own poem's reader. How, the latter asks, can the former meaningfully reveal the " 'sun-colored' " real, or things in public light, and himself still remain " 'In the midst of sleep,' " which is to say: all the while staying focused on private, meta-poetic affairs?

The poem provides one answer to the question in the way Stevens figuratively addresses himself as if " 'wander[ing]' " or browsing " 'the bushy plain' " of his *Harmonium* poems with their own lush poetic foliage. At bottom written simply to *happen* within private scenes of writing, these poems, just as "Of the Surface of Things" proposes, now appear no less sealed from him than to his imagined readers. Nonetheless, the poems are doubly private for that, since only he can register their former and now uncannily absent process of composition:

> "You [Stevens] that wander . . .
>
> . . . .
>
> Forget so soon.
> But I [the Stevens poem] set my traps
> In the midst of dreams."

Stevens needs to remind himself that he wrote his *Harmonium* poems using tropes that, by design ("I set my traps"), would preserve his ability to go "Berserk," to let himself go, his imagination unrestricted by public performance, externally or internally construed. He sets his meta-poetic "traps" to write like a "Prince," an "Emperor," a "Hoon," but only in private.

A meta-poetic commentary on his other *Harmonium* poems, "Anecdote of the Prince of Peacocks" resists surrendering its own private point in the process. First, by staging himself as reader of his works, Stevens again "blocks" by displacing the poem's *other* readers, and in that way effectively reinforces *its* private compositional scene:

> I knew from this
> That the blue ground
> Was full of blocks
> And blocking steel.

Second, if Stevens stands for the most in-the-know reader of his poems, they all the same come back to him rife with peacock-strutting tropes shorn of meaning. The "Forms, flames, and the flakes of flames" ("Nomad Exquisite") defining his former compositional acts have become reduced to a "blue ground." Signifying only the cold residue of his once self-enlivening poetic acts, Stevens' poems now emit to himself and imagined readers alike a semantically empty or impersonal aura, an effect that "Anecdote of the Prince of Peacocks" itself reproduces.

In the present case, however, Stevens' bird-poet gambit paradoxically sets up, as he regards it, his and other readers' positive imaginative relation to his poems. To be sure, similar to the anxiety he experiences in "Domination of Black," the *Harmonium* poem's resistance to reading can result in readers' "dread / Of the bushy plain." But it can also lead to their happening upon

> the beauty
> Of the moonlight
> Falling there

in the poem's post factum appearance. From Stevens' viewpoint, the *Harmonium* poem's beauty for readers, not unlike his experience in writing "In the Carolinas," exactly lies in the poem's withholding the very meanings it initially provokes them to seek. The conclusion seems clear: he can in fact allow himself to go public without fear of violating or sacrificing his "Berserk" or private mode of composition.

"Hymn from a Watermelon Pavilion" (*CP* 88–89) advances a concise, meta-poetic manifesto of his revised, Poesque poetics of privacy:

> You dweller in the dark cabin,
> To whom the watermelon is always purple,
> Whose garden is wind and moon,
>
> Of the two dreams, night and day,
> What lover, what dreamer, would choose
> The one obscured by sleep?

Writing in private ("the dark cabin") and preferring skewed visions of reality (watermelons "always purple") need not exclusively absorb Stevens' poetic attention. After all, indulging commonplace, watermelon-like subjects in accessible ways also carries the possibility of self-invigoration:

> A feme may come, leaf-green,
> Whose coming may give revel
> Beyond revelries of sleep.

Viewed from public perspectives, a Stevens poem may even seem like a "blackbird spread[ing] its tail," refracting and showing us how "the sun may speckle." His poetry, that is, can just as easily frame the real in beautiful ways for others as dwell on its Poesque doom in meta-poetic terms. Why not, then, engage and for that matter openly greet ("hail") others in writing, especially since doing so leaves the more private dreams "Of the two" intact?

> You dweller in the dark cabin,
> Rise, since rising will not waken,
> And hail, cry hail, cry hail.

Coming out of the closet (cabin), at least becoming convinced that what one writes only *might* have value for others, can support instead of imperil a poem's private ambience. The public is no enemy to poetic privacy. Indeed, if "Hymn from a Watermelon Pavilion" refers to the fictive moment when his intention to go private or public appears in abeyance, doesn't that moment here again constitute a quintessentially private poetic concern?[26]

In retrospect, Stevens' rationale applies to his other *Harmonium* poems, too. It finally doesn't matter to him or his imagined readers whether he pursues poetic privacy or not. Stevens' métier and intention occasionally seem to pull these poems *more* toward their public import. As he writes in "To the One of Fictive Music,"

> so retentive of themselves are men
> That music is intensest which proclaims
> The near, the clear, and vaunts the clearest bloom,
> And of all vigils musing the obscure,
> That apprehends the most which sees and names,
> As in your name, an image that is sure.
>
> (*CP* 88)

He recognizes that readers want images resonating with "the obscure" alongside familiar and precise ("The near, the clear") references and meanings. Readers want images inducing imaginary, identitarian investments or, as personified, images "in whom / We give ourselves our likest issuance." But Stevens quickly imagines that readers also want more:

> Our feigning with the strange unlike, whence springs
> The difference that heavenly pity brings.

This is no qualified public poetics, a sensible accommodation of his private modus operandi with poetic visions others want or like. "To the One of Fictive Music" finally addresses his own intimate muse, but as if *also* his imagined reader's own desire for "the strange unlike"—for acts of imagination as yet absent others.

By means of his "private" logic, Stevens recovers for his poetics one aspect of Poe's Eurekan vision: its predication not of final "nothingness" but of "periodicity."[27] In a universe of never-ending process, one's private because radically heterogeneous or "wrong" relation to things forever constitutes an ineluctable truth-position. That is why Poe can assert that "no one soul is inferior to another," or that "each soul is, in part, in its own God" (*P&T* 1357). Willing to keep intact each one's private relation to things, Stevens similarly positions himself and readers in "Two Figures in Dense Violet Night" (*CP* 85–86) as similarly regarding his own works through a glass darkly.

For its main poetic principle, the poem prescribes that he "Say that the palms" or his *Harmonium* poems be "clear" to him "and . . . obscure" or "dense" to others. Here, his muse addresses *him*,[28] asking that he do better than his first and apparently unsatisfactory effort at writing a poem. We can infer that his initial attempt sprang from an overeager and perhaps a sentimental ("moist") impulse, resulting in verse accessible to any commonplace ("hotel") public:

> I had as lief be embraced by the porter at the hotel
> As to get no more from the moonlight
> Than your moist hand.

Instead, his muse would have him write densely, in "violet" obscurity:

> Use dusky words and dusky images.
> Darken your speech.

Obscuration would eliminate his sense of self-conscious crafting, the construction of his poem for its public effects. Thus, she also requests that he "Speak, even, as if I did not hear you speaking."

Guided by her prescriptive poetics, his musings would have him and us ("Two Figures") abide in a softly darkened—a private—imaginative ambience. In short, he calls for nothing less than an "in . . . violet" state of mind, something far denser than Warren and Brandeis' notion of an "inviolate" social privacy. Stevens' poetics would thereby neutralize his own and our propensity to prey buzzard-like on the real, or his wish to make, and ours to find, publicly significant visions of it in his poems. For all of the reasons I have previously rehearsed, one can never rid that impulse entirely. But for him, "one eye" of blackbird poets and readers ought always to attend the sheer, aesthetic perception of reality's contingent (here Key West) occurrence:

> Say, puerile, that the buzzards crouch on the ridge-pole
> And sleep with one eye watching the stars fall
> Below Key West.

In designating himself a "puerile," Stevens scarcely confesses to his literary anxiety as a poetic novitiate. Akin to Poe's artistic desideratum traced in "The Domain of Arnheim" and his "watching the stars fall" in *Eureka,* Stevens' poetics would disarm *any* professional poetic ambition. The private "sleep" of writing requires nothing less than that he instead exercise "the courage," as the epigraph to the present chapter has it, "to be an amateur."

4

After reading proofs for the 1923 *Harmonium* volume, Stevens felt "such a horror of it that I have hardly looked at it since it was published" (*L* 279; 1928). I agree with Joan Richardson's assessment of his remark, that while it reflects "a common experience with authors and their first products, the strength of Stevens's reaction was unusual."[29] But his reaction, I think, bespeaks less an embarrassment over *Harmonium*'s public merit than a complaint about its published appearance per se. If only during this period, writing and publishing poems count as two different matters for Stevens, the first immediate and unshared, the other abstract or theoretically shared with an anonymous public. As I have tried to argue, *Harmonium* relentlessly testifies to his early preference for private writing over its public disseminations.

Stevens wrote his "amateur" aphorism later in his career, after a period of notable poetic abstinence following the 1923 publication of *Harmonium*. In part, pressing financial and family obligations accounted for the hiatus. He subsequently resumed writing poetry for publication in the heightened public contexts of the Depression era and World War II, not to mention his own growing poetic reputation. Various critics have discussed Stevens' success or failure as a poet engaging those critical social circumstances,[30] but one thing seems difficult to deny. Despite the central role that privacy plays in his *Harmonium* regimen, one can deduce that his concerted pursuit of it became a moot issue, perhaps untenable and even scandalously irrelevant. On the contrary, the crisis-ridden times doubtless fueled Stevens' efforts to justify his writing's public value, although still in meta-poetic terms. Whatever the reason, in his later poetry, the public-private issue appears to give way to what he himself termed the reality-imagination complex and his capital quest for a "Supreme Fiction," which many critics have taken as Stevens' authorized key for decoding his entire *Collected Poems*.

The one qualification has to be *Harmonium*, where the code arguably plays a secondary role. The speaker's brash "supreme fiction" credo in "A High-Toned Old Christian Woman" suggests that Stevens there makes it serve his private poetic interests. The same motivation marks *Harmonium* poems that more explicitly thematize the binary relation of imagination and reality. If the latter looks as if it wholly grounds the former—for instance

> The mandoline is the instrument
> Of a place

—"Anecdote of Men by the Thousand" tells of imagination's "invisible" musings to the contrary:

> Are there mandolines of northern moonlight?
>
> The dress of a woman of Lhassa,
> In its place,
> Is an invisible element of that place
> Made visible.
> (*CP* 52)

Poetic imagination also negates mundane modes of imagination in "Explanation" (*CP* 72–73), where one's "embroidering / French flowers on" an "old, black dress" for a common muse figure ("Mutter") leaves in its wake a muttering option not taken:

> It would have been different,
> Liebchen,

> If I had imagined myself,
> In an orange gown,
> Drifting through space,
> Like a figure on the church-wall.

On the other hand, imagining "magnificent" imagination as "the one reality / In this imagined world" inevitably leads to the "bitter" disappointment of "Another Weeping Woman," or to a dependence on the other's imaginative response to hers that

> Leaves you
> With him for whom no phantasy moves,
> And you are pierced by a death.
>   (*CP* 25)

By contrast, Stevens represents imagination in "The Apostrophe to Vincentine" (*CP* 52–53) as the "nameless" middle term between dull, mundane reality and its "Heavenly" transfigurations:

> I figured you as nude between
> Monotonous earth and dark blue sky.
> It made you seem so small and lean
> And nameless,
> Heavenly Vincentine.

Stevens figures his own imagination to resemble a baby, an innocent relation to things, "as warm as flesh," and dressed in "whited green," i.e., in clear and lush tropes. Even if difficult to understand at first glance—

> Brunette,
> But yet not too brunette

—his tropes of imagination resonate with accessible, communicative significance. Consonant with their linguistic-literary medium, they instantiate talk with others:

> Then you came walking,
> In a group
> Of human others,
> Voluble.

In short, through language, the poet's imaginative visions, his poem's "walking" and "talking," accrue a public identity:

> And what I knew you felt
> Came then.
> Monotonous earth I saw become
> Illimitable spheres of you,
> And that white animal, so lean,
> Turned Vincentine.

Still, the "I," not others, perceives such "Illimitable" metaphoricity. As if addressing the *Harmonium* poem at large, Stevens alone comes to know "what . . . you felt." The present poem, that is, expresses his private response to the quasi-public appearance of his other poems. Their language ("talking") reflects back to him "that white animal so lean," or his own all-but-invisible, i.e., pre-public, process of composition. In relation to a public gaze that he himself internalizes, language only registers his now unidentifiable or bare ("white animal") acts of imagination. Moreover, the poem inverts both the public convention and trajectory of poetic apostrophes. If they address absent and almost always significant persons or personifications, "The Apostrophe to Vincentine" at once invokes Stevens' other *Harmonium* poems and configures them in "Heavenly" or "Vincentine" terms. Already cryptic meta-poems to readers, they become different meta-poems to him. In one sense, "Vincentine" echoes "Valentine," "[a] written or printed letter or missive, a card of dainty design with verses," and especially "of an amorous or sentimental nature, sent on St. Valentine's day to a person of the opposite sex."[31] With its allusion to the "dark blue sky" in "Heavenly" splendor, Stevens' poem also connotes a small, versified version of *Vincent* Van Gogh's *Starry Night* painting, the mini-verbal *impression* of which Stevens sends to and receives himself.

So *Harmonium*'s poetics of privacy qualifies his early imagination of imagination, too. Considering the fact that he wished to entitle his later collected poems *The Whole of Harmonium: The Grand Poem,* one can at least wonder whether Stevens doesn't also presuppose the first collection's memorable "private" motivation as affecting *their* composition as well.[32] Does he simply incorporate the penumbra of his earlier poetics in his more openly meta-poetic poems after *Harmonium*? In the event, perhaps his later abstract ruminations about imagination effect a rhetorical shield behind which he remembers "the cry of the peacocks," the inaugural élan of writing the private poem and garnishing whatever it confers on private experience at large.

To be sure, his later, scattered allusions to the public-private issue at best take the form of a Warren-Brandeis anxiety about the invasive threat that a social-technological American public sphere poses for a liberal sense of privacy:

> We no longer live in homes but in housing projects and this is so whether the project is literally a project or a club, a dormitory, a camp or an apartment in River House. It is not only that we are actually close together. We are close together in every way. We lie in bed and listen to a broadcast from Cairo, and so on. There is no distance. We are intimate with people we have never seen and, unhappily, they are intimate with us. (*NA* "Noble Rider" 18; 1942)

At other times, Stevens endows the abstract modern public with ogre-like proportions. Just as it strikes many today, so a runaway publicity-compulsion marks his mid-twentieth-century United States milieu and affects people and poets alike:

> I did not see Time magazine, but from what you say gather that someone has taken a crack at Eliot. Someone takes a crack at everybody sooner or later: not only at everybody but at everything. In the long run, as Poe said in one of his essays which nobody reads, the generous man comes to be regarded as the stingy man; the beautiful woman comes to be regarded as an old witch; the scholar becomes the ignoramus. The hell with all this. For my own part I like to live in a classic atmosphere, full of my own gods and to be true to them until I have some better authority than a merely contrary opinion for not being true to them. We have all to learn to hold fast. (*L* 606; 1947)

To his now more pervasive, media-inflated public world, Stevens responded with a rigorously consistent, private lifestyle. He surely would have known how to answer the question "Where have you gone, Joe DiMaggio?" For all its assertive tone, Stevens' practiced and stated proclivity for personal privacy resembles the harassed aspect of wider social responses to its threatened status in the modern American public realm. Privacy here becomes defensive, resigned, doomed to the expressive half-shelf-life that he formerly finessed as but one passing trope, itself part of a more offensive, private project in *Harmonium*. If his later work confronts an abstract public with an abstract private rhetoric, it does it as if coerced, like the Poe work he cites "which nobody reads."[33]

In point of fact, Stevens continued to write poetry in private scenes of writing, and not just in his well-kept-private domestic room. While walking to work alone, he wrote down poetic lines on scraps of paper in script difficult to decipher; and he wrote poems in the social milieu of fellow insurance-workers befuddled by them, and who in any case represented anything but a serious literary public.[34] He sometimes telescopes those scenes in his later poetry, for example in "An Ordinary Evening in New Haven":

> The ephebe is solitary in his walk.
> He skips the journalism of subjects, seeks out
> The perquisites of sanctity, enjoys
>
> A strong mind in a weak neighborhood and is
> A serious man without the serious,
> Inactive in his singular respect.
>
> He is neither priest nor proctor at low eve,
> Under the birds, among the perilous owls,
> In the big X of the returning primitive.
>
> (*CP* 474)

Despite his poetic successes, Stevens still prefers to regard himself an "amateur" or (in his terms) an "ephebe" poet who eschews noticeably public topics ("the journalism of subjects"). "A serious man without the serious," he poeticizes his subjects not to elicit social action by others ("the birds"), or, like owl-like thinkers, to gain a purchase on "perilous" truths about life. Instead, he seeks "the returning primitive" moment of noticing reality in "singular" terms.

A private sentiment, then, arguably informs his later as well as his early formulation of what would become his poetic conception of the "First Idea." All of us, he would state, not only live "private lives," but all our thoughts occur within an endlessly recessive private ambience: "I think that I should continue to write poetry whether or not anybody ever saw it, and certainly I write lots of it that nobody ever sees. We are all busy thinking things that nobody ever knows about" (*L* 339; 1936). One thinks *things* in private, although they devolve on the background privacy familiar enough to everyone, and so always remain prone to instant conversion into withheld thought, incipiently formed or more. Whether or not they ever get literally expressed, such thoughts abide in some Public Lost and Found Archive, at least theoretically recoverable, explainable, or quasi-accessible.

Different it is to *think* things privately and to make *that* the end of think-ing, as Poe suggests doing in "The Power of Words" (1845): "not in knowl-edge is happiness, but in the acquisition of knowledge! In for ever knowing, we are for ever blessed" (*P&T* 822). Beyond *Harmonium,* Stevens likewise can still hold to private, poetic process at the expense of its condensed and interpretable formations. A de facto public occasion, his writing can mean to elicit non-significant poetic thought, of first value to him because it redounds to a private thereness:

> It is only the way one feels, to say
> Where my spirit is I am . . .
>
> .   .   .   .
>
> To expunge all people and be a pupil
> Of the gorgeous wheel and so to give
> That slight transcendence to the dirty sail . . .
>
> .   .   .   .
>
> And then rush brightly through the summer air.
>   ("Sailing after Lunch," *CP* 120–21)

My argument has it that Stevens' affinity with Poe lies not in a different but analogously belated Romantic insistence on anti-self-conscious feeling over thought, but in their sustained literary pursuits of thought and feeling's private yield. The self-regenerating if continually elusive goal is to arrive at an enlightened ignorance of anything that discursively orients the two writers' feeling or thinking primarily toward any cohesive "public," large or small, abstract or intimate. Poe's remarks on Shelley accordingly befit a reading of Stevens' *Harmonium* poems: "His rhapsodies are but the rough notes—the stenographic memoranda of poems—memoranda which, because they were all-sufficient for his own intelligence, he cared not to be at the trouble of writing out in full for mankind. For this reason he is the most fatiguing of poets" (*E&R* 1445). Stevens' private "memoranda" might have fatigued Poe the reader, too, but not prevented him from judging them, as he does Shelley's work, "profoundly original" for the same private reason.

One needs to emphasize that Poe and Stevens write to *imagine* a write to privacy. Both writers never "rush" to literary privacy in precipitous reaction to a multi-identifiable American public's reach into their very scenes of writ-ing. In writing, both writers appreciate what Stevens terms the "heavy histor-ical sail," and both offer what to them signifies "the slight transcendence" of it for the public to share, reject, or not notice at all. Beyond that, to paraphrase Emily Dickinson's well-known poem #303, Poe and Stevens shut "the Door" to the "Divine Majority"—even to those who represent and work for whatever a good public sphere might be—and become as if "Present no more."

Notes

Introduction: Going Private

1. John Carlos Rowe rehearses the case against Poe's alleged racism in his *At Emerson's Tomb* (New York, 1997), 42–62. Terence Whalen, *Edgar Allan Poe and the Masses* (Princeton, 1999), 111–46, supplies an important corrective to the more egregious aspect of such allegations. Poe's "aesthetic ideology" appears in his critical remarks throughout his career. See, for example, "Letter to B——" (*E&R* 11): "A poem, in my opinion, is opposed to a work of science by having, for its *immediate* object, pleasure, not truth" (his emphasis). Jane Tompkins discusses Hawthorne's literary politicking in her *Sensational Designs* (New York, 1985), claiming that his literary "canonization was the result of a network of common interests—familial, social, professional, commercial, and national" (32). The political problems attached to Twain's *Adventures of Huckleberry Finn* are well known. Jonathan Arac traces their "hyper"-canonical manifestations in *Huckleberry Finn as Idol and Target* (Madison, 1997).

2. Seyla Benhabib provides a representative statement of this position: "All struggles against oppression in the modern world begin by redefining what had previously been considered private, nonpublic, and nonpolitical issues as matters of public concern . . . that need discursive legitimation." "Models of Public Space," *Habermas and the Public Sphere*, ed. Calhoun (Cambridge, Mass., 1992), 84.

3. David Freeman Hawke, *Everyday Life in Early America* (New York, 1988), 58, 19.

4. See Charles Sykes, *The End of Privacy* (New York, 1999), 99.

5. Julie C. Inness, *Privacy, Intimacy, and Isolation* (New York, 1992), 6.

6. Arendt formulates this private-public distinction in relation to the ancient Greek *polis* in *The Human Condition* (Chicago, 1956), esp. 22–37.

7. Jeff Weintraub, "The Theory and Politics of the Public/Private Distinction," *Public and Private in Thought and Practice,* ed. Weintraub and Kumar (Chicago, 1997), 37.

8. To a certain extent, this situation repeats the older association of "private" with "privative," or "a state of being deprived of something," as noted by Arendt, *The Human Condition,* 38. Focused on challenging the historical dominance of (dominant) males in defining and ad-

judicating matters of public import, feminist studies tend to valorize public over private spheres by framing the latter as always already public in some sense, e.g., "the personal is political." For an overview of feminist work on the issue of domestic privacy, see Kathy Peiss, "Going Public," *ALH* 3 (winter 1991). Peiss also worries whether "the blurring of boundaries between public and private [might] erase meaningful distinctions between the two terms" (826).

9. Nancy Dunlap Bercaw argues, for instance, that "[b]y the 1850s the household had become an extrusion of the state, involved in the institutionalization of charity, health, and childcare." "Solid Objects/Mutable Meanings," *Wintherthur Portfolio* 26 (1991), 238–39. Also see Tamara Hareven, "The Home and the Family in Historical Perspective," in *Home: A Place in the World*, ed. Mack (New York, 1993), 238–39. Hannah Arendt observes that in modern societies, "all matters pertaining formerly to the private sphere of the family have become a 'collective' concern" (*The Human Condition*, 33).

10. See the essays collected in *American Literature* 70, no. 3 (September 1998), devoted to contesting the "separate spheres" ideology.

11. Samuel Warren and Louis Brandeis, "The Right to Privacy," *Killing the Messenger*, ed. Goldstein (New York, 1989), 8, 21, 13.

12. *Ibid.*, 7. In a strictly legal context, the linkage I speak of has led to what Charles Sykes terms privacy's "decidedly mixed record in the [United States] courts" (80), the history of which he rehearses in Chapter 5 of *The End of Privacy*.

13. Carl D. Schneider succinctly depicts left-political complaints against privacy's being "a recent historical phenomenon, a luxury available only to bourgeois capitalism. The private is seen as a form of false consciousness in which communal life is sacrificed for personal possession and property claims." *Shame, Exposure, and Privacy* (New York, 1992), 152. Patricia Boling airs her "liberal" suspicion about privacy in *Privacy and the Politics of Intimate Life* (Ithaca, 1996), xi. Jeffrey Rosen argues that the private sphere marks "personal boundaries that the [liberal] state may not overstep, interior regions into which it cannot penetrate"—in other words makes government "express its respect for the inherent dignity, equality, individuality, interiority, and subjectivity of the individuals who compose it." *The Unwanted Gaze* (New York, 2000), 219.

14. Gurstein points to various media as the culprits, ranging from "mass-circulation newspapers, photographs, and advertising," to "realist" literary fiction. *The Repeal of Reticence* (New York, 1996), 47, 32.

15. Publicity of this kind existed, of course, before the nineteenth and twentieth centuries in the Western world, but as an "underground" or illegitimate occurrence directed at political leaders and disseminated among lower-class people. Robert Darnton, for example, provocatively tracks how, among other informal venues in Louis XV's eighteenth-century regime, French folk-ballads, pamphlets, and longer *libelles*, as well as plain oral gossip, penetrated "the *secret du roi* itself, even to observe the King (Louis XV) between the sheets." "Paris: The Early Internet," *New York Review of Books*, June 29, 2000, p. 46.

16. Neal Gabler, *Life the Movie* (New York, 1998), 8.

17. Foucault's "Panopticon" account occurs in *Discipline and Punish*, trans. Sheridan (New York, 1977), 195–228. The demise of privacy due to ever more sophisticated computers and advances in surveillance equipment has become a commonplace topic in legal and popular journalism. Besides Charles Sykes' book of the same title, see, for example, Reg Whitaker, *The*

End of Privacy (New York, 1999), and "The End of Privacy," *The Economist,* May 1999. Whitaker's second chapter explicitly links the modern "technologies of surveillance" to Foucault's Panopticon thesis. Of course, to define the self in terms of his/her reducibility to "information" already testifies to the panoptic inroads made by such technologies. For example, Shaun MacNeill thinks normative definitions of privacy are too "context-specific," but still proposes that we define privacy as "the condition which obtains to the degree that new information about one's self is not acquired by others." "A Philosophical Definition of Privacy," *Dalhousie Review* 78, no. 3: 438.

18. Nagel supports Wittgenstein's position in *The View from Nowhere* (New York, 1986), 36–37. Nagel also remarks how "[m]ental phenomena . . . are located, despite their subjectivity, in the objective order" (32). Dennett effectively reduces the phenomenological notion of private experience to "physical effects of the brain" in *Consciousness Explained* (Boston, 1991), 16, passim. Inness, *Privacy, Intimacy, and Isolation,* 89, states the psychoanalytic situation quoted. Postmodern strategies like Jean-François Lyotard's contest the legitimacy of any single public sphere (including Habermas' well-known ideal of a consensual one), but remain negatively entwined with it by proposing to deconstruct its discursive practices. See *The Postmodern Condition* (Minneapolis, 1984), esp. 66.

19. Henry Sussman, "A Note on the Public and the Private in Literature," *MLN* 104 (April 1989): 597. Sussman, 599–605, also uses Poe's "The Tell-Tale Heart" as a primary example of "acting out" the private in public.

20. *Oxford English Dictionary,* 2nd ed., s.v. "privacy." Other *OED* definitions of *privacy* include "places of retreat," the "[a]bsence or avoidance of publicity or display; a condition approaching to secrecy or concealment . . . reticence," "[a] private matter, a secret," and "[i]ntimacy, confidential relations." Patricia Boling discusses in detail the *OED* etymologies and variable meanings of public and private in *Privacy and the Politics of Intimate Life,* 43–47, passim.

21. Theodor Adorno and Max Horkheimer would later assign the twentieth-century "culture industry" with both organizing these disciplinary practices and propagating a commodified public complex from which no cultural activity was exempt, whether artistic, critical, or otherwise. Within that complex, the concept of "culture" itself serves a professionalized, bureaucratic function that helps construct a pervasive public realm. See *Dialectic of Enlightenment,* trans. Cumming (New York, 1972), 131. I am indebted to Michael Denning for bringing my attention to this passage, although he is not responsible for my application of it here.

22. Gurstein, *The Repeal of Reticence,* 88. Gurstein's "party of exposure" consisted of late-nineteenth- and early-twentieth-century progressives opting for "aggressive" exposés of private affairs as facilitated by new modes of public surveillance. In opposition, the late-Victorian "party of reticence" "venerated a set of intense relations in the conjugal family" (32, 28).

23. Karen Halttunen, *Confidence Men and Painted Women* (New Haven, 1982), 172. Halttunen also cites "[t]he growing theatricality of middle-class funeral ritual after 1850, with its *dramatic* focus on the corpse" (170; her emphasis).

24. Stuart Sperry, "Wallace Stevens and Poetic Transformation," *Raritan* 17 (winter 1998): 25.

25. Richard Poirier, *The Renewal of Literature* (New York, 1987), 49. James M. Cox notes

how Hawthorne initially construed writing as a "matter of secrecy—or, better, intense privacy," in his essay "Reflections on Hawthorne's Nature," in *American Letters,* ed. Kennedy (Baton Rouge, 1987), 141. In an unpublished paper (1999), " 'The manliest relations to men,' " Milette Shamir argues that Thoreau struggles in *Walden* to articulate the relation between writer and reader vis-à-vis the period's social synonyms for privacy, including those of physical distance, literal concealment, silence, and gendered friendship. Allan Silver attaches the privacy issue to Melville's "Bartleby" in "The Lawyer and the Scrivener," *Partisan Review* 3 (1991): esp. 421. Emily Dickinson (cf. poem 326, "I cannot dance upon my Toes") and Henry James also come readily to mind in this context. See Nancy Walker, " 'Wider than the Sky,' " *The Private Self,* ed. Benstock (Chapel Hill, 1988), 272–303, passim; Brook Thomas, *American Literary Realism* (Berkeley, 1997), 55–88; Janna Malamud Smith, *Private Matters* (Reading, Mass., 1997), esp. 145–72; Gurstein, *The Repeal of Reticence,* 35, passim; and Barbara Hochman, "Disappearing Authors," *ELH* 63 (1996). Twentieth-century literary examples abound, and not simply of the notorious sort, such as J. D. Salinger's and Thomas Pynchon's resistance to becoming public celebrities. For example, in pre–World War II contexts, the issue of privacy inflects Hart Crane's poetic compositions as well as the James Agee and Walker Evans' literary-photo-journalistic work on Depression sharecroppers, *Let Us Now Praise Famous Men.* See Tim Dean, "Hart Crane's Poetics of Privacy," *ALH* 8 (spring 1996), and Joseph J. Wydeven, "Photography and Privacy," *Midwest Quarterly* 23 (autumn 1981).

26. Robert C. Post, "The Social Foundations of Privacy," *California Law Review* 77 (October 1989): 964; his emphasis.

27. Harold Bloom, *The Western Canon* (New York, 1994), 288, 518–20, 36. Kent Ljungquist terms Stevens Poe's "twentieth-century cousin," although in different terms from mine. Not unlike Bloom on Stevens, Ljungquist notes that "Poe's sharp focus on individual consciousness suggests that such a battle must be fought . . . alone." *The Grand and the Fair* (Potomac, 1984), 209, 208.

28. Stevens also revises a different aspect of this Emersonian moment in "The Snow Man," which I discuss in Chapter 3.

29. Cf. Bloom's view of Stevens' "The Snow Man": "the text he produces is condemned to offer itself for interpretation as being already an interpretation of other interpretations, rather than as what it asserts itself to be, an interpretation of life." *Poetry and Repression* (New Haven, 1976), 270.

30. W. H. Auden provides indirect support for this surmise: "Occasionally I come across a book which I feel has been written especially for me and for me only. Like a jealous lover, I don't want anybody else to hear of it. To have a million such readers, unaware of each other's existence, to be read with passion and never talked about, is the daydream, surely, of every author." *The Dyer's Hand* (New York, 1962), 12. I am indebted to John William Price for bringing my attention to this passage.

31. From a Bloomian viewpoint, Stevens' clearing of the square might yet bespeak the literary-oedipal strategy Bloom terms *kenosis,* or the ephebe poet's self-interested leveling of his and major texts to commonplace status. I briefly discuss this revisionary ratio in my essay "Influence," *Critical Terms,* ed. Lentricchia and McLaughlin (Chicago, 1995), 190.

32. My thanks to Maurice Rapf, from the Department of Film Studies at Dartmouth College, whose recollections of the period helped confirm this fact.

33. James Longenbach, *Stevens: The Plain Sense of Things* (New York, 1991), 69.

34. Robert Murphy maintains that even in cross-cultural social situations, withholding oneself "while communicating" or "communicat[ing] through [physical] removal is not a contradiction in terms but a quality of all social interaction." "Social Distance and the Veil," in *Philosophical Dimensions of Privacy,* ed. Schoeman (New York, 1984), 51.

35. Frank Lentricchia, *After the New Criticism* (Chicago, 1980), 223–24.

36. Of course, not all so-called New Critics went this far. In retrospect, for example, Murray Krieger's criticism argues for art's teleological transformation of "real" history. See his *Theory of Criticism* (Baltimore, 1976), 164–65. But as noted by Bruce Henrickson, Krieger's position still implies history's subservience to poetic mandates. "Murray Krieger and the Question of History," in *Murray Krieger and Contemporary Critical Theory,* ed. Henrickson (New York, 1986), 132.

37. W. K. Wimsatt, Jr., "The Intentional Fallacy," in *The Verbal Icon* (Lexington, 1967), 5.

38. Murray Krieger, *A Reopening of Closure* (New York, 1989), 75. In *Poetry and Pragmatism* (Cambridge, Mass., 1992), Richard Poirier, citing the textual scholar G. Thomas Tanselle, notes "that 'no text—embodied on paper or film or in memory—of a literary, musical, choreographic, or cinematic work' can in fact be fully synonymous with that work, which, besides, is not itself the same as the 'work' or performative activity or thought that produced it" (16–17).

39. Louis Montrose, "Professing the Renaissance," in *The New Historicism,* ed. Veeser (New York, 1989), 20.

40. Mark Bauerlein, *Literary Criticism* (Philadelphia, 1997), 103–109. Bruce Henrickson, for example, exhibits the suspicion I speak of when he "laments the constricted and private scope" of Murray Krieger's close readings of Shakespeare's sonnets. "Murray Krieger and the Question of History," 132.

41. Ernesto Laclau and Chantal Mouffe, *Hegemony and Socialist Strategy* (London, 1985), 181.

42. For example, Mark Poster argues that "[t]he vast ability of the established authorities to gather information about individuals or groups places in question or even eliminates the distinction between the public and the private." *Foucault, Marxism, and History* (Cambridge, Eng., 1984), 114. From a neo-historical viewpoint, Brook Thomas allows that critics in bourgeois society can "designate literature as a space in which the imagination has free play," although that, too, finally "indicates that literature's freedom is defined by social practices and institutions in which the imagination is not free." *The New Historicism* (Princeton, 1991), 169, 170.

43. Henrickson, "Murray Krieger and the Question of History," 133.

44. W. J. T. Mitchell, "The Violence of Public Art," in *Art and the Public Sphere,* ed. Mitchell (Chicago, 1992), 47; his emphasis.

45. Michael North, *The Final Sculpture* (Ithaca, 1985), 221.

46. Terence Whalen adopts this critical angle in discussing Poe's "average racism" in *Edgar Allan Poe and the Masses.* See n. 1 above. Poe was a pronounced anti-abolitionist, but in his tale "The Thousand-and-Second Tale of Scheherazade," he remarks on " ' "the detestable passion of mankind for enslaving other creatures, and confining them in horrid and solitary prisons until the fulfilment of appointed tasks" ' " (*P&T* 798). Regarding the interpellative

ramifications of literary texts, Brook Thomas observes that "[i]nsofar as a text's work is measured by its popularity, a text's complexity might actually limit the amount of [cultural] work that it can do." (*The New Historicism,* 160).

47. Adam Veeser, Introduction to *The New Historicism,* ed. Veeser (New York, 1989), xi.

48. Steven Mailloux maintains that "[w]hen we focus only on the text, an author's intention, or a reader's interpretive conventions . . . there is a strong tendency to view interpretation as a private reading experience involving only an independent text (and author) and an individual reader. . . . [But] interpretation is always a politically-interested act of persuasion." "Interpretation," in *Critical Terms,* ed. Lentricchia and McLaughlin (Chicago, 1995), 126–27.

49. James M. Cox, "Reflections on Hawthorne's Nature," 142. Cox here refers to writing about Hawthorne's works.

50. Stanley Fish, *Is There a Text in This Class?* (Cambridge, Mass., 1980), 172.

51. Cf. Michael Warner's argument in "The Mass Public and the Mass Subject," *Habermas and the Public Sphere,* ed. Calhoun (Cambridge, Mass., 1992): "Public discourse from the beginning offered a utopian self-abstraction, but in ways that left a residue of unrecuperated particularity, both for its privileged subjects and for those it minoritized" (384).

52. Barbara Herrnstein Smith, *Contingencies of Value* (Cambridge, Mass., 1988), 109; her emphasis. With respect to my next point, Smith maintains that when we judge literary texts, we are "(a) articulating an estimate of how that work will serve certain implicitly defined functions (b) for a specific implicitly defined audience, (c) who are conceived of as experiencing the work under certain implicitly defined conditions" (*Contingencies of Value,* 13). Henry Simoni-Wastila discusses the philosophical implications of "radical particularity" in "Particularity and Consciousness," *Philosophy Today* 44 (winter 2000), 415–25. Retrieved April 28, 2001, from the World Wide Web:

http://www.dartmouth.edu/perl/dcis/ej-access?UMI-28241

53. V. N. Vološinov, *Marxism and the Philosophy of Language,* trans. Matejka and Titunik (Cambridge, Mass., 1986), 93.

54. Ludwig Wittgenstein, *Philosophical Investigations,* trans. G. E. M. Anscombe (New York, 1958).

55. Wittgenstein, *Philosophical Investigations,* proposition 280.

56. Henry Sussman, "*Maxima Moralia,*" *MLN* 110, no. 4 (1995): 868, 869.

57. Geoffrey Madell, *The Identity of Self* (Edinburgh, 1981), 68, 24 (his emphasis). Also cf. Simoni-Wastila's section "Causation and Particularity" in his article "Particularity and Consciousness," and Richard Rorty, *Contingency, Irony, and Solidarity* (New York, 1989), 91–92. Simoni-Wastila references Wittgenstein and Nagel (cf. n. 18 above) to support the position of phenomenological privacy. For a criticism of Rorty's inability to keep his notion of an "ironic" private realm separate from his desired "liberal" public realm, see Shane O'Neill, "Private Irony and Public Hope," in *Public and Private,* ed. d'Entrèves and Vogel (London, 2000), esp. 60–65. American Pragmatism generally accepts the epistemological aporia of the public-private distinction. For example, William James in his "Talk to Teachers" argues that "[e]very Jack sees in his own particular Jill charms and perfections to the enchantment of which we stolid onlookers are stone-cold. . . . For Jack realizes Jill concretely, and we do not." Quoted in Margaret Peterson, *Stevens and the Idealist Tradition* (Ann Arbor, 1983), 140.

58. Wittgenstein, *Philosophical Investigations,* proposition 272; Wittgenstein's emphasis.

59. *Ibid.*, proposition 248.

60. Stevens later remarked that "The Place of the Solitaires" "is a poem in motion: in motion with the activity of thought in solitude" (*L* 504; 1944).

61. A similar purposeless play defines the tenor of "Homunculus et La Belle Étoile." In the "Good light for drunkards, poets, widows / And ladies soon to be married," one can think

> the salty fishes
> Arch in the sea like tree-branches;
> Going in many directions
> Up and down.

Trope-play can even momentarily charm

> philosophers,
> Until they become thoughtlessly willing
> To bathe their hearts in later moonlight,
>
> Knowing that they can bring back thought
> In the night that is still to be silent.
> (*CP* 25, 26)

62. Henry Simoni-Wastila suggests an ethics of privacy "closely related to questions concerning self-awareness and how one should treat the subjectivity of others." "Particularity and Consciousness." But his philosophical conception risks reduction to the Warren-Brandeis axiom of an inviolate selfhood, which runs counter to the performative pursuits of privacy exhibited in my understanding of Poe's and Stevens' works. Debra Morris tries to formulate privacy as a "perverse singularity" on social-democratic principles. She uses D. W. Winnicott's "understanding of culture as a vast transitional space—neither subjective nor objective, both imagined and real. . . . by which we assert a 'right *not* to communicate.' " For Morris, the private designates "the intractable, the incongruous, the incommensurate" experience, and "signifies the necessity for a reprieve from scrutiny and public judgement, a dispensation no less real and valuable for being contingent." Morris nonetheless regards such privacy as a matter that needs to be "asserted in manifestly public ways." "Privacy, Privation, Perversity," *Signs* 25 (winter 2000): 346, 330.

Chapter 1: Poe's Secret Autobiography

1. Stephen Rachman, for instance, discusses in detail Poe's fixations on other writers' plagiarism and his own recourse to them as a strategy of his fiction, particularly as a way to "question . . . the origin of *his* language and a problem with his own 'originality.' " " 'Es Lässt Sich Nicht Schreiben,' " in *The American Face of Edgar Allan Poe,* ed. Rosenheim and Rachman (Baltimore, 1995), 51–52; Rachman's emphasis.

2. On Saussure's critically seminal notion of the anagrammatic specular name encoded in literary texts, see Geoffrey H. Hartman, "Psychoanalysis: The French Connection," in *Psychoanalysis and the Question of the Text,* ed. Hartman (Baltimore, 1978), 94, passim.

3. John T. Irwin cites this quotation in his *American Hieroglyphics* (New Haven, 1980), 42. Edward Wagenknecht, in *Edgar Allan Poe: The Man behind the Legend* (New York, 1963), 4, quotes another oft-cited and here relevant passage from Poe's *Literati* sketch of Margaret Fuller: "The supposition that the book of an author is a thing apart from the author's self is . . . ill-founded."

4. In my former essay on which the present chapter is based, I suggested "Tyler" might well have been Poe himself. See "Poe's Secret Autobiography," in *The American Renaissance Reconsidered*, ed. Pease and Benn Michaels (Baltimore, 1985), 86 n. 14. In a more informed study of Poe's "cryptographic" writings, Shawn J. Rosenheim subsequently agreed with my surmise about Tyler a.k.a. Poe. *Secret Writing* (Baltimore, 1997), 36, passim. But cf. the end of the following note.

5. This is the case with "Tyler's" putatively undecipherable cryptogram, which Terence Whalen has brilliantly deciphered: "The stars shall fade away, the sun himself grow dim with age and nature sink in years, but thou shalt flourish in immortal youth, unhurt amid the war of elements, the wreck of matter and the crush of worlds." Whalen originally deciphered the cryptogram in his article "The Code for Gold," *Representations* 46 (Spring 1994), and thought it a covert message to Virginia Poe. In *Edgar Allan Poe and the Masses,* however, he notes that "for Poe, cryptography was never entirely separate from political intrigue and political advancement" (203). Cf. W. K. Wimsatt, Jr., "What Poe Knew about Cryptography," *PMLA* 58 (1943), 759. Supporting his contention, Whalen uses John Hodgson's discovery that the cryptogram is in fact a quotation from Joseph Addison's political play *Cato* (211–15). But assuming that Poe indeed constructed the cryptogram, I agree with Whalen's first surmise that the cryptogram's deciphered message likely addresses Virginia Poe. This would make it a literary-political, i.e., relatively public, cryptogram of a still more private one, and all the more so since its reference to "the wreck of matter" adumbrates Poe's vision in *Eureka* seven years later. In any case, the Tyler/Poe cryptogram has deferred its solution (for 150 years!), making it impossible to determine either its illocutionary context or, thanks to Poe's (?) plagiarism (?) of Addison, its authorial source. With the same effect, Poe also included a second putatively undecipherable message from "Tyler," which Gil Broza finally deciphered in October 2000. "The [solved] text," Shawn Rosenheim remarks, "is clearly not by Poe, but from some unidentified novel or story of the period. But like the first cipher text, its themes (enclosure, the dangers of exposure, immortality) are absolutely typical of Poe's writing." Bokler Software, "October 13, 2000, Announcement: The E. A. Poe Cryptographic Challenge has been solved." Retrieved November 9, 2000, from the World Wide Web:
http://www.bokler.com/eapoe_challengesolution.html.
Stephen Rachman has since added a further twist to the entire Poe-alias-"Tyler" critical episode. In a personal conversation at the American Literature Association Conference, May 24, 2001, Rachman informed me and Shawn Rosenheim that he had uncovered a sentimental poem on "kissing" attributed to "W. B. Tyler," which *Graham's Magazine,* under Poe's editorship, published in 1840 before the appearance there of the two "Tyler" cryptograms. Rachman has not yet found any contemporary United States listing (including a later obituary notice) of the said personage, although his search, unlike my earlier one in 1984, promises to be far more thorough. Yet whether or not one accepts the Poe/Tyler identification (in Poesque fashion, after all, the name "Tyler" reduces to a phonetic anagram for "letter"), Tyler's two

encrypted messages suggest an intimate familiarity with Poe's style and manner of "secret writing," a marked trait of which was to provoke virtually endless speculation (*sic*) about a text's subtextual messages and/or their sources. One might argue, then, that even some actual "W. B. Tyler" perhaps wished to communicate to Poe this, his own secretly written and private or entre-nous awareness of Poe's doubly encrypted mode of such writing.

6. Paul de Man, "Autobiography as De-facement," in *The Rhetoric of Romanticism* (New York, 1984), 70.

7. For the monetary-metaphoric significance of "The Gold-Bug," see Marc Shell, *Money, Language, and Thought* (Berkeley, 1982), 5–23, and also Michael J. S. Williams, *A World of Words* (Durham, 1988), 127–40. Williams suggests that the tale, like the parchment Legrand deciphers, "reflects a hierarchy of increasing complexity and privacy of language requiring radical shifts of perspective on the part of the interpreter" (135). Unlike Legrand's attempt to limit the context in which words can mean, "The Gold-Bug" "resists a reading that would recuperate a 'lost' or 'entombed' meaning from it" (140).

8. My thanks to James M. Cox, who called my attention to this additional, anagrammatic pun.

9. Eric Partridge, *Origins* (New York, 1984), 12. Among other places, Poe expresses his distaste for allegory in his 1841 review of Edward Lytton Bulwer's *Night and Morning:* "Pure allegory is at all times an abomination—a remnant of antique barbarism—appealing only to our faculties of comparison, without even a remote interest for our reason, or for our fancy" (*E&R* 159).

10. Arthur Hobson Quinn, *Poe: A Critical Biography* (New York, 1941), 331.

11. For example, in their annotated edition of Poe's tales, Stuart and Susan Levine regard the tale's narrator in an ironic light. Introduction to "The Oval Portrait," in *The Short Fiction of Edgar Allan Poe* (Indianapolis, 1976), 62. G. R. Thompson argues for a more pervasive romantic-ironic vision in Poe's tales, only *one* of whose manifestations was the "device" of the ironic narrator. *Poe's Fiction* (Madison, 1973), 9ff, passim.

12. Mabbott 3:919–20 cites some of these sources, some literary, some in newspaper accounts of the day that "would have been familiar to most contemporary readers" (920).

13. Summarizing an argument by Albert J. von Frank, Andrew Delbanco notes that copies of European masterpieces, many of them " 'cheap engravings,' " were the sole means by which Americans during the period became familiar with them, mostly via traveling exhibitions. "Sunday in the Park with Fred," *The New York Review of Books,* January 20, 2000, p. 55 n. 2. Also cf. Poe's comment in his 1846 "Marginalia" regarding translations: "Is it not clear that . . . *a translation may be made to convey to a foreigner a juster conception of an original than could the original itself?*" (*E&R* 1405; Poe's emphasis).

14. The narrator in Poe's article imagines the small, feminine fay inspiring it as finally disappearing "into the region of the ebony flood," until he can "behold *her* magical *figure* [or trope of poetic inspiration] no more" (*P&T* 938; my emphasis).

15. Daniel Hoffman, *Poe Poe Poe Poe Poe Poe Poe* (New York, 1978), 245, passim.

16. See Clark Griffith, "Poe's 'Ligeia' and the English Romantics," *University of Toronto Quarterly* 24 (October 1954): 8–25. Thompson, *Poe's Fiction,* 82–83, agrees with Griffith's contention that Ligeia stands for a figure of German "transcendentalism" and Rowena of "dull" English "worldliness."

17. Terence Martin, "The Romance," in *The Columbia History of the American Novel*, ed. Davidson et al. (New York, 1991), 82.

18. Sidney P. Moss makes this point in *Poe's Literary Battles* (Durham, 1963), ix; also see 108 n. 63.

19. Throughout my discussions of Poe and Stevens, I use the term "fantasy" not in its pejorative sense, but akin to Richard Rorty's definition: "We call something 'fantasy' rather than 'poetry' or 'philosophy' when it revolves around metaphors which do not catch on with other people . . . because of the contingencies of some historical situation, some particular need which a given community happens to have at a given time." *Contingency, Irony, Solidarity*, 37.

20. I wish to thank Bruce Duncan, Eivind Allan Boe, and Hermann Schnackertz for providing me with information about the German word in question. The following German-English dictionaries defining the word *ritzen* as "scribe" and "scribing" were retrieved from the World Wide Web, July 2001: LEO English/German Dictionary, http://dict.leo.org; German-English On-Line Dictionary. http://www.travlang.com/GermanEnglish; and German to English Dictionary, http://dict.tu-chemnitz.de. Nineteenth-century usage allowed that *ritzen* could mean to cut or carve one's name, as on a hard surface. *Der grosse Duden: Stilwörterbuch der deutschen Sprache* (Leipzig, 1937). As Eivind Boe reminds me, variations of spelling for German words existed in different German-speaking countries until the twentieth century. This fact, combined with uncertainty about the extent of Poe's specific knowledge of German (aside from his having raided German tales), makes my connections about Poe's here a matter of pure surmise, but one I think well worth making.

21. Cf. Poe's "Supplementary Marginalia 6": "The enormous multiplication of books in every branch of knowledge, is one of the greatest evils of this age; since it presents one of the most serious obstacles to the acquisition of correct information." *The Brevities*, in *Collected Writings of Edgar Allan Poe*, ed. Pollin (New York, 1985), 521. I wish to thank Burton R. Pollin for helping me locate this reference.

22. "Magazine Writing—Peter Snook," in *Complete Tales and Poems* (New York, 1975), 564; Poe's emphasis.

23. Using Abraham and Torok's psychoanalytic framework to discuss Poe's tale in the context of "the concealment of [a repressed family] secret," Esther Rashkin notes the pun on Madeline's name. *Family Secrets* (Princeton, 1992), 136, 148, 126.

24. Quoted in Mabbott 3:1266; Poe's emphasis.

25. Ellison's personal use of nature effectively negates Emerson's ideal "transparent" relation to the "Not Me." In the spirit of Poe, one can perversely argue that his choice of Ellison's very name bears on this revision. Ellison's "l" alphabetically just so happens to come right before—hence is more literally "original" than?—*Em*erson's "m." I discuss the further ramifications of Poe's internalized revision of Emerson's vision of Nature in Chapter 3.

26. *The Viking Portable Edgar Allan Poe*, ed. Stern (New York, 1976), 21. Poe also states in this letter that "I am not ambitious—unless negatively," a point that I presently discuss.

27. Poe's religious beliefs are hardly clear, although certain critics suspect they smack of a racially motivated biblical fundamentalism. See, for example, Sidney Kaplan's introduction to *The Narrative of Arthur Gordon Pym* (New York, 1960), xxiii. Needless to say, I do not share this view, even if, to tweak scientific rationalists, Poe's comments sometimes smack of Christian

apologias, to wit: "Skepticism, in regard to apparent miracles, is not, as formerly, an evidence either of superior wisdom or knowledge. In a word, the wise now believe" (*E&R* 1386).

28. If only in retrospect, a similar motivation arguably applies to Poe's other tales. In "The Oblong Box," for example, the narrator's flippant surmise about the box's *Last Supper* contents unwittingly conveys, as I have intimated, his sense of Wyatt's Judas-like betrayal of their putative friendship. But from the revisionary perspective of "The Domain of Arnheim," it is the narrator who exemplifies a Judas-like impulse. In effect, he would betray, by wanting to make public, the artist's private relation to his artistic act, here (dis-)embodied by the wife who inspired it. Failing to grasp "her" non-representable, i.e., spiritual, status for the artist, the narrator figures both a surrogate public audience and that aspect of Poe himself who writes cryptogrammatic tales to outwit his public instead of to focus primarily on their spiritual point.

29. Jonathan Auerbach, *The Romance of Failure* (New York, 1989), 71, 38. Cf. Donald E. Pease's argument that Poe resists his American individualistic environment by inscribing in his tales a wish for a pre-nineteenth-century aristocratic community—an imaginary public sphere not beset by competitive individualism. *Visionary Compacts* (Madison, 1987), 186–91.

30. *The Brevities,* 527.

31. Poe's ironic framing of the narrator's rhetoric becomes more tenable if one keeps in mind Burton R. Pollin's observation "that Poe was fully aware of the semantics of criticism and concerned with a proper critical vocabulary. Repeatedly he condemned excess and exaggerations, which he called 'hyperism.' " *Poe, Creator of Words* (Baltimore, 1974), 16.

32. By "social order," I do not mean coercive or otherwise state-controlled forms of regulation, but rather Habermas' notion of the eighteenth-century bourgeois public sphere as depicted throughout *The Structural Transformation of the Public Sphere* (Cambridge, Mass., 1989). For example, Habermas argues: "the bourgeois public sphere may be conceived above all as the sphere of private people come together as a public," in order to "debate over the general rules governing relations in the basically privatized but publicly relevant sphere of commodity exchange and social labor" (27). Robert Holub succinctly characterizes Habermas' well-known position on critical-rational communication: "The interactive use of language compels us to provide justification. . . . The expressive use of language brings with it the obligation to demonstrate trustworthiness." *Jürgen Habermas* (New York, 1991), 15.

33. Edward A. Shils, *The Torments of Secrecy* (Glencoe, Ill., 1956), 34–35. Shils argues that the public hates "not only . . . the actions carried out and thoughts harbored in [the] private sphere," but also "the very idea of privacy." Shils makes his observation regarding Cold War espionage in mid-twentieth-century America, but I think it generally befits Poe's imaginary depiction of the mid-nineteenth-century public realm as I see it invoked in "The Imp of the Perverse."

Chapter 2: Furniture and Murder in Poe's Private Rooms

1. Regarding the issue under discussion, Alexis de Tocqueville relevantly observed: "[Americans] prefer books which may be easily procured, quickly read, and which require no learned researches to be understood. . . . Accustomed to the struggle, the crosses, and the monotony of practical life, they require strong and rapid emotions, startling passages, truths

or errors brilliant enough to rouse them up and to plunge them at once, as if by violence, into the midst of the subject." *Democracy in America,* 2 vols., trans. Reeve, ed. Bradley (New York, 1949), 2: 62. David S. Reynolds argues that Poe simultaneously took aim against the sensationalist fiction dominating his literary milieu. *Beneath the American Renaissance* (New York, 1988), 229. In the second chapter of his *Reading at the Social Limit* (Stanford, 1995), Jonathan Elmer provides a finer-wrought argument regarding Poe's position toward literary "sensationalism" as it crossed swords with "the sentimental tradition."

2. See, for example, Poe's 1842 review of Griswold's anthology of American poets in *E&R,* 553, where Poe argues for the necessity of anthologies in order for the American "public voice" to "decide upon" American poetry's "merits." Many critics have discussed Poe's predicament as a magazinist and an embattled littérateur, for example William Charvat, "Poe: Journalism and the Theory of Poetry," in *The Profession of Authorship in America* (Columbus, Ohio, 1968); Michael Allen, *Poe and the British Magazine Tradition* (New York, 1969); and Robert Jacobs, *Poe: Journalist and Critic* (Baton Rouge, 1969). Sidney Moss, *Poe's Literary Battles,* describes in detail Poe's beleaguered literary-social context.

3. Tocqueville, *Democracy in America,* 2:275. Tocqueville additionally notes how, "[a]s men grow more alike, each man feels himself weaker in regard to all the rest."

4. Michael Schudson, "Was There Ever a Public Sphere?" in *Habermas and the Public Sphere,* ed. Calhoun (Cambridge, Mass., 1992), 149.

5. Tocqueville, *Democracy in America,* 1:194. An 1836 article from the Philadelphia *Public Ledger* supports Tocqueville's observation, especially regarding the changing role of the media in the early nineteenth century: "Formerly, when politics presented only two parties, public acts and measures were the only subjects of discussion, and rigid examination of private life was deemed illiberal. . . . Now, the current and sounder doctrine is that private vice and public virtue are inconsistent." Quoted in J. M. Smith, *Private Matters,* 201–202.

6. Gordon S. Wood makes this point in *The Radicalism of the American Revolution* (New York, 1992), 83.

7. Tocqueville, *Democracy in America,* 1:136, 165. Remarking on concealed social " 'atrocities,' " a character from Jane Austen's 1818 novel *Northanger Abbey* (New York, 1971), 151, lends credence to Tocqueville's observation: " 'Could they be perpetrated without being known in a country like this where . . . every man is surrounded by a neighbourhood of voluntary spies and where roads and newspapers lay everything open?' " (151). David Flaherty argues that while early American Puritan communities promoted privacy by emphasizing the importance of individual conscience, their "communal spirit" also led them to contest privacy via "a pervasive moralism, the concept of watchfulness, the encouragement of mutual surveillance, and the suppression of self to community goals." *Privacy in Colonial New England* (Charlottesville, 1972), 15. In Gordon Wood's view, such communal vigilance continued throughout the pre-Revolutionary colonial period in America. *Radicalism of the American Revolution,* 59, passim.

8. Richard Hixson, *Privacy in a Public Society* (New York, 1987), 9, 35. Relating it to Hawthorne's works, Milette Shamir discusses the " 'penumbra' " of privacy rights in the Bill of Rights in her "Hawthorne's Romance and the Right to Privacy," *American Quarterly* 49 (December 1997): 754.

9. Hixson, *Privacy in a Public Society,* 9; Richard Sennett, *The Fall of Public Man* (New York, 1974), 54.

10. Hixson, *Privacy in a Public Society*, 18.

11. James R. Beniger, *The Control Revolution* (Cambridge, Mass., 1986), 17, 128. Beniger also cites the change from face-to-face to impersonal modes of commercial trading induced by the advent of the auction system between the 1820s and 1830s, which not only reduced the businessman's control over the United States market (144), but also led to the "publication of false news [about products and markets], fictitious bidding, and false reports of sales" (151). Poe analogously suffered loss of authorial control over his literary labor in the "magazine prison-house," yet also promoted a kind of "false" fiction by plying literary hoaxes. Cf. Michael T. Gilmore, *American Romanticism and the Marketplace* (Chicago, 1985), esp. 13: "Disappointment impelled the romantics toward textual strategies of difficulty and concealment, causing them to reconstruct in their relations to their audience the alienation they criticized in modern society." See n. 13 below.

12. Karen Halttunen describes the mid-century American middle-class "cult of sincerity" in *Confidence Men and Painted Women*, 51, passim.

13. Shamir, "Hawthorne's Romance and the Right to Privacy," 748. Michael Newbury pertinently notes how the antebellum market also produced an abstract if "conspicuous cultural stage," a social space that now allowed authors to achieve "celebrity" status beyond commercial notions of success. But this new possibility also instigated the "anonymous public's demands" for intimate knowledge of the authors themselves. In response, romantic (male) and literary-domestic (female) writers alike ambivalently played to and resisted public "intrusions" into their putatively private literary labor. Antebellum authorship thus no longer operates on the model of economic exchange, i.e., readers/consumers with a writer's work-product. Instead, literary labor repeats the contemporary slavery situation in which Southern masters could use enslaved bodies less for "free" labor than for denying any private selfhood to the other. *Figuring Authorship in Antebellum America* (Stanford, 1997), 83, 84, passim. Newbury's thesis plausibly accounts for what I have termed Poe's "private" rhetorical ploys, permitting the surmise that they reflect antebellum American society's ambivalent concerns at large about the market's alienation of both private and public spheres. As I proceed to argue throughout the present chapter, however, the problem is that Poe transgresses these concerns, too. Using Newbury's terms, one might say that Poe's fictional scenarios deliberately *invite* to make moot the anonymous public's demands to know the authorial self. On the other hand, he does so by voiding the self that the author's imagined public would appropriate, and also that he/she might think to retain in private.

14. William J. Novak, *The People's Welfare* (Chapel Hill, 1996), 117.

15. "Morning on the Wissahiccon," in *P&T*, 943. Karen Halttunen remarks that "[i]n antebellum Philadelphia, most areas were a jumble of occupations and classes, of shops and homes, of immigrants and native-born Americans." *Confidence Men and Painted Women*, 39. Sam Bass Warner, Jr., catalogues the various forms of urban "privatism" (his term) affecting mid-nineteenth-century Philadelphia in *The Private City* (Philadelphia, 1968), esp. 20, 28, 57, 62, 102 (on the public waterworks system), and 125ff.

16. Richard D. Brown, *Knowledge Is Power* (New York, 1989), 230. Regarding the publicly threatened nature of private correspondence, cf. John Quincy Adams' comments during the 1828 presidential campaign: "I write few private letters. . . . I can never be sure of writing a line that will not someday be published by friend or foe. Nor can I write a sentence suscepti-

ble of an odious misconstruction but it will be seized upon and bandied about like a watchword for hatred and derision." Quoted in Paul Johnson, *The Birth of the Modern* (New York, 1991), 932.

17. Sennett, *The Fall of Public Man*, 168.

18. Terry Castle, "Phantasmagoria," *Critical Inquiry* 15 (autumn 1989): 43. Castle discusses how a tale like "The Fall of the House of Usher" deploys the phantasmagoria-model to "destabiliz[e] the ordinary boundaries between inside and outside, mind and world, illusion and reality" (50). Paul Johnson cites both the phantasmagoria and the panorama as "devices . . . essentially aimed at increasing verisimilitude," which "the public wanted" more than "Gothic terror and romantic emotion." *The Birth of the Modern*, 154, passim. Also cf. Katherine C. Grier, *Culture and Comfort* (Washington, D.C., 1988), 171. From one angle, the new "visual media and techniques of communication" underscore the impersonality of the public marketplace. According to James Beniger, contemporary advertisers, for instance, employed them "to stimulate and control consumption" (*The Control Revolution*, 274), a situation satirized by Poe in "The Business Man" (1840). From another angle, visual media add invasive potential to the economic-industrial complex insofar as they ideologically induce persons to regard themselves as commodities for public consumption.

19. Edgar Allan Poe, "The Daguerreotype," in *Classic Essays in Photography*, ed. Trachtenberg (New Haven, 1980), 37, 38; Poe's emphasis. Cf. Johnson, *The Birth of the Modern*, 158.

20. William A. Pannapacker, "A Question of 'Character,' " *Harvard Library Bulletin* 7 (fall 1996): 18.

21. Sennett, *The Fall of Public Man*, 27.

22. Halttunen, *Confidence Men and Painted Women*, 36.

23. Elmer, *Reading at the Social Limit*, 172.

24. Robert H. Byer, "Mysteries of the City," in *Ideology and Classic American Literature*, ed. Bercovitch and Jehlen (New York, 1986), 226, 227.

25. Most notably among Poe critics, J. Gerald Kennedy discusses Poe's relation to the period's fascination with death and its effect on his writing. See *Poe, Death, and the Life of Writing* (New Haven, 1987), esp. 5.

26. Kennedy, however, sees Poe's tale expressing a proto-Heideggerian notion of "anticipation," wherein "one's own death is the origin and principle of individual Being." *Poe, Death, and the Life of Writing*, 179.

27. Reynolds, *Beneath the American Renaissance*, 238.

28. Mabbott 2:679 notes that Poe's tale explicitly referred to the *Blackwood's* genre, and that Poe "sought and combined with modifications stories in the *Blackwood* manner—that is, sensational accounts of terrible experiences usually told in the first person" and using "some factual material" whose "sources were stories that had wide circulation at the time."

29. Poe refers to "lateral passes" as entrancing the eponymous character in "The Facts in the Case of M. Valdemar" (1845; *P&T* 836). With the reader's attention solely focused on the narrative "I," Poe also can be said to adopt another common inductive method of mesmerism, namely the eye-fixation of the mesmerist on the subject. To a certain extent, the tale's pendulum-like movement evokes the monotonous, eye-tiring use of an object to hypnotize subjects. Although that technique arose largely from the work of a Scottish physician, James

Braid, in the mid to late 1840s, one might say that Poe presciently transforms his narrative into just such an object. See William Edmonston, *The Induction of Hypnotism* (New York, 1986), 62–103.

30. Jeremy Bentham, *The Panopticon Writings,* ed. Bozovič (London, 1995), 48; his emphasis.

31. Foucault, *Discipline and Punish,* 205.

32. Quoted in Robert Post, "The Social Foundations of Privacy," 996.

33. See, for example, Poe's 1844 "Marginalia": "The *identical* arguments used to sustain Mr. Bentham's positions, might, with little exercise of ingenuity, be made to overthrow them" (*E&R* 1339; his emphasis).

34. Foucault, *Discipline and Punish,* 200.

35. One work was by Thomas Dick, published in 1815. Juan Antonio Llorente had written the other historical work on the Inquisition, first published in English in 1829, from which "The Pit and the Pendulum" takes "some unifying threads and one of its most outstanding features" (Mabbott 2:679–80).

36. Poe frequently puns on proper names throughout his tales, and not just in early comic-satirical ones like "Loss of Breath" (1832) and "King Pest" (1835). I have already referred to his puns on "Dupin," "William Wilson," and "William Legrand" in Chapter 1.

37. John Limon makes this connection in a different context. He regards the "room" allusion as an epistemological trope for the narrator's being "trapped within [empirical] consciousness," so that Lasalle's "name may imply that one is never quite removed from the locked and Lockean room." *Fiction in the Time of Science* (New York, 1990), 110, 111. Cf. Steven Carter, "From Room to Room," *Poe Studies* 31 (1998): 35. As for Poe's use of bilingual puns, see n. 65 below.

38. Norbert Elias refers to this "La Salle" throughout his book *The Civilizing Process,* trans. Jephcott (New York, 1978).

39. See Whalen, *Edgar Allan Poe and the Masses,* 157. A serialized section of *The Journal of Julius Rodman* appeared in the same 1840 volume of *Burton's Gentleman's Magazine* as "The Philosophy of Furniture." Kenneth Silverman notes that *The Journal* was taken to be "factual" by the United States Senate in the same year. *Poe: Mournful and Never-ending Remembrance* (New York, 1991), 147.

40. Halttunen, *Confidence Men and Painted Women,* 58.

41. Clifford E. Clark, "Domestic Architecture," in *Material Life in America, 1600–1860* (Boston, 1988), 538, 539. Conflating frontier with domestic literary topoi admittedly elides their combustible associations with gendered ideology. Throughout *West of Everything* (New York, 1992), Jane Tompkins argues that the nineteenth-century American frontier symbolized an ever-vanishing, idealized refuge for males precisely *from* a feminized domestic sphere, particularly as associated with the northeastern cultural establishment.

42. Shamir, "Hawthorne's Romance and the Right to Privacy," 752. Shamir emphasizes Hawthorne's attempt to strike a balance between private and public concerns. Michael P. Kramer similarly discusses Hawthorne's view of language in *Imagining Language in America* (Princeton, 1992), 164–84. Richard Sennett, *The Fall of Public Man,* 91, notes how the private and public spheres worked to check each other in pre-nineteenth-century European societies. David Leverenz reads Hawthorne's tale in an opposite sense to Shamir, arguing that the

Minister/tale's "inscrutable veil . . . arouses in [us an interpretive] will to power." *Manhood and the American Renaissance* (Ithaca, 1989), 230. The Minister, that is, wears the veil as a *public* exemplum: to show others how people wrongfully veil their privacies from each other and God. But if the Minister (or tale) at all represents this public charge, he does so in such an ambiguous, misinterpretable manner as to make even more intractable the very privacy he would "out." Cf. Newbury, *Figuring Authorship in Antebellum America*, 97–105, where he discusses Hawthorne's internalization of this issue through Dimmesdale in *The Scarlet Letter*.

43. Silverman, *Poe: Mournful and Never-ending Remembrance*, 149.

44. Shamir, "Hawthorne's Romance and the Right to Privacy," 756.

45. All references to Loudon's work are from *Loudon Furniture Designs* (Yorkshire, England, 1970). Grier, *Culture and Comfort*, 132, cites the work's contemporary influence and frequent reference in magazines like *Godey's*, as does Gail Kaskey Winkler and Roger W. Moss, *Victorian Interior Decoration* (New York, 1986), 3.

46. On these subjects, Poe takes the high if still modest and unexceptional aesthetic road on middle-class decorative habits. For example, according to William Seale, *Recreating the Historic House Interior* (Nashville, 1979), 81, the "most frequently used" Brussels carpet "had strong colors . . . and it was produced in intricate designs"—precisely the two elements to which Poe objects in carpets.

47. Loudon, *Loudon Furniture Designs*, 131.

48. So, too, the room lacks the aura of Romantic angst that Yves Bonnefoy thinks marks Poe's enigmatic furnishings in his fiction and poetry. "Igitur and the Photographer," *PMLA* 114 (May 1999): 334. According to Bonnefoy, this anxiety derives from the pervasive gestalt of the period's new photographic technology. In contrast to paintings, photographs delineate things such that they become vulnerable to chance. But as we have seen, Poe in fact touts the eclipse of pictorial art by the daguerreotype.

49. Grier, *Culture and Comfort*, 3; Halttunen, *Confidence Men and Painted Women*, 59. Halttunen provides a rationale for linking Poe's piece on etiquette, an even shorter magazine filler appearing six years later in *Godey's Lady's Book*, with "The Philosophy of Furniture." She argues that "after 1830, etiquette, like fashionable dress, was becoming a powerful force shaping the social life of the American middle-class parlor" (92).

50. Ronald J. Zboray and Mary Saracino Zboray, "Books, Reading, and the World of Goods in Antebellum New England," *American Quarterly*, 48 (December 1996): 621, 603. The Zborays further note how household "literary goods" mostly served "traditional social ends" by "maintaining networks of family and community," rather than fostered any "self-centered connection to literature" (603–604). The exception was the ersatz privacy associated with a certain kind of literary activity. For example, in some of the period's middle-class homes, a "library [was] usually located . . . in a more quiet part of the house . . . for the gentleman who 'has either professional occupations, or literary taste.' It had its own side entrance so that his comings and goings would not disturb the rest of the family." Clark, "Domestic Architecture," 542.

51. Schivelbusch, *Disenchanted Night* (Berkeley, 1988), 28. This situation dovetails with Poe's mention of the Philadelphia waterworks system (see n. 15 above). At the time Poe wrote his article, Philadelphia had in fact inaugurated a publicly visible because "controversial and very expensive Schuylkill water works . . . the first of their kind in the nation" to prevent "recurrent summer fevers." S. B. Warner, *The Private City*, 81.

52. Seale, *Recreating the Historic House Interior,* 83.

53. As the century progressed, curtains or window shades to block out " 'prying eyes' " were used more and more, thus to minimize the " 'fear at imagining some outside spectator gazing into our apartments during the evening hours.' " Quoted in Winkler and Moss, *Victorian Interior Decoration,* 162. Johnson, *The Birth of the Modern,* 155, notes the period's attraction to "the most gigantic effects" of public-theatrical panoramas and the like. Burton R. Pollin has reminded me that Poe's "Kaleidoscope" culprit was actually David Brewster, not Bentham. Kenneth Ames discusses how furniture items like Poe's served as "props" for "the major performances that took place in the highly self-conscious realm of the highly furnished parlor." Ames also remarks on the gendered significance of "two large chairs" typically found in Victorian American parlors. *Death in the Dining Room* (Philadelphia, 1992), 190, 194, 195. These furnishings are notably absent in Poe's room.

54. David Leverenz persuasively discusses the competitive ethos besetting the period's constructions of "manhood" and their effect on the works of male "American Renaissance" writers. See *Manhood of the American Renaissance,* esp. Chapter 3. Elaine Tyler May also cites the anxiety of "economic self-mastery" attendant on "manhood" during this period. "Myths and Realities of the American Family," in *A History of Private Life,* vol. 5, *Riddles of Identity in Modern Times* ed. Prost and Vincent (Cambridge, Mass., 1991), 542–43. Explicating Angelina Grimké's antebellum views of domestic privacy as espoused by white middle-class women writers like Catharine Beecher, Katherine Henry notes its "theatrical" or pseudo-private formation and its de facto support of political-ideological quiescence. "Rhetoric of Exposure," *American Quarterly,* 49 (June 1997): 337, 331, passim. Karen V. Hansen argues that domesticity itself constituted a kind of informal public sphere composed of men and women exchanging "numerous goods and services," all "built on the principle of mutual obligations binding neighbors and kin" alike. "Rediscovering the Social," in *Public and Private,* ed. Weintraub and Kumar, 280.

55. In his 1848 "Marginalia," Poe speaks about punctuation in a similar manner: "There seems to exist a vulgar notion that the subject is one of pure conventionality, and cannot be brought within the limits of intelligible and consistent *rule.* . . . I shall, hereafter, make an attempt at a magazine paper on 'The Philosophy of Point' " (*E&R* 1425; Poe's emphasis).

56. Jack Larkin, *The Reshaping of Everyday Life* (New York, 1988), 11.

57. Rochelle Gurstein, for example, argues that such activities "leave us defenseless precisely because we are not our usual selves at those moments: a person asleep, like a person lost in pleasure or pain, surrenders normal consciousness." *The Repeal of Reticence,* 11.

58. Robert Gerstein, "Intimacy and Privacy," in *Philosophical Dimensions of Privacy,* ed. Schoeman (New York, 1984), 267.

59. Laura Saltz, " '(Horrible to Relate!),' " in *The American Face of Edgar Allan Poe,* ed. Rosenheim and Rachman (Baltimore, 1995), 255. Cf. my remarks on "The Purloined Letter" in the Introduction.

60. Tocqueville, *Democracy in America,* 1:99.

61. John T. Irwin, "A Clew to a Clue," in *The American Face of Edgar Allan Poe,* ed. Rosenheim and Rachman (Baltimore, 1995), 141, 143.

62. It also does more than this, of course. Burton R. Pollin points out the many plot-mishaps (geographical, architectural, the ape's alleged vocal sounds resembling human ones,

and so on) that Poe commits in this tale, most of them bound to be overlooked given the reader's desire for mystification. "A Web Unravelled," in *Insights and Outlooks* (New York, 1986), 101–21.

63. John T. Irwin makes the same connection in *The Mystery to a Solution* (Baltimore, 1994), but for the purpose of psycho-biographical exposé, specifically Poe's "need to be mothered" turning into his "fear of being smothered, of being buried alive in the womb of the family" (231).

64. Pollin, *Poe: Creator of Words*, 15. See my discussion of "Ritzner" in Chapter 1.

65. Pollin, "A Web Unravelled," 109, suggests that the women's surname possibly derived "from Marshal Timoléon d'Espinay or perhaps from the more celebrated female Louise Florence Epinay, writer and intimate friend of Grimm and Rousseau." But Poe sometimes uses cross-linguistic puns as well as plays on proper names (see n. 36 above). In *Arthur Gordon Pym*, for example, the dog Tiger's arbitrarily invoked rescue of Pym (*P&T* 1027) all but literally represents a deus ex machina, where "deus" = "god" = anagram for "dog." Regarding the present tale, John T. Irwin notes how Dupin solves the crime on the basis the window's nail, the French word for which is *clou*. "A Clew to a Clue," 148. But if the pun evinces a plausible word-game that Dupin plays with the narrator (both of them being French), it remains implausibly detectable by the American mass-reader. The tale also positions readers able and avid to detect such puns to enact a word-hunting that mimics, or "apes," Dupin's deductive method. Just as he does with his cryptograms generally, so Poe does with *clou*, the point of which, one-upmanship of readers or simply a pro tem playful literary concealment, finally remains indeterminable.

66. Karen Halttunen catalogues the period's popular journalistic accounts of domestic homicides, many committed by husbands against wives, in Chapter 5 of *Murder Most Foul* (Cambridge, Mass., 1998). She argues that the "privatization of the family enhanced the mystery" genre by showing how "deeply familiar, mundane household activities" could "become terrible, alien, mysterious, once they were exposed as preludes to domestic murder." Raising the issue of how "the competing demands of the new domestic privacy and traditional communal surveillance and intervention" ought to "be negotiated," the often lurid accounts at once worked to reinforce "the sentimental family ideal" and to expose its vulnerability to the violent reactions stemming from the loss of the "traditional patriarchal family." *Murder Most Foul*, 143–44, 168. Poe's tale superficially lends itself to Halttunen's thesis. Yet with its emphasis on Dupin's analytic perspective, "The Murders in the Rue Morgue" hardly supports sentimental notions of domestic privacy, nor does it adopt the genre's sensationalist ploy to capture the public's prurient curiosity or need "to discover that other American families were really getting [the domestic ideal] wrong" (*Murder Most Foul*, 169). At the same time, Dupin effectively exposes the inadequacy of "communal surveillance" (e.g., the neighbors and the police) in resolving the domestic murders. The tale also turns the issue of any patriarchal threat into the contingent happenstance of a dumb animal. In short, if Poe would in effect murder the ideal of domestic privacy, he does the same with its recidivist, public alternatives.

67. Allan Silver, " 'Two Different Sorts of Commerce,' " in *Public and Private*, ed. Weintraub and Kumar (Chicago, 1997), 48–49.

68. "Disappearing Authors," 186.

Chapter 3: Falling Stars

1. Unless otherwise specified, all emphasis in quotations from *Eureka* refer to Poe's.

2. *Poe: Mournful and Never-ending Remembrance,* 531.

3. Joan Dayan, *Fables of Mind* (New York, 1987), 20–21, 33, passim. Dayan gives a close reading of *Eureka*'s epistemological influences. Cf. Daniel Hoffman, *Poe Poe Poe,* 286. Hoffman also makes the Freudian connection, 239. Jonathan Elmer situates *Eureka* in its mass-cultural context, *Reading at the Social Limit,* 222. Barbara Cantalupo provides a valuable overview of past and recent critical takes on *Eureka* in "*Eureka:* Poe's 'Novel Universe,' " in *A Companion to Poe Studies,* ed. Carlson (Westport, Conn., 1996), 323–44.

4. Edward H. Davidson, *Poe: A Critical Study* (Cambridge, Mass., 1957), 226.

5. Dayan, *Fables of Mind,* 32, and Hoffman, *Poe Poe Poe,* 274.

6. The public orientation of *Eureka* seems all the more true for Poe's having first delivered it as a two-hour-plus lecture in February 1848. Moreover, its topic alone points in that direction. For example, Habermas notes that "[w]hereas the scholastic concept of science referred only to 'disciplines designed in view of certain optionally chosen ends,' the cosmical concept of science was one 'which relates to that in which everyone necessarily has an interest.' " *The Structural Transformation of the Public Sphere,* 106.

7. Quoted in Dayan, *Fables of Mind,* 35.

8. Dayan conversely argues that in "choosing the limited vista [the Universe of stars] rather than the indefinite extent," Poe ventures something "quite unorthodox in American thought," in effect opposing "manifest destiny ideology, as well as . . . the sublime nature of the Hudson River painters and the godlike eye of the Orphic poets." *Fables of Mind,* 25.

9. *Eureka,* 1271, 1335, 1342, 1321, and 1353, respectively.

10. Two months before *Eureka*'s publication, Poe underscored this point in a reported conversation with someone otherwise supportive of his work, exclaiming " ' "My whole nature utterly *revolts* at the idea that there is any Being in the Universe superior to *myself*." ' " Dwight Thomas and David K. Jackson, *The Poe Log* (New York, 1987), 731; emphasis included.

11. Poe's disquisition arguably competes for public attention with Nichol's "popular" work on nebular cosmology. According to Kenneth Silverman, a week before Poe's lecture on "The Universe," Nichol actually "began a series of lectures on astronomy" in New York City, which were "widely praised" in the press. By comparison, Poe's received "only a brief account." *Poe: Mournful and Never-ending Remembrance,* 531, 532. In positing a non-locatable or divine center, Poe specifically revises Nichol's theory about an actual central orb toward which cosmic bodies are being drawn by gravity (*Eureka* 1287, 1346–47).

12. See Limon, *Fiction in the Time of Science,* esp. 82–93. Dayan, *Fables of Mind,* 52–53, shows Poe's reliance on Kantian thought despite his sarcastic allusion to "Cant" in *Eureka.* Even the text's quasi-scientific grounding flirts with being a coded riposte to favored American genres of science. For example, Tocqueville noted how "hardly anyone in the United States devotes himself to the essentially theoretical portion [of science] which is immediately requisite to application." *Democracy in America,* 2:43. Of what practical value is cosmology, especially given Poe's formulation of it?

13. Ralph Waldo Emerson, *Nature,* in *Emerson: Essays and Lectures,* ed. Porte (New York, 1983), 10; my emphasis. All references to Emerson's essays are taken from this edition.

14. Emerson, "Experience," 480, 481, 474, 481, and 489, respectively. Cf. Emerson, *Nature*, 9: "I am not solitary whilst I read and write, though nobody is with me."

15. John Dewey would later formulate the issue in precisely these "public" terms: "Human beings combine in behavior as directly and unconsciously as do atoms . . . from external circumstances, pressure from without. . . . But no amount of aggregated collective action constitutes a community. . . . 'I' and 'mine' appear on the scene only when a distinctive share in mutual action is consciously asserted or claimed." *The Public and Its Problems* (Athens, Ohio, 1954), 151–52.

16. *Nature*, 9, 10.

17. Poe clearly associates atomic effects with language-use. In "The Power of Words" (1845), one of the two posthumous speakers states: "And while I thus spoke [in my past life to you], did there not cross your mind some thought of the *physical power of words?* Is not every word an impulse on the air?" (*P&T* 825; Poe's emphasis).

18. W. C. Harris takes an obverse view of *Eureka*, arguing that it "is socially marked" by the foundational texts of the American republic, the Declaration of Independence and the Constitution, and in particular addresses the "the federal enigma" of "*e pluribus unum.*" "Poe's *Eureka* and the Poetics of Constitution," *American Literary History*, 12 (spring/summer 2000): 22, 3. But in engaging the social-political charge Harris attributes to it, *Eureka* perforce instigates the kind of ambition Poe simultaneously attempts to arrest here and elsewhere in his work. Quite literally, *Eureka*'s abstract cosmological discourse displaces—places off-stage or privatizes—its social-political imbrication and the literary ambition endemic to it by framing *them* as fictions.

19. Elmer, *Reading at the Social Limit*, 222.

20. See Käte Hamburger's discussion of "genuine" and "non-genuine," i.e., fictional, uses of the preterite in *The Logic of Literature* (Bloomington, 1974), 80, passim. Regarding the connection between cosmic "lightning-flashes" and poetry, cf. Wallace Stevens' "Adagia": "A poem is a meteor" (*OP* 185).

21. Timothy Scherman, "Authorship and the Problem of Poe's Public Double," unpublished paper delivered at the International Edgar Allan Poe Conference (Richmond, Va., October 1999). For a succinct review of the tale's criticism, see Scott Peeples, *Poe Revisited* (New York, 1998), 148–51.

22. Peeples, *Poe Revisited*, 150.

23. Jonathan Elmer, "The Jingle Man," in *Fissions and Fusions* (Rondebosch, South Africa, 1997), 144.

24. For the Symboliste connection, see, for example, A. Walton Litz, *Introspective Voyager* (New York, 1972), 144–45, and Melita Schaum, *Stevens and the Critical Schools* (Tuscaloosa, 1988), 35. In Stevens, *The Making of "Harmonium"* (Princeton, 1967), Robert Buttel argues generally that Stevens overcame the Symboliste influence in his later *Harmonium* poems (240–41, 247). Recent critics have pointed out Stevens' rejection of the Symboliste poets' quest for "transcendent" meaning (Bové) along with "the absolute authority" (Rae) they accorded themselves in revealing it. Paul Bové, *Destructive Poetics* (New York, 1980), 200, and Patricia Rae, *The Practical Muse* (Lewisburg, 1997), 33–34.

25. *Stevens and the Critical Schools*, 55.

26. Powys, quoted in Schaum, *Stevens and the Critical Schools*, 42; Yvor Winters, "Wallace Stevens; or the Hedonist's Progress," in *In Defense of Reason* (Denver, 1947), 439.

27. Joseph Riddel, "The Climate of our Poems," in *Critical Essays on Wallace Stevens,* ed. Axelrod and Deese (Boston, 1988), 151.

28. Eleanor Cook, "Riddles, Charms, and Fictions," in *Critical Essays on Wallace Stevens,* ed. Axelrod and Deese (Boston, 1988), 173.

29. Walt Whitman, "Passage to India," in *Poetry and Prose,* ed. Kaplan (New York, 1982), 531. Subsequent references to Whitman's work are from this edition.

30. See n. 30, Chapter 6.

31. "Song of Myself," 88.

32. Harold Bloom, *Stevens: The Poems of Our Climate* (Ithaca, 1976), 83; Eleanor Cook, *Poetry, Word-Play, and Word-War* (Princeton, 1988), 71; Longenbach, *Stevens: The Plain Sense of Things,* 81.

33. Margaret Peterson tries to mitigate this reading of the poem by suggesting its ironic depiction of "the idealist's . . . wholly conceptual world of abstractions which admit no perceptual reality." *Stevens and the Idealist Tradition,* 108.

34. Cf. "Grand Is the Seen," in which Whitman contemplates the universe's "multiform, puzzling, evolutionary" laws, and claims that "the soul of me" comprehends "all those, / Lighting the light, the sky and stars" (653).

35. Andrew Lakritz, *Modernism and the Other* (Gainesville, 1996), 33. On different grounds, George S. Lensing also links "The Snow Man" with "Stars at Tallapoosa." He argues that the former "sets forth the possibility of the psyche divesting itself of subjectivity in the act of embracing pure something," yet that the poem ultimately acknowledges one cannot escape the pathetic fallacy inasmuch as "that ultimate decreation remains unachievable this side of mortality." Lensing reads the trajectory of "Stars at Tallapoosa" similarly, but without the alternative "misery" response implicit in "The Snow Man." In "Stars," Stevens' "intensely joyous rendezvous with reality"—for example, the image of his eye's beholding its black lid suggests his wish to emulate the "purer" star-lines—"is not absolute and hence imperfect"; but the secretive poetic hunter's quest for such perfection clearly holds a positive and even an "erotic" attraction for Stevens, as manifested "by the force of the poem's own dazzling and breathless display." Lensing, *Wallace Stevens and the Seasons* (Baton Rouge, 2001), 137, 141, 162.

36. Peterson, *Stevens and the Idealist Tradition,* 182.

37. Bloom, *Stevens: The Poems of Our Climate,* 61.

38. Cook, *Poetry, Word-Play, and Word-War,* 48.

39. Ibid., 28.

40. Mervyn Nicholson, "The Riddle of the Firecat," *Wallace Stevens Journal* (hereinafter *WSJ*) 22 (fall 1998): 134. Kia Penso, argues that "Earthy Anecdote" resists explanations and itself strives to become "an object of experience." Penso specifically claims that the poem expresses the opposite view of poetry espoused by Poe in "The Philosophy of Composition": in effect reducing poetry to its "most transparent mechanical effects," Poe denies "Stevens' concept of the 'potency' or 'resistance' of a poem." *Stevens, "Harmonium," and the Whole of "Harmonium"* (Hamden, Conn., 1991), 23, 24. But by clearly allegorizing that resistance, "Earthy Anecdote" in fact mimics the "private" effect of Poe's *commentary* on "The Raven."

41. Peeples, *Poe Revisited,* 96–97.

42. Ibid., 97.

43. Milton J. Bates, *Stevens: A Mythology of Self* (Berkeley, 1985), 152. John Miles agrees that the poem's resistance to "the interpretations it evokes is its essential quality." But Miles goes on to read the poem as "an epistemological parable" along the lines of American pragmatist thinkers. He argues that the "nonexistent firecat" finally embodies "the animal faith that keeps us on the move" in a God-less, modern world. "An Encounter with the Firecat," *WSJ* 22 (fall 1998): 118, 117, 119, 129.

44. Cook's observation about Oklahoma occurs in *Poetry, Word-Play, and Word-War,* 29. Regarding my surmise, cf. Richard Hixson's association of the frontier with private pursuits in Chapter 1.

45. Bates, *Stevens: A Mythology, of Self,* 152.

46. Cook, *Poetry, Word-Play, and Word-War,* 114, and Buttel, *Making of Harmonium,* 129.

47. Cook, *Poetry, Word-Play, and Word-War,* 113.

48. Bates, *Stevens: A Mythology, of Self,* 103.

49. Cook, *Poetry, Word-Play, and World-War,* 113.

Chapter 4: *Harmonium:* Private Man, Public Stage

1. The title of my chapter plays on that of Mary Kelley's important work on nineteenth-century American "literary domestic" writers, *Private Woman, Public Stage* (New York, 1984). Kelley's book focuses on the difficulties women writers encountered in translating their private domestic lives into public venues. Stevens' temperamental penchant for privacy appears throughout his career, for example in an early journal entry for 1906: "Took my customary ramble yesterday—with three, for company. I detest 'company' and do not fear any protest of selfishness for saying so" (*SP* 163–64). He acted the same way in workplace and personal situations, including those with artistic friends during the *Harmonium* period. Besides Stuart Sperry's previously cited article in n. 24 of the Introduction, see Thomas C. Grey, *The Wallace Stevens Case* (Cambridge, Mass., 1991), 16, and John T. Newcomb, *Wallace Stevens and Literary Canons* (Jackson, Miss., 1992), 69, 70.

2. Untermeyer's remarks are quoted in Schaum, *Stevens and the Critical Schools,* 45; Schaum further cites Mark Van Doren's prediction that on the basis of his *Harmonium* poems, "Stevens would never become popular" (54). Other citations in this paragraph are respectively from: Newcomb, *Wallace Stevens and Literary Canons,* 9; Thomas B. Byers, *What I Cannot Say* (Urbana, 1989), 21–22; C. Roland Wagner, "Wallace Stevens: The Concealed Self," in *Wallace Stevens and the Feminine,* ed. Schaum (Tuscaloosa, 1993), 122; and Mark Halliday, *Stevens and the Interpersonal* (Princeton, 1991), 5.

3. William Sullivan, *Reconstructing Public Philosophy* (Berkeley, 1986), 19–21, 76–79, passim, argues that the liberal-individualist ethos as derived from Hobbes and Locke helped underwrite the separation between public and private realms by assuming that the individual's "contract" with society submits private life to a scientific-economic regimen. Habermas notes how in capitalism's configuration of the nineteenth-century public sphere, "[p]rivate persons came to be the private persons of a public rather than a public of private persons." *The Structural Transformation of the Public Sphere,* 128–29.

4. Beniger cites these occurrences in *The Control Revolution,* 19, 424–26, passim. Also see his Table 8.1 on 353.

5. Hixson, *Privacy in a Public Society,* 35.

6. Thomas Schlereth, *Victorian America* (New York, 1991), 116; Harvey Green, *The Uncertainty of Everyday Life* (New York, 1993), 170, 9.

7. Beniger, *The Control Revolution,* 271–74, 356; about statistical data, 309. Joan Richardson notes Wilson's use of advertising in *Stevens, a Biography: The Early Years* (New York, 1988), 461. Demonstrating a cultural-imperialist bent, so-called World Expositions, begun in the nineteenth century, advertised United States technological prowess vis-à-vis an international public arena. See Robert W. Rydell, *All the World's a Fair* (Chicago, 1984), 3.

8. Michael Kimmel, *Manhood in America* (New York, 1996), 197.

9. "The Right to Privacy," 8, 13.

10. Tim Dean, "Hart Crane's Poetics of Privacy," 103.

11. Rochelle Gurstein discusses many of these topics in compelling detail throughout her *Repeal of Reticence.*

12. For Sennett, "the fall of public man" was due to the "profound dislocation which capitalism and secular belief produced in the last century. Because of this dislocation, people sought to find personal meanings in impersonal [i.e., public] situations." *The Fall of Public Man,* 259. From civic-republican as well as social-democratic perspectives, privatization constitutes a symptomatic disorder within an idealized notion of a public sphere, akin to Christopher Lasch's famous indictment of "the culture of narcissism."

13. Antoine Prost, "Public and Private Spheres in France," in *A History of Private Life,* vol. 5, ed. Prost and Vincent (Cambridge, Mass., 1991), 137.

14. Walter Lippmann, *Public Opinion* (New York, 1965), 122.

15. Dewey, *The Public and Its Problems,* 137; my emphasis.

16. Lippmann, *Public Opinion,* 196; Walter Lippmann, *The Phantom Public* (New Brunswick, N.J., 1993), 54–55.

17. Dewey, *The Public and Its Problems,* 180 (his emphasis), 137, 104.

18. Longenbach, *Stevens: The Plain Sense of Things,* 7.

19. Stevens' business work undoubtedly entailed what Beniger defines as "the modern, functionally departmentalized bureaucratic structure developed first among life insurance companies." *The Control Revolution,* 391–92. Such companies, of course, further initiated an egregious mode of publicization in determining the actuarial status of people, places, and things. Stevens conspicuously distinguished his "masculine" business-work from his private "ladylike" activity of writing verse, a distinction that some critics read as an anxiously gendered one. See Richardson, *Stevens, a Biography: The Early Years,* 436, and Frank Lentricchia, *Ariel and the Police* (Madison, 1988), 147. I view Stevens' division of labor as his attempt to keep separate his work's public and private orientations. The same separation perhaps pertains to his early publication practice. By submitting his poems to small, avant-garde journals when deciding to publish at all, Stevens averts literary-public venues evocative of mass-circulation. The American publishing industry, John Newcomb notes, had exponentially increased book publications since the turn of the century. *Wallace Stevens and Literary Canons,* 28. See n. 32 below.

20. Lentricchia, *Ariel and the Police,* 16, 20. Taking William James' pragmatist viewpoint,

Patricia Rae demurs at Lentricchia's thesis and regards the poem, if not its speaker, as "condemn[ing] the practice of cognitive imperialism." *The Practical Muse,* 215. Andrew Lakritz reads the poem in terms of Walter Benjamin's notion of modern story-telling narratives and their political significance. By designating his poem an "anecdote, a mere fragment of experience," Stevens underscores the disjunction between thing and nature, indicated by the speaker's placing a jar in Tennessee. The disjunction points to "the larger argument about the inability of the human subject to tell his or her own story about the atrophy of experience" in the modern world due to "the rift between human and nature . . . that Stevens' poetry of destruction attempts to clear." *Modernism and the Other,* 37.

21. Rae, *The Practical Muse,* 215.

22. Glen MacLeod, *Stevens and Modern Art* (New Haven, 1993), 22.

23. Lentricchia, *Ariel and the Police,* 145. Daniel O'Hara argues that Stevens' "imaginary politics" results in a "poetry . . . firmly in opposition to the reductive modern commodification of aesthetic objects for ideological or commercial purposes of any stripe." "Imaginary Politics," in *Wallace Stevens and the Feminine,* ed. Schaum (Tuscaloosa, 1993), 68. Also cf. Lentricchia, *Modernist Quartet* (New York, 1994), 141, and Charles Altieri, "Why Stevens Must Be Abstract," in *The Poetics of Modernism,* ed. Gelpi (New York, 1985). Altieri thinks that Stevens' poetry instantiates a democratic ethos by fostering "dreams of appropriation . . . formed out of powers we all share, powers we can even imagine forming a community around" (114). Conrad Aiken had argued something similar, suggesting that Poe's as well as Stevens' works embodied a "communal concern" and "social consciousness." Quoted in Schaum, *Critical Schools,* 39, 38.

24. In "The Paltry Nude Starts on a Spring Voyage" (*CP* 5–6), Stevens telescopes his present *Harmonium* verse as "meagre play / In the scurry and water-shine." He compares it with an as yet unwritten poetry that will be inspired by a "goldener nude," a muse "Of a later day," more purposeful in intention, who

> Will go, like the centre of sea-green pomp,
> In an intenser calm,
> Scullion of fate.

In one sense, the sentiment reflects Stevens' ephebe-like status or lack of poetic self-confidence. In another, it effectively justifies his writing in a private scene, apart from any pretensions to literary "pomp" or for public approbation in the present.

25. Buttel thinks Stevens left "Architecture" out because he "decided that 'A High-Toned Old Christian Woman' used the imagery of architecture to much better effect." *Stevens: The Making of "Harmonium,"* 145. I think that he did so with respect to the Depression era's leftist political scene, which of course then dominated the critical reception of literary works.

26. Patricia Rae reads the poem as a metaphor of a "theoretical edifice," the totalization of which Stevens here resists. *The Practical Muse,* 167. But "Architecture" self-evidently concerns the social agenda of political art at large.

27. Cf. his 1907 journal entry: "I must think well of people. After all, they are only people.—The conventions are the arts of living. People know. I am not the only wise man.—Or if I cannot think well, let me hide my thoughts.—It is of no consequence to explain or to assert one's self. . . . Life is not important.—At least, let's have it agreeable" (*SP* 176–77).

28. A similar utopian imaginary figures the communal "chant of paradise" the speaker envisages in Section VII of "Sunday Morning," but which Stevens arguably frames as only a temporary vision, subject to the descending, all-pervasive evening darkness evoked in the poem's last stanza. See Newcomb, *Wallace Stevens and Literary Canons,* 66.

29. This is Melita Schaum's paraphrase of Frank Lentricchia's grievances against Stevens in *After the New Criticism. Critical Schools,* 158.

30. MacLeod, *Stevens and Modern Art,* 21, and Kevin Stein, *Private Poets* (Athens, Ohio, 1998), 10. MacLeod argues that Stevens adapts other attention-getting techniques of Duchamp (the two were personally acquainted), such as titling many of his works in puzzling, whimsically non-sequitur ways, e.g., "The Emperor of Ice-Cream." *Stevens and Modern Art,* 16. Critics usually attribute the influence of Modernist painting on Stevens' poetry to two particular sources: the 1913 Armory Show exhibit of Cubist and post-Impressionist paintings in New York City, which he likely attended, and his friendship with Walter Arensberg and his group's artistic interests. See Buttel, *Stevens: The Making of "Harmonium,"* 81; MacLeod, *Stevens and Modern Art,* 4–7; Richardson, *Stevens, a Biography: The Early Years,* 400–402, 464, passim. Examples of Stevens' other Modernist-pictorial practices abound. Buttel remarks that certain images in his "Anecdote of the Prince of Peacocks" mimic "Cubistic angularity." *Stevens: The Making of "Harmonium,"* 164. One cannot help but note the surrealistic, day-long perambulation of a doctor from Pacific Ocean to a Swiss city in "The Doctor of Geneva."

31. Not all Modernist writers adhered in principle to this "manifesto." Gertrude Stein, for instance, writes about and ostensibly for a middle-class public: "I have it, this interest in ordinary middle class existence, in simple firm ordinary middle class traditions, . . . with no fine kind of fancy ways inside us, no excitements to surprise us." *The Making of Americans* (Normal, Ill., 1995), 34. Stein also protests her "writing for myself and strangers. . . Everybody is a real one to me, everybody is like some one else too to me" (289). Stein's style, of course, belies her intention, since her text hardly constitutes the fare of "ordinary" readers. Yet the "private" associable with her Modernist style contradicts the thrust of Stevens' no less perplexing poetic work. Whereas he fantasizes privacy, Stein fantasizes a public of "strangers" for her work.

32. Quoted in Schaum, *Stevens and the Critical Schools,* 11. Stevens expressed uneasiness with the public attracted by Modernist paintings. In an unpublished letter, circa 1916–17, he refers to his having attended an art exhibition of the Society of Independent Artists in New York City, and states how "it has grown fashionable and attracts large crowds. . . . It is well to live in Hartford . . . and not be bothered by any public[,] even the public of a small group of friends." Quoted in Longenbach, *Stevens: The Plain Sense of Things,* 120. John Newcomb notes Stevens' reticence to publish his poetry. Stevens also conspicuously eschewed "campaigning" for poetic "attention" or status in the *Harmonium* period, despite his "chummy" connections in the "mutually reinforcing network of editors, poets, and readers" associated with contemporary avant-garde publications. *Wallace Stevens and Literary Canons,* 30, 70. George S. Lensing makes many of the preceding points in *Wallace Stevens: A Poet's Growth* (Baton Rouge, 1986), 100, 90–94. Lensing also goes on to note how "the encouragement of editors and challenge of competition were major incentives in his emergence before *Harmonium*" (95).

33. Subsequent sections in "Landscapes" traffic in Symboliste dreams (IV), Cubist constructions (V), and anti-positivist riposte (VI). Besides the examples provided below, one can point to how Crispin abandons his poetic-colonialist project in "The Comedian as the Letter

C." According to Margaret Peterson, the abandonment concerns Stevens' "assessment of the modernist movements in American poetry, and of his own participation in them." *Stevens and the Idealist Tradition,* 122–23. Cf. Lensing, *A Poet's Growth,* 97–100.

34. Lentricchia, *Ariel and the Police,* 17.

35. Stevens abjured other aspects of Modernist artistic practices such as dadaism (Schaum, *Stevens and the Critical Schools,* 12) and—a favorite of W. C. Williams and other contemporaries—the American "localist" movement. Martha Strom, "Crispin's Journal," *Critical Essays on Wallace Stevens,* ed. Axelrod and Deese (Boston, 1988), 131, 134. The slippages I refer to occur in certain sections of "Six Significant Landscapes." For example, in Section III, Stevens declares his Modernist poetic independence from precursors like Whitman. On one hand, he mimics Whitman:

> For I reach right up to the sun,
> With my eye,
> And I reach to the shore of the sea
> With my ear.
> (*CP* 74)

Yet Stevens ends the section by averring that "I dislike / The way the ants crawl," refusing, that is, to write as if one of or for the masses. In the next section, he again reverses poetic fields when imputing a Symboliste, abstract uniqueness to his imaginative vision: "When my dream was near the moon." But it turns out otherwise, for his dream coalesces into a poetic, human form, highlighted by tropological colorations (yellow-lit gown, red-soled feet, "hair filled / With certain blue crystallizations") deriving from notable imaginative lights emitted by other literary precedents—

> From stars,
> Not far off.

In *Harmonium,* as I have argued, such lights include poetic ones like Whitman's, or simply those of a Bonnie and Josie in Oklahoma ("Life is Motion").

36. Bates, *Stevens: A Mythology of Self,* 106.

37. Longenbach, *Stevens: The Plain Sense of Things,* 35; Fredric Jameson, "Wallace Stevens," *Critical Essays on Wallace Stevens,* ed. Axelrod and Deese (Boston, 1988), 184; Peterson, *Stevens and the Idealist Tradition,* 120. Theodore Sampson regards Hoon as Stevens' own "unmistakably Whitmanesque" persona through whom he "poses as a joyously self-assertive celebrant of his burgeoning poetic powers and mind." For Sampson, the poem's "exotic" scene and figure exemplify how Stevens "resorts to disjunctive troping" throughout *Harmonium* "in order to express and also alleviate his awareness of a [modern] chaotic world—including his own self." *A Cure of the Mind* (New York, 2000), 24–25, 35. Georg Lukács termed Modernism's sin "abstract potentiality," arguing that such literature thrives on an unalleviated subjectivism associable with the "negation of outward reality," the reduction of "Man . . . to a sequence of unrelated experiential fragments." "Ideology of Modernism," in *20th Century Literary Criticism,* ed. Lodge (London, 1972), 479, 480, 481. Cf. Irving Howe's similar view "of the modern," cited in Kevin Stein, *Private Poets,* 11. Stevens hardly denied himself bourgeois pleasures. He not only liked commodities, but preferred observing

rather than engaging others even in public situations: "My idea of life is a fine evening, an orchestra & a crowd *at a distance,* a medium dinner . . . and a soft, full Panatella" (*SP* 136; 1904; his emphasis).

38. Cf. Martha Strom: "Crispin is a burlesque figure who performs his routines in language before an audience of readers." Strom, "Crispin's Journal," 136.

39. Bloom, *Stevens: The Poems of Our Climate,* 87. Sampson, *A Cure of the Mind,* 23, sees the poem celebrating "an Emersonian 'inner leap' or edenic envisioning of reality," in other words, Stevens' coming upon "an original relation to the universe" vis-à-vis the "chaotic randomness and irrational and disorder of things" that mark his Modernist vision.

40. Eleanor Cook observes that the poem "encourage[s an] allegorical reading," but of what the poem's "narrative and linguistic plot" consists she remains uncertain. *Poetry, Word-Play and Word-War,* 37, 30. Cook also hears Whitmanian echoes in the poem, especially in the third girl's dialogue. She accordingly surmises that the "giant" signifies Stevens' reference more to Whitman than to himself (he occasionally signed his letters as the "Giant"), and that he finally sides with "the girls [who] remain dominant after all [so that] we anticipate the giant's undoing." I read the poem as referring entirely to Stevens, and not to his "undoing," with the Whitmanian echo a reference to a poetic mode identified with a certain type of literary-public expectation that Stevens attempts to finesse rather than deny.

41. This poetics helps account for the distinction between Stevens' private, poetic effects and, say, Eliot's at the time. According to John Newcomb, unlike Stevens' poetic hermeticism, "Eliot's . . . excluded the reader who did not follow its allusive texture, but . . . also clubbishly admitted those who did follow it into the priesthood of a prestigiously erudite tradition." *Wallace Stevens and Literary Canons,* 78.

42. Longenbach, *Stevens: The Plain Sense of Things,* 61.

Chapter 5: *Harmonium:* Dying to Love (in Private)

1. George S. Lensing, *A Poet's Growth,* 211–13, traces the poem's source via its epigraph to an essay on the life of Teodor de Wyzewa, a Polish "journalist and music critic." For Lensing, the poem accordingly consists of an imagined colloquy between Wyzewa and his revered aunt, who herself was memorable to him for her reverential view of saints' legendary lives. "Stevens emphasizes, rather, the seductiveness of saints beautified instead of beatified," and thus treats the aunt's words ironically. My reading of "Colloquy" suggests that Stevens instead recovers the aunt's authority on his own "private" terms.

2. Buttel notes the title's irony in *Stevens: The Making of "Harmonium,"* 115; Bloom, *Stevens: The Poems of Our Climate,* 15.

3. Cook, *Poetry, Word-Play, and Word-War,* 65.

4. Ibid., 66.

5. Stevens often addresses female figures like Susannah as internalized muse-figures (his "interior paramour"). See Barbara M. Fisher, "A Woman with the Hair of a Pythoness," *Stevens and the Feminine,* ed. Schaum (Tuscaloosa, 1993), 48. Other critics emphasize the negative aspect of Stevens' figurations of women. Mark Halliday bluntly argues that Stevens fears "female sexuality" and wants to control it. *Stevens and the Interpersonal,* 48. Also in Schaum's

collection, Celeste Goodridge, "Aesthetics and Politics," 157, notes that Stevens' women resemble mere "objects of desire," whom he voyeuristically "watches, stills, silences, dehumanizes, and transforms." Mary B. Arensberg, " 'A Curable Separation,' " 32, discusses how they mirror Stevens' creative desires, but as if engaged in a wholly separate "primal scene of creation," which he "can only gaze at but never participate in." Cf. Stevens' uncollected poem, "Dolls," written sometime between 1913 and 1914: "The thought of Eve, within me, is a doll / That does what I desire" (*OP* 4). Patricia Rae holds that Stevens' "radically empirical conception of the muse" mitigates any apparent "sexism." *Practical Muse,* 143, 139, passim. Regarding feminist interpretations of Stevens' poems, I refine what I note here when discussing "Peter Quince at the Clavier" in Chapter 6.

6. "Sex," as Alan Ryan notes, "breeds a desire for privacy, creates an intense interest in something to which the doings of the state are entirely irrelevant, makes one person care more for the fate of another person than for the fate of the collectivity. The pursuit of private happiness is likely to be an obstacle to social reconstruction." "Dream Time," review of *A Tale of Two Utopias,* by Paul Berman, *New York Review of Books,* October 17, 1996, p. 40.

7. Richardson, *Stevens, a Biography: The Early Years,* 283, 433.

8. Ibid., 498. Mark Halliday, *Stevens and the Interpersonal,* 126, charges that Stevens makes "racist and sexist jokes" of this sort throughout his poems.

9. Longenbach, *Stevens: The Plain Sense of Things,* 43.

10. Buttel, *Stevens: The Making of "Harmonium,"* 164.

11. Jon Rosenblatt, "Stevens' 'The Cuban Doctor,' " *Explicator* 37 (summer 1979): 15. Rosenblatt considers the poem "a small, fantastic allegory of retreat from nature and fate. The Cuban hides in Egypt, the country of the past; in summer, the season of plenitude; in sleep, the mental state oblivious to reality [ironically counterpointed by the last line's allusion to 'the gates of horn through which true dreams of reality pass']. Yet having escaped into these three alternate worlds, he still finds the Indian haunting him."

12. Ibid.

13. With his reference to those "dreadful sundry of this world, / The Cuban, Polodowsky, / The Mexican women, / The negro undertaker" found proliferating in Florida's "venereal soil" (CP 47), Stevens explicitly plays on ethnic stereotypes in "O Florida, Venereal Soil," written a year after "The Cuban Doctor."

14. Cook, "Riddles, Charms, and Fictions," 163–68.

15. Joan Gomez, *A Dictionary of Symptoms,* ed. Gersh (New York, 1968), 235.

16. The *OED* defines "clap" as "To make the hard explosive noise. . . . Said of agents, instruments, thunder, etc." With reference to venereal disease, the *OED* also cites Addison and Steele's reference in *Tatler* 260 to a "Clap Doctor." Eleanor Cook, "Riddles, Charms, and Fictions," 166, stresses Stevens' use of double entendres throughout his poetic career, citing for justification a passage from "Notes toward a Supreme Fiction" (I.viii): "Logos and logic, crystal hypothesis, / Incipit and a form to speak the word / And every latent double in the word, / Beau linguist."

17. *OED* definition.

18. In his article's section on "Wittgenstein on Privacy and Beetles," Henry Simoni-Wastila argues that Wittgenstein's recourse to the example of physical pain regarding the privacy issue "show[s] that two people have radically distinct subjectivities," and in general that the

"sensation of pain is private or, in our terms, radically particular." "Particularity and Consciousness," 415–25.

19. Poe, *P&T,* 268–69. Buttel, *Stevens: The Making of "Harmonium,"* 192 n. 12, also cites in passing the connection between Stevens' "The Cuban Doctor" and Poe's "The Conqueror Worm." Poe inserted the poem into his 1845 re-publication of "Ligeia." See Mabbott 2:308–309.

20. A Freudian reading might argue, for example, that the Indian represents the as if god-like because unpredictable attacks of Id. The "I" or Ego goes "to Egypt," i.e., tries to repress or embalm the Id's eruptions. But at most, the Ego can only drowse "in summer's sleepiest horn," that is, find respite in moments when sexual excitation (the phallic horn) seems to have abated. Along with the defensive doubling of "I," the dash near the end of line 8 marks the Id-besieged Ego's anxiety in attempting to repress the endlessly potential threat of the Id's return ("my enemy was near—I, / Drowsing . . ."). Contrary to Freudian formulation, then, Stevens' poem argues that: for the Ego or "I," where Id was, Id will be again. My thanks to John William Price for discussing this aspect of the poem with me.

21. Jameson, "Wallace Stevens," 178.

22. R. P. Blackmur, "Examples of Wallace Stevens," in *Selected Essays,* ed. Donoghue (New York, 1986), proposed an equally befuddling paraphrase: "The less obvious sense of the [poem's final] couplets . . . is, perhaps, that ice-cream and what it represents is the only power *heeded,* not the only power there is to heed. The irony recoils on itself: what seems *shall* finally be; the lamp *shall* affix its beam. The only emperor is the emperor of ice-cream. The king is dead; long live the king" (79; Blackmur's emphasis).

23. Aside from the poem's "to be or not to be" allusion ("Let be be"), the very image of "the emperor of ice-cream" recalls Hamlet's "Your worm is your only emperor for diet: we fat all creatures else to fat us . . . for maggots; your fat king and your lean beggar is but variable service; two dishes, but to one table: that's the end" (*Hamlet* IV, iii, ll. 22–27). Eleanor Cook, *Poetry, Word-Play, and Word-War,* 91, hears the same allusion. In confronting death without "the trappings and the suits of woe"—hence the speaker's call for a party-like wake—the Hamlet-like speaker in "The Emperor of Ice-Cream" also eschews "seems" (I, ii, ll. 75–87). Stevens held a similar position on the matter near the time he wrote the poem (1922): "From time immemorial the philosophers and other scene painters have daubed the sky with dazzle paint. But it all comes down to the proverbial six feet of earth in the end" (*L* 244; 1921). Also see n. 19, Chapter 6.

24. William Bysshe Stein, "The Requiem of the Romantic Muse," *NMAL* 1 (spring 1977): [no pagination]. The notes by Kenneth Lash and Robert Thackaberry appear in *Explicator* 6 (April 1948): #36.

25. The preceding citations occur respectively in the following works: Baird, *The Dome and the Rock* (Baltimore, 1968), 249; Vendler, *Stevens: Words Chosen* (Cambridge, Mass., 1986), 50; Haas, "Wallace Stevens," in *Hiding in Plain Sight,* ed. Lesser (San Francisco, 1993), 62; Burney, *Wallace Stevens* (New York, 1968), 59; Chavkin, " 'The Vaguest Emotion,' " *West Virginia Philological Papers* 28 (1982): 114; S. Silverman, "The Emperior of Ice-Cream," *Western Humanities Review* 26 (spring 1972): 168; Ellmann, "Wallace Stevens' Ice-Cream," *Kenyon Review* 19 (winter 1957): 95; Neill, "The Melting Moment," *Ariel* 4 (January 1973): 90; Strobel, "Stevens' 'The Emperor of Ice Cream' " (*sic*), *Explicator* (summer

1983): 33; Coyle, "Aphorism in Wallace Stevens' Poetry," *PMLA* 91 (March 1976): 213; R. Viswanathan, "Stevens' 'The Emperor of Ice-Cream,' " *Explicator* 50 (winter 1992): 85; Piccioto-Richardson, "By Their Fruits" (Ph.D. diss., CUNY, 1977), 605; Beckett, *Wallace Stevens* (London, 1974), 79; W. B. Stein, "Requiem of the Romantic Muse"; and Kravec, "Let Arcade Be Finale of Arcadia," *Wallace Stevens Journal* 3 (spring 197): 10.

26. Among other things, "privacy" can also mean "taken in isolation, singular, owned by one person." Partridge, *Origins*, 527.

27. Supporting a less ironic view of the speaker, the cigar image undoubtedly alludes to Stevens' own pleasure in smoking cigars. Richardson, *Stevens, a Biography: The Early Years*, esp. 76, 380, 475. See n. 37, Chapter 4, and n. 43 below.

28. Roy Harvey Pearce suggests that the cigar-rolling figure derives from Stevens' 1917 visit to Tampa, Florida, where, being an inveterate walker, he likely saw "cigar rollers" in a "cigar-manufacturing section" close to his hotel. Most of these "were Cuban, Spanish, and Sicilian emigres who had together created a genuine community," and who no doubt partook of the " 'pleasures of Sicilian *gelati* . . . and even more exotic ice creams.' " " 'The Emperor of Ice-Cream,' " *Wallace Stevens Journal* 3 (fall 1979): 53, 54. Richardson analogously traces one source of the poem back to Stevens' encounter, recorded in his journal twenty-two years earlier (*SP* 74; 1900), with Italian immigrants on the streets of New York City. *Stevens, a Biography: The Early Years*, 108–109. Both critics assign the poem's origins to Stevens' communitarian longings.

29. Alluding to home-based or cottage-industry activities in the nineteenth century, the poem's cigar-rolling and ice-cream-making contrast with the abstract, mass-mechanizing procedures endemic to the early-twentieth-century American marketplace. See Schlereth, *Victorian America*, 126, and Green, *The Uncertainty of Everyday Life*, 160–61. Even consuming ice-cream was becoming a mass-public affair. By 1916, for example, the chain-drugstore Walgreen's had opened with "soda fountains, lunch counters . . . ice cream." Beniger, *The Control Revolution*, 334.

30. Dewey, *The Public and Its Problems*, 180.

31. See my related remarks on "The Emperor of Ice-Cream" in the Introduction. One can claim that the poem plies two alternatives regarding the intimacy associated with American funeral situations. Contemporary middle-class "funeral services . . . became more private, isolating the family and intimate friends from the more public ceremonies of earlier times." Harvey Green, *The Uncertainty of Everyday Life*, 141. Cf. Philippe Ariès, *The Hour of Our Death* (New York, 1981), 575. But the scene hardly bespeaks a middle-class situation. Laid out without apparent benefit of embalming, the dead woman has only an old sheet "to cover her face"—certainly no fancy casket, which, in addition to embalming corpses, was becoming a common middle-class feature at wakes. Green, *The Uncertainty of Everyday Life*, 140. And yet the speaker conspicuously fails to call familial figures ("boys" and "wenches"?) to attend the poem's homely wake, suggesting his rejection of even communally intimate sorts of consolation.

32. *The Economist* (April 15, 1913) designated Morgan, an American capitalist par excellence, with this Napoleonic title, and notably during the period when Stevens lived and worked in New York City. See Ronald Chernow, *The House of Morgan* (New York, 1990), 160, and Jean Strouse, *Morgan: American Financier* (New York, 1999), 704. In December 1901, Ray

Stannard Baker had written an article on Morgan in the *Windsor Magazine,* an "Illustrated Monthly for Men and Women," entitled "The Emperor of Trusts." The "Emperor"-Morgan connection becomes more feasible to entertain when one considers that Morgan originally came from Hartford, Connecticut, Stevens' home when writing the poem. Stevens visited museums frequently, and not only was Morgan renowned for his art collection, but he contributed some of it to Hartford's Wadsworth Atheneum.

33. Grey, *The Wallace Stevens Case,* 99; Beckett, *Wallace Stevens,* 79; and Longenbach, *Stevens: The Plain Sense of Things,* 68.

34. Richard Ellmann, "Stevens' Ice-Cream," 91, 90, 92; Peterson, *Stevens and the Idealist Tradition,* 100.

35. Ellmann, "Stevens' Ice-Cream," 93, 91.

36. William Carlos Williams, *Collected Earlier Poems* (Norfolk, Conn., 1991), 130–31.

37. Strobel, Stevens' " 'The Emperor of Ice Cream,' " 35.

38. Piccioto-Richardson takes a more serious view of the "ice-cream" pun: "I scream" falls within the poem's most accessible thematic, its abjuring any "inherited Christian concept of death," whether theological or literary. "By Their Fruits," 602. Burney, *Wallace Stevens,* 59, and Stuart Silverman, "The Emperor of Ice-Cream," 167, also notice the poem's child-like tonality. Based on Blackmur's citation of a letter that Stevens had written him stating "that his [young] daughter put a superlative value on ice-cream" (Blackmur, "Examples of Wallace Stevens," 79), Ellmann speculates that she may have "asked [Stevens] to write a poem about it," which could not have been the case, since Holly Stevens was not born until 1924. In contrast to my following discussion of the poem, Ellmann also observes that "there is a child-like quality about the poem—its absence of taboo." "Stevens' Ice-Cream," 94.

39. Anne Martin-Fugier, "Bourgeois Rituals," in *A History of Private Life,* vol. 4, ed. Perrot (Cambridge, Mass., 1990), 333, notes the coroner's function. J. E. Lighter cites a 1918 American reference to "cig" or "cigar" as a "coffin nail" in his *American Slang* (New York, 1994), 1:422.

40. Bronislaw Malinowski, *Magic, Science, and Religion* (New York, 1948), 48; Gérard Vincent, "A History of Secrets?" in *A History of Private Life,* vol. 5, ed. Prost and Vincent (Cambridge, Mass., 1991), 264.

41. Thackaberry, *Explicator,* and Beverly Coyle, "Aphorism in Wallace Stevens' Poetry," 213. Theodore Sampson also notes "the diffuse sexual atmosphere pervading the entire scene," but with its function being to show how "sex and death" together "share the horrendous facticity and alienation to which they have been reduced in the modern world." *A Cure of the Mind,* 32, 33.

42. The scene might more specifically refer to an early 1920s apartment speakeasy, with the "concupiscent curds" a pleasure-inducing alcoholic concoction (Lash), here disguised—a not at all unusual occurrence—from law-enforcement officials by means of common household containers. Cf. Sampson, *A Cure of the Mind,* 32, 33.

43. Jacqueline V. Brogan makes the point about the poem's grotesque sexist humor in " 'Sister of the Minotaur,' " in *Stevens and the Feminine,* ed. Schaum (Tuscaloosa, 1993), 5. Around 1920, newspaper articles appeared linking the WCTU's efforts at Prohibition of alcohol to cigar and pipe tobacco sales as well. See "Plan Amendment to Outlaw Tobacco," *New York Times,* August 8, 1919, p. 5. One can also surmise that Stevens somehow includes his

wife in his poem's feminine violations, since after they were married, Elsie "lived by the most puritanical laws, banned alcohol periodically, [and] frowned at smoking." Richardson, *Stevens, a Biography: The Early Years,* 264. As for the poem's resorting to a coded homosocial idiom, Antoine Prost notes how Frenchmen in cafés during the same period would communicate with each other in "a kind of code" about their private lives, and primarily "about women" in a ribald if "formalized exchange governed by the rules of propriety." "Public and Private Spheres in France," 103.

44. W. B. Stein, "Requiem of the Romantic Muse," also notes Stevens' pun "on the polarizing etymological and semantic meaning of 'cream,' from chrism to semen."

45. Kravec, "Let Arcade Be Finale of Arcadia," 10, sees fantails as at once containing a "sexual reference" and alluding to "the peacock as symbol of Christ."

46. Thackaberry, *Explicator.*

47. This is Francis Barker's view of the "tremulous private body." Adopting his viewpoint, one might claim that the woman in Stevens' poem, whether understood as corpse or sexual object, reflects a common, Western ideological attitude that, underwritten by Cartesian epistemology (the self as isolated ego), reduces the body to "a hypostatized object . . . a simple biological mechanism of given desires and needs." *Tremulous Private Body* (Ann Arbor, 1995), 10. What Barker claims about the woman addressed in Andrew Marvell's "To His Coy Mistress" might also apply to the woman in "The Emperor of Ice-Cream." She, too, is "an objectified body at which speech is aimed . . . but whose being is . . . sub-discursive: dumb, reduced, corporeal matter," despite the fact that the feminized body remains "tremulous," or that "gendered reduction[s] cannot be total" (84). But as I am reading it, Stevens' poem plays out that very qualification.

48. Stevens later claimed that the embroidered fantails in "The Emperor of Ice-Cream" referred to "fantail pigeons" (*L* 387; 1939).

Chapter 6: *Harmonium:* A Private Poe-session

1. Eleanor Cook, *Poetry, Word-Play, and Word-War,* 65.

2. Joseph Riddel, *The Clairvoyant Eye* (Baton Rouge, 1965), 71. Melita Schaum cites William Van O'Connor's formalist view of "Peter Quince at the Clavier" "as an example of a modern poem which fulfills criteria of inclusivity, tension, and the use of antithesis for the purpose of final resolution into an 'instantaneous whole.' " *Stevens and the Critical Schools,* 89.

3. Patricia Rae and B. J. Leggett refer to Nyquist's influential feminist view of the poem. *Practical Muse,* 141; *Early Stevens: The Nietzchean Intertext* (Durham, 1992), 71–73. Nyquist focuses on the poem's "specular gaze, which makes the imagined or visual object the Other." Mary Nyquist, "Musing on Susanna's Music," in *Lyric Poetry,* ed. Hosek and Parker (Ithaca, 1985), 314.

4. Using a Nietzschean gloss, Leggett attempts to justify the discrepancy between Stevens' Susanna and her depiction in the Apocrypha, along with the strained narrative analogy, cited by Nyquist, between Quince's woman and Susanna. Leggett maintains that the poem need not possess narrative logic, since "these passages" actually represent "the musical mood seeking its discharge in [Apollonian] pictures." He interprets the poem's final theme as the "acceptance

of a world of becoming" wherein "individual desire is transient, but . . . life is infinitely desirable." *Early Stevens: The Nietzschean Intertext*, 68–63, 71, 73, and 77.

5. Bates, *Stevens: A Mythology of Self*, 117.

6. Regarding the privacy issue, Poe's take on poetry differs from Stevens'. Poe like Stevens sees poetry as indigenously elegiac, insofar as through it we experience "our inability to grasp *now*" any full vision of "Supernal" Beauty. "The Poetic Principle," *E&R*, 77; Poe's emphasis. But fostered by a Romantic credo, writing poetry for Poe spontaneously generates the desire to represent that Beauty for everyone. Other "souls fittingly constituted" will acknowledge the special accomplishment by poets (presumably like himself) to give "the world all *that* which it (the world) has ever been enabled at once to understand and *to feel* as poetic" (Poe's emphasis). If privacy at all pertains to Poe's poetry, it does so after the fact, for example in the way that "The Philosophy of Composition" frames "The Raven" in terms of a *now* occluded process of writing.

7. Helen Vendler reads the poem as an ironic aggression against the "Victorian" speaker, whom she regards as privileging virginal gentility over the negress's Blakean sexual "heat." *Words Chosen Out of Desire*, 18–19. From my viewpoint, Stevens' *Harmonium* poems often resist anti-Victorian and pro-Modernist stances alike. Thus, Vendler's otherwise plausible interpretation of "A Virgin Carrying a Lantern" arguably exemplifies the kind of reading that the poem both stages and finesses.

8. Bates therefore thinks the speaker succeeds in penetrating reality, the poem's process consisting in a movement "from reference to attitude." *Stevens: A Mythology of Self*, 137.

9. Buttel, *Making of "Harmonium,"* 131–32; Rae, *Practical Muse*, 196.

10. Peterson, *Stevens and the Idealist Tradition*, 94.

11. Peterson, for instance, specifically argues that Stevens adopts William James' "pragmatist" vision as a counter to Idealist conceptions of God, and persuasively cites a passage from James referring to the latter in terms of an "absolute bird." *Stevens and the Idealist Tradition*, 98.

12. Bates, *Stevens: A Mythology of Self*, 116.

13. Cook, *Poetry, Word-Play and Word-War*, 70.

14. See n. 35, Chapter 4.

15. Cook, *Poetry, Word-Play, and Word-War*, 100.

16. *Ibid.*, 34.

17. Cook, "Riddles, Charms, and Fictions," 166.

18. Vendler, *Stevens: Words Chosen*, 52.

19. "The Emperor of Ice-Cream" also echoes Duke Ferdinand's response to the death by murder of his twin sister—a Poesque motif—in John Webster's *The Duchess of Malfi*: "Cover her face: mine eyes dazzle: she died young" (IV.ii.274). In Ligeian fashion, moreover, the Duchess briefly revives after this moment, only to expire one final time (IV.ii.352–65).

20. Cf. Stevens 1936 brief and humorously ironic remark on Poe's poetry in "The Irrational Element of Poetry": "The slightest sound [in poetry] matters. The most momentary rhythm matters. . . . We no longer like Poe's tintinnabulations. You are free to tintinnabulate if you like. But others are equally free to put their hands over their ears." *OP* 230–31.

21. One finds this "rhythm" more indecisively mused in unpublished lines from "Le Monocle de Mon Oncle," cited in the present chapter's epigraph. There the speaker wonders

whether he should opt for Whitman's "sunshine" vision in *Leaves of Grass* or Poe's "melancholy" one.

22. Buttel, *Stevens: The Making of "Harmonium,"* 189.

23. With a no less Poesque "blackbird" inflection, the last stanza of "Thirteen Ways of Looking at a Blackbird" also argues his poem's beautiful failure to communicate in any conventional sense:

> It was evening all afternoon.
> It was snowing
> And it was going to snow.
> The blackbird sat in the cedar-limbs.

24. See Chapter 4.

25. Bates, *Stevens: A Mythology of Self*, 116; Bloom, *Stevens: The Poems of Our Climate*, 84.

26. Leggett thinks that "Hymn from a Watermelon Pavilion" results in a thematic standoff: "since the external world shares the quality of the imagined world, the artist might just as well (or better) dwell in the richer illusion of that dream of which life itself consists." *Early Stevens: The Nietzschean Intertext*, 61–62. But the public-private paradigm seems to me more appropriate to use for this poem than the subject-object binary on which Leggett relies. Subjective appearances differ from objective ones only in degree. Both are arguably motivated by impulses to go public on the basis of a transpersonal, Apollonian principle. In my formulation, private appearances remain different from their public manifestations, even if that difference finally "doesn't matter."

27. Poe entertains "a hope" that the entire process of God's " 'Infinite Self-Diffusion,' " via stars, things, and us, into " 'Concentrated Self' " will endlessly result in "another creation and radiation." *Eureka*, 1356, 1358.

28. See n. 4, Chapter 5, and n. 3 above. Patricia Rae reads the speaker of "Fictive Music" as Stevens addressing his female muse. For Rae, the poem provides more evidence for feminist charges that "Stevens' faceless women resemble pornographic mistresses, performing exactly as their men desire," a charge that she tries to disarm by claiming that such figures are specifically "muses." *Practical Muse*, 141, 142. Her claim strikes me as too defensive, and in any case unnecessary for both "Fictive Music" and, as I presently discuss it, "Two Figures in Dense Violet Night."

29. Richardson, *Stevens, a Biography: The Later Years* (New York, 1988), 51.

30. Longenbach accounts for Stevens' post-*Harmonium* poetic hiatus essentially in terms of his sense of economic insecurity. *Stevens: The Plain Sense of Things*, 118, passim. As predicted by "The Comedian as the Letter C," Eleanor Cook finds Stevens hitting a poetic dead-end by the time of his later *Harmonium* poems. *Poetry, Word-Play, and World-War*, 114. Also see George S. Lensing, *A Poet's Growth*, 119–21. Lakritz, *Modernism and the Other*, 20, Longenbach, 98, 159, and esp. Alan Filreis throughout *Modernism from Right to Left* (New York, 1994), discuss the literary-political movements that impinged on Stevens' writing poetry during the 1930s and before.

31. *Oxford English Dictionary,* 2nd ed.

32. Richardson, *Stevens, Biography The Later Years,* 412. Lensing maintains that Stevens' practice of "[p]privacy, relative secrecy, and solitude" in writing and publishing his early *Har-*

monium poems primarily derived from his "uncertainty about his verse experiments," but also "would remain necessary conditions for his art in the years ahead." Lensing, *A Poet's Growth,* 92, 90–91.

33. I have not been able to locate the source of Stevens' reference to Poe, notwithstanding much appreciated help from J. Gerald Kennedy and Burton R. Pollin. Poe's anti-progress pieces ("Some Words with a Mummy," for instance) sometimes express outrage at anyone's assumption that being born in the modern period makes one superior to past thinkers. Cf. n. 10, Chapter 3. Stevens' reference to the beautiful woman becoming a witch may partially derive from Poe's "The Black Cat," in which the narrator mentions "the ancient popular notion, which regarded all black cats as witches in disguise" (*P&T* 598), and that he attributes to his wife's "superstition." As I noted in Chapter 3, since he kills both wife and feline (a displaced target of his aggression toward his wife), he perforce manifests a love-hate ambivalence toward the "feminine." In any case, Stevens' overall recollection appropriately remains a private fiction.

34. Peter Brazeau's *Parts of a World* (New York, 1983) renders oral profiles of Stevens' relations with his fellow office-workers. See esp. 12–39.

Bibliography

Critical Works

Adorno, Theodor W., and Max Horkheimer. *Dialectic of Enlightenment.* Trans. John Cumming. New York: Seabury Press, 1972. Orig. German publication, 1944.

Allen, Michael. *Poe and the British Magazine Tradition.* New York: Oxford University Press, 1969.

Altieri, Charles. "Why Stevens Must Be Abstract; or, What a Poet Can Learn from Painting." In *Wallace Stevens: The Poetics of Modernism,* ed. Albert Gelpi, 86–118. New York: Cambridge University Press, 1985.

Ames, Kenneth L. *Death in the Dining Room and Other Tales of Victorian Culture.* Philadelphia: Temple University Press, 1992.

Anonymous. "The End of Privacy." *Economist,* May 1, 1999, pp. 15–16, 21–23.

———. "Plan Amendment to Outlaw Tobacco." *New York Times,* August 8, 1919, p. 5.

Arac, Jonathan. *Huckleberry Finn as Idol and Target.* Madison: University of Wisconsin Press, 1997.

Arendt, Hannah. *The Human Condition.* Chicago: University of Chicago Press, 1958; paperback edition 1989.

Arensberg, Mary B. " 'A Curable Separation': Stevens and the Mythology of Gender." In *Wallace Stevens and the Feminine,* ed. Melita Schaum, 23–45. Tuscaloosa: University of Alabama Press, 1993.

Ariès, Philippe. *The Hour of Our Death.* Trans. Helen Weaver. New York: Alfred A. Knopf, 1981.

Auden, W. H. *The Dyer's Hand and Other Essays.* New York: Random House, 1962.

Auerbach, Jonathan. *The Romance of Failure: First-Person Fictions of Poe, Hawthorne, and James*. New York: Oxford University Press, 1989.

Baird, James. *The Dome and the Rock: Structure in the Poetry of Wallace Stevens*. Baltimore: Johns Hopkins University Press, 1968.

Baker, Ray Stannard. "The Emperor of Trusts: J. Pierpont Morgan and His Career." *Windsor Magazine,* December 1901, 179–91.

Barker, Francis. *The Tremulous Private Body: Essays on Subjection*. Ann Arbor: University of Michigan Press, 1995.

Bates, Milton J. *Wallace Stevens: A Mythology of Self*. Berkeley: University of California Press, 1985.

Bauerlein, Mark. *Literary Criticism: An Autopsy*. Philadelphia: University of Pennsylvania Press, 1997.

Beckett, Lucy. *Wallace Stevens*. London: Cambridge University Press, 1974.

Benhabib, Seyla. "Models of Public Space: Hannah Arendt, the Liberal Tradition, and Jürgen Habermas." In *Habermas and the Public Sphere,* ed. Craig Calhoun, 73–98. Cambridge, Mass.: MIT Press, 1992.

Beniger, James R. *The Control Revolution: Technological and Economic Origins of the Information Society*. Cambridge, Mass.: Harvard University Press, 1986.

Bentham, Jeremy. *The Panopticon Writings*. Ed. Miran Bozovič. London: Verso, 1995.

Bercaw, Nancy Dunlap. "Solid Objects/Mutable Meanings: Fancywork and the Construction of Bourgeois Culture, 1840–1880." *Winterthur Portfolio* 26 (1991): 231–47.

Blackmur, R. P. "Examples of Wallace Stevens." In *Selected Essays of R. P. Blackmur*. Ed. and intro. Denis Donoghue, 71–100. New York: Ecco Press, 1986.

Bloom, Harold. *Poetry and Repression: Revisionism from Blake to Stevens*. New Haven: Yale University Press, 1976.

———. *Wallace Stevens: The Poems of Our Climate*. Ithaca: Cornell University Press, 1976.

———. *The Western Canon: The Books and School of the Ages*. New York: Harcourt Brace, 1994.

Boling, Patricia. *Privacy and the Politics of Intimate Life*. Ithaca: Cornell University Press, 1996.

Bonnefoy, Yves. "Igitur and the Photographer." Trans. Mary Ann Caws. *PMLA* 114 (May 1999): 332–45.

Bové, Paul. *Destructive Poetics: Heidegger and Modern American Poetry*. New York: Columbia University Press, 1980.

Brazeau, Peter. *Parts of a World: Wallace Stevens Remembered: An Oral Biography*. New York: Random House, 1983.

Brogan, Jacqueline Vaught. " 'Sister of the Minotaur': Sexism and Stevens." In *Wallace Stevens and the Feminine,* ed. Melita Schaum, 3–22. Tuscaloosa: University of Alabama Press, 1993.

Brown, Richard D. *Knowledge Is Power: The Diffusion of Information in Early America, 1700–1865.* New York: Oxford University Press, 1989.

Burney, William. *Wallace Stevens.* New York: Twayne Publishers, 1968.

Buttel, Robert. *Wallace Stevens: The Making of "Harmonium."* Princeton: Princeton University Press, 1967.

Byer, Robert H. "Mysteries of the City: A Reading of Poe's 'The Man of the Crowd.' " In *Ideology and Classic American Literature,* ed. Sacvan Bercovitch and Myra Jehlen, 221–46. New York: Cambridge University Press, 1986.

Byers, Thomas B. *What I Cannot Say: Self, Word, and World in Whitman, Stevens, and Merwin.* Urbana: University of Illinois Press, 1989.

Cantalupo, Barbara. "*Eureka:* Poe's 'Novel Universe.' " In *A Companion to Poe Studies,* ed. Eric W. Carlson, 323–44. Westport, Conn.: Greenwood Press, 1996.

Carter, Steven. "From Room to Room: A Note on the Ending of 'The Pit and the Pendulum.' " *Poe Studies* 31. 1–2 (1998): 35–36.

Castle, Terry. "Phantasmagoria: Spectral Technology and the Metaphorics of Modern Reverie." *Critical Inquiry* 15. 1 (autumn 1988): 26–61.

Charvat, William. "Poe: Journalism and the Theory of Poetry." In *The Profession of Authorship in America, 1800–1870: The Papers of William Charvat,* ed. Matthew J. Bruccoli, 84–99. Columbus: Ohio State University Press, 1968.

Chavkin, Alan. " 'The Vaguest Emotion' of Wallace Stevens' 'The Emperor of Ice-Cream." *West Virginia Philological Papers* 28 (1982): 114–18.

Chernow, Ronald. *The House of Morgan: An American Banking Dynasty and the Rise of Modern Finance.* New York: Atlantic Monthly Press, 1990.

Clark, Clifford E. "Domestic Architecture as an Index to Social History: The Romantic Revival and the Cult of Domesticity in America, 1840–1870." In *Material Life in America, 1600–1860,* ed. Robert Blair St. George, 535–49. Boston: Northeastern University Press, 1988.

Cook, Eleanor. *Poetry, Word-Play, and Word-War in Wallace Stevens.* Princeton: Princeton University Press, 1988.

————. "Riddles, Charms, and Fictions in Wallace Stevens" [1983]. In *Critical Essays on Wallace Stevens,* ed. Steven Gould Axelrod and Helen Deese, 162–76. Boston: G. K. Hall, 1988.

Cox, James M. "Reflections on Hawthorne's Nature." In *American Letters and the Historical Consciousness: Essays in Honor of Lewis P. Simpson,* ed. J. Gerald Kennedy and Daniel Mark Fogel, 139–57. Baton Rouge: Louisiana State University Press, 1987.

————. " *The Scarlet Letter:* Through the Old Manse and the Custom House." *Virginia Quarterly Review* 51 (1975): 432–47.

Coyle, Beverly. "Defining the Role of Aphorism in Wallace Stevens' Poetry." *PMLA* 91 (March 1976): 206–22.

Darnton, Robert. "Paris: The Early Internet." *New York Review of Books,* June 29, 2000, pp. 42–47.

Davidson, Edward H. *Poe: A Critical Study.* Cambridge, Mass.: Belknap Press, 1957.

Dayan, Joan. *Fables of Mind: An Inquiry into Poe's Fiction.* New York: Oxford University Press, 1987.

Dean, Tim. "Hart Crane's Poetics of Privacy." *American Literary History* 8 (spring 1996): 83–109.

Delbanco, Andrew. "Sunday in the Park with Fred." *New York Review of Books,* January 20, 2000, pp. 55–57.

de Man, Paul. "Autobiography as De-facement." In *The Rhetoric of Romanticism,* 67–81. New York: Columbia University Press, 1984.

Dennett, Daniel C. *Consciousness Explained.* Boston: Little, Brown, 1991.

Dewey, John. *The Public and Its Problems.* 1927; reprint, Athens, Ohio: Swallow Press, Ohio University Press, 1954.

Edmonston, William E. *The Induction of Hypnotism.* New York: Wiley, 1986.

Elias, Norbert. *The Civilizing Process: The History of Manners.* Trans. Edmund Jephcott. New York: Urizen Books, 1978.

Ellmann, Richard. "Wallace Stevens' Ice-Cream." *Kenyon Review* 19 (winter 1957) 89–105.

Elmer, Jonathan. "The Jingle Man: Trauma and the Aesthetic." In *Fissions and Fusions: Proceedings of the First Conference of the Cape American Studies Association, 4 July 1966,* ed. Lara Dunwell, 131–45. Belville, South Africa: Cape American Studies Association, 1997.

———. *Reading at the Social Limit: Affect, Mass Culture, and Edgar Allan Poe.* Stanford: Stanford University Press, 1995.

Filreis, Alan. *Modernism from Right to Left: Wallace Stevens, the Thirties, and Literary Radicalism.* New York: Cambridge University Press, 1994.

Fish, Stanley. *Is There a Text in This Class? The Authority of Interpretive Communities.* Cambridge, Mass.: Harvard University Press, 1980.

Fisher, Barbara M. "A Woman with the Hair of a Pythoness." In *Wallace Stevens and the Feminine,* ed. Melita Schaum, 46–57. Tuscaloosa: University of Alabama Press, 1993.

Flaherty, David H. *Privacy in Colonial New England.* Charlottesville: University Press of Virginia, 1972.

Foucault, Michel. *Discipline and Punish: The Birth of the Prison.* Trans. Alan Sheridan. New York: Vintage Books, 1977.

Gabler, Neal. *Life the Movie.* New York: Alfred A. Knopf, 1998.

Gerstein, Robert. "Intimacy and Privacy." In *Philosophical Dimensions of Privacy: An Anthology,* ed. Ferdinand David Schoeman, 265–71. New York: Cambridge University Press, 1984.

Gilmore, Michael T. *American Romanticism and the Marketplace.* Chicago: University of Chicago Press, 1985.

Gomez, Joan. *A Dictionary of Symptoms.* Ed. Marvin J. Gersh. New York: Stein and Day, 1968.

Goodridge, Celeste. "Aesthetics and Politics: Marianne Moore's Reading of Stevens." In *Wallace Stevens and the Feminine,* ed. Melita Schaum, 155–70. Tuscaloosa: University of Alabama Press, 1993.

Green, Harvey. *The Uncertainty of Everyday Life, 1915–1945.* New York: Harper Perennial, 1993.

Grey, Thomas C. *The Wallace Stevens Case: Law and the Practice of Poetry.* Cambridge, Mass.: Harvard University Press, 1991.

Grier, Katherine C. *Culture and Comfort: Parlor Making and Middle-Class Identity, 1850–1930.* Washington, D.C.: Smithsonian Institution Press, 1988.

Griffith, Clark. "Poe's 'Ligeia' and the English Romantics." *University of Toronto Quarterly* 24 (October 1954): 8–25.

Gurstein, Rochelle. *The Repeal of Reticence: A History of American Cultural and Legal Struggles over Free Speech, Obscenity, Sexual Liberation, and Modern Art.* New York: Hill and Wang, 1996.

Haas, Robert. "Wallace Stevens." In *Hiding in Plain Sight: Essays in Criticism and Autobiography,* ed. Wendy Lesser, 57–65. San Francisco: Mercury House, 1993.

Habermas, Jürgen. *The Structural Transformation of the Public Sphere: An Inquiry into a Category of Bourgeois Society.* Trans. Thomas Burger with Frederick Lawrence. Cambridge, Mass.: MIT Press, 1989.

Halliday, Mark. *Stevens and the Interpersonal.* Princeton: Princeton University Press, 1991.

Halttunen, Karen. *Confidence Men and Painted Women: A Study of Middle-class Culture in America, 1830–1870.* New Haven: Yale University Press, 1982.

———. *Murder Most Foul: The Killer and the American Gothic Imagination.* Cambridge, Mass.: Harvard University Press, 1998.

Hamburger, Käte. *The Logic of Literature,* 2nd rev. ed. Trans. Marilynn J. Rose. Bloomington: Indiana University Press, 1974.

Hansen, Karen V. "Rediscovering the Social: Visiting Practices in Antebellum New England and the Limits of the Public/Private Dichotomy." In *Public and Private in Thought and Practice: Perspectives on a Grand Dichotomy,* ed. Jeff Weintraub and Krishan Kumar, 268–302. Chicago: University of Chicago Press, 1997.

Hareven, Tamara K. "The Home and the Family in Historical Perspective." In *Home: A Place in the World,* ed. Arien Mack. New York: New York University Press, 1993.

Harris, W. C. "Edgar Allan Poe's *Eureka* and the Poetics of Constitution." *American Literary History* 12 (spring–summer 2000): 1–40.

Hartman, Geoffrey H. "Psychoanalysis: The French Connection." In *Psychoanalysis and the Question of the Text,* ed. Geoffrey H. Hartman, 86–113. Baltimore: Johns Hopkins University Press, 1978.

Hawke, David Freeman. *Everyday Life in Early America*. New York: Harper and Row, 1988.

Henrickson, Bruce. "Murray Krieger and the Question of History." In *Murray Krieger and Contemporary Critical Theory,* ed. Bruce Henrickson, 119–34. New York: Columbia University Press, 1986.

Henry, Katherine. "Angelina Grimké's Rhetoric of Exposure." *American Quarterly* 49 (June 1997): 328–55.

Hixson, Richard F. *Privacy in a Public Society: Human Rights in Conflict*. New York: Oxford University Press, 1987.

Hochman, Barbara. "Disappearing Authors and Resentful Readers in Late Nineteenth-Century American Fiction: The Case of Henry James." *ELH* 63 (1996): 177–201.

Hoffman, Daniel. *Poe Poe Poe Poe Poe Poe Poe*. New York: Avon Books, 1978.

Holub, Robert C. *Jürgen Habermas: Critic in the Public Sphere*. New York: Routledge, 1991.

Inness, Julie C. *Privacy, Intimacy, and Isolation*. New York: Oxford University Press, 1992.

Irwin, John T. *American Hieroglyphics: The Symbol of the Egyptian Hieroglyphics in the American Renaissance*. New Haven: Yale University Press, 1980.

———. "A Clew to a Clue: Locked Rooms and Labyrinths in Poe and Borges." In *The American Face of Edgar Allan Poe,* ed. Shawn Rosenheim and Stephen Rachman, 139–52. Baltimore: Johns Hopkins University Press, 1995.

———. *The Mystery to a Solution: Poe, Borges, and the Analytic Detective Story*. Baltimore: Johns Hopkins University Press, 1994.

Jacobs, Robert. *Poe: Journalist and Critic*. Baton Rouge: Louisiana University Press, 1969.

Jameson, Fredric. "Wallace Stevens." In *Critical Essays on Wallace Stevens,* ed. Steven Gould Axelrod and Helen Deese, 176–91. Boston: G. K. Hall, 1988.

Johnson, Paul. *The Birth of the Modern: World Society, 1815–1830*. New York: HarperCollins Publishers, 1991.

Kaplan, Sidney. Introduction to *The Narrative of Arthur Gordon Pym,* ed. Sidney Kaplan. New York: Hill and Wang, 1960.

Kelley, Mary. *Private Woman, Public Stage: Literary Domesticity in Nineteenth-Century America*. New York: Oxford University Press, 1984.

Kennedy, J. Gerald. *Poe, Death, and the Life of Writing*. New Haven: Yale University Press, 1987.

Kimmel, Michael. *Manhood in America: A Cultural History*. New York: Free Press, 1996.

Kramer, Michael P. *Imagining Language in America: From the Revolution to the Civil War*. Princeton: Princeton University Press, 1992.

Kravec, Maureen. "Let Arcade Be Finale of Arcadia: Stevens' 'The Emperor of Ice-Cream.' " *Wallace Stevens Journal* 3 (spring 1970): 8–11.

Krieger, Murray. *A Reopening of Closure: Organicism against Itself.* New York: Columbia University Press, 1989.

———. *Theory of Criticism: A Tradition and Its System.* Baltimore: Johns Hopkins University Press, 1976.

Laclau, Ernesto, and Chantal Mouffe. *Hegemony and Socialist Strategy: Towards a Radical Democratic Politics.* London: Verso, 1985.

Lakritz, Andrew M. *Modernism and the Other in Stevens, Frost, and Moore.* Gainesville: University Press of Florida, 1996.

Larkin, Jack. *The Reshaping of Everyday Life, 1790–1840.* New York: Harper and Row, 1988.

Lash, Kenneth. *Explicator* 6 (April 1948): #36.

Leggett, B. J. *Early Stevens: The Nietzschean Intertext.* Durham: Duke University Press, 1992.

Lensing, George S. *Wallace Stevens: A Poet's Growth.* Baton Rouge: Louisiana State University Press, 1986.

———. *Wallace Stevens and the Seasons.* Baton Rouge: Louisiana State University Press, 2001.

Lentricchia, Frank. *After the New Criticism.* Chicago: University of Chicago Press, 1980.

———. *Ariel and the Police: Michel Foucault, William James, Wallace Stevens.* Madison: University of Wisconsin Press, 1988.

———. *Modernist Quartet.* New York: Cambridge University Press, 1994.

Leverenz, David. *Manhood and the American Renaissance.* Ithaca: Cornell University Press, 1989.

Levine, Stuart, and Susan Levine. Introduction to "The Oval Portrait." In *The Short Fiction of Edgar Allan Poe: An Annotated Edition,* ed. Stuart Levine and Susan Levine, 62–63. Indianapolis: Bobbs-Merrill, 1976.

Lighter, J. E., ed. *Random House Historical Dictionary of American Slang,* vol. 1. New York: Random House, 1994.

Limon, John. *The Place of Fiction in the Time of Science: A Disciplinary History of American Writing.* New York: Cambridge University Press, 1990.

Lippmann, Walter. *The Phantom Public.* 1927; reprint, New Brunswick, N.J.: Transaction Publishers, 1993.

———. *Public Opinion.* 1922; reprint, New York: Free Press, 1965.

Litz, A. Walton. *Introspective Voyager: The Poetic Development of Wallace Stevens.* New York: Oxford University Press, 1972.

Ljungquist, Kent. *The Grand and the Fair: Poe's Landscape Aesthetics and Pictorial Techniques.* Potomac: Scripta Humanistica, 1984.

Longenbach, James. *Wallace Stevens: The Plain Sense of Things.* New York: Oxford University Press, 1991.

Loudon, John Claudius. *Loudon Furniture Designs.* Intro. Christopher Gilbert. Yorkshire, England: S. R. Publishers, 1970.

Lukács, Georg. "Ideology of Modernism." Trans. John and Necke Mander. In *20th Century Literary Criticism: A Reader,* ed. David Lodge, 474–87. London: Longman, 1972.

Lyotard, Jean-François. *The Postmodern Condition: A Report on Knowledge.* Trans. Geoff Bennington and Brian Massumi. Minneapolis: University of Minnesota Press, 1984.

MacLeod, Glen. *Wallace Stevens and Modern Art: From the Armory Show to Abstract Expressionism.* New Haven: Yale University Press, 1993.

MacNeill, Shaun. "A Philosophical Definition of Privacy." *Dalhousie Review* 78.3: 437–57.

Madell, Geoffrey. *The Identity of the Self.* Edinburgh: University Press, Edinburgh, 1981.

Mailloux, Steven. "Interpretation." In *Critical Terms for Literary Study,* ed. Frank Lentricchia and Thomas McLaughlin, 121–34. Chicago: The University of Chicago Press, 1995.

Malinowski, Bronislaw. *Magic, Science, and Religion.* New York: Doubleday, 1948.

Martin, Terence. "The Romance." In *The Columbia History of the American Novel,* ed. Cathy N. Davidson, Patrick O'Donnell, Valerie Smith, and Christopher P. Wilson. New York: Columbia University Press, 1991.

Martin-Fugier, Anne. "Bourgeois Rituals." In *A History of Private Life,* vol. 4, *From the Fires of Revolution to the Great War,* ed. Michelle Perrot, trans. Arthur Goldhammer, 261–338. Cambridge, Mass: Harvard University Press, 1990.

May, Elaine Tyler. "Myths and Realities of the American Family." In *A History of Private Life,* vol. 5, *Riddles of Identity in Modern Times,* ed. Antoine Prost and Gérard Vincent, trans. Arthur Goldhammer, 539–92. Cambridge, Mass: Harvard University Press, 1991.

Miles, John. "An Encounter with the Firecat: Wallace Stevens' 'Earthy Anecdote.'" *Wallace Stevens Journal* 22 (fall 1998): 116–32.

Mitchell, W. J. T. "The Violence of Public Art: *Do the Right Thing.*" In *Art and the Public Sphere,* ed. W. J. T. Mitchell, 29–48. Chicago: University of Chicago Press, 1992.

Montrose, Louis A. "Professing the Renaissance: The Poetics and Politics of Culture." In *The New Historicism,* ed. H. Aram Veeser, 15–36. New York: Routledge, 1989.

Morris, Debra. "Privacy, Privation, Perversity: Toward New Representations of the Personal." *Signs* 25 (winter 2000): 323–51.

Moss, Sidney P. *Poe's Literary Battles: The Critic in the Context of His Literary Milieu.* Durham: Duke University Press, 1963.

Murphy, Robert. "Social Distance and the Veil." In *Philosophical Dimensions of Privacy: An Anthology,* ed. Ferdinand David Schoeman, 34–55. New York: Cambridge University Press, 1984.

Nagel, Thomas. *The View from Nowhere*. New York: Oxford University Press, 1986.

Neill, Edward. "The Melting Moment: Stevens' Rehabilitation of Ice Cream." *Ariel* 4 (January 1973): 88–96.

Newbury, Michael. *Figuring Authorship in Antebellum America*. Stanford: Stanford University Press, 1997.

Newcomb, John Timberman. *Wallace Stevens and Literary Canons*. Jackson: University Press of Mississippi, 1992.

Nicholson, Mervyn. "The Riddle of the Firecat." *Wallace Stevens Journal* 22 (fall 1998): 133–48.

North, Michael. *The Final Sculpture: Public Monuments and Modern Poets*. Ithaca: Cornell University Press, 1985.

Novak, William J. *The People's Welfare: Law and Regulation in Nineteenth-Century America*. Chapel Hill: University of North Carolina Press, 1996.

Nyquist, Mary. "Musing on Susanna's Music." In *Lyric Poetry: Beyond New Criticism*, ed. Chavia Hosek and Patricia Parker, 310–27. Ithaca: Cornell University Press, 1985.

O'Hara, Daniel T. "Imaginary Politics: Emerson, Stevens, and the Resistance of Style." In *Wallace Stevens and the Feminine*, ed. Melita Schaum, 58–79. Tuscaloosa: University of Alabama Press, 1993.

O'Neill, Shane. "Private Irony and the Public Hope of Richard Rorty's Liberalism." In *Public and Private: Legal, Political, and Philosophical Perspectives*, ed. Maurizio Passerin D'Entrèves and Ursula Vogel, 51–65. London: Routledge, 2000.

Pannapacker, William A. "A Question of 'Character': Visual Images and the Nineteenth-Century Construction of Edgar Allan Poe." *Harvard Library Bulletin* 7 (fall 1996): 9–24.

Partridge, Eric. *Origins: A Short Etymological Dictionary of Modern English*. New York: Greenwich House, 1964.

Pearce, Roy Harvey. " 'The Emperor of Ice-Cream': A Note on the Occasion." *Wallace Stevens Journal* (fall 1979): 53–55.

Pease, Donald E. *Visionary Compacts: American Renaissance Writings in Cultural Context*. Madison: University of Wisconsin Press, 1987.

Peeples, Scott. *Edgar Allan Poe Revisited*. New York: Twayne Publishers, 1998.

Peiss, Kathy. "Going Public: Women in Nineteenth-Century Cultural History." *American Literary History* 3 (winter 1991): 817–28.

Penso, Kia. *Wallace Stevens, "Harmonium," and "The Whole of Harmonium."* Hamden, Conn.: Archon Books, 1991.

Peterson, Margaret. *Wallace Stevens and the Idealist Tradition*. Ann Arbor: UMI Research Press, 1983.

Piccioto-Richardson, Joan. "By Their Fruits: Wallace Stevens, His Poetry, His Critics." Ph.D. diss., City University of New York, 1977.

Poirier, Richard. *Poetry and Pragmatism*. Cambridge, Mass.: Harvard University Press, 1992.

————. *The Renewal of Literature: Emersonian Reflections.* New York: Random House, 1987.

Pollin, Burton R. *Insights and Outlooks: Essays on Great Writers.* New York: Gordian Press, 1986.

————. *Poe, Creator of Words.* Baltimore: Enoch Pratt Free Library, Edgar Allan Poe Society, and Library of the University of Baltimore, 1974.

Post, Robert C. "The Social Foundations of Privacy: Community and Self in the Common Law Tort." *California Law Review* 77 (October 1989): 957–1010.

Poster, Mark. *Foucault, Marxism, and History.* Cambridge, England: Polity Press, 1984.

Prost, Antoine. "Public and Private Spheres in France." In *A History of Private Life: Riddles of Identity in Modern Times,* vol. 5. ed. Antoine Prost and Gérard Vincent, trans. Arthur Goldhammer, 3–143. Cambridge, Mass: Harvard University Press, 1991.

Quinn, Arthur Hobson. *Edgar Allan Poe: A Critical Biography.* New York: Appleton-Century-Crofts, 1941.

Rachman, Stephen. " '*Es Lässt Sich Nicht Schreiben*': Plagiarism and 'The Man of the Crowd.' " In *The American Face of Edgar Allan Poe,* ed. Shawn J. Rosenheim and Stephen Rachman, 49–87. Baltimore: Johns Hopkins University Press, 1995.

Rae, Patricia. *The Practical Muse: Pragmatist Poetics in Hulme, Pound, and Stevens.* Lewisburg: Bucknell University Press, 1997.

Rashkin, Esther. *Family Secrets and the Psychoanalysis of Narrative.* Princeton: Princeton University Press, 1992.

Renza, Louis A. "Influence." In *Critical Terms for Literary Study,* ed. Frank Lentricchia and Thomas McLaughlin, 186–202. Chicago: University of Chicago Press, 1995.

————. "Poe's Secret Autobiography." In *The American Renaissance Reconsidered: Selected Papers from the English Institute, 1982–83,* ed. Walter Benn Michaels and Donald E. Pease, 58–89. Baltimore: Johns Hopkins University Press, 1985. 58–89.

Reynolds, David S. *Beneath the American Renaissance: The Subversive Imagination in the Age of Emerson and Melville.* New York: Alfred A. Knopf, 1988.

Richardson, Joan. *Wallace Stevens, a Biography: The Early Years, 1879–1923.* New York: Beech Tree Books, 1986.

————. *Wallace Stevens, a Biography: The Later Years, 1923–1955.* New York: Beech Tree Books, 1988.

Riddel, Joseph N. *The Clairvoyant Eye: The Poetry and Poetics of Wallace Stevens.* Baton Rouge: Louisiana State University Press, 1965.

————. "The Climate of Our Poems." In *Critical Essays on Wallace Stevens,* ed. Steven Gould Axelrod and Helen Deese, 145–62. Boston: G. K. Hall, 1988.

Rorty, Richard. *Contingency, Irony, and Solidarity.* New York: Cambridge University Press, 1989.

Rosen, Jeffrey. *The Unwanted Gaze: The Destruction of Privacy in America.* New York: Random House, 2000.

Rosenblatt, Jon. "Stevens' 'The Cuban Doctor.' " *Explicator* 37 (summer 1979): 14–15.

Rosenheim, Shawn J. *Secret Writing from Edgar Allan Poe to the Internet: The Cryptographic Imagination.* Baltimore: Johns Hopkins University Press, 1997.

Rowe, John Carlos. *At Emerson's Tomb: The Politics of Classic American Literature.* New York: Columbia University Press, 1997.

Ryan, Alan. "Dream Time." Review of *A Tale of Two Utopias,* by Paul Berman. *New York Review of Books,* October 17, 1996, pp. 39–42.

Rydell, Robert W. *All the World's a Fair: Visions of Empire at American International Expositions, 1876–1916.* Chicago: University of Chicago Press, 1984.

Saltz, Laura. " '(Horrible to Relate!)': Recovering the Body of Marie Rogêt." In *The American Face of Edgar Allan Poe,* ed. Shawn Rosenheim and Stephen Rachman, 237–67. Baltimore: Johns Hopkins University Press, 1995.

Sampson, Theodore. *A Cure of the Mind: The Poetics of Wallace Stevens.* New York: Black Rose Books, 2000.

Schaum, Melita. *Wallace Stevens and the Critical Schools.* Tuscaloosa: University of Alabama Press, 1988.

Scherman, Timothy. "Authorship and the Problem of Poe's Public Double." Unpublished paper delivered at the International Edgar Allan Poe Conference, Richmond, Va., October 9, 1999.

Schivelbusch, Wolfgang. *Disenchanted Night: The Industrialization of Light in the Nineteenth Century.* Trans. Angela Davies. Berkeley: University of California Press, 1988.

Schlereth, Thomas J. *Victorian America: Transformations in Everyday Life, 1876–1915.* New York: HarperCollins, 1991.

Schneider, Carl D. *Shame, Exposure, and Privacy.* New York: W. W. Norton, 1992.

Schudson, Michael. "Was There Ever a Public Sphere? If So, When? Reflections on the American Case." In *Habermas and the Public Sphere,* ed. Craig Calhoun, 143–63. Cambridge, Mass.: MIT Press, 1992.

Seale, William. *Recreating the Historic House Interior.* Nashville: American Association for State and Local History, 1979.

Sennett, Richard. *The Fall of Public Man.* New York: W. W. Norton, 1992; orig. pub. 1974.

Shamir, Milette. "Hawthorne's Romance and the Right to Privacy." *American Quarterly* 49 (December 1997): 746–79.

———. " 'The manliest relations to men': Thoreau on Privacy, Intimacy, and Writing." Unpublished paper delivered at the Dartmouth Humanities Institute, Hanover, N.H., August 1999.

Shell, Marc. *Money, Language, and Thought: Literary and Philosophic Economics from the Medieval to the Modern Era.* Berkeley: University of California Press, 1982.

Shils, Edward A. *The Torments of Secrecy: The Background and Consequences of American Security Policies.* Glencoe, Ill.: Free Press, 1956.

Silver, Allan. "The Lawyer and the Scrivener." *Partisan Review* 3 (1981): 409–24.

———. " 'Two Different Sorts of Commerce'—Friendship and Strangership in Civil Society." In *Public and Private in Thought and Practice: Perspectives on a Grand Dichotomy,* ed. Jeff Weintraub and Krishan Kumar, 43–74. Chicago: University of Chicago Press, 1997.

Silverman, Kenneth. *Edgar A. Poe: Mournful and Never-ending Remembrance.* New York: HarperCollins, 1991.

Silverman, Stuart. "The Emperor of Ice-Cream." *Western Humanities Review* 26 (spring 1972): 165–68.

Simoni-Wastila, Henry. "Particularity and Consciousness: Wittgenstein and Nagel on Privacy, Beetles, and Bats." *Philosophy Today* 44 (winter 2000): 415–25.

Smith, Barbara Herrnstein. *Contingencies of Value: Alternative Perspectives for Critical Theory.* Cambridge, Mass.: Harvard University Press, 1988.

Smith, Janna Malamud. *Private Matters: In Defense of the Personal Life.* Reading, Mass.: Addison-Wesley, 1997.

Sperry, Stuart M. "Wallace Stevens and Poetic Transformation." *Raritan* 17 (winter 1998): 25–46.

Stein, Gertrude. *The Making of Americans.* Normal, Ill.: Dalkey Archive Press, 1995.

Stein, Kevin. *Private Poets, Worldly Acts: Public and Private History in Contemporary American Poetry.* Athens, Ohio: Ohio University Press, 1998.

Stein, William Bysshe. "Stevens' 'The Emperor of Ice-Cream': The Requiem of the Romantic Muse." *NMAL* 1 (spring 1977).

Strobel, Shirley H. "Stevens' 'The Emperor of Ice Cream' [*sic*]." *Explicator* (summer 1983): 33–35.

Strom, Martha. "Wallace Stevens' Revisions of Crispin's Journal: A Reaction against the 'Local.' " *Critical Essays on Wallace Stevens,* ed. Steven Gould Axelrod and Helen Deese, 130–45. Boston: G. K. Hall, 1988.

Strouse, Jean. *Morgan: American Financier.* New York: Random House, 1999.

Sullivan, William M. *Reconstructing Public Philosophy.* Berkeley: University of California Press, 1986.

Sussman, Henry. "*Maxima Moralia*: Millennial Fragments on the Public and Private Dimensions of Language." *MLN* 110.4 (1995): 856–887.

———. "A Note on the Public and the Private in Literature: The Literature of 'Acting Out.' " *MLN* 104 (April 1989): 597–611.

Sykes, Charles. *The End of Privacy.* New York: St. Martin's Press, 1999.

Thackaberry, Robert. *Explicator* 6 (April 1948): #36.

Thomas, Brook. *American Literary Realism and the Failed Promise of Contract.* Berkeley: University of California Press, 1997.

———. *The New Historicism and Other Old-Fashioned Topics.* Princeton: Princeton University Press, 1991.

Thomas, Dwight, and David K. Jackson. *The Poe Log: A Documentary Life of Edgar Allan Poe, 1809–1849.* New York: G. K. Hall, 1987.

Thompson, G. R. *Poe's Fiction: Romantic Irony in the Gothic Tales.* Madison: University of Wisconsin Press, 1973.

Tocqueville, Alexis de. *Democracy in America.* Revised ed., 2 vols. Trans. Henry Reeve. Ed. Phillips Bradley. New York: Vintage Books, 1945.

Tompkins, Jane. *Sensational Designs: The Cultural Work of American Fiction, 1790–1860.* New York: Oxford University Press, 1985.

———. *West of Everything: The Inner Life of Westerns.* New York: Oxford University Press, 1992.

Veeser, Adam. Introduction to *The New Historicism,* ed. H. Aram Veeser, ix–xvi. New York: Routledge, 1989.

Vendler, Helen. *Wallace Stevens: Words Chosen Out of Desire.* Cambridge, Mass.: Harvard University Press, 1986.

Vincent, Gérard. "A History of Secrets?" In *A History of Private Life,* vol. 5, *Riddles of Identity in Modern Times,* ed. Antoine Prost and Gérard Vincent, trans. Arthur Goldhammer, 145–281. Cambridge, Mass: Harvard University Press, 1991.

Viswanathan, R. "Stevens' 'The Emperor of Ice-Cream.' " *Explicator* 50 (winter 1992): 84–85.

Vološinov, V. N. *Marxism and the Philosophy of Language.* Trans. Ladislav Matejka and I. R. Titunik. Cambridge, Mass.: Harvard University Press, 1986.

Wagenknecht, Edward. *Edgar Allan Poe: The Man behind the Legend.* New York: Oxford University Press, 1963.

Wagner, C. Roland. "Wallace Stevens: The Concealed Self." In *Wallace Stevens and the Feminine,* ed. Melita Schaum, 117–39. Tuscaloosa: University of Alabama Press, 1993.

Walker, Nancy. " 'Wider than the Sky' ": Public Presence and Private Self in Dickinson, James, and Woolf." In *The Private Self: Theory and Practice of Women's Autobiographical Writings,* ed. Shari Benstock, 272–303. Chapel Hill: University of North Carolina Press, 1988.

Warner, Michael. "The Mass Public and the Mass Subject. In *Habermas and the Public Sphere,* ed. Craig Calhoun, 377–401. Cambridge, Mass.: MIT Press, 1992.

Warner, Sam Bass, Jr. *The Private City: Philadelphia in Three Periods of Its Growth.* Philadelphia: University of Pennsylvania Press, 1968.

Warren, Samuel, and Louis Brandeis. "The Right to Privacy." In *Killing the Messenger: 100 Years of Media Criticism,* ed. Tom Goldstein, 5–21. New York: Columbia University Press, 1989. Originally published in *Harvard Law Review,* December 15, 1890.

Weintraub, Jeff. "The Theory and Politics of the Public/Private Distinction." In *Public and Private in Thought and Practice: Perspectives on a Grand Dichotomy,* ed. Jeff Weintraub and Krishan Kumar, 1–42. Chicago: University of Chicago Press, 1997.

Whalen, Terence. "The Code for Gold: Edgar Allan Poe and Cryptography." *Representations* 46 (spring 1994): 34–57.

———. *Edgar Allan Poe and the Masses: The Political Economy of Literature in Antebellum America.* Princeton: Princeton University Press, 1999.

Whitaker, Reg. *The End of Privacy: How Total Surveillance Is Becoming a Reality.* New York: New Press, 1999.

Williams, Michael J. S. *A World of Words: Language and Displacement in the Fiction of Edgar Allan Poe.* Durham: Duke University Press, 1988.

Williams, William Carlos. *The Collected Earlier Poems of William Carlos Williams.* Norfolk, Conn.: New Directions, 1951.

Wimsatt, Jr., W. K. "The Intentional Fallacy." In *The Verbal Icon: Studies in the Meaning of Poetry.* Lexington: University of Kentucky Press, 1967.

———. "What Poe Knew about Cryptography." *PMLA* 58 (1943): 754–79.

Winkler, Gail Caskey, and Roger W. Moss. *Victorian Interior Decoration: American Interiors, 1830–1900.* New York: Henry Holt, 1986.

Winters, Yvor. "Wallace Stevens; or the Hedonist's Progress" [1943]. In *In Defense of Reason,* 431–59. Denver: Alan Swallow, 1947.

Wittgenstein, Ludwig. *Philosophical Investigations.* Trans. G. E. M. Anscombe. New York: Macmillan, 1958.

Wood, Gordon S. *The Radicalism of the American Revolution.* New York: Alfred A. Knopf, 1992.

Wydeven, Joseph J. "Photography and Privacy: The Protests of Wright Morris and James Agee." *Midwest Quarterly* 23 (autumn 1981): 103–15.

Zboray, Ronald J., and Mary Saracino Zboray. "Books, Reading, and the World of Goods in Antebellum New England." *American Quarterly* 48 (December 1996): 587–622.

Other Sources Used

Austen, Jane. *Northanger Abbey.* New York: Oxford University Press, 1971.

Dickinson, Emily. *The Complete Poems,* ed. Thomas H. Johnson. Boston: Little, Brown, 1960.

Dylan, Bob. *Lyrics, 1962–1985.* New York: Alfred A. Knopf, 1985.

Emerson, Ralph Waldo. *Emerson: Essays and Lectures.* Ed. Joel Porte. New York: Library of America, 1983.

Fitzgerald, F. Scott. *The Beautiful and the Damned*. New York: Penguin Books, 1998.

Frost, Robert. *Selected Letters of Robert Frost*. Ed. Lawrance Thompson. New York: Holt, Rinehart, and Winston, 1964.

Hawthorne, Nathaniel. "Prophetic Pictures." In *Hawthorne: Tales and Sketches*, ed. Roy Harvey Pearce, 456–69. New York: Library of America, 1982.

Holy Bible, Old King James Version.
http://dciswww.dartmouth.edu:50080/?&&&301&s/

Jewett, Sarah Orne. "From a Mournful Villager." In *Country By-Ways*, 116–38. Reprint: Freeport, N.Y.: Books for Libraries Press, 1969.

Kerouac, Jack. "The Vanishing American Hobo." In *Lonesome Traveler*, 172–83. New York: Grove Press, 1960.

Kierkegaard, Søren. *The Present Age and of the Difference between a Genius and an Apostle*. Trans. Alexander Dru. New York: Harper and Row, 1962.

Melville, Herman. *Billy Budd, Sailor, and Other Stories*. Ed. Harold Beaver. New York: Penguin Books, 1983.

Oxford English Dictionary. 2nd ed. Ed. J. A. Simpson and E. S. C. Weiner. New York: Oxford University Press, 1989.

Poe, Edgar Allan. *The Brevities: Pinakidia, Marginalia, and Other Works*. Vol. 2 of *Collected Writings of Edgar Allan Poe*, ed. Burton R. Pollin. New York: Gordian Press, 1985.

———. *Complete Tales and Poems of Edgar Allan Poe*. New York: Viking Books, 1975.

———. *The Complete Works of Edgar Allan Poe*, 16 vols. Ed. James A. Harrison. 1902; reprint, New York: AMS Press, 1965.

———. "The Daguerreotype." In *Classic Essays on Photography*, ed. Alan Trachtenberg, 37–38. New Haven: Leete's Island Books, 1980.

———. *The Short Fiction of Edgar Allan Poe: An Annotated Edition*. Ed. Stuart and Susan Levine. Indianapolis: Bobbs-Merrill, 1976.

———. *The Viking Portable Edgar Allan Poe*. Ed. Philip Van Doren Stern. New York: Viking Press, 1945.

Shakespeare, William. *Hamlet. In The Oxford Shakespeare: Complete Works*, ed. W. J. Craig. London: Oxford University Press, 1964.

Thoreau, Henry David. *A Week on the Concord and Merrimack Rivers, Walden, the Maine Woods, Cape Cod*. Ed. Robert F. Sayre. New York: Library of America, 1984.

Webster, John. *The Tragedy of The Duchess of Malfi*. In *English Drama, 1580–1642*, ed. C. F. Tucker Brooke and Nathaniel Burton Paradise, 645–86. Boston: D. C. Heath, 1933.

Whitman, Walt. *Poetry and Prose*, ed. Justin Kaplan. New York: Library of America, 1982.

Index